MW01235686

REASONING FROM FAITH

INDIANA SERIES IN THE PHILOSOPHY OF RELIGION
Merold Westphal, *editor*

REASONING
from *Faith*

Fundamental Theology in
Merold Westphal's Philosophy of Religion

JUSTIN SANDS

INDIANA UNIVERSITY PRESS

This book is a publication of

Indiana University Press
Office of Scholarly Publishing
Herman B Wells Library 350
1320 East 10th Street
Bloomington, Indiana 47405 USA

iupress.indiana.edu

The paper used in this publication meets the minimum requirements of the American National Standard for Information Sciences—Permanence of Paper for Printed Library Materials, ANSI Z39.48-1992.

Manufactured in the United States of America

Cataloging information is available from the Library of Congress.

ISBN 978-0-253-03193-8 (cloth)
ISBN 978-0-253-03195-2 (ebook)
ISBN 978-0-253-03194-5 (paperback)

1 2 3 4 5 23 22 21 20 19 18

To Terry and Debbie Cave

CONTENTS

ACKNOWLEDGMENTS

Portions of chapter 2 appeared as "The Concept of *Aufhebung* in the Thought of Merold Westphal: Appropriation and Recontextualization," in *International Journal in Philosophy and Theology*, June 25, 2015 (doi: 10.1080/21692327.2015.1057197). Portions of chapter 3 appeared as "Hegelians in Heaven . . . but on Earth? Westphal's Kierkegaardian Faith," in *Journal for the History of Modern Theology* 26, no. 1 (2016): 1–26 (doi: 10.1515/znth-2016-0018). Portions of chapter 7 appeared as "Radical Eschatology: Westphal, Caputo, and Onto-Theology," in *Louvain Studies* 38 (2014): 246–268 (doi: 10.2143/LS.38.3.3105907). I thank these journals for their permission to include these texts in this monograph.

I thank Lieven Boeve and William Desmond for their help with this project and for guiding my research. I am especially grateful to Joeri Schrijvers for his friendship, critique, and advice. Patrick Eldridge was an essential reader for this project and his fingerprints are all over this text. I am also indebted to KU Leuven and the research group Theology in a Postmodern Context, and to the School for Philosophy at North-West University–Potchefstroom. The people at both institutions were instrumental in the creation of this work. I am particularly obliged to Marijn de Jong and Anné Verhoef for their friendship, good humor, and critical eyes.

Importantly, I am indebted to my family and loved ones. I thank my mother and father, Debbie and Terry Cave; my sister, Oshen Wallin; and my grandparents, Margaret and Thomas Butcher. Last, I warmly thank all my friends and colleagues in the United States, Belgium, and South Africa. I am truly blessed with my network of love and support, and I thank you all.

ABBREVIATIONS

IPG   Westphal, Merold, Thomas Ludwig, Robin Klay, and David Myers. *Inflation, Poortalk, and the Gospel.* Valley Forge: Judson Press, 1981.

GDD   Westphal, Merold. *God, Guilt, and Death.* Bloomington: Indiana University Press, 1984.

KCRS   Westphal, Merold. *Kierkegaard's Critique of Reason and Society.* Macon: Mercer University Press, 1987.

HFM   Westphal, Merold. *Hegel, Freedom, and Modernity.* Albany: SUNY Press, 1992.

BS   Westphal, Merold. *Becoming a Self.* West Lafayette, IN: Purdue University Press, 1996.

HT   Westphal, Merold. *History and Truth in Hegel's Phenomenology.* 3rd ed. Bloomington: Indiana University Press, 1998.

SF   Westphal, Merold. *Suspicion and Faith.* Grand Rapids, MI: Eerdmans, 1998.

OCOT   Westphal, Merold. *Overcoming Onto-Theology.* New York: Fordham University Press, 2001.

TST   Westphal, Merold. *Transcendence and Self-Transcendence.* Bloomington: Indiana University Press, 2004.

LKD   Westphal, Merold. *Levinas and Kierkegaard in Dialogue.* Bloomington: Indiana University Press, 2008.

GTPD   Putt, B. Keith, ed. *Gazing through a Prism Darkly: Reflections on Merold Westphal's Hermeneutical Epistemology.* New York: Fordham University Press, 2009.

WCWI   Westphal, Merold. *Whose Community? Which Interpretation? Philosophical Hermeneutics for the Church.* Grand Rapids, MI: Baker Academic, 2009.

KCF   Westphal, Merold. *Kierkegaard's Concept of Faith.* Grand Rapids, MI: Eerdmans, 2014.

REASONING FROM FAITH

INTRODUCTION

Merold Westphal stands as one of the preeminent thinkers in North America concerning Continental philosophy of religion. Moreover, together with John Caputo and Richard Kearney, Westphal can be thought of as one of the main philosophers who popularized postmodern thought on religion in North America. The present work reviews Westphal's contributions to philosophy, what possible offerings those may have for theology, and how his work might best be understood within these discourses.

Although Westphal often fashions himself as a Christian philosopher—and hence it may seem simple to situate him between philosophy and theology—this is not so easily the case. What I will show is that his Christian philosophy, while being thoroughly Christian and heavily founded in philosophical thinking, is better understood as a theology proper. This is because Westphal's thought functions less as a philosophical reflection on the Christian faith and more as an active engagement of philosophy that begins from within the Christian faith. At first, this may sound as if I am splitting hairs concerning what a philosophy (or theology, for that matter) can and cannot do, yet this distinction is essential for best understanding the faith that Westphal wishes to pronounce and the ways in which that faith is enacted. Westphal, these chapters will show, does not seek a rational or apologetical justification of faith. Rather, he begins from a faith solely initiated by an acceptance of God's revelation, which thereby resists any rational foundation. From this anti-apologetical faith, Westphal then proceeds to rationally develop its implications. Faith is always the first act of the believing soul, Westphal argues; it begins as unreasonable, and reason only aids in one's understanding of faith. Finally, Westphal finds that this understanding, as commanded by God's revelation, is always oriented as a loving task toward the concern of those at the margins of society.

I argue that it may be better to understand his Christian philosophy as theology because Westphal rejects an apologetical defense of faith and that his understanding of faith is an active response to revelation with the above command for praxis. Furthermore, by aligning it with theology, one situates Westphal's work in a discourse that can better appropriate, adapt, and further his thought. This is especially so since Westphal is often confessional in his work, which is reflected in his thoughts on the praxis of faith. In this regard, he often addresses Christian believers by correcting and directing this praxis in the process of faith seeking understanding.

Our Course of Action

If one were to read Merold Westphal as a scholar of philosophical texts, one would see that his career follows three acts: first, he establishes himself as one of the premier American readers of Hegel; he then embraces Kierkegaard's critique of Hegel and Christendom; and finally, he completes his career by moving toward Continental philosophy of religion. Where at first one sees a Hegelian in ascension, one eventually finds Westphal pivoting toward a philosophy that heavily critiques Hegel, and this critique continues through a postmodern philosophy of religion. However, while Westphal's career evolved, the most interesting facet of this evolution is that nothing is ever abandoned or completely discarded. He never just leaves Hegel. In fact, with everything he reads, Hegel is always peering over Westphal's shoulder—with Kierkegaard always right by Westphal's side. More precisely, we can see in Westphal's work a continual process of recontextualization: he continually takes up the thought of those he critiques and uses that thought to find solutions to those criticisms.

This process of recontextualization is especially evident in his reading of Kierkegaard. Kierkegaard is at the core of Westphal's work, but Kierkegaard is always read through a Hegelian lens. Westphal's own critique of philosophy—be it Hegelianism, onto-theology, or what stands as 'modernity'—often involves a Hegelian reading of Kierkegaard. Like Kierkegaard himself, Westphal always assumes Hegel as a starting point. This is especially true regarding how Westphal understands the concept of *Aufhebung*, which he argues is an operation not just in Hegel's thought but also in Kierkegaard's. What we shall see is that Westphal appropriates Hegel's *Aufhebung* to understand Kierkegaard, and he later recontextualizes it in his own philosophy of religion. Even if one were to dispute whether his use of *Aufhebung* is faithful to Hegel's own conception—and Westphal is explicit that his use of *Aufhebung* is Hegelian—it is quite clear that understanding Westphal's own philosophy requires thoughtful consideration of his scholarly work on Hegel and Kierkegaard.

Somewhat surprisingly, there has been little attention paid to the importance of his early scholarly work when considering his philosophy of religion, and the present text seeks to remedy that by giving a thorough account of Westphal's philosophical evolution. Westphal's work is widely read in Hegelian, Kierkegaardian, and philosophy-of-religion academic circles. Yet his work in each academic circle is often siloed, meaning that scholars in one field rarely read Westphal's contributions to other fields.[1] Therefore, bridging these gaps will be one of our underlying tasks in this book; by exploring Westphal's maturation we will gain insights into his philosophy as a whole. Thus, we will see how interrelated themes emerge from his readings of other philosophers, revealing how Westphal's career transitions from one act to another. Stretching the metaphor a little, one cannot quite understand the finale without the preceding plot points, although many have tried. Therefore, the initial seven chapters of this book provide an intellectual history of Merold Westphal's thought. Chapters 1 and 2 begin with how to understand Westphal's reading of texts and his style of recontextualization. These chapters set for us a guide for understanding how Westphal develops his thought in light of Hegel and Kierkegaard, the focus of chapters 3–5. Chapters 6 and 7 connect our findings to his philosophy of religion, thus presenting a more comprehensive understanding of Westphal's theological and philosophical voice.[2]

It is important to note, however, that our present interest is in Westphal's thought and not whether his reading of Hegel and Kierkegaard are correct; even though we will approach Westphal's reception and contribution to those academic circles when necessary. Our intellectual history will not be a critique of his scholarly readings, since doing so would require a separate book-length treatment of its own. Rather, it will be a close reading of Westphal himself, and this reading will retrieve and connect various strands of his thought into a cohesive, intellectual narrative.

Such an overview is a necessary project in its own right. However, it comprises only part of the objective of this work. As the intellectual history will show, Westphal's mature thought fashions itself on a hermeneutical line of postmodern philosophy and on a process of transcendence through self-transcendence as a response to the critique of onto-theology. Fashioned as such, there are numerous movements in his thinking that require a thorough examination to be properly understood, hence our intellectual history. From there we will explore the possible fruitfulness of Westphal's thought as a fundamental theology. This goal is the primary concern of chapters 8 and 9, but it will also be addressed from time to time through the previous chapters. On a final note, it is important to remember that Westphal understands his work as residing within the academic discipline of philosophy and that his goal is a philosophical inquiry into faith. Therefore, we begin our assessment of his work under these presumptions by reading him as a philosopher. What will emerge from our inquiry, however, is something quite different as his theological colors become more vivid and begin to shine through. However, we must give him due diligence through reading his work in the style and genre that he intended before pronouncing where to best situate his thinking.

The Command of Faith: Westphal's Challenge to Theology and Philosophy

Does theology have something to say to philosophy and, in particular, to phenomenology? If so, then what will it have to say and on whose terms? Westphal's philosophy argues for a blurring of the lines between philosophy and theology, showing that each has something to say to the other and that these domains, though not the same, are not necessarily incompatible. Westphal's concept of faith speaks to these questions.

What it says is that faith is not taken seriously enough in philosophy and that faith can be just as radical as the suspicion of Freud, Marx, and Nietzsche; through a hermeneutics of suspicion, Westphal argues that faith can serve as a critique of ideology not just for Christendom but for philosophy as well. In his later works, he addresses faith as ideology critique through Heidegger and onto-theology, where he sees philosophical thinking dictating "the rules that God must play by."[3] For Westphal, onto-theology is manifest in the way humanity directs how God can and/or should enter into the world, thus seeing God no longer as *mysterium tremendum et fascinans*. This imprisoned god, conceived as *causa sui*, leads to self-legitimization, becoming a tool in our own will to power.[4] In response, Westphal argues for a radical faith that creates at once a self-transcendence and a transcendence beyond the world toward God. He argues that this faith is epistemological: it involves gathering knowledge through participation in revelation while accepting that this knowledge will never make God completely intelligible.

For some, doing theology presupposes having faith, yet Westphal does not let the theologians off the hook too easily, and he critiques them for under-appreciating faith itself. Far too often faith is explained away through apologetics or is sidetracked in tangential discussions. For Westphal, reason should always aid faith in discipleship, not prop it up—something that theologians often forget. Moreover, the obligation faith imposes on the believer to love God first and to always love the other as one's self serves as a potent reminder to theologians that theology's primary task should always be one of liberating the oppressed. It should always maintain a preferential option for the poor.

Westphal could not be more explicit regarding the Christian's duty to the poor. In "Levinas, Kierkegaard and the Theological Task," he lays out his own understanding of proper theology. In his estimation, theology should always be confessional and praxis based, and that *"all theology should be liberation theology, a guide to the practice of overcoming oppression in all its forms."*[5] The content of this essay effectively lays out Westphal's personal argument that theology's primary function is to fulfill the love commandment. Theology, here, is not concerned with apologetics or the particulars of doctrine. Westphal will continually designate apologetics as a Greek-influenced style of thinking, with its primary designation being "Athens" from Tertullian's famous question, "What does Athens have to do with Jerusalem?"[6] On the contrary, he believes that theology should follow its Hebraic tradition, which he also believes is immersed in a hermeneutics of suspicion yet is praxis based and always focused on welcoming the widow, orphan, and stranger. Summarizing the issue, Westphal states:

> Theology will inevitably give priority either to a Greek inspired ontology of war and violence or to a Hebrew inspired eschatology of messianic peace. It ought to orient itself to the latter, and it will find sufficient rational motivation to do so if, and only if, it pays sufficient attention to the ethical encounter with the Other that presupposes neither of the two.[7]

As if laying the issue to rest, Westphal continues:

> The first implication of all this for theology has been stated negatively: if theology would be a theology of liberation rather than of domination, it must not orient itself to the philosophical framework inherited from the Greeks and expressed in our own time most powerfully by Husserl and Heidegger.[8]

Needless to say, these are bold claims that will require elaboration. For now, one can see that Westphal's theology will be a liberation theology, and that it should be judged as such. Moreover, Westphal's separation of Hebrew thinking from Greek thinking will need to be examined, since those statements can be taken as oversimplifications of a much more complex relationship. Therefore, we will continually revisit the relationship between Hebrew and Greek thinking throughout this text. We will find that Westphal believes Jerusalem needs Athens, and vice versa; it is just that each has particular functions in the life of faith. While they must work together, they cannot be collapsed into one and the same.[9]

It should not be forgotten that Westphal is essentially arguing for a separate (one could say "privileged") space for faith in both theological and philosophical discourses. For Westphal, faith initiates theology, yet it also cannot be excluded from philosophical discourse merely because it is unreasonable. It is, in fact, because faith is unlike reason that it must be explored and understood in philosophical terms. Faith thus becomes something that is at once a theological concern and a philosophical one. Therefore, while this present work intends to focus primarily on Westphal's thinking as a theology, it cannot go unnoticed that the divide between philosophy and theology for Westphal is rather thin.

To accomplish a thorough examination of the whole of his thought while respecting the ever-blurring divide between philosophy and theology, Westphal's philosophical concept of liberation theology is continually addressed and revisited throughout this book. I have not fashioned the text as a discourse on liberation theology and do not address how Westphal's thought might be critiqued by those in the academic field of liberation theology. However, I anticipate a future discussion or dialogue between Westphal and liberation theology and present possible points of contact between the two.

Because Westphal often presupposes theism and revelation through faith in his work, I find theology to be the best genre to understand his thinking. In postmodern, phenomenological discourses in philosophy, these sorts of presuppositions are extremely circumspect. Following Dominique Janicaud's critique of the 'theological turn' in French phenomenology as 'crypto-theology,' I argue that philosophy is an academic discipline that founds its presuppositions on methodology (especially in phenomenology) and reason.[10] Through a fidelity to method and reason, philosophy seeks to uncover the underlying concepts, implications, and predispositions within concepts, individuals, and society at large. In so doing, it must bracket out any specified religious or theistic conception. True, philosophers and phenomenologists address the question of God and the possibility of revelation, but the methods to which they adhere do not allow for them to begin from a standpoint that revelation has occurred and that their job is to better understand it. Philosophy, in this way, attempts to maintain an agnostic or a-theistic position in order to adhere to its discipline. I understand that this might be a contentious stance and one with which Westphal might disagree. Therefore, I further address and clarify my distinction between philosophy and theology throughout the text.

Chapter 9 will aid in this clarification through a dialogue between Westphal and Richard Kearney. There, I argue philosophy's task as one that is faithful to methodological reasoning through Kearney's work: while the philosopher might be a believing soul, one must begin by a stepping out of this belief in order to maintain and sustain one's intellectual project. Theology, however, requires a different sort of fidelity: one that is concerned with the faith tradition from which one works. Theology can presuppose revelation and the existence of God so as to better understand each and how they relate to believers and to the church as a whole. Theology thus concerns itself with praxis and reflects on the faith tradition to better understand both God and how to be more faithful to God. Westphal's thought follows this theological line as he frequently leaves his philosophical methodology to appropriate philosophy for theological ends: to better understand God and to learn how to be more faithful to God.[11]

Throughout the text, I argue that Westphal's work can best be read as a fundamental theology, which admittedly is a foreign term in most American academic circles, especially Protestant ones. Furthermore, fundamental theology, like postmodernism, has many definitions. For the sake of simplicity, I understand fundamental theology as a theological discipline that operates through two movements. First is an inward, reflective exploration of the foundations of Christianity as a faith that is based upon God's revelation. In this movement, it seeks to understand Christianity's reception of revelation through Scripture and tradition. Second, it operates through an outward, dialogic exploration of understanding revelation (and subsequently doctrine) by engaging sources and disciplines that do not adhere to revelation as a basic principle. While this outward engagement often holds an apologetical line (and indeed fundamental theology has its historical roots in apologetics), it need not always be concerned with a rational defense. Even though it is primarily a Catholic theological term, I situate Westphal as a fundamental theologian through this latter, outward movement: while he does not give an apologetical defense of Christianity or revelation, he seeks to better understand both through an outward, philosophical engagement with postmodern thought.[12]

It is important to note that I am not trying to silo Westphal's thought into theology. Rather, I maintain that this is important for understanding his work because it allows a space for his ideas to flourish. Anecdotally, I have come to notice through conversing with other philosophers (phenomenologists in particular) at conferences, and by looking at the curricula at universities in North America and Europe, that many thinkers who are not a part of Westphal's academic circles find his works hard to understand and thus do not completely read them. However, once I engage their critique by explaining Westphal's theological starting position, they begin to see its value and can accept his presuppositions, even if they do not themselves, and thus proceed in a thoughtful consideration of his ideas. Although this does not found the basis of my arguing that Westphal lends himself to be read as a theologian, it does inform it. The issue of situating Westphal in a genre is one of reception: how can other thinkers best understand and come to engage Westphal? I find that this is by noting that he reasons from faith; an unfounding and unreasonable beginning to exploring what faith might entail.

NOTES

1. A notable exception of this is Christina Gschwandtner's work *Postmodern Apologetics? Arguments for God in Contemporary Philosophy* (New York: Fordham University Press, 2012).

2. Westphal is often dependent on his sources to make his point, which is an integral part of his style of recontextualization, and he often fashions his texts in a manner where source A is in dialogue with sources B, C, D, and E. This, as it will be shown, is one of the major weaknesses of Westphal's thought, as his dialogues often occlude his stated intentions and major points in his arguments. To simplify this arrangement, and to get at the heart of Westphal's thinking, we will review only how Westphal treats the particular insights he has retrieved from these authors, forgoing a critique of whether his reading is entirely correct or novel. This means that Westphal's work will be treated as a complete whole, as a project in its own right, and not as a commentary on other thinkers.

3. *TST*, 34–37.

4. Westphal sees Kierkegaard's critique of Christendom as a prime example. See *OCOT*, 156–158, 205–207, and 273–275. See also, *TST*, 36, 148. Also, Westphal states: "The task of God is to make science possible and metaphysics will treat any God who shirks this responsibility as an illegal immigrant in the brave new world of modernity" (*TST*, 21).

5. Merold Westphal, "Levinas, Kierkegaard, and the Theological Task," *Modern Theology* 8, no. 3 (July 1992): 246.

6. Here "Athens" and "Jerusalem," as terms, are interchangeable with the "Greek" and "Jewish" traditions of philosophy and theology, respectively. See Merold Westphal, "The Canon as Flexible, Normative Fact," *Monist* 76, no. 4 (October 1993): 436–449; Westphal, "Levinas, Kierkegaard, and the Theological Task," 249; *LKD*, 38–41, 88–90, 121 (when talking about Levinas, Westphal often refers to Levinas's "Greek" writings as separate from his "Hebrew" writings. Although this is customary in certain corners of Levinas scholarship, Westphal's work intentionally makes this distinction for theological and philosophical reasons); *GTPD*, 86–92.

7. Westphal, "Levinas, Kierkegaard, and the Theological Task," 249.

8. Ibid.

9. See chapter 1 for how he develops a concept of hermeneutics of prophecy, and chapter 5 for how he develops a concept of faith in light of Kierkegaard's 'logic of insanity'; Westphal, "Canon as Flexible, Normative Fact," 444–448; *KCRS*, "Kierkegaard's Logic of Insanity."

10. Dominique Janicaud, "The Theological Turn of French Phenomenology," in *Phenomenology and the "Theological Turn"* (New York: Fordham University Press, 2000), 18–22.

11. Westphal's hermeneutical phenomenology moves from a philosophical description of faith to a theological prescription for faith: he fashions concepts such as a hermeneutics of suspicion not to correct any unperceived bias imparted by the phenomenologist, but as a way for Christians to reflect on their misuses of faith. Philosophically, this is problematic because he recontextualizes methodologies outside of established philosophical principles. I explain the implications and reasons behind these recontextualizations in the latter part of this work. I will argue that this is not a problem with his work; it is rather where his work shines the brightest.

12. See chapter 6, where I discuss this in greater detail. See also Jean-Yves Lacoste, ed., *Encyclopedia of Christian Theology* (London: Routledge, 2005), 593–599.

1. OF HERMENEUTICS AND STYLE

How to Read Westphal

TEXTUAL FIDELITY: WESTPHAL'S PHILOSOPHICAL STYLE

Beginning our investigation by understanding how Westphal thinks of and approaches philosophy and theology will inform us of his motivations and the subsequent implications of his writing. We start by investigating Westphal's hermeneutics and his earlier writings to gain a particular 'Westphalian' perspective for things to come. What is important is to look at how he first receives his intellectual influences and carefully parses out their meaning before crafting his own original thinking. From here, one should see the foundations of Westphal's own hermeneutics.

First and foremost, Westphal is primarily a scholar rather than an original thinker; he maintains a textual fidelity by always investigating the author's original intention and how the text in question was received in its day. It is only from that position that he moves toward a contemporary interpretation or his own critique. His first book, *History and Truth in Hegel's Phenomenology*, published in 1979, is a superbly close reading of Hegel's *Phenomenology of Spirit*. Westphal constructs his text around Hegel's structure, crafting his work as a companion study of Hegel with the only goal of explaining *Phenomenology*, not developing any contemporary critique or adapting it for any other project.[1] This is the same case for his next primary influence, Søren Kierkegaard, in the book *Becoming a Self*, a commentary on *Concluding Unscientific Postscript*. Once he turns to Emmanuel Levinas, he follows a similar style, but this time fashions the work as a dialogue between

Levinas and Kierkegaard in the aptly titled *Levinas and Kierkegaard in Dialogue*.[2]

Westphal carries this scholastic style throughout all of his work, often focusing on one author at a time and then adding his own critique through linking to either another author or a converging concept. When reading his work, one can get the sense that it is a dialogue on another dialogue: Westphal and Author X, who also happens to be "talking" to another thinker, be it Kierkegaard talking to Hegel (more exactly, Danish Hegelians), Hegel to Spinoza, Levinas to Heidegger (or Kierkegaard), Aquinas to Pseudo-Dionysius, and so on. This pattern is especially seen in *Transcendence and Self-Transcendence*, Westphal's most original text, where each chapter title refers to an author whose concept(s) accounts for the central theme of the chapter (e.g., "Hegel: The Onto-Theological Pantheism of Spirit"), with subsequent chapters continuing Westphal's line of reasoning by engaging another author.[3] He abandons this style only when dealing with a single issue, for example, in *God, Guilt, and Death*, where he seeks to find the existential meaning of religion. All of this is to say that Westphal is a reader of texts first, a philosopher second: he initially is concerned about the text or author, and then either comments on it or links the text to another.

Rarely does he diverge from this style and rarely does he ever form any completely novel concepts or neologisms. Even with his particularly innovative use of *Aufhebung*, Westphal still maintains that term's connection to Hegel and, by way of comparison, to Kierkegaard's teleological suspension. For Westphal, the keys to overcoming particular problems or to advancing our understanding are given in the texts handed down through our intellectual history.[4]

This might seem like a typical strategy for a philosopher, but it is an important acknowledgment for us to make at the headwaters of our investigation because it tells us what terrain lies ahead and how to best navigate it. Whereas some philosophers, such as his contemporaries John Caputo and Richard Kearney, are keen on creating their own concepts and/or stretching the limits of their influences, Westphal is more conservative: he sticks closely to his sources, and when he ventures away from reading other authors in their own contexts, he does so by appropriation.[5] In relation to our present inquiry, the books *History and Truth in Hegel's Phenomenology of Spirit*, *Becoming a Self*, and, to a lesser degree, *Levinas and Kierkegaard in Dialogue* are like eddies or landmarks along a riverbank that reveal changes in the course of Westphal's thinking. Furthermore, the subjects of these books are thinkers, not topics. The thinkers whom Westphal explores, and whom he places into dialogue, become just as important for mapping Westphal's thinking as what he says about them.

This is significant for three reasons: First, it shows the evolution of his thinking—seeing how he progresses from one dialogue partner to another uncovers what he sees as most philosophically problematic in contemporary life while also revealing his insights into how to address those issues. Second, his most important contributions often come from how he connects certain authors—how he reads Kierkegaard with a Hegelian lens, for example, and how that discloses the tension between *Aufhebung* and the teleological suspension. Looking at these dialogues as a progression uncovers certain themes that run throughout his own thinking and through that of his interlocutors.[6] A particular example, which will become a central theme of ours in the coming chapters, is the relationship between politics and biblical faith. Whether it is Hegel, Kierkegaard, Levinas, or, collectively, Freud, Marx, and Nietzsche, Westphal sees that each of these authors has something to say about how a 'believing soul' should live out faith and the ethical choices that must be addressed within faith.[7] Looking at these engagements—not just how he reads authors but with whom he reads them—gives us a greater understanding of Westphal's own perspective on these issues. Finally, his dependence on the texts themselves reveals the founding principle for his hermeneutics—the primacy of the text or author over application is the underlying theme behind his whole thinking. This perhaps stems from his Protestant background, where Scripture and its interpretation are primary and essential guides for faith. This is relevant because the interpretation of Scripture forms most of his theological concepts. In *Suspicion and Faith*, for example, he links the Freud, Marx, and Nietzsche's hermeneutics of suspicion to the biblical prophets of suspicion who levy similar critiques against religious praxis. This is also true of *Whose Community? Which Interpretation?* in which he appropriates Gadamer as a heuristic for reading the Bible.

B. Keith Putt's concluding interview in Westphal's Festschrift, titled *Gazing through a Prism Darkly*, solidifies how this concern for the text, and this appeal to Scripture, weave themselves together to create the canvas for Westphal's work by highlighting his concern for canonicity and suspicion.[8] Referring back to Westphal's article "The Canon as Flexible, Normative Fact," in which he argues that canons should be considered with "both

affirmation and suspicion," Putt asks Westphal about the relationship between canonicity and interpretation, particularly interpretations that are
informed through a hermeneutics of suspicion.[9] Westphal responds:

> Your question suggests, "Well, what about the texts themselves? Does one
> approach them with suspicion?" Of course, it seems to me that the first
> thing to emphasize is the point that you have already suggested. We never
> have the texts themselves; we always have interpretations . . . on interpreta-
> tions . . . on interpretations, and those are certainly subject to suspicion.
> But then there still remains the question, "What about the production of
> the texts themselves?" Granted, in terms of deciphering its meaning, we are
> always working in a tradition of interpretation, but what about the possibil-
> ity that things went into composition of those texts of which we should be
> suspicious?[10]

Referring back to the Bible, Westphal states that his own opinion is that
the Bible was written with human hands, which problematizes the reception of those texts; "God's involvement in [their] production" makes them
"the Word of God" but that does not entail that everything in the Bible fell
"directly down from heaven." In this way, Scripture, analogous to Christ, is
both human and divine. The cleavage in the analogy is whether the Bible,
like Christ, is sinless. On this issue, Westphal is somewhat ambivalent; he
leaves the question open, stating that he does not "feel an overwhelming
compulsion to deny that human sinfulness was part of the process by which
the Scriptures came to be," noting that biblical exegetes might uncover
what role human sinfulness played in their writing. However, he states, "I
wouldn't want to lose the faith perspective, which seems to be the bottom
line, that God was involved in the production of those writings in such a way
that we can turn to them and expect to hear God speaking to us."[11]

By referring to biblical sources, their various interpretations, then relating those to one's own, we can begin to see that central to Westphal's hermeneutics is the relationship between a given text's authority and the suspicion
against the text itself. To make this connection between Westphal and his
sources a bit clearer, it is necessary to further examine the article that Westphal and Putt are referencing, "The Canon as Flexible, Normative Fact."

Authority and Suspicion: Westphal's Canonicity

In "The Canon as Flexible, Normative Fact," Westphal addresses the tension
between the general consensus that establishes particular works as classics
and the arbitrariness of what and who creates that consensus. For Westphal

the most pressing questions are, What gets to be considered a classic? and, Who decides? Following David Tracy's definition of a classic, he argues that these texts "belong to *our* story, are part of the narrative of *our* identity. They belong to *us* in a special way because we belong to them in a special way."[12] For Westphal, this process is not a binary either-or development but a situation of continuous plurality in which consensus and disagreement cause changes in gradations between "the center and the periphery," or moves texts out of the conversation all together (as if the texts move "up and down the charts, as well as on and off").[13] The principle of all this is that our story is interwoven with these texts, they are a part of our story, and our story also helps sustain and designate them as classics. Furthermore, because our story is unfolding, the classics themselves change and new ones emerge. Westphal emphasizes this last notion, stating that "to call a contemporary text a classic is to make a prophecy," a bold statement about where our story is heading while also a claim about what we wish it to become.[14]

Within this tension between a future-oriented becoming and tradition-oriented, historical worldview, Westphal refers back to Derrida's concern about the violence inherent in canons. This is where a hermeneutics of suspicion enters his thinking. Westphal appeals to Derrida's arguments that canons are based on a notion of legality and are "the origin or institution of legal systems.... [A]s the very term 'canon' suggests, there is an analogy between legal systems and literary canons in the roles they play in the formation of social identity and the maintenance of social integration."[15] This formation, for Derrida, is a violent formation: a struggle between the individuals in a society to form the identity and course of that society. Which laws (and classics) each society (dis)establishes tell us a great deal about that society. With regard to our concern about how to read Westphal, this point should not be missed: the authors he engages, and to whom he links with others in dialogue, reveal as much about his philosophical thinking as does his own singular critique of those authors.[16] His selection of authors and his subsequent dialogues are themselves a commentary and a critique.

Referring back to the violent nature of these canons, neither Westphal nor Derrida argues that this violence is necessarily physical. Westphal states that Derrida's first concern is the "'differential character of force' since it can be 'direct or indirect, physical or symbolic, exterior or interior, brutal or subtly discursive and hermeneutic, coercive or regulative, and so forth.'"[17] Westphal backs off from Derrida's strong phrasings of violence and terrorism but still holds to the principle that establishing such a canon is a struggle of becoming by way of exclusion and hierarchy. In summarizing his assessment of Derrida, Westphal states:

> [Derrida's] point, as I understand it, is to remind us of the social force of norms that are interpretations, that cannot claim the legitimacy of ultimate justification. The formal question about the canon as such, about any canon, can be framed in terms of its violence, in terms of the establishment of hierarchy and exclusion which, without ultimate justification, play a significant role in social identity and integration.[18]

Throughout the article, Westphal continues to explore the inherent violence in the concept of the canon while also understanding the importance and social necessity of that canon. His conclusion is that rather than disassembling and doing away with canons altogether, one must subject them to constant scrutiny and revision.

By way of explaining how these critiques should work, he refers back to the Athens and Jerusalem controversy between Greek philosophy and Jewish religious thought (primarily found in the Old Testament) that rose up simultaneous to Christian theology and philosophy.[19] Here he highlights how badly "Athens needs Jerusalem" as a critical dialogue partner, because both are integrated into the Western Christian tradition, albeit from different perspectives and convictions, thus helping revise, overturn, and add to that tradition and its canon of texts.[20] In this argument one can again see Westphal appealing to a dialogue between authors and texts and the community at large that establishes canons: authors (and/or their texts) need to be read in relation to others in order to gain a balanced understanding of the texts themselves and to see how those texts relate to one's own communal narrative.[21] In cementing this emphasis on dialogue between sources, he makes a final appeal toward multiculturalism by arguing that sources outside of the tradition or canon in question can prove vital in revising the canon itself. This appeal to multiculturalism, however, works in the same way as the Athens and Jerusalem model in that the canonical text in question is placed in dialogue with another extracanonical text addressing a similar issue, thus opening the text to external critique. Here again one can see the nature of dialogue in Westphal's hermeneutics while also seeing him employ a (conservative) hermeneutics of suspicion as an appeal to alterity: by placing the canonical text into dialogue with another, we disregard neither the text nor the authoritative weight that the canon lends to it, but we do revise our reception of it.[22] We renew its importance, or, if we hold that the text no longer represents our story, we decrease its authority. It moves up, down, or off the charts. However, the reader still judges the text itself; therefore, a careful appraisal of it is necessary first, then one can make an appeal to alterity by placing it into dialogue with another.

Westphal, speaking about Gadamerian hermeneutics with regard to biblical interpretation, reiterates this point, albeit with less emphasis on external, multicultural critique.[23] In *Whose Community? Which Interpretation?* Westphal summarizes thus:

> Classic texts found communities, are sustained by communities, and in turn sustain communities. But this means that their interpretation is also a communal affair, a dialogical and not a monological process. It takes place among individuals within a community and among communities. If the Bible is the "classic text" of the Christian church, that church, in turn, is the community of the Bible's interpretation. It belongs to the church's identity that it is the conversation in which its members and communities seek to understand the Bible and its subject matter: God and our relation to God.[24]

One's interpretation is communal and not definitive, so even with a closed canon, as he claims the Bible to be, an interpretation of those texts shifts as it is placed into dialogue with others. What texts we read, when we read them (more technically, our "historically effected consciousness," our *wirkungsgeschichtliches Bewusstsein*) and in relation to what else we have read, allow us to revise our interpretation.[25]

Westphal's hermeneutics hews closely to its sources, and he is focused on letting the text, through its own context, speak for itself. Moreover, Westphal's style of placing the text in dialogue with others reveals the (dis)continuities between the texts in question while also allowing them to speak to different audiences without displacing those texts from their historical-cultural contexts. Thus, Westphal is keenly aware of how texts are often lifted from their context to unjustly support ideas and ideologies. Moreover, in the case of prophetic texts, the author's biting critique can effectively be neutered if, on the one hand, the author's words are considered historically dated and no longer relevant, or, on the other hand, the author's words are "sanitized" by readers who attempt to "update" a text by revising it into a particular "context."[26]

The following section supports this claim by exploring how Westphal employs both Marx and the Hebrew prophet Amos to develop his critique of ideology, revealing three things: First is the way contextual awareness plays a pivotal role in his thinking. Second, Westphal—always a scholar first—is perpetually concerned with the consequences of removing his sources from their own context in support of his project. Third is an emphasis on Westphal's concern over losing the personal, contextual experience found in the texts that he places into dialogue, revealing that the act of placing them into dialogue enables him to recontextualize them into contemporary culture.

Masters of Suspicion and Biblical Critique: Outlining an
Appropriation of Suspicion through Dialogue

In *Suspicion and Faith*, Westphal takes the prophet Amos's historical context as inseparable from his writings. Therefore, because of our historical and cultural distance from Amos, there are certain aspects of our life for which he can serve only as a model of prophetic speech and not as a contemporary, primary prophet. Here, Westphal attempts to keep the identity of our shared history with Amos while acknowledging the differences between our circumstances. Amos is a part of our history, but that does not make him one and the same with us.

Throughout the work, he frequently compares Amos's prophetic speech to that of the so-called masters of suspicion, arguing that they all actually make similar critiques of religious praxis. For instance, Westphal centers on Amos's fight against an "unholy alliance of church and state against the poor," emphasizing how Amos preaches against the high priest Amaziah's corrupt practices.[27] Here, Westphal quickly pairs Amos's story with Marx's critique of the "church, through its silence, join[ing] the state in upholding economic exploitation," jokingly stating, "If Marx had been my student and had turned in his theory in the form of a term paper, I would have searched the notes for references to Amos. In their absence I would have called young Karl in for a serious discussion about plagiarism."[28]

Clarifying his intentions, Westphal argues that "we," his contemporary audience, cannot simply refer back to either Amos or Marx but need to utilize both, because each author speaks to us from within his own context in different ways and on different terms but with the same covalent theme. Amos and Marx can be employed together to make the critique that they share sharper for the believing soul. For Westphal, this is a great example of how the prophetic speech in biblical sources like Amos and secular, contemporary voices like that of Marx can be placed in dialogue to help others gain insight into critical self-reflection and ideology critique. Speaking as to why we need both, Westphal argues:

> We need Marx as well as Amos, perhaps Marx as a commentary on Amos, because Marx is about us in a way that Amos is not. I have been Christianizing and modernizing Amos to remind us that his message is not just about wicked people long ago and far away. We do not have that hurdle to overcome with Marx. His critique of religion is about Christians in capitalist society. We know he is talking about us. . . . Amos may understand our hearts as well as Marx does, but Marx understands our society in a way that Amos could not. If we intend to let Amos really address us, we will probably have to read him with a generous dose of Marx thrown in. The converse is equally true.[29]

We cannot merely appropriate biblical prophets to speak to present conditions; they must be read alongside others who better know our context—even others who directly critique our own beliefs—in the service of correcting our Christian praxis and fulfilling the love commandment.

In a sense, he wants to maintain the personhood and individuality of his sources, preventing them from merely becoming cogs in his own project. As Westphal's argument reveals, one cannot just "modernize" Amos to open his prophetic voice; one has to approach Amos through a commentary or dialogue to make him relatable to our current context. Furthermore, Westphal is concerned that if one makes the Hebrew prophets *the* rubric for the ethical, then their words will become a religious system just as ideological as the ones they critique; indeed, this has been the case at various points of our history. Hence, the critiques of the masters of suspicion against religion are "all too true too much of the time," and "a modern echo of an ancient assault on the devotion of the devout, the one developed by Jesus and the prophets of Israel."[30]

Instead, one relies on the prophets as guides, but they should not be mistaken for a closed narrative of living one's faith. B. Keith Putt, summarizing Westphal's conception of prophetic speech, hints at this by stating that "a prophetic philosophy of religion can never assert the same authority as the God-called prophet. Instead, it should be construed as a 'thought experiment' dedicated to making philosophy of religion more practically therapeutic and more intellectually honest."[31] Westphal does not want to close off one's life by preaching that they must "live prophetically" or hold to any closed system of ethics. Instead, he argues that prophetically inspired self-critique helps open one toward becoming a more godly ethical self.

Through Amos and Marx one can see how primary that other authors' text are to Westphal's philosophy while also seeing the interplay between authority and suspicion in his hermeneutics. However, what remains is understanding how he incorporates authors and texts into his own original thinking through dialogues. This speaks to his progressive recontextualizations, which is why the following chapter explores Westphal's use of *Aufhebung*.

NOTES

1. *HT*, xvii–xx.

2. Westphal authored two other books that follow this format of sticking close to an author, further revealing his scholastic tendencies: *KCRS, HFM*.

3. *TST*, 66. In *TST*, he begins with Heidegger and onto-theology, and then moves to Spinoza and Hegel to show forms of onto-theology, then moves to non-onto-theological concepts of God by investigating Augustine, Pseudo-Dionysius, Thomas Aquinas, and Karl Barth, respectively. He continues this style throughout the book, and it can also be seen in *SF*.

4. This is especially prevalent in Westphal's appeal to revelation in *TST*, 147–151, and in his works on Gadamer, particularly throughout *WCWI*. See also Merold Westphal, "Nietzsche as a Theological Resource," *Modern Theology* 13, no. 2 (1997): 214–225 (reprinted as chapter 14 in *OCOT*).

5. However, when Westphal does stretch the limits of his influence, it is in dialogue with another author and his or her perspective.

6. Broadly speaking, the concepts are historical consciousness; freedom and the interrelation of religion and politics (Hegel); faith, existential selving, and a religious hermeneutics of suspicion (Kierkegaard); and ethics, phenomenological transcendence, and immediacy (Levinas). For Hegel, see *HFM*, vi–iii, 8–10, 34, 43, 55; *HT*, 41, 47, 86–87. For Kierkegaard, see *BS*, 20–25, 41, 49–52; Merold Westphal, "Kierkegaard's Climacus—A Kind of Postmodernist," in *Concluding Unscientific Postscript to "Philosophical Fragments,"* ed. Robert L. Perkins, International Kierkegaard Commentary (Macon, GA: Mercer University Press, 1997), 53–71, esp. 54–56; Westphal, "Johannes and Johannes: Kierkegaard and Difference," in *Philosophical Fragments and "Johannes Climacus,"* ed. Robert L. Perkins, International Kierkegaard Commentary (Macon, GA: Mercer University Press, 1994), 13–32, esp. 18, 20–25. For Levinas, see *TST*, 178–-181, 184–187; *LKD*, 4–6, 10–12, 15–16, 18; Merold Westphal, "Levinas and Kierkegaard and the Theological Task," *Modern Theology* 8, no. 3 (July 1992): 241–261, esp. 253–254.

7. The term "believing soul" is one that Westphal appropriates from Paul Ricoeur and uses for the self who professes religious (typically but not essentially Christian) faith.

8. *GTPD*, 204.

9. Merold Westphal, "The Canon as Flexible Normative Fact," *Monist* 76, no. 4 (October 1993): 436–449. See also *GTPD*, 204.

10. *GTPD*, 205.

11. Ibid.

12. Westphal, "Canon as Flexible, Normative Fact," 438. Also David Tracy, *Plurality and Ambiguity: Hermeneutics, Religion, Hope* (San Francisco: Harper and Row, 1987), 12: "On historical grounds, classics are texts that have helped found or form a particular culture. On more explicitly hermeneutical grounds, classics are those texts that bear an excess and permanence of meaning, yet always resist definitive interpretation."

13. Westphal, "Canon as Flexible, Normative Fact," 437.

14. Ibid., 438.

15. Ibid., 441–442.

16. A key to understanding Westphal's appropriations is to explore why he places certain authors into dialogue with others. By looking at his motivations, one can also see their importance.

17. Ibid., 442. Westphal quotes from Jacques Derrida, "The Force of Law: 'The Mystical Foundation of Authority,'" in *Deconstruction and the Possibility of Justice*, ed. Drucilla Cornell, Michel Rosenfeld, and David Gray Carlson (New York: Routledge, 1992), 28. This is the primary text he cites to understand Derrida's concept of canonicity.

18. Westphal, "Canon as Flexible, Normative Fact," 442.

19. Ibid., 444.

20. Ibid., 445. He makes this claim by appealing to Jerusalem's emphasis on alterity: either by showing how contemporary Christian philosophy has shown the exclusionary character of its own tradition in making a rational justification for the faith or by arguing how Levinas's alterity criticizes Husserl and Heidegger.

21. I separate authors and texts here because Westphal typically discusses an author's entire body of work when he links thinkers together. However, he is also aware that an author's intent is one of only many readings of a text, and he attempts to understand that intent in relation to the other possible readings of a given text. On the relationship between the author and his or her text, and on the so-called death of the author, Westphal sees this as a question of "legitimation" and as the "death of the subject—not every possible subject, but that autonomous subject for whom the world is transparent and whose knowledge is final and certain." Merold Westphal, "Blind Spots: Christianity and Postmodern Philosophy," *Christian Century*, June 13, 2003, 34–35. Moreover, he does not separate the author and text completely, allowing that "every text speaks with multiple voices, some of which, but not all, are the author's," and he sees deconstruction as a "strategy for opening oneself to the many and even contradictory meanings of a text." Westphal, "Blind Spots," 35.

22. "We," here, should be interpreted to be any community that posits a canon, per Westphal's use of the term.

23. This is because, as Westphal says to Putt, the question of which books belong in the Bible—the canonicity of the Bible—is a question that is "closed"; therefore, external critique of the Bible belongs within biblical interpretation (or exegesis broadly) and its authority as a text within other canons. It is not a matter of revising the Bible with the addition or subtraction of different texts (*GTPD*, 204). In *WCWI*, Westphal is more concerned with interpretation and how Christians interpret their own founding texts than about multiculturalism. Therefore, he fashions external critique as that between Christian communities. Westphal never goes into why the Bible as a canon should be considered closed whereas others are open.

24. *WCWI*, 118.

25. Ibid., 74.

26. For example, to "Christianize" an Old Testament text, thus reframing its prophecy as one of foretelling the coming of Christ, not a prophetic critique of religious praxis.

27. *SF*, 212–213, referencing Amos 7:10–17. Amos is Westphal's primary example of prophetic speech throughout *SF*; he even references Amos in his concluding interview in *GTPD*, 186–188.

28. *SF*, 212–213.

29. Ibid., 213.

30. Ibid., xiv.

31. *GTPD*, 3.

2. RECONTEXTUALIZATION
A Westphalian Aufhebung?

Reconstituting and Despoilment: Westphal's Appropriations

William Desmond describes Westphal's style of appropriation as similar to the Israelites' despoilment of the Egyptians. However, Westphal's is a gentle despoilment: the fidelity he shows superficially to sources appears to be an agreement between him and his source, but he is actually enacting a piece-meal acquisition of certain key ideas within that source.[1] It is not a hostile takeover—it is not a takeover at all—rather, it is a form of retrieval; he takes parts of an author's idea while also diligently critiquing the idea as a whole. A charitable reading of this method would call it a recontextualization, but perhaps "gentle despoilment" is more honest.[2]

Nowhere is this despoilment more evident in Westphal's thought than in his reading of Hegel and Westphal's use of *Aufhebung*. As Desmond notes, Westphal will take *Aufhebung*, that contentious term, and, in a gentle despoilment, he will make it do all sorts of "productive, indeed benign, work for him."[3] Therefore, we continue our exploration of Westphal's herme-neutics by exploring how he appropriates Hegel's concept of *Aufhebung*, to reveal how his appropriation reconstitutes the concept itself. Moreover, the exploration here highlights three important facets of Westphal's style of philosophy: First, it shows how Westphal employs a Hegelian structure within his philosophy, which makes a further exploration of Westphal's cri-tique of Hegel all the more necessary. Second, it problematizes Westphal's textual fidelity by revealing the (hermeneutical) gap between the text in question and Westphal's own reading. While there is a hermeneutical gap for all readers, it is important for our study because we now know that Westphal grants heavy authority to the text itself, particularly when that text is Scripture. Last, and most important, our exploration in this chapter will give us insight into the way this type of recontextualization works across Westphal's thought, demonstrating how Westphal's dialogues between texts and authors build toward a central idea while also negating arguments found within those texts or made by those authors. In short, his dialogues often function as ("Westphalian") *Aufhebungen*.[4]

To understand Westphal's appropriation, we first need to understand Hegel's own use of *Aufhebung*. Once we have a grasp on what is admittedly a tricky word, let alone concept, we can explore and compare Westphal's reconstitution of the term. Doing so will reveal the differences in usage, as we first explore how Westphal uses the term in his Hegelian writings, to prove that he has a solid grasp of how Hegel used the term himself. From there, we will see how Westphal employs the term to understand Kierkegaard in order to prove how his own *Aufhebung* differs from Hegel's. We conclude by analyzing how Westphal's *Aufhebung* reveals his recontextualization of his sources, recontextualizing them—or despoiling them, if you prefer—into his own thought.

Hegel's use of Aufhebung

The German word *Aufhebung* is a word with a common meaning that is not philosophical, yet its tricky double meaning quickly lends itself to becoming one. The definition of *Aufhebung* is to cancel out something while simultaneously preserving it; however, this overly simple definition does not completely encapsulate its everyday use or its appropriation by Hegel. Therefore, we must begin by unpacking the term itself. As Ralph Palm notes, the trickiness of understanding the concept of *Aufhebung* in Hegel's works confounds several scholars, particularly English translators of Hegel, who do not know whether to translate the word as *suspension* or *sublation*, or to simply leave it in its German form.[5] While *suspension* does not quite do justice to the negation involved in *Aufhebung*, the use of *sublation* in English is all but obsolete, thus rendering it little to no help in explaining the word's meaning. Likewise, use of the German form can appear to evade the question of its meaning while also causing headaches between the German-English grammatical crossover when conjugating the term (i.e., *aufheben, aufgehoben*).[6]

When Hegel uses the term, he explains it only in four sections of his works, the most important being in *Science of Logic*, in the first chapter of book 1, titled "The Doctrine of Being."[7] In the *Zusätz*, Hegel refers to its everyday German usage, which implies that there is a preservation—the picking up can be seen as a form of preserving—and also a cessation, but what matters most to him is the simultaneity of this action; it is not an if-then movement, but a double action. "That which is sublated," Hegel remarks, "is thus something *at the same time* preserved, something that has lost its immediacy but has not come to nothing."[8] As Walter Kaufmann notes, this is akin to picking up a fallen book from the floor and putting it on a shelf: you have removed the book from its present state (the negative or cancelling action) and have preserved its condition (the positive or conserving action).[9] However, this explanation goes only so far, given that after Hegel notes the double action of *Aufhebung*, he goes on to add a third element to the term: it not only cancels and preserves but also *elevates* the object in question. He does this through contrasting *Aufhebung* with the related but etymologically distinct Latin term *tollere*.[10] *Tollere* means "to take or lift up," as in placing the book on the shelf, but *Aufhebung*, through its negating act, goes one step further and implies an elevation of the book's concept, its bookness, into something else altogether. More precisely, Hegel characterizes *tollere* as merely an affirmative action, whereas *aufheben* involves the unity of affirmation and negation. Something is taken away in the act, which makes *aufheben* a much more impactful concept since the object in question is no longer the same.

Although *Aufhebung* is directly related to the dialectic—Palm goes so far as to call it "the heart of the dialectic"—it should also be understood as its own distinct, speculative (i.e., infinite) term.[11] This is perhaps best seen in Hegel's concept of becoming found within being and nothingness, the topic that Hegel addresses in *Science of Logic*, where he first reflects on *Aufhebung*. Therefore, let us pivot our examination of *Aufhebung* to his concept of becoming in order to better grasp the term's meaning. However, it is important to note that because our interest is not in Hegel's concept of becoming, our treatment will be all too brief and simplistic, focusing primarily on *Aufhebung* and not the larger implications of Hegel's thought.

Becoming and Being: A Case Study of Hegel's Aufhebung

For Hegel, being (*Sein*) begins with the concept of pure being (*reine Sein*), which is distinct from any concept of determinate being, where existence takes shape and forms into a thing unto itself.[12] In other words, before there is 'a being' (determinate being), there must be a general concept of pure being, indeterminate and unconstructed, from which a being emerges. Pure being, according to Hegel, cannot have "any determination with respect to an other, so too it cannot have any within"; it is devoid of content and thus has no mediated distinction with or against an other.[13] Any distinction or determination would thus render it as something else, a being, that would exist with other beings (from which it is distinct and determined).

Interestingly, this sounds much like nothingness but for one great difference: the intuitive *meaning* behind the concept of nothingness. Hegel calls this "pure nothingness," which he goes on to describe as "complete emptiness, complete absence of determination and content; lack of all distinction within."[14] So far, pure being and pure nothingness sound like the same thing; however, to think of nothing intuits a meaning—even if it is the absence of meaning. "So," Hegel concludes, "nothing *is* [i.e., concretely exists] in our intuiting or thinking; or rather it is the empty intuiting and thinking itself, like being."[15] Paradoxically, this renders pure being and pure nothing as the same—both are indeterminate and empty—but they are different with respect to their intuitive meaning, and therefore they are not the same.[16] Pure being intuits an existence, however indeterminate, whereas pure nothingness intuits an absence of existence.

This paradox exists because of the unity of pure being and pure nothingness. This unity, however, dissolves in an instant when pure being "passes over" pure nothingness in its becoming determinate being.[17] As far as becoming is concerned, the 'purity' of being is thus negated through this passing over into determinate being. Hegel plainly sees that his notion of being and nothingness coming together to create a being is paradoxical and astonishing to most people, since they fail to see the relationship between indeterminacy and determinacy. So, to clarify, he remarks on how this paradox correlates with various creation motifs and concepts of existence within Christianity, which uses similar *ex nihilo* concepts, and Buddhism, which emphasizes a similar notion of indeterminate nothingness.[18] Let us turn now to how paradoxes function as a transitional aspect of Hegel's logic and its relationship to *Aufhebung*.

As Palm notes, the key to understanding the paradox of pure being and pure nothing becoming a determinate being is in noticing the location of the paradox within the transition (or becoming) itself.[19] In becoming, two things happen: (1) pure, indeterminate being and nothing are distinct and opposing yet also the same, and, as such, (2) they immediately proceed to cancel out the contradiction of the paradox (their 'opposite-yet-the-sameness') while preserving and forming a determinate being. As Hegel states:

> But the truth is . . . that they *are the not the same,* that they are absolutely distinct yet equally separated and inseparable, and that *each* immediately *vanishes into its opposite.* Their truth is therefore this *movement* of the immediate vanishing of the one into the other: *becoming,* a movement in which the two are distinguished but by a distinction which has just immediately dissolved itself.[20]

The coexistence of pure being and pure nothingness *immediately* causes a reaction that becomes something new, a distinct determinate being. This unity is better understood through its double sense: at the level of sameness they are an abstract unity (*abstrakte Einhheit*), and at the moment of union, in their becoming, they are a determinate union (*bestimmte Einheit*). Therefore, in their becoming or unifying, the indeterminacy of being and nothingness is removed—their 'pureness' is taken away or ceased—as pure being passes over pure nothingness into becoming something: a determinate, distinct, and individual being. For Hegel, this is an *Aufhebung*: "In this unity, therefore, *they are,* but as vanishing, only as *sublated* [*aufgehoben*]. They sink from their initially represented *self-subsistence* into moments which are *still distinguished* but at the same time sublated."[21]

Aufhebung, therefore, is what makes this process of becoming a determinate being possible. More precisely, it is the key to explaining what happens *in* becoming a determinate being. The *in* here is operative since the *Aufhebung* is not an external happening; rather, it happens within the unity of being and nothingness; there are no outside influences or forces causing the negation. Pure being and pure nothingness, Palm remarks, "sublate themselves" through an "internal determination from within a given moment operating on itself."[22] This is absolutely crucial to understanding *Aufhebung* because one must recognize that no outside factor can cause the negating act, only the two concepts (either concretely or abstractly) coming into union within themselves. Nothing from the outside causes this sublation, nor can another factor catalyze this unionizing: they come together, negate and preserve, and elevate by their own attraction. This may not be applicable to pure, indeterminate being and nothingness, which are abstract concepts that Hegel uses to convey a particular thought, but, for our purposes of understanding *Aufhebung*, we must remember that Hegel sees this movement as contained in the process itself.

Regarding the dialectic, this process of becoming can be reasonably deduced from determinate being to indeterminate being and nonbeing. The dialectic, in this manner, presupposes a negation within this becoming, where the process inherently posits a negation of another concept, in this case indeterminate being's negation of indeterminate nonbeing.[23] As David Gray Carlson notes, "According to Dialectical Reason, Becoming has a second aspect. It is *ceasing-to-be* (*Verstehen*), which starts from Being and ends at Nothing. It concedes the Understanding's point that Nothing turns into Being. But it embarrasses the Understanding by pointing out that the opposite is just as true: Being turns into Nothing. It has 'ceased to be.'"[24] *Embarrassed*, here, is how dialectical reasoning challenges the understanding by revealing what it has negated and, consequently, that this negation could have been an opposite movement from being to nothing.

Dialectical reasoning thus reveals the negative aspect of these movements within the *Aufhebung*, which enables one to deduce what has been negated. Just as speculative reasoning enables one to explore the act of becoming in the *Aufhebung*, its counterpart, dialectical reasoning, allows one to explore the exact opposite by reasoning back from this act of becoming to discover what was negated, and also what was preserved or elevated, in this process.[25] In regard to this negative aspect of the dialectic, Hegel states:

> Taken quite generally, this determination can be taken to mean that what is at first *immediate* is therewith posited as *mediated*, as *referred* to an other, or that the universal is posited as a particular. The *second* universal that has thereby arisen is thus the *negative* of that first and, in view of subsequent developments, the *first negative*. From this negative side, the immediate has *perished* in the other; but the other is essentially not an *empty negative*, the *nothing* which is formally taken to be the result of dialectic, but is rather the *other of the first*, the *negative* of the *immediate*; it is therefore determined as the mediated—*contains as such the determination of the first* in it.[26]

Dialectical reasoning matters to understanding Westphal's use of the *Aufhebung* because it shows how the *Aufhebung* can be deconstructed: rather than two opposing concepts moving to create a new idea, one can also reason from the final idea to the two opposing concepts that created it. Westphal's *Aufhebung* works against this dialectical aspect in that the concepts he elevates or suspends into another concept cannot be dialectically reasoned back to the moment of sublation, since they are not contradictory, antithetical concepts. For example, when Westphal claims that the teleological suspension of the ethical in *Fear and Trembling* is synonymous with the concept of *Aufhebung*, Westphal does not show how the ethical is directly antithetical to the religious; thus, one cannot dialectically reason toward the moment of sublation of the ethical into the religious. His use of the term through Kierkegaard, as shown later in this chapter, lacks this opposition and thus is not exactly a Hegelian *Aufhebung*. Rather, Westphal recontextualizes Hegel's *Aufhebung* to connect opposing (yet still not antithetical) concepts.

Through exploring Hegel's concept of determinate being, we have thus come to the following understanding of *Aufhebung*: two distinct, opposing, and antithetical (hence, related) concepts pass through a moment together in which each immediately cancels out the other while also simultaneously preserving the essential, elemental concept that formed the union in the first place. This preservation, while negating that which initially caused the opposition, elevates the essential, elemental concept insofar as what is preserved holds a different, rational status. This status, as seen in the example of a determinate being, still holds a hint of the negation in that the primary opposites (pure being and pure nothingness) can be dialectically traced back to the moment before the sublation (and so it is a speculative-rational moment). This explanation of *Aufhebung* has given us enough of a foothold with the term to allow for us explore how Westphal utilizes it and how he sees it working within the writings of others, particularly in the works of Kierkegaard, who is often seen as Hegel's greatest critic and historical counterpoint.

Westphal's Aufhebung: *A Suspension of Hegel in Kierkegaard?*

As previously noted, Westphal uses *Aufhebung* throughout his work and not only in reference to Hegel, but he first uses the term within his early scholarship on Hegel, as in *Hegel, Freedom, and Modernity*. This book is therefore a good starting point for our exploration of Westphal's *Aufhebung* because it shows that his original use of the term was strictly Hegelian in nature, and only in his more mature works does he reconstitute it.

Merold Westphal's 1991 address to the Hegel Society of America (expanded on in *Hegel, Freedom, and Modernity*) is an examination of Hegel's theory that society, in its proper function, is an *Aufhebung* of church and state articulated through the term *Sittlichkeit*.[27] He sets up this *Aufhebung* by quoting Hegel, stating that Hegel repeatedly claims that "religion is the foundation of the state" and that "the state is the foundation of religion."[28]

Not unlike Hegel's understanding of being and nothingness, both hold to the fact that the other is united but different, as in two sides of the same coin. From these two quotes, Westphal then pivots from Hegel to his own sociohistorical context in 1991, at the end of both the Cold War and the Gulf War, to reflect on what he sees as opposing yet inextricably linked forces at work in society.

Westphal articulates these opposing forces as "old secularism" and "new theocracy," both inhabiting the respective spaces of Hegel's concepts of state and religion.[29] Westphal's aim in coining the term *old secularism* is that he wishes to highlight the state's current movement toward "absolutizing pre-ethical goods"—namely, pleasure (food, sex), wealth (materialism), and honor (social class, prestige)—and this is indeed an old thread that has been woven into the function of the state for some time.[30] Autonomy without moral (i.e., religious) constraints emerges as the state's primary motivation since it is "central to the pursuit of wealth and status," revealing that old secularism (in its deification of pleasure, wealth, and honor) is liable to be charged with idolatry. Or, in the case of its instrumental use of religion, old secularism can often perversely fashion a god as an enabler of our desires.[31]

In opposition to old secularism, Westphal describes a new theocracy arising as an "ethico-religious" movement, popularly known through its "charismatic television personalities and massive, computerized direct-mail fund raisers"; this became known as "the Moral Majority," a political movement in the 1980s and 1990s based on religious, so-called family values rhetoric.[32] The new theocracy's emphasis on morality rather than religion puts them on equal footing with old secularism's absolutizing of pre-ethical goods; thus setting up a good-versus-evil narrative that fashions new theocracy as the advocate for "right" morality. Westphal, in line with his caveats on using the term *old secularism*, recognizes the differences between traditional theocracy and his own use of the term, noting that none of these members of the "Moral Majority" wishes to establish a state church. However, he does state that "the spirit of theocracy is present" in their political actions, particularly in their appeal to religious authority.[33]

However, in their ethico-religious protest, the new theocracy echoes old secularism's sectarian pursuit of personal interest by advocating a "selective morality," that is, a morality that appeals only to the tastes and causes that reflect those they hold themselves.[34] They are against the aforementioned pre-ethical goods, but only selectively and when it is in their self-interest to be against them. Therefore, in their distaste for old secularism's sexual revolution, for example, the new theocracy comes out tenfold to protest, but when that new theocracy comes to challenge other ethical offenses such as the unreserved pursuit of wealth and status, it actually *moralizes* those pursuits and reframes them as godly, making itself just as idolatrous.[35] The result of this idolization is an approving god for our personal pursuits, such that, Westphal sarcastically exclaims, "God wants us to be rich, personally and nationally, and God wants us to have a bigger military budget, for we are the shining city set on a hill to save the world from the evil empire."[36]

Hegel enters the scene for Westphal via his notion of *Sittlichkeit*, which is a sublation of private, personal religion into a common sense of reason, to create an ethical society—often expressed and understood through the customs and mores of that society. In the case of old secularism and new theocracy, Westphal notes that each opposes the other not as contradiction, where one "must be true, but as contraries, both of which may be, and in this case are, false."[37] Through his prior quotations of Hegel that church and state must be separate but are also inseparable, Westphal first peels back any idea that Hegel would support a theocratic state as contrary to his concept of freedom, the very essence of the state's existence.[38] This results, more or less, in a comparative relationship between old secularity and Hegel's concept of a purely secular state.

Yet just as the relationship is established, Westphal retreats from the notion that Hegel's *Sittlichkeit* would support an entirely secular enterprise given that, just like the new theocracy, old secularism is "only selectively critical of the primacy given to pre-ethical goods."[39] Moreover, and again in line with the critique of new theocracy, old secularism—through its unchallenged elevation of certain pre-ethical goods—encourages a de facto "civil religion which hovers around the fringes of political life and in churchly religion which hovers around the fringes of everyday life in general"; paradoxically, and as foreshadowed by the critique of idolatry, old secularism has turned into a self-legitimating religion whose foundation is just as inept as new theocracy.[40] Thus, for Westphal, old secularism and new theocracy are contrary opposites but not such that the denial of one entails the affirmation of the other.

For Westphal, these oppositions show what can go awry when a society overly concerns itself with being either too secular or too religious: idolatrous self-legitimization and selective enforcement of principles go unchecked in both, inevitably leading to an unjust, unequal society.[41] Contrariwise, Hegelian *Sittlichkeit* gives the state an ethical foundation that unites the core principles of religious life with that of the greater society. Regarding old secularism and new theocracy, he utilizes the well-established self-legitimizing nature that unites them to argue that, in their unity, the inherent paradox of each holding an opposing, cynically pious pursuit of selfish fulfillment is canceled out. What is preserved is 'the ethical': the desire to orchestrate a cohesive theory of governance.[42] Westphal argues that the ethical that is described here is a version of Hegelian *Sittlichkeit*. "Correspondingly," Westphal argues, "the state is not to be the instrumentalism of the secular life but its *Aufhebung*." Religion's "universal principle of truth" thus infiltrates "all the particular realms of national life," and therefore its critique of the secularity within "old secularism is also the critique of" religion's own idolatry: "The *Aufhebung* of secular life in the Hegelian state, whose foundation is religion, is the systematic de-absolutizing of pre-ethical goods and their subordination to and incorporation into a life determined by ethico-religious values."[43]

In sum, Westphal's concepts of old secularism and new theocracy are simply contemporary versions of an existing problem in modernity, and Hegel's *Sittlichkeit*, "as the ethico-religious *Aufhebung* of pre-ethical goods into their truly human form," serves as a theory of the state that holds up the best of what these contrary movements have in common while negating their destructive self-interests. Note that this negation or preservation happens *within* their unity and not by virtue of an outside source. What is significant for us is not Westphal's correlation of contemporary politics and religion, or his creative use of Hegel to describe them and to address a remedy through Hegel's *Sittlichkeit* (even though this further emphasizes the political nature of Westphal's philosophy). Rather, what we can see here is an example of Westphal using Hegel's *Aufhebung* in a manner somewhat faithful to Hegel himself. We can see that his use of the term in his later work is intentional and deliberate and that he is, in the vein of despoilment, taking the term from Hegel and making it his own.[44]

Suspending Hegel: Westphal's Kierkegaardian use of Aufhebung

Westphal's primary use of *Aufhebung* typically centers on his critique of Hegelian *Sittlichkeit* as the end point of a religiously based ethics. In sounding out his critique, Westphal often employs Kierkegaard's critique against Hegelian ethics and *Sittlichkeit* as a challenge to the types of cultural theocracies and secularities as mentioned earlier. In numerous places, Westphal will also relate *Sittlichkeit* to Christendom.[45] Furthermore, Westphal often finds himself agreeing with Kierkegaard on the idea that one must go beyond *Sittlichkeit* (or, in Kierkegaard's words, 'the ethical') to get to a truly religious based morality that places faith in, and obedience toward, God above all political, secular ethical systems.

One of the surprising ways that Westphal expands on his critique of *Sittlichkeit* is through detailing the interplay between Kierkegaard's pseudonymous 'authors,' where he sees each author as an individual voice discussing with another Kierkegaardian author.[46] In this vein, Westphal addresses the Kierkegaardian corpus as a whole, attempting to tease out the prevailing themes that run through it. It is as if Kierkegaard is performing a dialogue with himself and Westphal is moderating it for his readers.[47] For example, he sees Judge William in *Either/Or* discussing Hegelian *Sittlichkeit*, which informs him of the idea of the ethical that is taken up by Johannes De Silentio in *Fear in Trembling*. Likewise, the teleological suspension in *Fear and Trembling* informs him of the teleological suspensions first seen in Frater Taciturnus's section in *Stages on Life's Way*, which Johannes Climacus expands on in *Concluding Unscientific Postscript*. Finally, all of these works culminate in Kierkegaard's self-authored *Works of Love*, in which Kierkegaard details how the love commandment is the highest act of faith and a task of a lifetime. In this way, Westphal sees Kierkegaard's pseudonymous dialogue reaching its conclusion through Kierkegaard himself, who gets the final word.[48]

Westphal introduces the concept of *Aufhebung* through Judge William's account of marriage in *Either/Or*, which Westphal describes as a form of ethical *Sittlichkeit*, given how marriage tames sexual desire. For Judge William, this is where the sensual, pleasure-seeking desires of sex are "ennobled" through marriage, which is "the transfiguration of the first love [i.e., aesthetic love, sex] and not its annihilation."[49] Sexual pleasure is seen as a preethical good that is *aufgehoben* in marriage as an ethical or 'rightly ordered' act. Marriage elevates—transfigures even—sexual desire into something beautiful, just, and worthy. This structure leads Westphal to argue that Judge William is a Hegelian, "whether he knows it or not."[50] In *Philosophy of Right*, for example, Hegel notes that "marriage, as the elementary social relation, contains firstly the factor of natural life" and that "marriage is essentially an ethical relation."[51] He goes on to remark that various accounts of marriage's relation to the foundation of the state are inadequate because they do not take into view the loving aspect of the relationship. Additionally, traditional thoughts on love as the foundation of marriage are also woefully inadequate.[52] Continuing, Hegel remarks that "the ethical side of marriage consists in the consciousness that the union is a substantive end. Marriage thus rests upon love, confidence, and the socializing of the whole individual existence."[53] Thus, it is an *Aufhebung* of the pre-ethical sexual desire, transfigured in love between the couple and ennobled in duty toward the family and state.

For Westphal, this is exactly the form of the ethical that Johannes De Silentio remarks is teleologically suspended by Abraham in *Fear and Trembling*. According to Westphal, De Silentio's commentary in *Fear and Trembling* marks the "transition from the ethical to the religious" where "Judge William falls short of the religious" through his fidelity to the ethical. *Sittlichkeit* can take one only so far, and it definitely cannot comfort Abraham as he walks toward Mount Moriah. The ethical, therefore, must be teleologically suspended for this journey to happen. On this matter, Westphal is explicit: stating that this suspension is "nothing but a Hegelian *Aufhebung*, in this case the relativizing of the ethical by recontextualizing it within the religious as its higher principle. But while the form of this teleological suspension is Hegelian, its content is anti-Hegelian, for it is an all-out assault on the Hegelian understanding of *Sittlichkeit*."[54]

How De Silentio remedies the epistemological ramifications of suspending the ethical—a mediated, reasoned ethics—into the religious is a discussion for chapter 4. What is important presently is that this reveals the paradigm for how Westphal sees subsequent teleological suspensions in Kierkegaard's writings. Westphal elaborates on this particular form of *Aufhebung*:

> Another Hegelian name for such mediation is *Aufhebung*; in the language of *Fear and Trembling*, we are talking about a teleological suspension. In both cases the process of recontextualization has negative and positive implications, cancellation and preservation. When X is *aufgehoben*, or teleologically suspended in Y, the immediate, self-sufficient form of X is canceled, and whatever belongs to that mode of its being is relativized as something insufficient by itself. But this has positive significance, for the claim is that Y is the truth, or *telos*, of X, and that in this process X realizes itself, or at least moves to a higher level of its normative development.[55]

Westphal sees an X that is taken up and recontextualized within Y, which thereby cancels or negates the *telos* of X—the true purpose or end goal for X—while also preserving some aspect of X. In other words, the aim of the ethical toward the good and righteous is preserved, recontextualized, and *taken up* into the religious. The self's walk toward righteousness falls short in and of itself because of humanity's fallen nature; however, when the self surrenders its claim on righteousness to God, then and only then can it truly feel that it is on the path toward righteousness, because the self is following God first and its own intellect second. This is why Abraham takes up his task and follows God's command toward Mount Moriah.

Two things are striking about Westphal's reading. First, it is remarkable and enlightening to see how Kierkegaard undoes Hegel's work through Hegel himself. This reading of Kierkegaard reveals the Dane's ingenious wit and clever critique by at once showing how Hegel is the greatest philosopher of them all while also showing that Hegel is still but a fallen man when compared to God and revelation.[56] Hegel is not wrong, but he is not right either; his concepts of *Sittlichkeit* and *Aufhebung* are correct when he talks about taking up and elevating a base notion, such as pre-ethical desires, but they fail once they mistake the true *telos* of the self (or selves) as one that is free and understood as ethical, communal living. Rather, the true *telos* of the self is to love God above all things and to love your neighbor as yourself.

This leads to the second striking element of Westphal's reading: that this is not *really* an *Aufhebung* in the strict Hegelian sense. In this reading, X and Y are not paradoxes of each other. Nowhere in Westphal's account (or in Kierkegaard's) is the religious or anything else paradoxically equated to the ethical. In Hegel's account of becoming, pure nothingness and pure being were exactly contrary. In his account of *Sittlichkeit*, this was somewhat or partially so, in that private religious sentiment and secular social ethics were equal in their aims (i.e., how should I live?) but contrary in their executions and goals. But in the teleological suspension of the ethical—if it is indeed *Sittlichkeit* as Westphal argues—the religious is hardly on par with the ethical as an opposing force, and making it into a dialectic somewhat softens Kierkegaard's critique of the ethical.

Westphal's rebuttal to this, I imagine, would follow that it *was* on par once Abraham received the command from God. "Should I follow what I've been told is right, which is to not kill my children," Abraham would have asked himself, "or should I follow what my God tells me to do, with the hope that God will give Isaac back to me or somehow make this all OK?" Westphal might argue that this dilemma poses *Sittlichkeit* and the ethical against the religious command to follow God. At the onset, this makes sense: *Sittlichkeit* is negated but preserved in the justness of God, and the religious is also thereby lifted into righteousness because it suspends all human ethics within faith and duty toward God. This is tenable and possible.

However, is it tenable throughout Kierkegaardian scholarship? That is a much more difficult question. As we have previously covered, Westphal argues that this teleological suspension is a paradigm that Kierkegaard follows throughout his work, particularly in his theory of stages. In short, the aesthetic (pre-ethical) is teleologically suspended in the ethical, which is then suspended in Religiousness A, which is then suspended in Religiousness B, and (for Westphal) completed in Religiousness C.[57] Westphal argues that these follow the exact same pattern of suspension or *Aufhebung* seen in *Fear and Trembling*. But again, what are the contraries in these patterns?[58] The critical questions thus become these: How and in what way does X negate Y? And once Y has taken up X, how does one *logically deduce* this moment of sublation? Furthermore, it appears as if Westphal often forgets the necessity of negation in the process. It almost reads as quasi-eschatological, where all things get taken up or otherwise reconciled into a higher, (more) complete purpose. Is there an actual negation happening in a Westphalian *Aufhebung*, or is it all merely suspension? Sometimes it can be hard to tell.

In *Concluding Unscientific Postscript*, Kierkegaard addresses Hegel's use of *Aufhebung* as a philosophical term through the pseudonym Johannes Climacus. Exploring Climacus's critique thus should provide clarification in regard to how Kierkegaard himself perceived the relationship between his teleological suspension and Hegel's *Aufhebung*. Following Hegel, Climacus places the concept within the realm of subjective thinking and inward speculation, and he then focuses on how it is perceived in Christian thinking, particularly in relation to Christianity's paradox of faith. What is at stake, for Climacus, is how the concept of *Aufhebung*, through its suspension of "various and indeed opposite meanings," functions as an explanation of paradoxes, which thus renders Christianity as something one can reasonably understand.[59] In regard to Christianity, Hegel's *Aufhebung* represents a hubristic attempt to logically grasp the truth held within the paradox of Jesus Christ. The speculative nature of *Aufhebung*, Climacus argues, reduces the paradox to a relation of opposites, which makes the paradox logical, thus no longer rendering it as a paradox. "But suppose," Climacus states, "that we let the word *aufheben* mean reduction to a relative factor, as indeed it does when what is decisive, the paradox, is reduced to a relative factor. What this says is that there is no paradox, no decision, for the paradox and the decisive are what they are precisely by being unyielding."[60] For Climacus, the problem with Hegel's concept of *Aufhebung* is not that it renders Christianity, and the paradox of Jesus as divine yet man (the primary paradox of Christianity, for Climacus), as false or untrue. Quite the opposite. Climacus's primary concern is that such speculation has the audacity to believe that it can grasp and logically understand this paradox, thus missing the point of Christianity altogether.[61] Relating this back to our exploration of determinate being in the prior section, Climacus might agree with Hegel that there is a paradox between the relation of being and nonbeing; however, he would criticize the reduction of becoming, or of the creation of determinate being, into this simple act of negation-preservation: there is more happening in becoming than a simple movement of being passing over into nonbeing. Although Hegel acknowledges that this is an abstract understanding, it still attempts to know too much and it assumes that the paradox can be understood, making it no longer a paradox.

Climacus argues that Hegelians are gullible. Specifically regarding Christianity, these great thinkers have mistaken logic as *the truth* rather than beholding the paradox of Christianity as the actual truth that the average Christian accepts naturally within faith.[62] One might kindly say that they have overthought the paradox; less charitably, one might argue that they have tried to seize the truth of Christianity as their own:

> For Christianity as it is understood by the speculator differs from what plain folk are presented. [For the plain folk] it is a paradox, but the speculator knows how to suspend the paradox. So it is not the Christianity that is, was and remains the truth, and the speculator's understanding is not that Christianity is the truth; no, Christianity's truth is the speculator's understanding of Christianity. *The understanding is thus something other than the truth*; it is not that once the understanding has understood everything contained in the truth, then truth is understood.... The truth is not first given and its understanding what one then awaits; *what is awaited is the completion of the speculative understanding as that which alone can bring about the truth.* Speculative knowledge thus differs from knowledge in general, as something indifferent to what is known, so that the latter does not change by being known but stays the same. No, speculative knowledge is itself the object of knowing.[63]

Climacus thus makes it clear that he has concerns about the use of *Aufhebung* to properly understand the paradox of Christianity, and this explains why he forgoes the use of the term in describing his theory of stages. It would be philosophically inconsistent to critique the speculator's use of *Aufhebung* to remove, or to 'render out,' the logical impossibility of the paradox, and then to go on to explain how one arrives at the paradox of Christianity through a process of stages that are *aufgehoben* in each other. This reveals a particular concern missing in Westphal's argument that the teleological suspension and *Aufhebung* are synonymous concepts: he does not explain why, if this is true, Kierkegaard opted to call these transitions teleological suspensions. As one can see with the passage just previous, Climacus's concern with *Aufhebung* runs parallel to De Silentio's concern against *Sittlichkeit*: Hegel is not wrong, but he is not right either. Through *Aufhebung*, Hegel and his followers make the correct observation that there is a dialectical relation between opposing concepts, but they fool themselves once they mistake this observation as a method to explain a paradox's full truth within a dialectical relation, especially within the paradox of Christianity and within Jesus' dual nature.

Westphal has received similar critiques from Jack Mulder, who argues against Westphal's conviction that the teleological suspension completes a dialectical movement, and Henry Piper, who argues that Westphal wrongly fashions Kierkegaard as quasi-Hegelian.[64] Mulder and Piper's arguments vary, but the covalent element of their critique is Westphal's use of Hegel to understand Kierkegaard: either Westphal reads Kierkegaard's pseudonyms too dialectically, as if they are Hegelian progressions of Kierkegaard's thinking, or he reads the teleological suspensions too dialectically, as if the suspensions themselves 'complete' the progression on life's way or that the self can otherwise 'return' to a respective stage as if it were a Hegelian dialectic.[65] In Westphal's rebuttal, he does not revise his position but essentially retraces his steps as detailed earlier.[66] Debates about the proper reading of Kierkegaard aside, what is important to our own investigation comes into view when Westphal addresses Piper's concern that Kierkegaard is not a Hegelian:

> So [after restating or proving that Kierkegaard is indeed using Hegelian themes, as seen with Judge William], a more careful formulation than "Kierkegaard is not Hegelian" would be that Kierkegaard is not *substantively* Hegelian even when he (or his pseudonyms) employ Hegelian forms. *The question is about the how: are these forms employed as Hegel employs them?* Piper understands this when distinguishing the "logical" dialectic of Hegel from the "non-dialectical," "existential" dialectic of Kierkegaard. The difference is between a dialectic in which differences are "mediated" and brought to 'resolution' and one in which they remain in "tension" and "paradox."[67]

Hegel does not have the final say on how Hegel's concepts can be used, according to Westphal. To say that something is Hegelian does not have to mean that it is Hegelian in the proper sense: the dialectic does not need to find resolution but can be in tension and taken up by another *Aufhebung*. Here, Westphal reveals himself as a despoiler of Hegel. Hegel no longer has control over his own concepts, and while we should be mindful of the way Hegel developed these terms, we do not need to limit their usage to Hegel's own. This is not to say that one can do whatever one wants with concepts such as *Aufhebung*; philosophical concepts have legacies, and to ignore their original usages is abuse. A proper appropriation is mindful of this legacy while still exploring its possibilities; appropriation explores the tensions within the concept's original meaning and context in relation to our own while not breaking the concept. Last, these tensions open up the elasticity of the term by placing its original meaning in relation to a contemporary, evolving usage: Hegel's *Aufhebung* is taken up by Kierkegaard's usage of the term (and in Kierkegaard's critique of Hegel), which is then taken up by Westphal and his own philosophy.

Consider whether this is what Hegel did with the term *Aufhebung* when he adapted it for his philosophy. In our first exploration of Hegel's use, we noted that he took the term in its everyday form and explored its philosophical 'usefulness' for understanding how things are, thereby canceling out its everyday usage for a higher purpose. The everyday, common *Aufhebung* is—once its paradox is genuinely reflected on—*aufgehoben* into a philosophical *Aufhebung*! The unity of the sublation here is the notion of paradox itself: on the one hand, the common, everyday perspective in which contrary actions have practical meaning (to pick up a fallen book), and, on the other hand, from a theoretical perspective in which paradoxes have a different but similar meaning (to say yes and no to the same question). The fact that the sublation happens *within* the term itself and with no external additions (or prefixes or suffixes) completes this idea.

Now, it would be perfectly sane to argue that this is grasping at straws and is linguistic sophistry—a charge that has been levied by several critics against Hegel.[68] Additionally, it could be argued that stretching a term to its limits—or, as I did earlier, turning a term against itself—is bad philosophy in the sense that it eschews rigor and fidelity for a (faulty) attempt to find meaning and understanding. Philosophy requires and demands from its practitioners a certain rigor in order to prevent concepts from falling into etymological wordplay and nonsense.

Westphal does not see this as softening or weakening rigor for the sake of finding understanding.[69] Rather, it is about being mindful of the sources and then recognizing the tension already within the source itself. Throughout his Kierkegaard scholarship, Westphal has, with remarkable consistency, characterized the connections and tensions between Kierkegaard and Hegel. His prior expertise in Hegel is undoubtedly the catalyst for this reading. It ultimately comes down to whether one finds his claims convincing. Moreover, his philosophy of religion may hinge on whether you grant him this understanding of *Aufhebung*, since it founds the structure of his all of his work.

Desmond is right in claiming that Westphal uses *Aufhebung* to do work—profound *and* benign work—and that there is a degree of despoilment in his philosophy as a whole. But Westphal does not arrive by taking any intellectual shortcuts: there is still a great admiration toward his sources (or the "Pharaoh," as Desmond puts it), and he does not blindly take from them. Rather, as Desmond notes, it is a gentle and agreeable despoilment. Yet, unlike the Pharaoh-Israel metaphor employed here, this is always a three-part dialogue between X, Y, and Westphal himself. The term *dialogue* could not be more important, because, for Westphal, what is happening here is grounded in a hermeneutics that simultaneously appropriates while also being faithful to its source: 'What does X say to Y, what is or would be negated in their dialogue, and what could be taken up from it into my own thought?' Westphal's thinking is, therefore, always a recontextualization of his sources into something else, something higher. However, it is a particular type of recontextualization; it is a Westphalian *Aufhebung*.

NOTES

1. *GTPD*, 21–23. Desmond is referencing Exodus 3:21–22, 11:2–3, 12:35–36, and Psalm 105:37. His intent is playful but also evocative of Westphal's biblical roots in its relationship to his politics and ethics.

2. *GTPD*, 26.

3. Ibid., 23. Westphal's most creative use of *Aufhebung* comes from his reading of Kierkegaard, particularly when describing Kierkegaard's concept of the teleological suspension. On several occasions and in varying contexts, Westphal equates the two terms as meaning the same thing. See, for example, *LKD*, 47; *TST*, 11n29; Merold Westphal, "Kierkegaard and the Role of Reflection in Second Immediacy," in *Immediacy and Reflection in Kierkegaard's Thought*, ed. Paul Cruysberghs, Johan Taels, and Karl Verstrynge (Leuven: Leuven University Press, 2003), 174.

4. Calling this a "Westphalian *Aufhebung*" should not conflate Merold Westphal's thought with the Germanic region of Westphalia or the Peace of Westphalia. I use the neologism to separate Westphal's *Aufhebung* from Hegel's and from those who use it in Hegel's own manner.

5. Ralph Palm, "Hegel's Concept of Sublation: A Critical Interpretation" (PhD diss., Katholieke Universiteit Leuven, 2009), 1–2, 8, 13–15. With regard to its resistance to translation, Palm gives a valuable anecdote (1n2) in which Hegel's translators had such a dispute over translating the term in Hegel's *Encyclopedia Logic* that they produced two different introductions. See G. W. F. Hegel, *The Encyclopedia Logic: Part I of the Encyclopedia of Philosophical Sciences with the Zusätze*, trans. and ed. T. F. Geraets, W. A. Suchting, and H. W. Harris (Indianapolis, IN: Hackett Publishing, 1991), xxvi, xxxv–xxxvi. See also Ralph Palm, "Hegel's Contradictions," *Hegel Bulletin* 32, nos. 1–2 (2011): 134–158.

6. For the sake of clarity, I use only *Aufhebung* except when specifically discussing its other forms, since Westphal's own work uses that term.

7. Palm, "Hegel's Concept of Sublation," 8. The three instances are PS, 68 (HW 3/94–TM); EL, 154 (HW 8/204–205); and SL, 107 (HW/114). The third of these instances pertains to the differences between the first and second editions of *Science of Logic*. Note that this is Hegel's explanation of the term, not its usage.

8. G. W. F. Hegel, *Science of Logic*, trans. and ed. George Di Giovanni (Cambridge: Cambridge University Press, 2010), 82 (*SL* 107; HW 5/114–EA), emphasis mine. To give easy references to nonspecialists, I cite direct quotations from Di Giovanni's translation while making every effort to cite other translations when referencing secondary sources such as Ralph Palm.

9. Walter Kaufmann, *Hegel: A Reinterpretation* (South Bend, IN: University of Notre Dame Press, 1965), 114. Taken from Palm, *Hegel's Concept of Sublation*, 9.

10. Hegel, *Science of Logic*, trans. Di Giovanni, 82 (SL 107 [HW 5/114–EA]).

11. Palm, *Hegel's Concept of Sublation*, 30. The use of *Aufhebung* here is understood as speculative or infinite reasoning, according to Hegel, insofar as its relation to thinking and metaphysics. In *The Encyclopaedia Logic*, Hegel distinguishes infinite reason from the finite reason that dominated philosophy before Kant. This finite form of reasoning had not yet understood what reason could or could not do (which is why Kant's critique of reason was so important for Hegel), and thus took for granted that one could reason about things-in-themselves with no attention to their predicates or relation to other things (EL §26–27). "The presupposition of the older metaphysics," Hegel summarizes, "was that of the naïve belief generally, namely, that thinking grasps what things are *in-themselves*, that things only are what they genuinely are when they are [captured] in thought" (EL §28Z). Accordingly, older metaphysics took up "the abstract determinations of thought immediately," which allowed the thinker to consider these predicates—these attachments to the thing-in-itself under consideration—as a part of what makes the thing a thing, what makes it "true" as a thing in relation to the thinker (EL §28Z).

In contrast, speculative thought after Kant opens the thing in question to be considered from an "infinite form of reason" by expressing that it has certain qualities that cannot "be brought to consciousness through what is finite"; that is, the thinker cannot fully bring about the abstract qualities of the thing in question through rationalization (EL §28Z). Infinite thinking thus turns inward toward speculation and sublates this acknowledgment of finite thinking, accepting its limitations—what reason can and cannot do—while also cancelling these limitations in respect to finite thinking's naïveté (that it can think of things-in-themselves). This allows the thinker to proceed toward an infinite speculation of the thing in itself. Hence, one transitions from thinking about things-in-themselves to thinking about thinking, which thus makes this an infinite form of thinking for Hegel: there is no limiting opposition when one is thinking about thinking since no object stands over against cognition as that which is not-cognition. Thus, Hegel states: "Infinite or speculative thinking, on the contrary [to finite thinking's restriction to determinations], makes determinations likewise, but, in determining, in limiting, it sublates this defect again. Infinity must not be interpreted as an abstract, ever-receding beyond" but in a simple manner of negation of limitation while cognizant of those limitations (EL §28Z). Quotes are from Hegel, *Encyclopaedia Logic* (trans. Geraets, Suchting, and Harris).

12. SL 82; HW 5/82; Hegel, *Science of Logic*, 48, 59.

13. Hegel, *Science of Logic*, 48.

14. Ibid., 59.

15. Ibid.

16. By 'intuitive meaning,' Hegel refers to the initial, primal meaning of being and nothingness. *Intuition*, and the verb *intuit*, pertain to their basic meanings: that being connotes that some-thing exists and that nothing connotes that no-one-thing exists.

17. Ibid., 60.

18. Ibid., 60–82. See also Palm, *Hegel's Concept of Sublation*, 42–56.

19. Palm, *Hegel's Concept of Sublation*, 51. *Location* here is to be understood as the paradox's position in the logical sequence of becoming.

20. Hegel, *Science of Logic*, 60 (cf. Palm, *Hegel's Concept of Sublation*, 51; Hegel, SL 83; HW 5/83–EA). The emphasis is Hegel's.

21. Ibid., 80 (SL 105; HW 5/112–EA); 53–54. The emphasis is Hegel's.

22. Palm, *Hegel's Concept of Sublation*, 56.

23. Hegel, *Science of Logic*, 741–744.

24. David Gray Carlson, *A Commentary on Hegel's Science of Logic* (New York: Palgrave Macmillan, 2007) 21.

25. Hegel, *Science of Logic*, 744–746.

26. Ibid., 744 (12.245). The emphasis is Hegel's.

27. HFM, 165. *Sittlichkeit* is also a difficult term that Hegel employs throughout his work. Perhaps an oversimplistic translation would be the concept of ethical life or order within society.

28. Ibid.

29. Ibid., 166.

30. Ibid. In an aside on page 166, Westphal readily admits that this is not the standard definition of secularism and that by calling into question the concept old secularism, his intention is "to call attention to an important observable feature of the secularization process," namely its relationship to the adage "if God is dead everything is permitted."

31. Ibid., 168–169. On the point of idolatry, Westphal argues this is particularly clear in the case of "nuclear nationalism," where "we are prepared to incinerate millions . . . simply because they happen to belong to another people." Invoking the term *holocaust*, a religious word used to denote burnt offerings and sacrifices for personal sins, he argues that it has come to stand for a sacrifice to a different god: "If we ask who is the god to whom human life on this unprecedented scale, along with human civilization and the earth's atmosphere, are to be sacrificed, the answer is clear: the nation" (169).

32. This American political movement gained in popularity through the 1980s and 1990s; Vice President Dan Quayle evoked it when reprimanding the television character Murphy Brown (in the eponymously titled show *Murphy Brown*) for having a baby out of wedlock. Westphal's example is dated but still relevant given the rise of popular conservative cable television news and radio programs that trace their roots to the rise of the Moral Majority. For a history, see David Bromley and Anson Shupe, *New Christian Politics* (Macon, GA: Mercer University

Press, 1984), esp. "Part II: Sources of Social Support for the New Christian Right," 61–113. For the specifically televangelical bent, see Doug Banwart, "Jerry Falwell, the Rise of the Moral Majority, and the 1980 Election," *Western Illinois Historical Review*, no. 5 (Spring 2013): 133–157.

33. *HFM*, 170.

34. Ibid., 172.

35. It seems that Westphal anticipated the "prosperity gospel" movement that emerged in the coming decade.

36. Ibid., 172.

37. Ibid.

38. Ibid., 172–174.

39. Ibid., 177.

40. Ibid.

41. Westphal calls this a sectarian epistemology, denoting that it is not just society turning a blind eye toward its own principles; instead, society comes to *know* and *understand* the world only through this self-interested selectivity. One not only sees what one wants to see, but one is fooled by one's own self-interests into thinking that this is all there is to see. See ibid., 174.

42. Ibid., 178.

43. Ibid., 178.

44. Looking at Westphal's source material on religion's role in the state, primarily Hegel's *Philosophy of Right*, helps us understand his use of the term. In section 270, Hegel details his notion of the state where, in the *Zusätz*, he states that religion can be used as a tool of indifference or, at worse, oppression. However, religion's necessity to the state can be seen "when we go back to their conception," or before religion is *taken up* by the state. "Religion has as its content absolute truth," Hegel continues, "and, therefore, also the highest kind of feeling." G. W. F. Hegel, *Philosophy of Right*, trans. S. W. Dyde (Kitchener, ON: Batoche Books, 2001), 206. Religion's orientation toward absolute truth found in God, as the "unlimited basis and cause of all things," lends itself to becoming the foundation of the state's ethics. However, the purely secular state concerns itself with laws and duties, Hegel argues, which lends the ethical system its determinate reality. "Religion, so interpreted," Hegel concludes, "is the foundation of the ethical system, and contains the nature of the state as the divine will; yet it is only the foundation. This is the point at which the state and religion separate. The state is the divine will as a present spirit, which unfolds itself in the actual shape of an organized world" (*Philosophy of Right*, 207). Hegel, here, is explicating the ethical system as an *Aufhebung* of religion and the secular state, which Westphal then takes as the paradigm for his old secularism and new theocracy.

45. *LKD*, 133: "Similarly," Westphal argues, "Kierkegaard's positive account of the self is in ethical terms, for example the absolute duty to God with which De Silentio explicates the teleological suspension of *Sittlichkeit* and Christendom." See also *LKD*, 53–54, 72, 105, 106, 133–136, 160n18; *KCRS*, 76–82, 109; *BS*, 29. These are but a few examples of a recurring theme.

46. Westphal is consistent when introducing his concept of Kierkegaard's teleological suspensions—as if he always takes the minority position (or, at least, is talking to non-Kierkegaardian scholars) and therefore has to explicate it nearly every time. This creates a pattern in his work, but to simplify things, we primarily examine Westphal's thought in *Becoming a Self*.

To find the pattern yourself, see *LKD*, 53–57; *BS*, 24–29, 91–93, 115–123, 154–158, 160–167, 194–199; *KCRS*, 30–32, 76–83; *TST*, 207–213, 217–219; Merold Westphal, "Johannes and Johannes: Kierkegaard and Difference," in *International Kierkegaard Commentary: Philosophical Fragments and Johannes Climacus*, ed. Robert Perkins (Macon, GA: Mercer Press, 1994), 14–15, 19–25, 31–31; Westphal, "Kierkegaard and Hegel," in *The Cambridge Companion to Kierkegaard*, ed. Alastair Hannay and Gordon D. Marino (Cambridge: Cambridge University Press, 1997), 76–101. This latter essay, in addition to describing the complicated relationship between the two thinkers, excellently describes how Westphal's sees the connections and dialogue between Kierkegaard's authors that develops into a cohesive narrative and discussion on Hegelian concepts such as *Sittlichkeit* and *Aufhebung*.

See also Merold Westphal, "Kierkegaard's Teleological Suspension of Religiousness B," in *Foundations of Kierkegaard's Vision of Community*, ed. George B. Connell and C. Stephen Evans (London: Humanities Press, 1992), 111–114; Westphal, "Kierkegaard's Religiousness C: A Defense," in *International Philosophical Quarterly* 44:4 (2004): 537–542, 546–548; Westphal, "Abraham and Sacrifice," in *Neue Zeitschrift für Systematische Theologie und Religionsphilosophie* 50:3–4 (2008): 320–321; Westphal, "Kierkegaard on Language and Spirit," in *Language and Spirit*, ed. D. Z. Phillips and Mario von der Ruhr (New York: Palgrave Macmillan, 2004), 72–73, 78–79 (see also the dialogue between Westphal and other scholars at 87–88).

47. For further elaboration on how these pseudonyms engage in dialogue with each other, see Westphal, "Johannes and Johannes."

48. Note the Hegelian character of Westphal's reading of these 'authors.' For reference, the first three chapters of *Becoming a Self* set the stage for Westphal's method of reading Kierkegaard's pseudonyms, see especially *BS*, 20–21, 25–26, 29–30. With regard to Kierkegaard having the final say in *Works of Love*, what Westphal will eventually call Religiousness C, see *BS*, 194–200. I explore these matters further in chapter 4.

49. *BS*, 24–25. He is quoting from Søren Kierkegaard, *Either/Or Part II*, trans. William and Edna Hong (Princeton, NJ: Princeton University Press, 1987), 31. See also *Either/Or Part II*, 21, 30, 56–57, 61, 94, 253.

50. Westphal, "Kierkegaard and Hegel," 106.

51. *Philosophy of Right*, §161. Westphal also uses this example of marriage in *HFM*, 179–180.

52. *Philosophy of Right*, §162.

53. Ibid., §163.

54. *BS*, 26, 39.

55. Ibid., 145. The context in which Westphal raises this comparison of *Aufhebung* and teleological suspension is in discussing the relationship between *Philosophical Fragments* and its sequel, *Concluding Unscientific Postscript*. On pages 303–309 of *Postscript* (Cambridge, 2009), Climacus—the author of both works—discusses the relationship between Hegel and Christendom, particularly as regards 'becoming' a Christian through baptism. The issue at hand is whether simply performing a ritual can legitimate the act of becoming Christian; the child cannot assent, and many baptize their children out of custom. This concerns Climacus (echoed by Westphal on pages 144–148 of *Becoming a Self*) about the role of mediation in faith, particularly with respect to *Sittlichkeit* and its 'regulating' of faith. See Kierkegaard, *Concluding Unscientific Postscript*, chapter 4, §1.

56. At page 102 of "Kierkegaard and Hegel," Westphal draws this out to show how Kierkegaard is simultaneously mocking and praising Hegel through his allegory of the dancer who could leap so high that he thought he could fly (Kierkegaard, *Concluding Unscientific Postscript*, 124). The dancer represents Hegel, and the dancer can clearly leap higher than any other dancer to great praise. The dancer fails by believing that a great leap is equal to flight.

57. For Religiousness C, see chapter 4. In short, Westphal discovers this hidden stage when placing the theory of stages alongside *Works of Love*.

58. For example, when Religiousness A (a religious sentiment with divine aims but settles for self-legitimization/*Sittlichkeit*) is taken up by Religiousness B (a Christ-centered religiousness

that focuses the believer toward living Christ-like), does it negate anything within Jesus Christ or his teachings?

59. Søren Kierkegaard, *Concluding Unscientific Postscript*, trans. Alastair Hannay (Cambridge: Cambridge University Press), 186.

60. Ibid., 187.

61. At page 187 of *Concluding Unscientific Postscript*, Climacus states: "Speculation says by no means that Christianity is untruth; on the contrary, it says that speculation grasps its truth." This, for Kierkegaard, is the greatest act of hubris (see 189–196).

62. Although Climacus regards this 'average Christian' as "plain folk," it is partially untrue; in various places Kierkegaard recalls the difficulty that all Christians face in accepting the paradox of Christianity and of Jesus' nature, which is why Religiousness B is the last stage. However, here the 'average Christian' is an idealized concept—like the term *simple soul* he uses on 191—to distance the true Christian from the Danish Hegelians and Christendom that is his primary target.

63. Kierkegaard, *Concluding Unscientific Postscript*, 187–188, emphasis is mine.

64. Jack Mulder Jr., "Re-radicalizing Kierkegaard: An Alternative to Religiousness C," in *Continental Philosophy Review* 35 (2002): 303–324; Henry Piper, "Kierkegaard's Non-Dialectical Dialectic or That Kierkegaard Is Not Hegelian," in *International Philosophical Quarterly* 44, no. 4 (December 2004): 496–518. See chapter 4.

65. Mulder, "Re-Radicalizing Kierkegaard," 304, 309, 311–312, 314, 321; Piper, "Kierkegaard's Non-Dialectical Dialectic," 498–499, 503, 510–518.

66. Westphal, "Kierkegaard's Religiousness C." For example, Westphal asks, "Is it not evident that a teleological suspension has the form of an Hegelian Aufhebung?" and notes that while "Judge William does not use the language of teleological suspension or *Aufhebung*, . . . the structure is plainly visible, the same structure that [De] Silentio calls a teleological suspensions in a case where it is the ethical (society's requirements) that is relativized *vis-à-vis* the religious (God's requirement)" (546).

67. Westphal, "Kierkegaard's Religiousness C," 547, emphasis is mine.

68. Also, picking up a fallen book is not paradoxical, but I stand with Kaufmann in believing that this is a typical everyday usage of the term.

69. "There is something (formally) Hegelian in my account of Kierkegaard's dialectic, but if by 'temporizing' is meant a softening that calls for a re-radicalization of Kierkegaard, as it clearly does for Piper, I ask the court for a verdict of directed acquittal on the grounds that a plausible *prima facie* case has not been made." Westphal, "Kierkegaard's Religiousness C," 547–548.

3. WESTPHAL AND HEGEL

Judging Religion through Politics

HEGEL AND POLITICS

Westphal's reading of Hegel reveals the political nature of his own philosophy. Moreover, Westphal's struggle with Hegel, as we shall see, can also be seen as a struggle with modernity and its resultant political, economic, and religious structures. With these thoughts in mind, Westphal's second book on Hegel, entitled *Hegel, Freedom, and Modernity*, is a prime source, as Westphal shapes the book to highlight these struggles, hoping to shed light upon the insights Hegel can give us and where he goes astray. This chapter explores Westphal's journey with Hegel by focusing on Westphal's political (and therefore religious) critique of Hegel. Additionally, we will look Hegel's influence in Westphal's political philosophy, noting how his critique of Hegel leads him to a better understanding of the relationship between faith and politics. For Westphal, saying must mean doing, and what one speaks about in one's religious discourse must be followed by political action.

To keep our focus on Westphal, we will not investigate how his work fits into existing Hegelian scholarship, even though we will address that when it becomes relevant to our primary concern. Our interest here does not lie in whether Westphal gives an accurate reading of Hegel, since doing justice to that task would be unwieldy for our present aims. Instead, we are primarily interested in how Hegel has influenced Westphal's own thinking.

In addition to the reasons mentioned already, using *Hegel, Freedom and Modernity* as our primary text for this exploration is ideal because Westphal crafted the book from his prior articles, which gives us several guideposts to follow when exploring his career trajectory. Published in 1992, the text refashions articles originally published between 1971 and 1989. This is important because, by 1992, Westphal had already moved steadfastly into his Kierkegaard studies and had established himself within the field of philosophy of religion.[1] Westphal utilizes this text as a sort of scenic overlook, viewing the path he traveled alongside Hegel early on in his own career.

Westphal hints at this in his preface when he proclaims that we are still 'moderns,' situating himself alongside Hegel, and that both he and Hegel are concerned with a political theology. From the outset, Westphal calls Hegel a "philosopher of freedom in the modern world." More specifically, he says Hegelian freedom champions a "political theology, a theory in which religion and society are always treated as inseparable," and this concept—the relationship between religion and society and the claims of both about freedom—makes up the book's central concern, broadly construed throughout thirteen essays.[2]

However, Westphal cannot follow alongside Hegel any longer, for several reasons. Chief of these is politics, particularly Westphal's own political dispositions and Hegel's lack of will to go further in his concept of freedom (and, by extension, justice).[3] On this issue of his political concerns, Westphal openly states:

> I speak of us as moderns because I cannot deny my modernity any more than I can deny my Americanness. But these essays were written during years when my identity as an American became increasingly problematic and when I came to see modernity as the larger context of my ambivalence. I was (and am) proud to be an American. But I came to be (and remain) ashamed of much that America does and stands for. At times my country has been the embodiment of its lofty ideals of "liberty and justice for all"; but at other times it has been their betrayal. My suspicion is that this ambiguity of the American experiment has its roots in the liberal modernism that is its ideology.[4]

He continues, placing Hegel on the spectrum of his own thinking, by stating:

> I cannot say that Hegel was the catalyst of my discomfort. That role has been played by the events of our recent history[5] and my attempts to make biblical faith my own. But I can say that Hegel has been enormously helpful to me as I have worked through these issues, even where I find his own views problematic. For I invariably find insight in his thinking, even when it is accompanied by oversight.[6]

These two passages hint at the fact that Westphal utilizes Hegel as a foil to discuss modernity itself and the subsequent failings of projects of modernity. Furthermore, I think Hegel becomes his primary foil because of how Hegelian freedom closely links politics and religion. Here, Hegel and Westphal both are trying to reconcile their biblical (i.e., theological) concerns with their philosophical and political worldviews. Therefore, before getting into Westphal's critique of Hegel, it is important to explore more thoroughly how Westphal understands the relationship between politics and religious convictions.

This notion of reconciling faith and politics is especially evident in Westphal's coauthored work *Inflation, Poortalk, and the Gospel*, published in 1981, during the time he was publishing articles that would eventually become *Hegel, Freedom, and Modernity*.[7] This book is a prime example of Westphal's desire to understand his biblical faith through a political lens. Written for a general audience, the text focuses on the economics of inflation (a major political issue of the 1980s), its psychological effects, and the biblical response to both overcoming inflation and its social repercussions. Hence, Westphal and his coauthors craft the text as theological source for everyday Christians who are concerned about their own welfare as well as that of others living in the United States. Christians, the book proclaims, are in a unique position "to serve as models of successful adaptation to the new economic realities" of their time and therefore must be "informed and active," since "the economic pressures in our society may be working against the biblical norms of justice and charity."[8]

After detailing the problem of inflation, the book then explains that, from both a psychological and theological perspective, a change in behavior is necessary to effect change in the country at large.[9] The authors emphasize behavior because, as they proclaim, "our behavior shapes our attitudes as much as our attitudes shape our behavior"; and "behavior contrary to biblical principles will contaminate the heart by generating attitudes consistent with that behavior."[10] Note the suspicion Westphal has regarding proclaiming Christian values and acting on them. One must behave biblically to pronounce a biblical attitude—or, one cannot claim to be Christian if one does not act like one. As we shall see, this concern runs throughout Westphal's writing.[11]

One can also say this is Westphal's grave concern about his "Americanness" and the ideals that the United States is supposed to stand for: declaring "liberty and justice for all" requires that one actually gives liberty and justice to all. The suspicion that Westphal holds toward texts, American-ness, and modernity is a suspicion based on accountability and esteem. One can imagine him asking: "Does this text really tell the story of those who give it authority? Do those who hold the text in authority actually follow what the text says (especially the Bible)? Does our modernity, with all its glittering machinations, actually bring out the best in us? Is this the most just and free system that we can create?" These questions are at the heart of Westphal's intellectual concerns, and Hegel helps him come to this cri-tique honestly. Through Westphal's grappling with Hegelian thinking, one can see his politico-ethical awareness emerge as a crucial motivator of his prophetic hermeneutics and, for that matter, a central reason he considers self-transcendence a first step toward transcendence.[12]

WESTPHAL'S UNDERSTANDING OF HEGELIAN FREEDOM AND ETHICS

The initial chapter of *Hegel, Freedom, and Modernity* tackles Hegel's concept of freedom by first working through what he means by the term *concept*. The initial four chapters are formatted as a mini-commentary on Hegel's *Phi-losophy of Right* in which Westphal uses the notions of friendship and love to explore what Hegel means by freedom itself.[13] However, some digging must be done to get to these concepts; to understand what Hegel means by friendship and love, and therefore freedom, one must also understand his idea of the concept through its distinct, relatable formations of "Universal-ity, Particularity, and Individuality."[14] In short, exploring Hegelian friend-ship and love, according to Westphal, will lead us to Hegel's understanding of the concept of the absolute, which is important for understanding what he means by freedom (which will then lead to a discussion on ethics). Here, Westphal is attempting to tease out how freedom, for Hegel, does not equal complete independence from obligations, rights, or duties.

Westphal begins by showing two equivalences—one between univer-sality and indeterminacy, and the other between particularity and determi-nation. He notes that the first holds to an understanding of freedom that is against all forms of particularity,[15] and the second acknowledges its own willing through a finite, particularization of the self, yet this makes the self only "a function of its [own] impulses and inclinations or of [those of] the other selves it encounters."[16] Universality and indeterminacy, as Westphal explains it, are relations that come to together to form a "one-sided freedom" that "professes to serve some new and better actuality but cannot do so"[17] because it annihilates any "particularity and objective characterization that the self-consciousness of this negative freedom" encounters.[18] Universality and indeterminacy, therefore, seek to turn everything into one concept, ultimate and universal, no matter the cost. Hegel here shows us a 'negative' form of freedom in which one withdraws or negates any otherness to be free from external influence.[19] Stephen Houlgate compares this form of freedom to the notion of "the 'classical liberal conception of freedom': I am free on this account, when I can and do as I please and others do not force me to do what I want to do."[20]

Contrariwise, the equivalency of particularity and determination moves in the opposite direction, toward willing a concrete, particular object of freedom instead of negating it. Yet this form of freedom runs into another set of problems where the self becomes, according to Westphal, "only a function of its impulses and inclinations," or the self becomes dominated by the impulses and inclinations of the other selves that it encounters.[21] In this form of freedom, the self's will has contents but is beholden solely to those contents and is driven to fulfilling them and nothing else. The finite will that one has, in this equivalence, has not sufficiently reached a fully developed concept of freedom because it lacks a proper understanding of mediation and self-reflection; the self is still susceptible to being dominated by the wills of others in pursuit of their own contents and drives because it cannot rationally control its own impulses.

As Hegel himself explains, "Through this establishment of itself as a definite thing the I becomes a reality," but "this second element in the characterization of the I [i.e., this movement of freedom] is just as negative as the first, since it annuls and replaces the first abstract negativity."[22] In other words, this particular and finite willing is an aspect of the self that is foreign to the self's own rational agency. In this form of freedom, the will lacks the self-discipline that comes with rational reflection, and thus the self is a slave to its own inclinations. Therefore, this form of freedom (particular, determinate) is inadequate as well. One is not free because one is being determined by something (or someone else); but in this equivalency one finally engages in reality, willing toward some concrete thing. So, on the one hand, there is a concept of freedom that is overdetermined and seeks to subsume everything, annihilating particularity in the process. On the other hand, there is a freedom that is too acutely aware of the particularity of all things, thus becoming underdetermined and subjected to the greater will of either its own impulses or those from others.

Hegel considers both of these to be caricatures of freedom. A unity is necessary between these two forms, as is seen in the third equivalence between individuality and self-determination. Self-determination, Westphal explains, is "the preservation of self-identity in the process of determination," which is important because individuation is necessary for "endur[ing] determination without becoming simply a function of those others through whom this determination is mediated."[23] Self-identity, therefore, goes through a process of mediation in its self-determining; this ultimately means that there is a dependence on an other (if there is no other, there is no mediation) in one's self determination. This other, Westphal continues, must in some way be on par with the self, of "qualitative similarity," so that both sides stand opposed.[24] If there is not an equivalency, then "we can see nothing . . . to weaken the understanding's suspicion that the self must either destroy the selfhood of the other by becoming its master or give up its own by becoming the slave, in neither case achieving freedom."[25] Westphal acknowledges that Hegel presents the idea that the self can posit "itself as its other yet remains by itself in this other," but Westphal claims this "provides us with no assistance in making sense out of [Hegel]," and therefore we are in a quandary: what is necessary for the self to have freedom while also securing itself (i.e., not becoming a slave) in relation to otherness?[26]

To grasp how this self-determination operates through an other without producing an other-determined self (namely, someone who is told what to do), Westphal employs Hegel's notion of friendship and love as a model to make this process intelligible. The issue is that the self imposes a restriction on itself. Quoting Hegel, Westphal argues, "we restrict ourselves gladly in relating ourselves to another, but in this restriction know ourselves as ourselves. In this determinacy a man should not feel himself determined, on the contrary, since he treats the other as other, it is there that he first arrives at the feeling of his own self-hood."[27] In this way, freedom lies within the synthesis of indeterminacy and determinacy happening at once. Again, for clarification, the will is determinate only by engaging with something and by relating to an other.

Yet for this to be *self-determination*, this other must somehow also be a self. For example, I restrict myself in relation to an other (i.e., my will becomes finite in relating to some other, and I give up certain impulses out of respect and recognition of this other), which is ultimately still a self-determination. In recognizing another self I choose to restrict my impulses, thus determining myself within my own limits. This is because the other is indeed another self, with whom each I forms a "we." This other within this "we" is a self I still identify with but that self is not a mere numerical identity; rather, it is a *qualitative* identity. It matters that I see this other as a person whose selfhood is equal to my own.

We therefore have a model of self-determination that is not self-enclosed. For Hegel, this is how a concrete freedom is revealed that is at once determinate and reflective.[28] In summary, let us review Hegel's own words:

> The third step [of freedom] is that the will, while in this limitation, i.e., in this other, is by itself. While it limits itself, it yet remains with itself, and does not lose hold of the universal. This is, then, the concrete conception of freedom, while the other two elements have been thoroughly abstract and one-sided. But this concrete freedom we already have in form of perception, as in friendship and love.[29]

This identity with difference opens the self (and the other in relation to the self) to concrete freedom. It also confirms Hegel's theory of the concept as a "theory of freedom, of personality, and of that sense of ego which the slave lacks."[30] So far we have seen how Westphal summarizes Hegel's concept of the transition from abstract to concrete freedom. Westphal has given an extremely close reading of Hegel's notion of freedom, paying special attention to the triadic relationship of universality, particularity, and individuality. He does so because he wants to turn toward Hegel's concept of love. Westphal sees in Hegel a tightly bounded relationship between love and freedom, and at this point Westphal intends to unpack that relationship to reveal how it has an impact on Hegel's political philosophy.

Westphal asserts that taking loving intersubjectivity as a basis for understanding Hegel's theory of the concept sheds light on its creative usages. Hegel frequently refers to the creative, formational, effecting activity of the concept. Westphal explains these rather mysterious formulations through reciprocal love, which he has been developing throughout this chapter.[31] According to Westphal, this reciprocal love, and its creative aspects, can best be explained through Hegel's own allegory of the biblical Creation motif.

Surprisingly, Westphal demonstrates that the reciprocal love between God the Father and Christ the Son is the model par excellence for understanding the creative activity of the concept. Quoting Hegel, this notion of creation is "expressed in the teaching of Christianity . . . not merely has God created a world which confronts Him as an other; He has also from all eternity begotten a Son in whom He, a Spirit, is at home with Himself [*bei sich selbst ist*]."[32] Reciprocal love (exemplified by the godly Father-Son relationship) generates a kind of identity, a kind of selfhood that preserves the alterity of the participants while holding them in communion. So this mode of generating an identity, a "we," befits the concept's creative activity because it is a self-determination.

Stepping back, this is a rather quick and bold move by Westphal, even though Hegel himself uses the comparison. It is quick in that Westphal presupposes a great deal, theologically, concerning the relationship of and within the Trinity. It is bold in that he briefly—perhaps too briefly—claims to fully grasp Hegel's understanding of the Trinity, which is a difficult matter given Hegel's complicated understanding of God and Spirit (*Geist*). Westphal's reading of Hegel here really does a disservice if one is trying to understand Hegel for the first time; in effect one supplies one's own concept of the Trinity to make Hegel's theory work since the reader may know neither Hegel's Trinitarian theology nor Westphal's. Just as quickly, Westphal then moves toward two other examples to clarify his point concerning Hegel. I bring this up here—at some risk of confusion—to highlight that the perspective from which Westphal reads Hegel is highly theological, residing particularly within a Protestant context.

After relating the concept's creativity to the Trinity, Westphal continues by comparing two other models of creation that fail to completely exemplify the self-determination of the concept. The first model is a child's imaginary play, and the second model follows God's creation of the world.[33] These models fail on several fronts: First, the creative activity of the concept does not literally create another thing that would be dependent on the concept for its existence. Second, and more precisely, the problem with the child's play model is that the other has no independence, no agency, no dignity, and the other can be discarded at a whim, as a child is wont to do with toys and imaginary friends. The problem with the creator-created model is that both are so radically different from the other that it is difficult to conceive how they are related to each other; this fails to achieve qualitative identity, as mentioned earlier. Going back to the model of the Father and Son, qualitative identity is established because reciprocal love creates an identity that can be reduced to neither an "I" trapped in its interiority (as seen in universality) nor an "I and you" that are threats to each other (as seen with particularity). A novel selfhood is created, a "we," through recognition of the dignity of the other.

Having said this, Westphal turns his attention to the transition from essence to concept in Hegel's *Encyclopedia Logic*. Specifically, Westphal claims that Hegel's notion of reciprocity can shed light on this transition. However, there is a caveat: there is more than one form of reciprocity, and the first form has nothing to do with freedom. The other form of reciprocity is one of causal necessity that is exemplified by physical, worldly cause and effects. This is because, in purely conceptual terms (following Hegel's logical approach), an entity is a substance, and a substance is totally self-sufficient. The only way that a totally self-enclosed substance can relate to another totally self-enclosed substance is through a purely *external* exchange that is totally without any interpenetration and is best understood through the model of the mechanistic transfer of force.[34] "Causal necessity," Westphal further elaborates, "involves a special form of identity" that is exclusive to independence since the effect (of a cause) becomes understood through its cause.[35] In this way, everything loses its identity because it becomes known solely through its cause. If everything is an effect, then nothing is a substance because nothing is self-sufficient. If one wanted to preserve a thing's identity, one would have to disregard its causal relations, thus destroying reciprocity, since nothing is related to anything. In this way, reciprocity as a category of essence fails to represent freedom because this form of reciprocity leaves us with either entities that either are "mutually indifferent to one another" or are "so tightly bound together by natural necessity" that they lose their own individualities.[36] Like falling dominoes, they are either so close that the first falling domino causes all others to tumble or so far away from each other that one cause effects none of the other dominos.

At this point, it is clear to Westphal that any concept of love in Hegel's system needs to be fleshed out in relation to identity, especially with how entities relate to or reciprocate others without either being a part of a causal chain or having done so without cause at all. For freedom to be possible, there must be a different form of identity that is irreducible to the definition of identity given in the logical approach. This identity must be able to include alterity within itself, as in recognition through the other.

Clarifying this relationship between recognition and self-consciousness, Robert Pippin interprets Hegel to be arguing that "our answerability to the world is inextricably bound with, even dependent for its possibility on, our answerability to each other."[37] What is at stake here is that, for Hegel, alterity is essential to relationally (i.e., affiliation with other selves by forming groups, memberships, tribes, and so on). Thus, the self is able to identify with others (mediation that generates groups and affiliations) and, in turn, gains a greater sense of its self: I am a person who is American, who likes the Boston Red Sox, who is Catholic, and so on, because of these identifications with others.

While other scholars may find this interpretation of mutual recognition problematic and more of a Fichtean reading of Hegel than a reading of Hegel himself,[38] for our purposes we must move on to complete our exploration of how Merold Westphal himself understands Hegel's theory of the concept. From this theory of mutual recognition in Hegel, Westphal then gives an account of the concept from the point of view of a theory of knowledge (Westphal simply calls this 'the Logic').[39] This point of view emerges predominantly when one takes into account how the self, as 'the concept,' has concepts of its own: the concept creates more and more intricate, connected relationships. Westphal leaves this somewhat open, which lends itself to the interpretation of how one understands Hegel's epistemology.[40] Yet Westphal still postulates that love is the key to Hegel's structure of the concept. To prove this, he must explain his own understanding of Hegel's epistemology so that he can prove his hypothesis by finding the same structure of loving relationship in the theoretical self as found in the practical self.

Clarifying this, Westphal states that "the theory of loving intersubjectivity which is the direct meaning of the Concept as a theory of the practical self is the guiding metaphor for the theory of knowledge which has reached the same level of philosophical insight." Therefore, we can understand Hegel's practical philosophy and his theoretical philosophy provided that knowing can also be a "nonviolent unity of the self and its other."[41]

Truth and love, it seems, are related to freedom as seen in Hegel's logic. According to Westphal, there are two forms of knowing: one at the level of the understanding (purely theoretical and not fully realized) and the other related to the concept (namely, a notion of self-determination and nonviolent mediation through the self and the other). Knowing at the level of the understanding is characterized by the subjective activity of imposing intelligible forms on inert content(s). Thus, knowledge from the point of view of the understanding encounters objects as "brute otherness which we must forge weapons to overcome." Westphal argues that these weapons, so forged, become "abstract universals" that enable us to "deprive the object of its original independence," thus subjugating it to our own domination and mastery; Hegel, here, has "described the essence of calculative thinking."[42] This calculative thinking, and its mastery of the other in hopes of controlling its otherness, will become one of Westphal's chief concerns as he moves toward a dialogue with Martin Heidegger and his critique of onto-theology.[43]

Knowledge at the level of the concept, however, is higher than that at the level of the understanding. Knowledge here is found, for Hegel, in art, religion, and philosophy. This is in sharp contrast to the violent imposition of the understanding. Knowledge is recognition of the truth that the other contains within itself. It acknowledges the other's own intelligibility. Thus, this form of knowing is characterized by the subject's "openness to the object . . . the impetus towards domination is undermined as a new identity takes shape."[44] This is a parallel to the previous discussion of love, wherein the relation between the self and the other is seen in light of mutual identity in which neither compromises the other; rather, each builds up the other, and no alterity is compromised.

Freedom, therefore, is a process of deepening our own sense of self-understanding, our consciousness, through our relationship with other entities and substances in the world. Because this relationship happens within the world, it is a historical process that does not necessarily mean continual progress; there are regressions and struggles as well. Westphal's concern, however, is that the way in which Hegel describes our becoming more aware selves, and thus freer selves, is that the thinking one utilizes to become self-aware quite often reduces the other to a mere foil for one's own self-understanding, making it easy for the self to slip into a role of dominating the other.[45] This can be mitigated, however, if one recognizes that knowledge at the level of the concept is more complete than that at the level of understanding.

For now, this reinforces our understanding of how Westphal reads his sources and has also set forth on a path of critique concerning Hegel's concept of freedom through the ideas and notions that comprise this idea. In chapters 2 and 3 of *Hegel, Freedom and Modernity*, Westphal continues this inquiry by asking which effects Hegel's concept of freedom has on human rights and on the ethical relationships or obligations among families, communities, and, ultimately, the state.

Westphal explains Hegel's role in crafting what is called modernity by couching it within postmodern critique: "What postmodernism rejects about modernity is its dalliance with the quest for absolute clarity (meaning) and certainty (truth) that, since Plato, has often been seen as the very heart of philosophy itself; more specifically, it is the rejection of two dominant modern strategies for achieving absolute knowledge, Cartesian immediacy and Hegelian totality."[46] Westphal casts suspicion on modernity by critiquing Hegel's politics. In this process Westphal comes to grips with his own philosophical thinking, leading him to develop his hermeneutics of suspicion and his concept of self-transcendence.

Chapter 2 of *Hegel, Freedom, and Modernity* begins Westphal's critique by looking at the theory of rational freedom that is central to Hegel's "theory of right."[47] Westphal argues that Hegel's theory of property, as the "first embodiment of freedom," ultimately relegates all other aspects of right into the indifferent realm of particularity. Westphal states that "it is because property" is considered "the first embodiment of rational freedom that everything must be excluded as of secondary importance that pertains to life needs and their satisfaction."[48] However, this is not the completely damning critique that it seems to be. To understand why it is not, we need to begin to understand Hegel's theory of property. For Hegel, property is freedom's first embodiment since it transcends the "subjectivity of personality."[49] In owning property, the self "exists for the first time" because it has moved beyond mere abstraction toward a more concrete, physical realization of the self.[50] Hegel places less emphasis on one's personal needs and more on property because he sees those needs as part of the particular and not rational aspect of freedom. Freedom begins with property because it needs to move away from the abstract to the actual or real.[51] As Hegel states it himself in *Philosophy of Right*:

> The reasonableness of property consists not in its satisfying our needs, but in its superseding and replacing the subjective phase of personality. It is in possession first of all that the person becomes rational. The first realization of my freedom in an external object is an imperfect one, it is true, but it is only the realization possible so long as the abstract personality has this firsthand relation to its object.... Since our wants are looked upon as primary, the possession of property appears at first to be a means to their satisfaction; but it is really the first embodiment of freedom and an independent end.[52]

Notably, owning property is not a naturally occurring phenomenon; one can own land only through others who recognize the ownership of that land (which may take some defending, either through legal deeds or even battle). Hence, property ownership is a primitive form of Spirit—a higher level of communal relationship—because the recognition of one's property involves a (minor) form of mutual respect and dignity.

Westphal continues by explaining the relationship this theory of right has with Spirit in Hegelian thinking; what is important for us, however, is to see that Hegel's concern for property as the embodiment of our freedom over and above all other concepts of economic and social welfare creates a dire lack of concern for the actual well-being of others. Westphal argues that this neglects those who have had their rights violated either through theft or dispossession, but also enables something much more damning:

> The property I own may be far from sufficient to provide for my subsistence needs; and my property rights will not have been violated as long as I own something. The society that refuses to bulldoze the shanty town in which I live so as to respect my rights as a "homeowner" will have done all that is required by Hegel's theory of property rights, even if it provides me with no work or with work at wages so low that I cannot feed and clothe my family.[53]

This relates to Hegel's concept of utility within the world, where Hegel sees the use of a thing as "my need being externally realized." However, "by identifying need as the 'particular' aspects of the will, he reminds us that, as before, it is not the essential (rational) thing."[54] This places Hegel into a position where "use is for the sake of ownership and not ownership for the sake of use," which, while it maintains his faithfulness to idealism, diminishes the priority of economic and social welfare within his system of right.[55]

Consequently, Hegel's concept of right ultimately fails to feed, clothe, or shelter anyone. In reaction to the "first liberty, then bread" argument made by the theologian Michael Novak,[56] which Westphal utilizes as an introduction to the chapter, Westphal claims that "Hegel's *Philosophy of Right* belongs with [John] Locke and Adam Smith among those classics of Western Liberalism that have 'a blind spot' to severe economic need."[57] His concern is that these thinkers helped craft a modern, liberal theology and philosophy of "corporate capitalism" that "ends up giving aid and comfort, even divine sanction, to the unholy alliance at the heart of the contemporary human rights crisis in the Western Hemisphere."[58]

However, as he shows us later in the same chapter, Hegel cannot be so easily pegged. Westphal then notes the tensions between Hegel's *Philosophy of Right* and the context of Western liberalism into which he has just placed it, finding that it is "incompatible with any theoretical interpretation of rights and political association as means to biological ends."[59] This places Hegel at odds with Western liberalism, and, Westphal explains, to clarify what he means by biological ends, "the term *good life* [has been] redefined [in modern liberalism] so that it no longer refers to virtue and freedom but to survival, security, and comfort. By giving priority to status over survival and thus to spirit over nature, Hegel gives expression to his lasting affinity for classical politics."[60] This affinity has Hegel pulling back toward any "first liberty, then bread" political philosophy since "the purpose of Hegel's theory of property rights . . . is not to legitimate liberalism's insensitivity to severe poverty, but to keep the theory of a rational society from lapsing to the subhuman level."[61]

More to the point, this intention to keep society together opens Hegel's theory of right to be developed: property rights are merely the first embodiment, not the last. This does not exclude other forms of freedom, Westphal argues, but it is the first "not because [it is] the causal condition of other modes of freedom, but because [it is] the least developed, least adequate, least rational form that freedom can take without ceasing to be freedom."[62] Going back to Hegel's intention to create a philosophy of rights to establish a cohesive, rational society, one can see Hegel's first embodiment of freedom via property rights establishes a connection between the abstract and physical reality. This does not absolve him from establishing a first principle that is indifferent to suffering, but it does allow for other rights and responsibilities to be developed. Westphal elaborates, "It is only as freedom becomes that of a person richly related to what is other than the self that freedom is properly understood, and that the true significance of property rights themselves can be grasped." One can see how these aspects develop: to "the Good (Morality), then the community based on love rather than self-interest (Family), then the community based on economic self-interest (Civil Society), and finally, the community based on the solidarity of a people sharing common laws and customs (State)."[63]

Westphal's critique of Hegel's notion of freedom and of human rights moves him toward Marx's critique of society, noting that Marx's critique "grows right out of Hegelian analysis" and that Hegel's notion of freedom and rights actually "goes a further crucial step. Because its theory of society is individualist and instrumentalist, civil society creates inhuman modes of life and interaction."[64] However, Hegel's notion of freedom and rights, as one can see in a Marxian analysis, has not achieved genuine welfare and happiness because of the problems sketched out earlier. Hegel (as well as Marx, Westphal adds) sees capitalism and capitalist societies as having foundational problems for which merely fine-tuning a system for bust periods or social inequality is not a cure: the system itself is not based on subsistence rights, and therefore its rationality as a political system for all people fails. This is plainly seen, for Westphal, in the fact that the "juxtaposition of wealth and poverty in liberal society gives the lie to its claim to be rational."[65]

This takes us back to the theme of pronouncing one thing—liberty and justice for all—and doing another, such as providing security, liberty, and justice for only a select (wealthy) group of individuals. However, Westphal actually *defends* Hegelian freedom and ethics over and against Western liberalism. This is why Hegel is such a struggle for Westphal, and also the perfect foil: Hegel is not easily tossed aside because is he not completely wrong about property being necessary to move rights from the abstract to the concrete.

In the next section, we explore this struggle further by looking into Westphal's understanding of Hegelian dialectic and intersubjectivity. From there, we briefly cover the ramifications of his conclusions, which will lead us to the final section of this chapter, where I summarize how Hegel has influenced Westphal's thinking overall, moving us forward to the next chapter on Kierkegaard. In *Hegel, Freedom, and Modernity*, Westphal presents his philosophical thinking as a struggle with modernity and, through this, his desire to wed biblical faith to politics, where saying and believing must mean doing. This, I argue, is why he embraces Kierkegaard's critique of society and Kierkegaard's unique understanding of faith.

Westphal's Theo-politics: Belief Is Praxis

For Hegel, the truth is the whole, but as the whole it is also a process of mediation between entities, which becomes the focus of the second part *Hegel, Freedom, and Modernity*. He critiques Hegel's understanding of truth on three grounds: first, its notion of intersubjectivity (its process of mediation); second, its sense of historicity (against Gadamer's concept of hermeneutical, historical development); third, its notion of the whole itself (against Husserl's critique of Cartesian foundationalism). Moreover, Westphal is alarmed that Hegel does not follow his own idea to its fullest extent (hence the title of the section, "A Failure of Nerve"), and consequently he emphasizes the second and third critiques: the truth is the whole, but Hegel's philosophy stops "short of the totality that it demands," and, failing to be a method for complete knowledge, it therefore is an inadequate comprehension of freedom.[66] This is the fatal flaw that Westphal sees in Hegel.

The totality Westphal describes rests upon the fact that Hegel's philosophy does not extend to the global whole; it moves from the "we" to the family, to the community, to the nation, but it falls short when assembling a global community. In short, there is no room for the United Nations in Hegel's philosophy: throughout his understanding of the whole, recognition reigns supreme where Hegel finds peace and harmony between individuals and in communities, but when it reaches the nation-states Westphal claims that it has been abandoned:

> [In the *Philosophy of Right* and *Philosophy of History*] the particular state is not absolute there, and Hegel retains a kind of universalism. But it is primarily the diachronic universalism of world history rather than the synchronic universalism of a global community; and while the states do belong (synchronically) to a community in which they recognize each other, the rationality of the world order does not seem, in Hegel's eyes, to be compromised by the fact that their relations are mediated by war and contractual relations, though the former is a fundamental violation of the concept of recognition and the latter Hegel has shown at smaller levels of totality to be entirely too abstract to constitute genuine recognition.[67]

For Westphal, Hegel abandons his previous philosophy to understand the relations between nation-states in order to integrate them into his thinking. What this failure indicates for Westphal, however, is something much larger. Westphal sees Hegel's failure of nerve as not merely a logical failure or mere oversight in constructing his holism; rather, it is a failure to be prescriptive. Hegel fails because he refuses to philosophically argue what nation states ought to do: Hegel gives no command or instruction for what nation-states should to be in relation to other nation-states.

This is a rather audacious claim, and to properly understand this critique, we need to better understand Hegel's own argument and how Westphal perceives it. Westphal lays out his appraisal over three chapters by first reevaluating what mediation means to Hegel's philosophy. Intersubjectivity, as dialectic, creates the whole of society and works entirely from a drive or desire for recognition. Westphal notes that "in Kantian language this [desire for recognition] can be expressed as dignity or respect, in biblical language as love." No matter the term one uses, the general aim is to be "treated as an end and not merely a means and it is to be united with another at the center of the circle of value and interest rather than pushed to the periphery by the self-assertion of the other."[68] As shown earlier, one finds Hegel's concept of freedom working within recognition, where self-determination is still the foundation of recognition. Hence, it is essential for any intersubjectivity to occur: one cannot make a whole out of society—or even a "we"—without it.

This reciprocal recognition serves as the foundation for Hegel's concept of Spirit in the *Phenomenology of Spirit*, where the Spirit becomes absolute and absolute knowing can be realized (a totality, a complete understanding of the whole and therefore complete truth). "Knowledge," Westphal explains, "no longer needs to go beyond itself when and only when it is embedded in a social praxis which no longer needs to go beyond itself, and when the social praxis occurs in the community whose distinctive mark is reciprocal recognition."[69] Recognition thus works through intersubjective mediation, and this mediation (two selves interacting as two equal yet distinct selves) is integral to understanding Hegel's vision of community as found in the Absolute Spirit. For this to work, however, recognition must be seen as a *universal* dialectic, since "to be a human individual is to be a part of a community (at first only a twosome) in which reciprocal recognition occurs. But once this process begins there is no stopping it short of universality."[70] An individual must recognize the humanity in an other who reciprocates, who then recognizes the same a different individual and so forth until larger and larger communities of mutually recognized individuals are created until a universal, holistic community in which all recognize others as selves. And so the dialectic found within reciprocal recognition progresses up the social scale: from families to tribes, to towns, to cities, to nations. However, as shown earlier, the holism works at an intranational level but falters at an international level. Accordingly, Westphal sees that this holism is not political, since it excludes foreign diplomacy altogether.[71]

Although this holism is not political itself, it does not exclude the political, since "that very same holism requires that our moral and religious life not be isolated from our political life, and the concept of recognition has very direct political implications."[72] Human selves can have a complete self-understanding (and thus relate to their concept entirely) only when they are a part of a violence-free, open (i.e., noncontrolling) "universal community."[73] This is not only a universal community without war but also one in which religious, political, and social influences are eliminated. Yet such a world has not been realized. So, in response to this lack, the dialectic of reciprocity, as found within intersubjectivity, consequently functions as a way of "pressing onward to a radically new form of social life."[74]

Hegel's concept of freedom leads to an intersubjective understanding and recognition of the self in an other, which leads to a utopian society, that is, the Absolute Spirit. Or so it should go. But Westphal notices that Hegel's thinking ultimately fails to evoke a political action of the whole. The totality required for such a utopian vision is never equally applied to states, and although the state represents a community, and Hegel does maintain his concept of holism from *Phenomenology of Spirit* to *Philosophy of Right*, he fails to develop how states follow the dialectic of reciprocal recognition as seen in smaller communities. From Westphal's reading of Hegel, a particular state is not an absolute, but it does hold to "a kind of universalism."[75] And even though for Hegel the state belongs "to a community in which they recognize each other," the critical oversight, as discussed earlier, is that Hegel fails to see that nations interact through contracts or war. War is a violation of Hegel's concept of recognition, and contracts are too abstract to concretize recognition. To be fair, Westphal explains that Hegel maintains his holism but that Hegel's concept of the state "as the genuine community of all the individuals and sub-communities which make it up, is abandoned without justification at paragraph 321 [of the *Phenomenology*] when Hegel turns from treating the state as the whole in relation to its parts and begins to treat it as a part of the larger international whole. This is the failure of nerve of which I spoke earlier."[76]

Westphal moves onward from this critique (rebuffing the possible defense that Hegel was abstractly talking about states as how they ought to exist) by arguing that for Hegel, philosophy's primary ambition is not giving advice, but to "comprehend what is, this is the task of philosophy, because what is, is reason."[77] Philosophy is descriptive, not prescriptive. Moreover, Westphal continues, "the object of philosophy," for Hegel, "is the Idea: and the Idea is not so impotent as merely to have a right or an obligation to exist without existing." These arguments, against the backdrop of his failure to take his concept of the state to its necessary and ultimate conclusion, definitively show that Westphal sees Hegel's framework as a system that is trying to do politics without activism. As we have seen before, for Westphal, one cannot claim (philosophically) that liberty and justice is for all without (actually) giving liberty and justice to all (or at least striving for this end). Reprising this belief, Westphal summarizes Hegel's failure of nerve thus:

> Finally, if philosophy sees the rose in the cross of the present, this can only be because it sees the cross, the pain which cries out for some kind of reconciliation.[78] This means that philosophy not only apprehends "the substance which is immanent and the eternal which is present" in "the show [*Schein*] of the temporal and transient," but also the degree to which

the substance remains transcendent and the eternal absent. And what does philosophy do then? In the first place, it transcends itself in action. *The time has come for understanding the world to become the guide for changing it.* If dialectical holism points to a mode of human intersubjectivity not yet actual, belief in the ability of the rational to actualize itself may well take the form of *hearing the call to do whatever one can to assist in the actualization. Philosophy becomes political action.*[79]

Keeping in mind that Westphal is our focus and not Hegel, the previous statement reinforces Westphal's argument that there must be a link between speaking and doing. Words matter, but only when actions back them up. Moreover, Westphal views the needs of the marginalized—those in pain and anguish—through the motif of the cross as well. He sees that our present (our contemporary liberal democracy) is the prize (the beautiful rose) that appears in the background of terror, pain, war, and slavery (the suffering on the cross). Although this is not the definitive statement Westphal makes about his own work, it shows a transition in his thinking from a hermeneutics of suspicion to a hermeneutics of prophecy. In the previous statement, and throughout the text as a whole, Westphal not only consistently reaffirms his critique of Hegel but also reveals himself to be a philosophical activist, thus blurring the line between Westphal the philosopher and Westphal the Christian or Westphal the theologian.[80]

Westphal's hermeneutics of suspicion and its relation to prophecy matters because he sees that there should be another form of philosophy of religion that is based on the concept of the prophet. In "Prolegomena to Any Philosophy of Religion That Will Be Able to Come Forth as Prophecy" (which later became the initial chapter to *Kierkegaard's Critique of Reason and Society*), Westphal argues that this is not just a Hegelian critique but a critique of the discipline of philosophy itself.[81] Speaking against the backdrop of philosophy as a "rigorous science of what is," beginning with Hegel but also including the philosophies of Edmund Husserl and Martin Heidegger, Westphal states that "if philosophers should not think of themselves primarily in terms of the scientist, then perhaps the Hebrew prophet provides a better model."[82]

Westphal makes his case by observing that phenomenology claims to be a purely scientific discipline within philosophy, as fashioned by Husserl, and that it has done so by bracketing out all outlying (theological) interests to become a purely descriptive discipline. However, he notices that often, despite the core principle of detached objective description, some phenomenologists who work within philosophy of religion follow an "underlying" interest in their own religious and spiritual concerns. Westphal remarks that, from time to time, "this is why phenomenology looks suspiciously like an indirect form of natural theology, slipping from the description of religious experience to an argument from religious experience."[83] As Westphal sees it, "If there are religious interests underlying the phenomenology of religion, then 'the *epoche* of all practical interests' may not have been achieved, and the bracketing of the question of religious truth may have been more apparent than real."[84]

Westphal spends some time considering whether or not phenomenology of religion can ever be as rigorous as its intentions, but he eventually leaves this for others to decide.[85] He focuses instead on the Hebraic tradition as a counterbalance to the "scientific ideal of the Greeks" that Husserl and others often champion as the paradigm for phenomenology and contemporary philosophy. Stating that "our society has its roots in biblical religion as well," Westphal considers that it is time for us to consider that the role of philosopher of religion might be something more than just a scientist. Even though there could be "numerous possibilities," he advocates for the "Hebrew prophet" as such a model.[86]

To be clear, Westphal does not want to make the philosopher a preacher, but he finds that there "are other characteristics of prophetic speech that philosophers of religion might well seek to imitate. I have in mind particularly its character as *personal, untimely, political, and eschatological.*"[87] We will detail how these prophetic traits can be incorporated into philosophy of religion in the following chapters on Westphal and Kierkegaard. For our current purposes, this is important because it reminds us of Westphal's struggle to wed biblical faith to politics and of how he forms his hermeneutics through that struggle. The fact that he consistently relies on a model of Athens and Jerusalem—the scientific and the prophetic, the objective and the personal—should not be glossed over, nor should the fact that one of his major critiques of Hegel is that he forsakes the personal (the well-being of other individuals) to describe society as completely rational.

Finally, we should also bear in mind Westphal's proclamation that all "*all theology should be liberation theology, a guide to the practice of overcoming oppression in all forms.*"[88] At this point, we can see how the concerns of the suffering and well-being of others matter to Westphal's own philosophy and to his reading of Hegel in particular. He continues this emphasis throughout the rest of *Hegel, Freedom, and Modernity* by searching for how Hegel views the community in relation to the Absolute Spirit. Even though West-phal goes on to develop various critiques of Hegel and apply his philosophy of freedom in different ways, this last section centers on how Hegel's work becomes a major influence in Westphal's whole philosophical project, and especially to his hermeneutics of suspicion and prophecy.

Promises Made, Promises Kept: The Wedding of Faith to Action

In *Hegel, Freedom, and Modernity*, Westphal furthers his exploration of com-munity and Spirit by looking at Hegel's views on Hinduism. He does so as a backdrop to explaining how Hegel's system can help us view society through a political lens, that is, through a concern for the well-being of all who constitute society. The initial interest for Hegel is seeing what freedom would look like if it were understood completely in terms of the equivalency universality = indeterminacy, which he sees at play in Hinduism. What this interest develops into, however, is a critique of religious and social praxis within Hinduism as a system that never expresses a "genuine spirit of per-sonhood."[89] In this critique, Westphal claims, "Hegel is never willing to isolate neither the individual from society nor the sacred from the secular. Hence the question of [religious] practice becomes the question of social practice in general, and the cultic critique becomes the political critique."[90] The upshot of this is that when Hegel criticizes the Hindu religion as a "so-cial system of unfreedom" that its adherents accept with little protest, he is implicating the religious structure as a source of the "enslavement" of the people as a whole.[91] We will not get into the details of Hegel's critique of Hinduism and will instead focus on the larger overall point that Westphal is getting at:[92] whether "there is a concept of freedom that can be held up as the criterion for all humanity and, if so, how well Hegel has expressed it."[93]

For Westphal, the result of Hegel's inquiry into Hinduism, even with its problems, is that it presents us with a surprising development: "in agree-ment with Marx and the liberation theologians, Hegel gives priority to the question, 'What kind of social order does this religion legitimize?'" West-phal notes that Hegel is reluctant to rigorously apply this scrutiny to his own religion and society, but he claims that, in spite of itself, this development "invites the suggestion that the ultimate test for any religion is neither theo-logical, nor ritual, but political."[94]

This becomes a litmus test for Westphal's philosophy of religion in the future, cementing itself as a key fixture in his hermeneutics. This is especially on point in *Suspicion and Faith*, an entire work dedicated to correcting religious praxis. At the beginning of the work, Westphal states that that the religious critique of Freud, Marx, and Nietzsche, the so-called masters of suspicion, can be utilized "as a stimulus for self-examination" and, if carefully and thoughtfully employed in that manner, can help us move from "an examination of conscience to penitence, and eventually to repentance."[95] Westphal examines and explains the critiques of religious practice made by these authors, thereby showing the potential traps and errors Christians often fall into. His primary concern here is that these masters levy a critique against adherents to Christianity that

> seem *all too true all too much of the time*. The prominence of various self-serving motives in our [Christian] piety, or at least in that of others, is all too easy to notice. Who can fail, for example, to see the self-deception in the Afrikaner attempt to portray apartheid as a divine mandate or in the "white man's burden," "manifest destiny," and "anti-communist" theologies that have shaped the colonial domination and even extermination of indigenous populations in North, Central, and South America? Or who can fail to notice the instrumental character of the piety of the politicians, especially at election time? Do they serve God for naught (Job 1:9)?[96]

Accordingly, one can see the political test Westphal teases out of Hegel: "What political actions does your religion validate?" Furthermore, one can see his attempt to combine this test with the conviction that one's professed beliefs must equal one's actions. Framing his exploration of these authors and their critique of Christianity as a Lenten journey, Westphal's intent is to guide the Christian in self-reflection. Moreover, he does this while tacitly restating that Athens and Jerusalem are interconnected. In support of why the Christian should seriously consider these critiques, Westphal argues that the masters of suspicion can find a "profound parallel" of their critiques in the Bible, where "the Spirit that speaks to the church also blows where it will. Is it possible that the Spirit would speak to the church through its worst enemies?"[97] Westphal believes so and he thinks that with the masters of suspicion, the Christian can find a critical voice that reminds her of the teachings (and admonishments) made by the prophets within the Bible.

This discussion will be covered in detail in chapter 6. For now, we can again see Westphal working out his political critique of religious praxis. With Hegel, despite his oversights, as Westphal has called them, he does show some great insights into the relationship between religion and politics. It has become clear that in Hegel, Westphal finds a thinker whose concerns line up with his own and even though he eventually rejects Hegel, Westphal's struggle with Hegel allows him to express and develop his political concerns through a religious, philosophical lens. He gives Westphal an opportunity to explore the relationship between his Christian beliefs and his political concerns, and how one affects the other.

Regarding the thesis that Merold Westphal is best read as a theologian rather than a philosopher, our present investigation has indeed proved a very philosophical one, albeit perhaps a Christian political philosophy, where Christianity grounds the political action that Westphal articulates through philosophical reasoning. This, in and of itself, is nothing new to philosophy. However, even though Westphal has yet to reveal his theological colors, one can begin to see cleavages between his thinking and philosophy as a discipline predicated on the use of reason and articulated through one's prescribed method. The most honest example of this is his argument for a prophetic hermeneutics within philosophy, yet this example is based on his concern that reason is not enough for philosophy; it must involve action. He focuses his critique of Hegel's philosophy (and, by extrapolation, modern philosophy) on a failure of nerve to do what is necessary to actually strive for liberty and justice for all, not just think about it. Postmodern philosophers from various traditions will eventually level similar critiques against modernity and modern philosophy as a whole. What separates Westphal from these other critiques is how his Christian faith motivates his critique as well as the fact that when he moves toward political action, his politics are always based on revelation and the theological principles gleaned from religious reflection on revelation. Faith in revelation, as we shall see, is at the heart of his political action.

NOTES

1. During this time he also coauthored *Inflation, Poortalk and the Gospel* and wrote *God, Guilt and Death* (1987) and *Kierkegaard's Critique of Reason and Society* (1987). Additionally, he continued publishing several articles on the postmodern critique of modernity, and on Christianity.

2. *HFM*, vii.

3. This is why he titles the book's second part "The Failure of Nerve," which reveals Hegel's "reluctance to allow the vision of freedom [Hegel] set forth . . . to unfold into the critique of modernity they contain." Ibid., x.

4. Ibid., vii.

5. Westphal does not go into detail as to what issues specifically concern him with regard to American politics, but for historical perspective, he is writing in 1991–1992, when the United

States had just engaged in Operation Desert Storm in Iraq. Economically, the United States was also in a recession, which would last into the middle of the 1990s.

6. Ibid., viii.

7. Thomas E. Ludwig, Merold Westphal, Robin J. Klay, and David G. Myers, *Inflation, Poortalk and the Gospel* (Valley Forge, PA: Judson Press, 1981).

8. *IPG*, 7.

9. Ibid., 69.

10. Ibid., 69–70.

11. It is unclear who authored which part of *IPG*, but coauthor Tom Ludwig mentions that he and his colleagues "obtained the collaboration" of Westphal in relation to "philosophical/theological matters." Ibid., 5. This, along with the fact that the work is written as a cohesive whole, gives me credence to assume that Westphal agrees with these statements and that he more than likely wrote the theology and philosophy parts of the work.

12. Westphal's early Hegelian work reveals his appreciation of a critique of ideology that reminds the self that he or she is far too human, far too often. As we shall see in chapters 6 and 7, this is the first step toward any meaningful self-transcendence, which opens the self to being taken up by God in transcendence.

13. *HFM*, x. Westphal bases this on the *Philosophy of Right*, which states, "Freedom, in this sense, however, we already possess in the form of feeling—in friendship and love, for instance" (quoting Hegel from *HFM*, 5).

14. Ibid., 5.

15. Ibid., 6, quoting Hegel, *Philosophy of Right*, §5. Westphal explains that "it is precisely out of the annihilation of particularity [*Besonderung*] and objective characterization that the self-consciousness of this negative freedom proceeds." Westphal also uses Hegel's example of the French Revolution's "irreconcilable hatred of everything particular" to explain this universal and indeterminate notion of freedom.

16. Ibid., 6–7.

17. Westphal does not clarify what he means by actuality, but, since he is working with Hegelian language, *actuality* here can be assumed to mean *die Wirklichkeit*. The actual, for Hegel, "is the concrete actualizing Idea" and "this realization is a dynamic, ever-unfolding act." Moreover, "Hegel holds that the world is eternally actualizing Idea, but that this actualization takes place within time and through change." See Glenn Alexander Magee, *The Hegel Dictionary* (New York: Continuum Publishing, 2010), 33–35.

18. *HFM*, 6

19. For more, see Isaiah Berlin, "Two Concepts of Liberty," in *Four Essays on Liberty: Isaiah Berlin*, ed. Henry Hardy (Oxford: Oxford University Press 2002), 166–218, esp. 178–180, 205–208. Hegel's notions of universality and indeterminacy show a freedom that is in constant negation. Westphal, to clarify this, brings up two of Hegel's own examples in *Philosophy of Right* (¶5Z): the contemplative ascetic Hindu who constantly negates the external world and all its beings to withdraw into himself, and at a political level, the terror wrought by Robespierre and Marat, who ruthlessly annihilated all particular instances of their cherished universal principles following the French Revolution.

20. Stephen Houlgate, *Freedom, Truth, and History* (London: Routledge, 1991), 80. Houlgate is referencing Peter Singer.

21. *HFM*, 7.

22. G. W. F. Hegel, *The Philosophy of Right*, trans. S.W. Dyde (Mineola, NY: Dover Publications, 2005), §6, ¶32

23. *HFM*, 7.

24. Ibid., 9.

25. Ibid.

26. Ibid.,

27. Ibid., 9–10. He is quoting Hegel from *Encyclopedia Logic*, §7.

28. *HFM*, 10.

29. Hegel, *Philosophy of Right*, §7 34.

30. *HFM*, 10. Westphal is quoting form *Encyclopedia Logic*, ¶163Z.

31. *HFM*, 10. *Das Wirkende* is taken from Hegel, *Encyclopedia Logic*, §163.

32. *HFM*, 11, Here Westphal is quoting *Encyclopedia Logic*, §1.

33. *HFM*, 11–12.

34. Curiously, Westphal refers to a world of cause and effect. Technically, this is impermissible because it references empirical reality while still trying to operate at the level of Hegel's logical approach. A separate approach—namely, a phenomenological one—is needed to bridge this gap between pure concepts and empirical reality.

35. Ibid., 13.

36. Ibid.

37. Robert Pippin, *Hegel on Self-Consciousness: Death and Desire in the* Phenomenology of Spirit (Princeton, NJ: Princeton University Press, 2011), 61.

38. For example, see Kenneth Westphal, "Mutual Recognition and Rational Justification in Hegel's *Phenomenology of Spirit*," *Dialogue* 48, no. 4 (December 2009): 753–799, esp. 756–758.

39. *HFM*, 14–15: "Of course, Hegel would not have called this part of the Logic by the name Concept if his theory were not a theory of knowledge (and the object of knowledge as well). But in spite of saying 'Concept' instead of 'Freedom' when naming the final level of categorical development, Hegel himself seems to give the epistemological part of his theory a secondary place."

40. Ibid., 15.

41. Ibid. Writing in a similar vein, Stephen Houlgate echoes this sentiment, particularly in relation to Hegel's theoretical ethics. He argues that "in the ethical will the moment of theoretical understand is finally given equal status to the practical will. . . . The ethical subject recognizes that the institutions that secure freedom and welfare only exist in the understanding and action of practical beings who labor in order to secure their rights and welfare. For the ethical will, therefore, ethical life has "its actuality through self-conscious action." See Stephen Houlgate, "The Unity of Theoretical and Practical Spirit in Hegel's Concept of Freedom," *Review of Metaphysics* 45, no. 4 (June 1995): 875.

42. *HFM*, 16.

43. See *TST*, chaps. 1 and 3. See also *OCOT*, chap. 10, "Laughing at Hegel," which was previously published in *Owl of Minerva* 28, no. 1 (Fall 1996): 39–58.

44. *HFM*, 16.

45. As we will see in later chapters, Westphal expands this critique through a hermeneutics of suspicion in *Overcoming Onto-Theology*.

46. Merold Westphal, "Postmodernism and Religious Reflection," *International Journal for Philosophy of Religion* 38, nos. 1–3 (December 1995): 127.

47. *HFM*, 21.

48. Ibid., 22.

49. Ibid., 28.

50. Ibid., 29.

51. Ibid., 22.

52. Hegel, *The Philosophy of Right*, §41Z, 45.

53. *HFM*, 25.

54. Ibid.

55. Ibid.

56. The line of reasoning that Novak is using is that "first bread, then liberty" as a political philosophy often falls into totalitarianism, denying both bread and liberty. Therefore, he argues, one must follow an economic and political philosophy that secures liberty first, which will then open economic developments, leading to bread, or economic well-being. This argument, as Westphal sees it, falls in line with the United States' political philosophy in the latter half of the twentieth century and has often led the United States to cooperate with dictatorships for its own economic and otherwise strategic gain. *HFM*, 19.

57. Ibid., 26.

58. Ibid., 26, 19.

59. Ibid., 27.

60. Ibid., 242n22.

61. Ibid., 27.

62. Ibid., 29.

63. Ibid., 30.

64. Ibid., 34.

65. Ibid., 34–35. *Rational*, here, means being consistent with the assertion to support all individuals' welfare.

66. Ibid., 81.

67. Ibid., 86.

68. Ibid., 84.

69. Ibid.

70. Ibid., 85.

71. Ibid., 85–86.

72. Ibid., 86.

73. Ibid.

74. Ibid.

75. Ibid.

76. Ibid., 86–87.

77. Ibid., 88. Westphal quotes from the preface of *Philosophy of Right*. Although Westphal does not give any page references, see G. W. F. Hegel, *Philosophy of Right*, trans. S. W. Dyde (Kitchener, ON: Batoche Books, 2001), 19.

78. The cross represents the Passion motif, particularly Jesus' crucifixion.

79. *HFM*, 89. The emphasis is mine.

80. Westphal's career vacillates between these concerns. In an exchange between myself and Westphal, he proclaimed, "Every once and a while a friend will say, 'You write for the academy. You should write something for the church.' My latest book, *Whose Community? Which Interpretation?*, is the result of just such prodding." Thus, he has produced *IPG*, *SF*, and *WCWI*. Furthermore, Westphal frequently gives workshops and lectures at churches on theological and political matters. *IPG*, 5.

81. Merold Westphal, "Prolegomena to Any Philosophy of Religion That Will Be Able to Come Forth as Prophecy," *International Journal for Philosophy of Religion* 4, no. 3 (Fall 1973): 129–150. Since Westphal incorporates this text into *KCRS*, the citations from this essay are cited to *KCRS* hereafter.

82. *KCRS*, 2.

83. Ibid., 8.

84. Ibid.

85. Ibid., 8–11. "Whether a discipline with such a discrepancy between methodology and subject matter could still be called scientific is a question I will leave to whomever is interested. My concern is whether such a discipline can serve as spiritual medicine in the crises of our time." Ibid., 11.

86. Ibid.

87. Ibid., 12.

88. Merold Westphal, "Levinas, Kierkegaard, and the Theological Task," *Modern Theology* 8, no. 3 (July 1992): 246. The emphasis is Westphal's; this article was published in the same year as *HFM*.

89. *HFM*, 144.

90. Ibid.

91. Ibid., 146.

92. See ibid., 145–147. Note that Westphal charges Hegel with bias; particularly given that Hegel, as a product of his time, utilized resources in his research on Hinduism that seemingly were prejudiced.

93. Ibid., 147.

94. Ibid.

95. *SF*, xiv, 4.

96. Ibid., 15.

97. Ibid., 12.

4. HEGELIANS IN HEAVEN, BUT ON EARTH . . .

An "Unfounding," Kierkegaardian Faith

BEGINNING WITH AN UNFOUNDING FAITH

Westphal is attempting to craft a prophetic line of philosophy he finds sorely lacking, particularly with Hegel. This is also the case for Husserlian phenomenology, which he sees as replicating Hegel by being purely descriptive, never prescriptive.[1] At this point, it is clear that Westphal aims to push philosophy into the realm of action: to not just reasonably argue but to move those arguments toward helping the widow, orphan, and stranger. Westphal sees in Kierkegaard a possible way to adapt this preferential option for the poor into a postmodern framework; with Kierkegaard, Westphal finds a Christian response to a society that superficially claims to care for these people in the name of liberalism and a just society. Revealing Kierkegaard's critique of ideology is typically considered Westphal's main contribution to Kierkegaardian studies; Westphal presents Kierkegaard as a "kind of postmodernist," a "proto-phenomenologist," and even a critical theorist whose Christian ideology critique is a rejoinder to those (particularly Marx and Nietzsche) who view religion as an ideology or an enabler of oppression.[2] The foremost result of Westphal's contemporary reading of Kierkegaard is his dialogue between Kierkegaard and Levinas, where he develops their critiques of Hegel (for Kierkegaard), and Heideggerian and Husserlian phenomenology (for Levinas) to establish a prophetic philosophy that critiques society's superficial regard for the other. Through this dialogue, Westphal is not attempting to rid completely the world of "philosophy as rigorous science"; rather, his reading of Levinas maintains that a scientifically rigorous philosophy can coexist alongside a prophetic philosophy.[3] Yet coexistence carves out a space for the philosopher who seeks to explore the ways philosophy can aid the world, and Westphal wants to appropriate the fruits of that "rigorous science" to do so. Westphal's reception in both Kierkegaardian and postmodern circles has been mostly positive, and those who disagree with Westphal largely accept the fertile nature of his project.[4]

It is not surprising that his work repeatedly returns to ethics, specifically to his conviction that saying must mean doing. His ethics centers on love for one's neighbor, especially for those at the margins. Westphal gathers this from Kierkegaard's interpretation of the love commandment (Mark 12:29), when Jesus proclaims that the greatest commandment is to love God "with all your soul" but also to "love your neighbor as yourself." Eventually, Westphal incorporates this commandment into a phenomenological process of becoming an ethical self, a process that he finds helps overcome onto-theology.

He initially discovers this process within the surprising connections between Kierkegaard's concept of faith and Levinas's ethics as first philosophy.[5] It is from this discovery that Westphal founds his own "phenomenology of faith" and its dual movement of transcendence and self-transcendence, where one's faith-bound responsibility toward the other at once decenters and surpasses the self's own understanding, thus opening the self to a possibly divine transcendence.

Interestingly, by reading this neighborly love commandment through Kierkegaard's existential philosophy and Levinas's phenomenology, Westphal avoids a systematic explanation of becoming an ethical self. His is a more personal approach that follows a similar path to that in the writings of Hebrew prophets and in the Gospels. Westphal's project, it seems to me, critiques any attempts made by a systematic philosophy or theology to reduce faith to a logical and coherent construct—or even to reason, for that matter, as we shall see. Essentially, Westphal is trying to break open systematic thinking when it becomes too rigid and ideological; he is constantly aware that any construction—philosophical or theological—can become ideological and so lose sight of the marginalized. Although systematic thinking may be inevitable, it needs to be corrected from time to time through a vigilant critique of ideology.

This critique of systematic thinking is why Westphal sees Kierkegaard as a "proto-postmodernist." Westphal, C. Stephen Evans argues, emphasizes that Kierkegaard's genius may have something to say to everybody, yet his concept of faith as the shibboleth that breaks open ideologies is what speaks the loudest.[6] Accordingly, within his own project, Westphal tries to present a concept of faith that can be called, at best, a framework. For Westphal, faith propels the task of a lifetime, and that task is always an ethical one that must always relate back to the faith that spurs it onward.

Therefore, investigating Westphal's faith-bound ethics presents two challenges: one has to tease out Westphal's notion of becoming an ethical self while concurrently resisting the temptation to systematize it—since this is a contradiction with his own project. Being mindful of this, we will focus on his two main ethical through lines: first, Westphal's Kierkegaardian faith, which finds its antithesis in sin and not reason; and second, Westphal's understanding that the onto-theological critique of metaphysics falls in line with Kierkegaard's critique of Christendom's faith and society's reason. Yet, to comprehend how he arrives at an unsystematic ethics, we initially have to understand how Westphal "unfounds" all of this upon a Kierkegaardian faith as a resistance to any foundation that reason may provide.[7] For Westphal, faith is where ethics begins for the believing soul, and it is also the unreasonable origin from which reason aids and guides the believing soul toward understanding and discipleship.

This leads into the following chapter 5, where we explore the ethical ramifications of Westphal's unfounding faith. Hence, both chapters focus on Westphal's Kierkegaard-centric texts. I find that these texts, most of which were published just before Westphal began to articulate his phenomenology of faith, are crucial to understanding the underlying impetus of Westphal's thinking. In Kierkegaard, Westphal finds his theological voice, and he reads Kierkegaard as a prophetic philosopher, finding in him an ally who also sees Hegelianism as merely proclaiming the possibility of liberty and justice for all while never actually striving to achieve that.

FEAR AND TREMBLING: WESTPHAL'S KIERKEGAARDIAN FAITH

Westphal draws from several philosophical and theological influences for his understanding of God, yet his notion of faith in that God is primarily derived from *Fear and Trembling*. Westphal cites Kierkegaard's *Fear and Trembling* throughout most of his writings, and it is the text that he turns to the most frequently in his philosophy; *Works of Love* and *Concluding Unscientific Postscript* are a close second and third, but Westphal almost always references those works in relation to the faith found in *Fear and Trembling*. The work is present throughout all of his writings, save for his those solely dedicated to Hegel.[8] Additionally, Westphal's most recent book, *Kierkeg-aard's Concept of Faith*, begins by exploring De Silentio's notion of faith in *Fear and Trembling* and then follows its development through Kierkegaard's subsequent pseudonymously written works by Johannes Climacus and Anti-Climacus.[9] Accordingly, to understand what a Westphalian faith looks like, one must first understand what a Kierkegaardian faith looks like, particularly in *Fear and Trembling*.

This exploration will reveal how Westphal refutes the claim that Kierkegaard is an irrational individualist while affirming that Kierkegaard's faith ultimately is a (ethical) task of a lifetime. In the preface to *Kierkeg-aard's Critique of Reason and Society*, Westphal autobiographically traces his own research into Kierkegaard and talks about how he once held these superficial views against Kierkegaard, but as he began to sift through the texts themselves, he realized that they were gross mischaracterizations.[10] Accordingly, our exploration will also reveal how Westphal's prior reading of Hegel helped him move beyond these mischaracterizations and how it becomes the lens from which he reads Kierkegaard. It is not so much that Westphal views Kierkegaard as an avid critic of Hegelianism—which is quite obvious—rather, Westphal uses Hegelian concepts like *Sittlichkeit* and *Aufhebung* to read Kierkegaard. This perspective, one that Kierkegaard himself might even reject, is at the heart of a Westphalian reading of Kierkegaard.

Hegel Trembles: Westphal's Reading of Fear and Trembling

The structure of *Fear and Trembling* reveals just as much about the concept of faith as the content of the essay itself. Johannes De Silentio sets out to give a meditation on Genesis 22 (often called the Akedah story), in which Abraham is called by God to sacrifice his son, Isaac.[11] De Silentio, through that meditation, explores a concept of faith that runs contrary to reason. It is a faith founded on a paradox that holds itself up by a promise in the absurd: that through God all impossible things are possible.[12]

De Silentio makes it clear that he cannot go about proclaiming the nature of faith through a series of propositional, linear arguments and instead is compelled to explain his views on faith through various stories that he then contrasts with Abraham's sacrifice of Isaac.[13] Structurally, De Silentio is illuminating the difference between faith and reason through his series of interrelated mediations—first through prefaces on the impossible situation of Abraham, then through various, smaller stories that relate back to

Abraham, and then returning back to the Akedah—sidestepping a straight forward, logical argumentation describing the truth nature of faith, which he finds too limiting. The structure's overarching goal is to describe faith while resisting a systematizating of faith into categories and justifications, which would negate De Silentio's premise. This breaks the philosophical tradition of writing in "logical," propositional arguments, and it is intentional, as De Silentio's concept of faith is a mode of thinking that operates through a nonlogical structure that ends in a paradox. Westphal appropriates this configuration, and when reading Westphal's other work, one gets a clear and undisputable sense that *Fear and Trembling* not only influences the content of his thought but also provides its structure.

De Silentio dramatically separates faith from reason, stating that, contrary to the arguments and proofs found in philosophical reasoning, "even if someone were able to transpose the content of faith into conceptual form, it does not follow that he has comprehended faith, comprehended how he entered into it or how it entered into him."[14] Through the Akedah, De Silentio finds that faith is independent of, and incommensurable with, universal reason. He further underscores this point by proclaiming, in a satirical fashion, that he himself is not a philosopher and cannot even begin to understand their system(s) that attempts to do in a book what faith requires a lifetime to achieve.[15]

Westphal unpacks the claim that faith cannot be a science, and therefore cannot be an epistemology, by unpacking the not-so-subtle jabs that De Silentio makes toward Hegel and, by extension, Plato. He begins by remarking that De Silentio's rejection of faith as an element of epistemology is a reference to Plato's theory of knowledge. De Silentio wants to overturn the subordination of faith to reason, as found within "Plato's divided line," since the call to faith comes from the outside, from God, as opposed to from some form of personally acquired knowledge.[16] Summarizing, Westphal states that "like Plato's belief (*pistis*) and opinion (*doxa*) and Hegel's representations (*Vorstellungen*) and understanding (*Verstand*), [De] Silentio's faith is not knowledge in the sense to which speculative philosophy aspires (*noesis, episteme, Wissenschaft,* system), or, to say the same thing in biblical language, faith is not sight."[17] If faith were sight, according to Westphal, then it would be caught in "the pure and total presence that is philosophy's pride" and, moreover, an "objective" faith would fail to retain the "mystery and subject (agent and subject matter) of revelation"; in both cases faith simply becomes merely a weaker form of reasoning, or rather, a form of wish fulfillment.[18]

By focusing on the Akedah, Westphal clarifies that De Silentio effectively challenges these models in two fashions:

> First, that the highest task is knowledge as pure insight and full presence, the untrammeled gaze at truth in the full daylight outside the cave, and second, that mere belief (*pistis*) is what you have to settle for when you're not good enough to raise yourself to such lofty heights. Thus Hegel, *the current form of the Platonic model for* [*De*] *Silentio,* will say, "religion is for everyone. It is not philosophy, which is not for everyone."[19]

For Westphal, De Silentio is trying to shatter the supremacy of reason over faith by further separating the two, making faith a distantly connected matter altogether. De Silentio does so by developing three interlocking concepts during his mediations on Abraham: the knight of infinite resignation, the knight of faith, and the paradoxical or absurd. The knight of infinite resignation comes close to the knight of faith in that he, too, like Abraham, boldly resigns himself to the task at hand and does so with the finite, totalizing, concepts of daily living. Unlike Abraham, though, he cannot attain the possibilities found in the infinite absurdity of faith. One could say that the desire for grounding his thinking has led the knight of infinite resignation up to the edge of infinity—to the point that he can accept his present task—but it prevents him from passing into infinity, which is the only place he can fulfill this paradoxical task. The knight of infinite resignation is tied too securely to his grounding reasoning to believe that his actions will be fulfilled through the absurdity of God.

De Silentio gives an example of such a knight in the story of a man who is in love with a princess but, because of various circumstances, can never enter into a romantic relationship with her.[20] Surpassing the "slaves of the finite," this man "assures himself that [this love] is the substance of his life," and he continues to love her, albeit from afar.[21] He passionately loves her but becomes reconciled to the fact that this existence is all that is possible.[22] Thus, De Silentio claims, the man paradoxically renounces his pursuit of the princess for the sake of his love: "The knight [of infinite resignation] does not cancel his resignation, he keeps his love just as young as it was in the first moment; he never loses it simply because he has made the movement infinitely."[23]

The knight of faith, however, performs the same movement of resignation while also performing the (seemingly impossible) movement of faith. Whereas the knight of infinite resignation accepts the fact that his love will

never reach fruition, the knight of faith believes that he will have his princess "by virtue of the fact that for God all things are possible."[24] This is belief
in the absurd—that the man will have his princess, and that Abraham will
get Isaac back—founded on the faith that God will make the impossible,
possible:

> Nevertheless, to the understanding this having [of faith] is no absurdity,
> for the understanding continues to be right in maintaining that in the finite
> world where it dominates this having was and continues to be an impos-
> sibility. The knight of faith realizes this just as clearly; consequently, he can
> be saved only by the absurd, and this he grasps by faith.[25]

Within this grasping by faith lies the ultimate paradox: through faith, God
will make the (seemingly) impossible happen. Abraham will get Isaac back.
The man in love will have his princess. For Abraham, the paradox cannot be
expressed in ethical terms since any explanation of his action would defy
logic and "common" behavior. De Silentio argues that the knight of faith
must teleologically suspend the ethical through this impossible paradox in
order to act out his faith; Abraham must be fully prepared to sacrifice Isaac
without reasonable justifications since there are none.

Explicating his point, De Silentio compares Abraham to three other fathers who have murdered their sons: Agamemnon, Jephthah, and Brutus.[26]
Each of these men, in varying ways, killed his son, and yet their actions
could be explained through a (Hegelian) ethical relationship that allowed
their actions to be judged, perhaps even rationalized as necessary or just.[27]
Abraham is not afforded such privileges since there is no ethical justification
for them, which leaves him completely alone with nothing to mollify him
on his journey to Mount Moriah, burdened with the task he must carry out.
Therefore, he takes to this task in silence, telling no one, not even Isaac, what
will happen when he draws his knife on the mountain.

Abraham's actions cannot be mediated (i.e., rationalized), and therefore
he cannot speak of them, since doing so requires words that hold interrelated
meanings governed by a socialized ethic. He is completely alone and speaking of what he must do, as commanded by God, would break his faith in the
absurd, as through language (mediation), he can only speak of his actions as
murderous or madness.[28] At this point, De Silentio's concept of the ethical
is mediated through culture and community (hence, language), which leads
Westphal to argue that the ethical that must be teleologically suspended is
Hegelian *Sittlichkeit* in which the laws and customs of one's culture dictate

what are just and proper actions.[29] The suspension of any mediation in tandem with the ethical leads Westphal to conclude that De Silentio sees them as intertwined concepts, as in Hegel's *Sittlichkeit*. This suspension of *Sittlichkeit* (of both the ethical and its required mediation) is what separates Abraham as a knight of faith from Agamemnon, Jephthah, and Brutus. While they can speak of their actions and mourn the loss of their sons with their countrymen, Abraham cannot because no one will understand him; therefore, he must go on in silence if he is to carry out his task at all.

Westphal's argument that Hegelian *Sittlichkeit* is the "ethical" suspended by De Silentio is a significant contribution to Kierkegaardian research, and it is also the linchpin he uses to place Levinas and Kierkegaard into dialogue.[30] Consequently, it is important for us to see how Westphal develops and defends this reading before moving forward. In "Kierkegaard and Hegel," Westphal argues that Kierkegaard is not antagonistically anti-Hegelian (as he is widely portrayed) but that his relationship is to Hegel is, ironically, an *Aufhebung*: "There is appropriation," Westphal remarks, "as well as negation, and Kierkegaard is never simply anti-Hegelian."[31] Although Kierkegaard often satirizes Hegelian philosophy, he also pays it tacit compliments throughout—an object has to be worthy of such a sustained satirizing, after all. A key example of this is found in Kierkegaard's analogy about the dancer (representing Hegel) who leaped so high he thought he could fly. Kierkegaard accepts that this dancer can leap higher than any other dancer, and, analogously, Hegel leaps higher than any other philosopher—however, the dancer only dances, never flies. For Westphal, this is a bittersweet compliment: Hegel's philosophy "is more comprehensive and more systematic than [any other]. . . . It is that he spoils his magnificent achievement by making an absurd claim about finality and completeness."[32]

Westphal continues with the complexities of Kierkegaard's relation to Hegel by noting that Kierkegaard's *The Concept of Irony* is quite Hegelian in nature.[33] In this early work one finds deep convergences in both Kierkegaard's and Hegel's appreciation of Platonic thinking (particularly concerning romanticism and its form of Platonism). Eventually, when completing his concept of irony, Kierkegaard begins to critique and diverge from Hegel's thinking. Referring to Robert L. Perkins for summary, Westphal quotes that both thinkers make "the move beyond irony . . . but, according to Kierkegaard, within the new human actuality of ethical existence there remains irony. Human existence is not simply rounded off in the sphere of the ethical as defined by the ethics of Hegel. The infinite still calls."[34]

Returning to the relation between *Sittlichkeit* and the teleological suspension of the ethical, Westphal begins making his case through Kierkegaard's Judge William, whose "The Esthetic Validity of Marriage" begins the
second volume of *Either/Or*. Westphal designates Judge William as a Hegelian, "whether he knows it or not," and he stakes this claim on Judge William's belief that marriage is the pinnacle of socialization and thus is the
key to the ethical.[35] Westphal advances by remarking that Hegel, as an Aristotelian, "repudiates the Platonic, Thomistic, and Kantian models in favor
of an ethics in which the self has no immediate relation to the Good but
only one mediated through the laws and customs of one's people. *Sittlichkeit*
(ethical life) signifies the social institutions that mediate the Good to the
individual." This is why *Either/Or*'s concluding sermon, "The Upbuilding
That Lies in the Thought That in Relation to God We Are Always Wrong,"
is so effective: "It is we," Westphal writes, "I and my *Sittlichkeit,* the laws
and customs, institutions and practices of my society, that are always in the
wrong once God is on the scene. For God is the infinite and eternal while we
are finite and sinful."[36] Just as in *The Concept of Irony*, the infinite still calls,
and no socialization (mediation) can adequately express one's relationship
to that call. Hence, Kierkegaard's use of *Sittlichkeit* carries over to *Fear and
Trembling*.

Westphal insists that many people gloss over this fact, thereby diminishing the major critique that Kierkegaard, through all his pseudonyms but
especially through De Silentio, has against Hegel: that Hegelian philosophy
is so incompatible to biblical faith that its "system is the abolition rather than
the perfection of Christian faith."[37] This, he finds, is where many people get
the concept that Kierkegaard is an irrationalist, since they assume De Silentio's teleological suspension of the ethical signifies "the Moral Law." These
faulty notions, he concludes, are "imported into the text by the reader" and
result in a misreading of the text.[38]

I think Westphal is correct that De Silentio, like Judge William, assumes
a Hegelian construction of the ethical. For further evidence, Westphal states
two key examples of this assumption: first, when De Silentio outright states
this in the phrase, "for if the ethical—that is social morality";[39] second,
when De Silentio distinguishes Abraham from Agamemnon, Jephthah, and
Brutus. Concerning these tragic heroes, Westphal finds that their aforementioned justifications and comforts are from a *Sittlichkeit* that is derived
from the laws and customs "not only *of* their people but also *by* their people
and above all *for* their people. Its highest requirements are the needs of the

nation, the state, and society; and these needs prevail over the otherwise protected needs of the family."[40] Abraham, without an appeal to such laws, is left to suspend or subordinate those laws to serve a higher law from God. De Silentio, Westphal states, is not making an argument that religious faith is against Moral Law but that "to be seriously religious is to have a higher allegiance than to my people and their conception of the Good. What is at issue is the ultimate source of the Moral Law, including my duties to God, neighbor, and self. Is it society or God?"[41]

Answering this question, De Silentio argues that the individual's absolute, infinite relation to God is always over and above that of society. So, when he states that "the ethical is reduced to the relative,"[42] Westphal summarizes that "he means that the believing soul never identifies the law of the land with the law of God but gives absolute allegiance to the latter and only relative allegiance to the former."[43] The fact that God's law is over and above every human law (*Sittlichkeit*) is why Hegel's philosophy is incompatible with biblical faith. De Silentio reveals how "Hegel has collapsed the difference between society and God, making the former absolute and the latter otiose. This is why each of the three 'Problemas' begins with the claim that if Hegel is right, Abraham is lost and can only be considered a murderer."[44]

Westphal is not alone in reading *Fear and Trembling* in light of Judge William from *Either/Or*, nor is he alone in his characterization of Judge William as a Hegelian proxy.[45] Alastair Hannay follows a parallel sentiment, arguing that Judge William's Hegelianism is integral to interpreting *Fear and Trembling* as well as Kierkegaard's other works around this time: *Either/Or, Fear and Trembling*, and *Repetition* were all published in 1843, and *Stages on Life's Way* in 1845 (Hannay, like Westphal, sees a connection between all four books). Hannay, however, directs his interpretation of Judge William and *Fear and Trembling* toward Kierkegaard's personal struggle with the fallout of his proposed marriage to Regine Olsen.[46]

Hannay argues that these texts are "the inspirational product of Kierkegaard's own attempt to come to terms with the conflicts surrounding his own failure to 'realize the universal' in respect of marrying Regine, along with the 'civic' side of the universal which Kierkegaard, the ecclesiastical 'drop-out,' also failed conspicuously to realize."[47] This leads Hannay to two different but intertwined interpretations: the more direct interpretation concerns the impossibility of achieving Judge William's or Hegel's universal absolute, and the second pointedly critiques the premises underlying the concept of the universal absolute. In short, one could say that Kierkegaard is wrestling with the impossibility of achieving the absolute while also questioning why the absolute is absolute. Westphal's and Hannay's interpretations of *Fear and Trembling* (at least in part) converge through their focus on Judge William, a character who is not even in the text itself. Westphal is not alone, then, in cross-referencing Judge William as a Hegelian proxy, placing him in the text as the anti-Abraham whose sole concern is following a universal *Sittlichkeit*. Given the pseudonymous nature of Kierkegaard's writing—where one pseudonym often contradicts another pseudonym to prove a point—it is hard to tease out what, exactly, Kierkegaard's intent was concerning the relationship between *Sittlichkeit* and the ethical. However, Westphal's argument holds firm given the evidence he provides, as well as Kierkegaard's sustained engagement with Hegel throughout his career.[48]

Revealing Revelation: From De Silentio to Climacus

Setting aside the issue of interpreting Kierkegaard, let us pivot back to our original discussion of a Westphalian faith in his reading of *Fear and Trembling*. De Silentio's distinction between society and God reveals that the discussion of faith and the teleological suspension of the ethical is also a discussion of mediation and revelation. The fact that Abraham must remain silent proves that mediation fails him and provides no comfort or justification; "none of the 'already saids,'" Westphal proclaims, "available to him will do the job," and "for Abraham the immediacy of revelation overflows the norms contained within these linguistic dikes, leaving him not alone . . . but, as with Levinas, alone before the traumatic alterity of divine revelation."[49]

Abraham, since he is outside of "the ethical universal" and thus beyond and outside mediation, cannot rely on it for comfort, but how does he know it is God who was testing him? The answer, for Westphal, is through revelation. Therefore, we must turn to the notion of revelation and its relationship to the immediate encounter with God. This moves us from *Fear and Trembling*, in which one first reads about the paradox of faith, to *Philosophical Fragments*, a work in which Kierkegaard's Johannes Climacus augments *Fear and Trembling*'s concept of faith by further describing the relationship of mediation, immediacy, and revelation. This description provides more insight into how revelation plays a deeply abiding role in faith, for both Kierkegaard and Westphal, and how revelation founds a particular interpretation of truth as subjectivity while culminating in the command to love one's neighbor.

According to Westphal, the immediacy of revelation cuts through everything in its path in *Fear and Trembling*, where the immediacy of Abraham's encounter with God compels Abraham to act in a way that can be understood only through the discourse of faith. This encounter comes by way of a command and voice—directly from God—and that voice breaches all forms of mediation between Abraham and the world:

> What is distinctive about this account is the immediacy [De Silentio] attributes to it. God expresses the divine will καθαυτό, and the message cuts through all of Abraham's defenses. No version of the *a priori*, the "already said" . . . enables Abraham to be the condition for the possibility of the authority of this command. So Silentio describes the whole situation as paradoxical, absurd, and sheer madness. It is "unreasonable," not in and of itself, but "humanly speaking" relative to "worldly understanding" and "human calculation."[50]

De Silentio shows that Abraham must accept this commanded revelation through faith by a teleological suspension of the ethical or *Sittlichkeit*. De Silentios thus exposes this as a matter of epistemic revelation, not an account of motive, even if he does not (or cannot) explain how. The actions resulting from this epistemic revelation do not account for any direct motive in the sense that they cannot be reasonably justified within an ethical system that is based on the normativity of culture. Moving from the what of this epistemic revelation to the how—namely, how revelation works in the world—propels Westphal to explore *Philosophical Fragments*, written under the name Johannes Climacus.[51]

Johannes Climacus explores the relationship between recollection and revelation through Socrates' account of knowledge as recollection in the *Meno*.[52] Recounting the story in which Socrates aids in the slave boy's discovery of the Pythagorean theorem, Climacus says that Socrates merely provides the occasion for the discovery. Socrates, Climacus assures us, insists that this discovery is a recollection made by the boy and not something implanted into him, thus separating Socrates from the source of knowledge and making him incidental to the boy's discovery. Socrates has merely presented the boy with the occasion, or opportunity, to discover the theorem.[53]

However, if the opposite were true, if the teacher was the sole source of knowledge and essential to the learning process, then this would be called revelation. Yet for this revelation to occur, the boy must still have the ability to recognize and accept this knowledge. Revelation, as Westphal reads it within Climacus's retelling of the story, is not just a presentation of ideas from the teacher to the student. There must be a "condition for recognizing it as truth. Only when the teacher gives the truth in this double sense does the relation to the teacher become essential."[54]

For Climacus (and by extension, Kierkegaard), revelation needs to be independent of the self and the self's a priori knowledge. Furthermore, the self must recognize, and be open to receiving, this event of revelation. Recognition and reception constitute the ability to be open to the impossible becoming possible (particularly but not necessarily through God), and hence are essential to accepting revelation. Moreover, they are necessary to accept the infinity found within the other that is opened (or revealed) through revelation. This other not only holds the possibility of revelation; he or she also holds the authority of revelation in that the self must accept that the self has no control over the message since revelation is immediate and cuts through the self's conditions of understanding. And it must accept this through faith. Therefore, revelation, as the authoritative voice coming from the outside, is the origin point of faith and of religion (which in this context is faith lived in the world).

This form of revelation is how Westphal connects Levinas to Kierkegaard, and from this concept of revelation Westphal eventually turns to the encounter with the other through and commanded by revelation—as that which enables self-transcendence. Kierkegaard's two accounts of revelation establish a tension between the self, who is receiving and enacting revelation, and the other, who is the infinite ends of revelation.

These two accounts make up what I later call Westphal's "three forms of revelation." I elaborate on this throughout our exploration, but for now, one can begin to see that Westphal understands revelation occurring in three modes: in a mediated immediacy (as in De Silentio's account of Abraham), through the self's recognition that God has revealed something within the self (as in the maieutic account in the *Meno* from Climacus's *Philosophical Fragments*), and through an encounter between the self and the other (as in Kierkegaard's Religiousness C, and in Levinas). We likewise save the concept of Religiousness C and how Levinas enters the picture for later exploration. What matters for us now is that Westphal, through two of Kierkegaard's pseudonyms, has discovered two different expressions of revelation that acknowledge both the need for reception within the self and the need for God to give that revelation. These dual concepts at once acknowledge the reception of the content of revelation (God's commandment to the believing soul) and content itself that is necessary for faith (God commands you to love the other as you love yourself, or, for Abraham, to sacrifice Isaac).

Returning to the issue of how revelation enters into faith, we must note that in *Philosophical Fragments*, Climacus claims that having faith—or taking a "leap" of faith rather—is a necessary condition for receiving and recognizing revelation.[55] Yet this condition of faith runs contrary to the immediacy of revelation within *Fear and Trembling*. Climacus's concept of revelation implies that the self needs faith in some kind of God in order to receive revelation, or at least must be able to accept revelation by an act of faith and not through reasonable knowledge. In other words, the self must accept revelation on God's terms, which requires a trust that this revelation comes from God, and not accept revelation on the self's terms, which relies too much on a reasonable justification for belief. If the latter happens, then revelation becomes a sort of ersatz recollection.

Interestingly, this condition for faith is not addressed or mentioned by De Silentio in *Fear and Trembling*, and it somewhat contradicts De Silentio's argument: if Abraham is called on by God through revelation to sacrifice Isaac—an act that he can legitimately perform only if he places God's command over any reasonable justification for his actions (i.e., the teleological suspension of the ethical, *Sittlichkeit*)—then Abraham's faith is either directly functional as an epistemic command or indirectly functional as a motive for an ethical action based on the occasion of revelation itself. In sum, Westphal's thesis becomes problematic in that in his first argument, that revelation comes as an epistemic command from God as found in *Fear and Trembling*, and his second argument, that recognition and reception of revelation within the self are essential as found in *Philosophical Fragments*, rely on two separate functions of revelation: one tells you what to do from a position of radical alterity (from an infinite God calling to you, a finite and mortal human, thus surpassing all human and hence ethical understanding), and the other tells you that you already know what to do but just need to recognize its truth. The latter form of revelation draws one, as a finite and mortal human, much closer, and much less radically opposed, to an infinite God. This highlights the tension mentioned previously: can revelation be two things at once? It seems that Westphal's reading of Kierkegaard is tangled in contradiction. However, for Westphal at least, this is not so much a contradictory reading but an opening to discuss the tension within revelation, to allow for a space for the self to be open to possibilities.

One could object that these separate, seemingly contradictory functions are further problematized by their pseudonymous authorship and the issue of trying to make Kierkegaard's philosophy a collective, systematic whole. As such, this contradiction problematizes the concept of revelation throughout Kierkegaard's work and how said revelation can be utilized as a foundation for a faith that emphasizes the love commandment. Not only is Abraham lost, as De Silentio likes to say, but so is Westphal's understanding of Kierkegaard.

In response to such an objection, one can almost hear Westphal proclaim, "Wait until I'm finished! This tension between authors and revelation is part of the point!" In "Johannes and Johannes: Kierkegaard and Difference," Westphal contends that Kierkegaard is clearly aware of the two seemingly contradictory positions and is trying to prove an essential point through that tension. Westphal is *not* giving a novel reading of revelation within Kierkegaard's work but rather is exploring a tension Kierkegaard consciously placed into his pseudonymous authorship. Kierkegaard's authors, in short, are in dialogue with each other (which is not a foreign concept in Kierkegaard scholarship), and within that dialogue, there are intentionally unresolved discussions that highlight aspects of concepts such as revelation but do not resolve them into a definition. Westphal explains that Kierkegaard precisely aims to disclose a tension "where the present age sees harmony, to juxtapose antithesis to its synthesis."[56] Rather than merely revealing their differences, Kierkegaard presses further: expressing how many reduce these opposing accounts to a simple identity of revelation and move on.

More pointedly, what Kierkegaard offers us through these two authors is a critique of modernity's metaphysics, which, as many postmodern authors have shown, has the tendency to reduce what is other to the same. This critique attempts to overcome or subvert metaphysics, according to Westphal, "by the desire to confront modernity (and very possibly postmodernity as well) with its other, to make philosophical reflection and social practice vulnerable to both God and neighbor in ways they have tended to foreclose."[57] We therefore turn to exploring this attempt to subvert and overcome metaphysics, which has crucial influence for Westphal's thinking. Afterward, we return to a consideration of how Westphal sees this as part of Kierkegaard's overarching project.

Recollection and Immediacy: Kierkegaard's Two Accounts of Revelation

Interestingly, Westphal takes from this supposed contradiction of revelation the notion that Kierkegaard is trying to appeal to difference but also, in doing so, is trying to develop a process of becoming an ethical self through a faith-based, critical theory.[58] This process is at once dependent on an inward faith—part of the hidden inwardness of faith—and an outward expression of that faith as seen in the love commandment.

Westphal explains that Kierkegaard's first step toward developing this is through De Silentio's *Fear and Trembling*. Here, Westphal argues that the teleological suspension of the ethical functions as a critique of ideology (Christendom), since the ethical is the "celebration and sanctification of some social status quo" and not a truly inspired desire for a moral and just concept of the Good.[59] Abraham's faith, as a form of religiously inspired critique, places this so-called status quo on trial before God and shows that it is found wanting. Christendom has been judged as merely legitimating its own interest rather than working humbly in service of loving God or the neighbor. It finds that the ethical fails because it implies some final, teleological end at which, if everyone were to follow all of its rules and processes, society could find perfection and complete harmony in its social order. "Another way to put this point," Westphal wryly summarizes, "is that we will all be Hegelians in heaven. But on earth . . . that is the question Kierkegaard wants us to ponder."[60]

Pondering this point on behalf of Kierkegaard, Westphal (anachronistically) muses that perhaps Kierkegaard's challenge to critical theorists, particularly those that follow a Marxian analysis of society, is to consider whether modernity's most fundamental error is its tendency to deify itself "as history's *telos*" and thus become immune to critique.[61] Everything gets swallowed in its self-fulfillment, and all minor narratives get assumed into its grand, master narrative. The critical theorist who critiques only capitalism, materialism, and social constructs—thus neglecting the spiritual dimension of society—does so at his or her own peril. "But what if," Westphal asks, "material injustice and oppression have their roots in spiritual pride?"[62] Going back to our exploration of his critique of Hegel, one can definitely see Westphal's spiritual litmus test emerging here; although the question "What kind of social order does this religion legitimize?" can now be expressed in the inverse: "What does your politics say about your spirituality?" Or, more exactly, "What does your politics uphold for the sake of all others?"[63]

Revisiting the case study of Amos and Marx where, in *Suspicion and Faith*, Westphal proclaims that the Christian cannot simply utilize Amos for a critique of ideology because "Marx is about us in a way that Amos is not," one can see more clearly that Amos is about "us" in a way that Marx is not; Amos knows the spiritual side of religious belief in a way that Marx cannot fathom just like Marx knows contemporary society's Christian, political, capitalist faults in a particular way that Amos cannot fathom.[64] Both are essential for a complete critique of the self. In other words, Westphal is revealing how he believes both that the political and the spiritual are intertwined—again wedding his biblical faith to politics—and that one needs to address both in tandem for a more complete understanding of oneself. Echoing his perspective that Athens needs Jerusalem, and vice versa, in "The Canon as Flexible, Normative Fact," perhaps one's spiritual concerns are just as pertinent to one's political and social life as one's material concerns, which is why Pope Francis's recent denouncement of the world's great idol—market capitalism—is apt and so bitingly true for so many people, religious or otherwise.[65] Athens needs Jerusalem, and Jerusalem needs Athens, because they are "about us" in different ways, and each judges religious believers (as well as society) with different measures.

Westphal gathers this more holistic form of critical theory from the fact that he sees not two competing concepts of revelation but rather two dialoguing concepts. De Silentio and Climacus are not presenting two different revelations that are mutually exclusive. On the contrary, they reveal an aspect of the other through a dialogue that resists reducing both to an identity of the same; in doing so, this dialogue presents a strong critique against society. Arguing this, Westphal finds *Fear and Trembling* to be an exercise in which De Silentio teases out the paradox of faith as something beyond reason and as the task of a lifetime. As a task of a lifetime, it challenges our often entrenched social-political worldviews—thus becoming a critical theory—and compels us first to hold our faith in God as absolute and everything else a distant second. Accordingly, the chief task of *Philosophical Fragments* is to explore the "epistemological ramifications" of De Silentio's thesis. In other words, in *Philosophical Fragments*, Johannes Climacus asks Johannes De Silentio, "How does the dichotomy between recollection and revelation map onto that between the ethical and the religious?"[66]

Westphal is quick to reply on De Silentio's behalf: "Not directly."[67] Explicating this tension further, Westphal appeals to two pivotal figures behind both works, Socrates and Gotthold Ephraim Lessing. Socrates, for

Kierkegaard, reveals a knowledge that is accessible only through recollection, and Kierkegaard's pseudonyms are quick to adapt this as a strident rebuke of "Athenian *Sittlichkeit*."[68] Keep in mind, however, that Climacus did not adopt Socrates' notion of recollection wholesale, he instead offers a higher form of recollection in divine revelation. Running parallel to this, Westphal argues that, despite Climacus's appreciation of Lessing (in *Philosophical Fragments*), he still levies a critique against Lessing's claim that human reason contains an a priori knowledge of God that supersedes all historical accounts of God's revelation.[69] Climacus would see this concept as a nice way to box God up, a way to make God a necessary part of our lives but only as a singular, fixed function. Therefore, in Climacus's writings on the epistemic implications of revelation, he simultaneously presents an alternative to both Socrates and Lessing, thus giving a primary alternative "to the whole Enlightenment project of which [Lessing's argument] is a classic expression."[70] In short, Westphal is arguing that Kierkegaard's *Fear and Trembling* and *Philosophical Fragments* criticize not only Hegelian *Sittlichkeit* but also a certain concept of God that finds traction in Enlightenment thinking and that locks God "out of a world pre-interpreted in our own image," making God merely a cog in in the wheel of our own human reasoning.[71] Presaging the critique of onto-theology, Westphal is concerned about humanity's desire for autonomy through naming what God is (and what God is not), effectively putting humanity in charge of its own destiny. By leaving intact the tension between *Fear and Trembling* and *Philosophical Fragments*, as far as recollection and revelation are concerned, Kierkegaard is able to explore the concept of revelation without reducing it to something that can be confined to human reason.[72] This tension allows for possibilities of difference and resists giving revelation a static identity while also giving believers a moment to reflect on what it is, how it works, and why they need it.

The irony, however, is that Kierkegaard utilized both Socrates and Lessing for his reflections and his criticisms. Again, as with Hegel, there is somewhat of an *Aufhebung* going on: Kierkegaard is negating their thought while also sublimating it into his own, for his own purposes. Here that purpose is to address a critique against Christendom. According to Westphal, Kierkegaard's work is utilizing the juxtaposition of "faith as essentially linked to a teleological suspension of the ethical" (for De Silentio) to faith "as the opponent of a Reason that makes such a suspension possible," which therefore makes De Silentio's critical theory possible. Yet in making this claim, Kierkegaard utilizes both theories of recollection, eventually superseding them with his own concept of revelation, while also keeping the spirit of their theories intact. In other words, both Socrates' and Lessing's theories of recollection are utilized and surpassed by Kierkegaard's own theory of revelation and the faith required for said revelation, but those theories of recollection are still present in and germane to Kierkegaard's theory. As Westphal argues, this is a quintessential example of Kierkegaard's appropriation of Hegel's concept of *Aufhebung*.

Christendom, and its underlying Hegelianism, thus becomes problematic because it fails to see the challenge faith poses to its structures. Westphal sees that Christendom is in the crosshairs of Climacus and De Silentio, since both can be read as a critique of the theory of recollection as a form of absolute knowing (presented in the *Phenomenology of Spirit*). Since Hegel's concept of revelation holds that "the transcendence of the limitations of the religious mode of knowing in absolute knowing is presented as recollection," one must move from revelation to recollection, thus making it the final movement of the Spirit in the *Phenomenology*. This is the primary target of both works in that, according to Westphal, "not only does Climacus reverse [this] direction in the *Fragments*, but in place of the harmony posited by Hegel he represents a radical otherness that recalls the radical otherness of *Fear and Trembling*."[73] In the concluding section of his "Johannes and Johannes," Westphal continues by detailing Hegel's view of the religious and how it is enacted by the Spirit in history (and in the life, death, and resurrection of Jesus). Westphal argues that Hegel's theory of necessary truth (i.e., ultimate truth, capital-*T* Truth) differs from Lessing and Socrates in that it attempts to integrate historical consciousness, "but this theory, like theirs, entails that insofar as the truth is necessary truth, it is within us and needs to be recollected. Even if such recollection is history comprehended rather than abandoned, the point about recollection that is essential to Johannes Climacus remains the same."[74] In making necessary truth a product of historical recollection—and therefore mediated through action, or religion—Hegel becomes the link between Johannes and Johannes. Again, the importance of holding faith in God and God's revelation to humanity over and above one's *Sittlichkeit* comes to the fore. Especially given that this is the only way for one to find the mediation necessary for recollection according to Hegel's theory. Westphal concludes:

> In arguing that religious *Vorstellungen* must achieve the form of universality, [Hegel] identifies what he calls the higher truth of Christianity with what Johannes De Silentio presents as the ethical in *Fear and Trembling*;

and in seeking to replace religious narrative with (his own very peculiar sort of) conceptual necessity, he identifies his version of religious truth with what Johannes Climacus presents as the Socratic recollection motif in *Philosophical Fragments*. Since they are, in Hegel's text, two sides of the same coin, that text invites us to read the works of Johannes and Johannes as two sides of a single attempt to spell out an alternative to an Hegelian understanding of Christianity.[75]

This gives Westphal ample evidence to believe that Johannes and Johannes should be read together as a bonded couplet with each illuminating the other and with a common critique against Hegel and Christendom. This is a remarkable argument for the coherency and unity of Kierkegaard's authorship, but for us, "Johannes and Johannes: Kierkegaard and Difference" sheds light on two aspects of how Westphal understands faith and revelation: First, it reveals how this hidden inwardness of faith, as seen in *Fear and Trembling*, becomes a critical theory, moving toward an outward expression of that faith in *Philosophical Fragments*. Second, it reveals how revelation can hold itself in tension through its various forms and functions. Revelation, so understood, prevents itself from being reduced it to merely one of those functions, thereby attempting to make it manageable or completely intelligible in service of human projects. For Westphal, revelation needs difference because it is wholly different from human reason. Moreover, human reason enters into the picture only once it comes as an aid to a revelation-steeped faith.

This does not mean that faith cannot use reason but, as we have seen through his concepts of recollection and revelation, reason's role in faith is to be utilized to understand faith and its contents, yet in no way should it ever see itself as superior to faith. Faith becomes an origin point for Westphal, it and its leap are tantamount to the headwaters of life and the source of all a Christian's actions. As an origin point, however, it holds no particular foundation since faith is a willing assent (leap) toward accepting God's commanded revelation. This is why I call it an "unfounding" faith: Westphal's faith is an origin point of thought for the believing soul, but since it is an assent and therefore a task, it holds no typical foundation.

Furthermore, an unfounding faith works as a critical theory since it consistently asks believers if they are truly performing God's will or their own: "Have you loved your neighbor as you love yourself today? Have you (mis)placed your needs over God's and others?" This critical reflection is one way the hidden inwardness of faith is expressed as a task of a lifetime:

it constantly demands the believing soul to love one's neighbor and to keep God's concerns paramount. Westphal sees his philosophical task as faith seeking understanding, and he bases his entire project on how philosophical reasoning—even from postmodern and atheistic perspectives—guides and aids one's faith; reasoning directs faith to understanding, as it were. This is how "atheism for Lent" becomes a useful tool for the believing soul and why overcoming onto-theology becomes a necessary task: both hold philosophical critiques that aid the believing soul toward understanding. What we have seen here is the apparatus, so to speak, that runs this process of faith seeking understanding.[76]

So how does this task of a lifetime express itself in society, and just as important, how does it work with reason? Westphal has clearly expressed how he thinks Athens needs Jerusalem, but questions remain about how, exactly, Jerusalem needs Athens, and following this, how one holds onto faith without falling into fideism, where faith alone justifies faith.

AN ATTACK UPON CHRISTENDOM: WESTPHAL'S KIERKEGAARDIAN CRITIQUE OF REASON AND SOCIETY

As already mentioned, Merold Westphal initially came to embrace Kierkegaard by noticing how he had often been misinterpreted as an irrationalist and an extreme individualist. The bulk of Westphal's early Kierkegaardian research explored alternative interpretations of Kierkegaard's work. Much of this went into his book *Kierkegaard's Critique of Reason and Society*, published in 1987 as a collection of reformatted journal articles originally published from 1971 to 1985.

This work is our primary text to explore Westphal's Kierkegaardian concept of reason and how the relationship between faith and reason further compels social action. As Westphal notes in the preface, these essays present less of a discovery "*about* Kierkegaard" and serve "primarily [as] discoveries *through* Kierkegaard, insights gained with his help," making this a great resource for our exploration of Westphal's Kierkegaardian faith and its social consequences.[77] What emerges from this is how Westphal sees a Kierkegaardian faith as an act of will, making the metaphor of a leap of faith such an apt explanation. Faith, for Westphal's Kierkegaard, is not a conclusion to a rational exercise but a trusting, inward movement of intuition and hope that is justified not solely by faith but, rather, by how it engenders actions of love toward God (as the object of the believing faith) and God's creation, the neighbor (as the action and works which solidify the believing faith, without which faith would be dead; see James 2:14–26).

Prophetic Critique: Seeing Society from the Eyes of Faith

In chapter 2 of *Kierkegaard's Critique of Reason and Society*, Westphal explains that the key to reading Kierkegaard is to read him as a prophetic philosopher, as an alternative to a philosophy that sees itself as a rigorous science that many, especially those in Hegelian and Husserlian camps, will outright reject. This is Kierkegaard's strength. Westphal calls Kierkegaard's work "personal, untimely [i.e., purposely inconvenient], political, and eschatological," and all of these characteristics make his work an expression of suspicion toward an overtly sterile, objective way of doing philosophy.[78] It constantly reminds philosophers of the humanly social aspects of their work and never lets them forget the foolhardiness of humanity's wisdom. This may work for prophets, Westphal concedes, but it "may be claimed that it is not properly philosophical" and therefore exists outside of the task of philosophy.[79] Westphal responds with four rebuttals, two of which we will immediately deal with and two that require further attention: first, perhaps we have created a "too tight . . . disciplinary division of labor" for philosophy, and this should make us constantly aware and "suspicious of boundaries when they become merely simplistic rationalizations."[80] Second, being suspicious of these boundaries, we must be aware that prophetic critique serves as a counterweight to "scientific" philosophy. Current philosophical scholarship often presumes that the critiques of Marx, Nietzsche, and Freud respectively fill this role, in various capacities and from different subdisciplines. Westphal is quick to place Kierkegaard among these masters of suspicion, since he speaks to philosophy from a position of faith and is thus able to give a perspective—steeped in its own particular brand of suspicion—that is often overlooked or presumed faulty by said masters. "Isn't it better," Westphal asks, "to hear the painful truth about God's people from those who are compelled to tell it by their faithfulness to God, rather than from those who would like to do away with Him in the name of Truth?"[81]

Sticking with this second rebuttal for a moment, one can begin to see how Westphal's prophetic-philosophical interpretation of Kierkegaard takes shape: Kierkegaard is about us in a way that the masters of suspicion are not, yet he agrees with their suspicion that religion more often than not legitimatizes social praxis. Kierkegaard, however, critiques Christendom from within Christianity, twisting the knife both ways: on the one hand, he accuses Christendom of being in service of itself, just like his fellow masters, and, on the other hand, as a believing Christian, he charges that Christendom has obliterated its own faith from within.

Westphal's third rebuttal argues that, although the masters are quick to take up the "prophetic task of subjecting popular religion to critical scrutiny," Kierkegaard pushes their critique from the perspective of the religious person who is also a critical theorist: he both examines what Christendom has legitimated in service of itself and attempts to reconfigure how the Christian can understand his or her faith.[82] This leads to Westphal's fourth and final rebuttal, arguing that Kierkegaard's work shines a light on the deeply social nature of Christianity and knowledge itself. Kierkegaard's critique of Christendom, parallel with the masters' critique of religion, targets this social aspect of knowledge (which Westphal calls "the sociology of knowledge"), finding that this social nature attempts to make Christianity morally reasonable and presentable.[83] In doing so, it has suppressed, subverted, or outright ignored core tenets of the Christian faith, such as the Incarnation. This, Westphal claims, is what causes Kierkegaard to bitingly state that "Christendom has abolished Christianity" and has turned it into "a superficial something which neither wounds nor heals profoundly enough."[84]

Hence, for both Kierkegaard and Westphal, faith comes from an inwardness that relies on a trust in, or leap toward, God in and through revelation. Abraham's faith came from an encounter with God, not from socially mediated and reasoned circumstances. He is no Pascal and there is no wager for him. Faith begins individually, *and then* it is expressed socially. Kierkegaard's so-called individualism, for Westphal, is merely his penultimate move, not the climax of his thinking, and only the final assessment before enacting faith through the commandment that the believing soul should love God above all things and love the neighbor as the believing soul loves herself.[85] Reason, however, is always expressed socially through the interpretation of texts, through an encounter with the other, through a reflection upon prior experiences or ponderings (*Nachdenken*).

For Kierkegaard, reason is a social phenomenon since it is entirely socially mediated, or, at least legitimated, through society; therefore, it is a social phenomenon. Faith, contrariwise, is able to break through these barriers since it originates inwardly first and then outwardly expresses itself. God is beyond social reasoning, even though we, the community of believers, at times have to employ reason to remind ourselves of this.[86] This is why Abraham's godly faith can teleologically suspend the ethical (*Sittlichkeit*), but it is also why we, as the faithful, can reflect on Abraham through works like *Fear and Trembling* to better understand our own faith.[87] With apologies to St. Anselm, who argued that both phrases should be interchangeable, for Kierkegaard it is clearly *fides quaerens intellectum* and not *intellectus quaerens fidem*.

This puts reason in a precarious role. Why does Jerusalem need Athens? It is certainly not because faith needs to be justified through (social) reasoning. Kierkegaard, for Westphal, makes this point about faith plain by arguing that those who try to apologetically and historically defend the viability of Christianity in Christendom are Judases guilty of blasphemy. Relating back to a familiar refrain throughout his work, Westphal quips, "Perhaps we are beginning to get a notion of how the priests felt when they saw Jeremiah or Amos coming to the temple."[88]

He is arguing how the faithful build and maintain worldviews upon human reason, which by its own nature is socialized and historically conditioned. Kierkegaard, through his attention to the "sociology of knowledge," as Westphal puts it, levies the damning critique against apologetics as "corrupted Christianity," since he recognizes that all factions within society propagate themselves through "belief systems in which the established order is justified" and that religions are often the most effective factions in doing this.[89]

Through reason, religions often sustain and maintain their influence in society not for the greater glory of God, but for their own survival and domination: for the greater glory of me. "For Kierkegaard," Westphal summarizes, "reason is man's capacity to recognize the authority of the established order, thereby participating in its self-deification. When this is what masquerades as Reason, Kierkegaard asks why one should pledge allegiance to it."[90] When this reasoning is employed to justify faith, what prevents one from thumping his or her chest after proving that God exists, and therefore that we, the believers in that God, are in the right and everyone else is in the wrong (and therefore must be converted to our worldview)? In effect, what does one gain to debate an atheist and win? Does that guarantee one's salvation or the salvation of others? Does it merely legitimize an established order and worldview? These are the critical questions arising from Kierkegaard's critique of apologetics, and Westphal sees them as a guard against creating God in one's self-image and thus an idol for one's selfish gain. The question again turns to the inverse of Westphal's litmus test— what does your politics place above all else?—since our (i.e., the Christian community's) apologetics propagates an established order in service of legitimating our beliefs (and thus ourselves, our worldview) and not toward the commandment to love God with all our hearts and to love our neighbor as we love ourselves.[91]

The answer to the question of why does Jerusalem need Athens therefore pivots away from legitimization through apologetics, moving toward discipleship. The epistemological question of faith, for Westphal (via Kierkegaard), is part of a much larger, ethical question concerning discipleship and becoming a follower of Christ. It is not (nor cannot be) concerned with ensuring Christianity's place in society, that is, Christendom. As a Christian, one emulates Christ's life as the paradigm of his or her own life; one becomes contemporaneous with Christ, according to Westphal.[92] This contemporaneous path of being at once spiritually with Christ while also living in the world places one's faith in tension with reason—Kierkegaard goes as far as to even say against reason—since, Westphal explains through Kierkegaard, "'faith is on the other side of death,' the death that dies to immediacy, selfishness, and worldliness."[93] Returning to *Fear and Trembling*, faith allows the self to do the impossible: to believe in a life after death, to believe in a God through whom this impossibility is made possible. In doing so, faith offends reason and society, which Westphal is quick to link with Christ's life and works that likewise offended his society (so much so that they crucified him). That this crucifixion and the subsequent resurrection are the source of faith for Christians is doubly offensive to society, which is why Christians are so quick to wrap their faith in a reasonable, apologetical defense.

Westphal abates this hasty inclination by highlighting what he calls Kierkegaard's "logic of insanity," nodding toward the Socratic notion of divine madness. Faith, as an act of will, not only explains how faith can be against reason without being fideist but also discloses how reason works as part of ethical discipleship. Therefore, the following section briefly covers how this logic, and its subsequent leap, fits into his concept of faith.

Logic and Leap: Kierkegaard's Antiapologetical Faith

Westphal points out that Kierkegaard regularly references Plato's *Phaedrus*, particularly with regard to the notion of madness.[94] In this work, Socrates opens his second speech with a commentary on madness that questions whether or not society has wrongly labeled "madness as an evil, but in reality, the greatest blessings come by way of madness, indeed of madness which is heaven-sent" (244a).[95] In questioning this, Socrates, and later Kierkegaard, argues for the elevation of "heaven-sent madness over man-made sanity."[96] The logic of insanity readily accepts that, according to reason, Christianity is absurd and implausible, but in a twist, it turns the question of credibility back onto reason by asking it where it acquires its authority and criterion to judge. Human reason, after all, is finite and limited. The question and critique becomes, for Kierkegaard and Westphal, why does such a humanist epistemology get to be the arbiter of all things?

The logic of insanity consequently inverts the roles between faith and reason and turns the critique of fideism on its head: it no longer asks if reason sustains your faith but if your faith sustains your reason. This clarifies what Kierkegaard meant by faith being against reason, since faith's trust in the implausible, improbable, and paradoxical constantly reminds reason of its finitude while faith trusts in the infinite understanding of God. Therefore, since it is a trust in the infinite, Westphal argues that it, not reason, should be the final arbiter of all things.

Westphal reminds us that this is a critique of a thoroughly modern enterprise. Interestingly, he references Kant to bolster the theological critique Kierkegaard makes against reason and its place as the final criterion of all that is true.[97] Westphal elaborates this point by showing that, by Kant's estimation, "human reason fails through its essential finitude to be an absolute (perspectiveless) perspective of the world."[98]

Westphal connects the two thinkers briefly *not* to show how each's projects are similar—Kant would not accept being affiliated with "divine madness," even though his work on the limits of reason touches on the logical proofs of God's existence (or lack thereof) and the nature of faith[99]—but to illustrate how Kierkegaard's divine madness rests upon the limits of human reason, thus contrasting Kierkegaard with the Enlightenment tradition. More clearly, in *Concluding Unscientific Postscript*, Kierkegaard continually mocks and satirizes philosophy's self-deification via its absurd claim to hold absolute knowledge as attainable. Westphal notes that, in the *Postscript*, Kierkegaard finds this to be "the acme of professional absent mindedness in which, forgetting their names, philosophers identify themselves with the pure I-am-I, the divine self-knowledge."[100] As if to make sure that the philosophers know that he is laughing at them and not with them, Kierkegaard turns serious by outright calling it "blasphemy again and again, thereby giving a theological twist to Kantian finitism."[101] Returning to Kierkegaard's parody of the dancer who could leap so high he thought he could fly, Westphal is showing that even our greatest philosophers are still always flawed and finite; taking a page from the concluding chapter of *Either/Or*, one could say that, in relation to the infinite knowledge of the divine, they are always in the wrong. This becomes the problem Westphal sees with the Enlightenment project and with modernity: in both we can see how far too often philosophy exceeds its grasp in its exploration of knowledge when it seeks to achieve absolute knowledge and, through that attempt, absolute autonomy. When Westphal eventually pivots toward a postmodern critique of modernity and the Enlightenment, this becomes a focal point. Westphal's primary appropriation of Kierkegaard's logic of insanity thus becomes a faith that at once critiques and remedies humanity's intellectual overreach for autonomy. So, Westphal's philosophy takes a theological turn to combat the philosophical hubris of absolute knowledge while combating an apologetics that assumes that, through God, one can obtain an absolute knowledge, albeit of a different kind. A finitism emerges throughout his thinking, and in these pages of *Kierkegaard's Critique of Reason and Society* Westphal discovers it within Kierkegaard's framework.[102]

Furthermore, this divine madness and its critique of finite reason becomes the locus from which he reads onto-theology. Briefly, his primary concern with onto-theology is that, quoting Heidegger, it pinpoints the tendency to only let "the deity . . . come into philosophy [i.e., human reasoning] only insofar as philosophy, *of its own accord and by its own nature,* requires and determines that and how the deity enters into it."[103] Westphal, again following Heidegger, is quick to point out that, by relying on apologetics and favoring reason over faith, one forgets the Pauline question: "Has not God let the wisdom of this world become foolishness?"[104] This highlights the connection between Kierkegaard's critique of reason and Westphal's thinking, particularly his later work on onto-theology and postmodern thought. In the onto-theological critique of metaphysics, Westphal sees a postmodern articulation of the finite nature of human reasoning seen in Kierkegaard, which is why it is important to elevate Kierkegaard's divine madness above human reasoning.[105]

Returning to *Kierkegaard's Critique of Reason and Society* for a deeper explanation, note how the acceptance of revealed divine madness is an act not of the understanding but of the will. With faith as an act of will or leap, Kierkegaard critiques not only an apologetically argued concept of faith but also a faith that falls in line with rationally defined deism, both of which he criticizes as attempts "to provide absolute guarantees that preclude even the possibility of being wrong."[106] Here, Westphal revisits the relationship between deism and Kierkegaard, contrasting Kierkegaard's views with Lessing's theological conceptions of God as the "necessary truths of reason."[107] For Lessing, historical data (meaning the stories pertaining to the faith, such as the Bible) and one's own historical narrative in the faith (one's own life of faith) must stand the scrutiny of reason that renders them not as evidence for the truth found in God but as occasions for recollecting truth about God. Basically, the question under scrutiny, for Lessing, is how a historical event can ever aspire to be the eternal truth. Lessing's answer, at the risk of oversimplification, is that it cannot because of the contingent nature of historical events.

Following a familiar pattern, Westphal compares this with Socrates' query of the slave boy in the *Meno*, finding that the argument draws a conclusion from the story that contrasts with Kierkegaard's. By making faith a product of recollecting truth from within the necessary truths of reason, this argument renders void anything miraculous or paradoxical since reason cannot comprehend it or, when it does, it has to shape it and warp it so that that it can conform and legitimate itself. Westphal summarizes Lessing's concept of faith thus:

Data as occasion + the Truth within = knowledge as recollected Truth.[108]

However, Westphal concludes, this formulation suffers from begging the question since its conclusion is latent within the second premise. In contradistinction, Westphal describes Kierkegaard's leap of faith as more a "resolution than a recollection" given that "voluntarism," or the willing act of believing, moves the believing soul toward accepting certain truths that are beyond one's own capacity to reasonably obtain or completely understand them. Additionally, because historical data (i.e., our empirical and evidential experiences) cannot serve as the occasion for recognizing Truth, we must rely upon a giver of that Truth, or what Westphal calls a teacher. Like Socrates, the teacher provides the occasion to recognize and accept truth, but moving beyond Socrates and beyond human reason, this teacher also gives the capacity to recognize a truth that surpasses understanding so greatly that it can be called only divine madness.[109] This is nothing short of a miracle for Westphal:

> We need therefore, not only a Teacher who can confront us with the Truth, but also one who can implant within us the condition for recognizing it as such. This fundamental remaking is nothing short of *an act of re-creation,*

and the one who performs it is *not just a Teacher but a Savior.* Thus instead of Lessing's formula we have a very different formula:

Data as occasion + *the giving of the condition* = *faith as miracle.*

That the end product is called both faith and miracle is appropriate since Kierkegaard emphasizes both the divine activity, the giving of truth and condition, and the human response, the act of obedience and trust that is a leap of faith, though he does not present a theory of how they are related.[110]

By both being the truth and giving us the conditions to recognize it as truth beyond reason, Westphal brings Kierkegaard's two notions of revelation back into the picture, particularly concerning the revelation occurring in Jesus as the Incarnation. This will be important once we arrive at Westphal's concept of Religiousness C. As discussed already, the concepts of revelation as epistemic knowledge (in *Fear and Trembling*) and as recognized and received knowledge (in *Philosophical Fragments*) are in tension with each other, which, Westphal argues, Kierkegaard maintains is necessary to provide a dynamic difference with our concept of (human, rational) knowledge. Here, that tension is exemplified with the giving and receiving of a miraculous faith, and it is also why Westphal understands why Kierkegaard did not give a theory of how they are related. The fact that there is tension in the giving and receiving deprives this miracle of any logical certainty that reason lends to itself.[111] Faith is a willing act of trust and acceptance best described as a leap.

One makes this leap of faith inwardly, trusting the internal recognition of revelation and truth, and therefore going beyond reason. This, then, is a move toward the infinite through faith. The evocation of movement or action within the concept of the leap of faith is apt: the only way one can grasp faith is through a willing, inward action that eventually expresses itself in an outward action of love. Here, faith's outward expression is in response to revelation's call to love God with all your heart (i.e., faith's inward movement) and to love your neighbor as much as you love yourself (i.e., faith's outward movement). Faith thus becomes a question of ethics and discipleship, which is where it meets reason and is why Jerusalem needs Athens. Reason becomes the way the self comprehends its faith and also ethically enacts its faith. Thus, one accepts the aforementioned inversion of fideism—that faith in the infinite God, as seen through revelation, is neither judged by reason nor claimed to support itself by itself. Rather, it is a voluntary trust in God and revelation that supports reason's contemplation of the infinite.

This brings us back to Westphal's claim that reason's primary objective is to understand and deepen faith through discipleship. Reason's role in faith is articulated through a contemplative discipleship that posits sin, not reason, as the antithesis of faith. Reason, when it supports faith in seeking understanding, can become enriched as it is taken up in the task of a lifetime. Therefore, if reason becomes enriched through faith's acceptance of God and revelation, then it cannot be the opposite of faith, as the question of faith and reason suggests. Thus, Westphal finds Kierkegaard arguing that faith is opposed to sin and this sin is typically characterized by "despair, disobedience, offense, and resignation."[112] Acts of sin, here, are articulated as moments when one's faith in God is weakened or lost, thus harming one's discipleship and one's willful hope that through God all things are possible. Suffice it to say, for our present purposes, the question no longer becomes one of faith and reason but one of faith and sin, with reason being the person's capacity to fully understand his or her faith and the person's faculty for ethically expressing that faith in society.

Sin, in contrast, becomes a deprivation of reason's ability to express one's faith, or in matters of despair, it becomes a total lack of faith.

Conclusion: An Unfounding Faith?

The following chapter explores faith's opposition to sin and its relation to reason in greater detail as this concept, for Westphal following Kierkegaard, explains how faith is related to discipleship. This can be summarized as a faith dependent on revelation, and through the aid of reason, revelation leads one on the course of faith seeking understanding. In doing so, it also leads the believing soul away from sin and despair, which are opposed to faith.

Presently, we should assess how Westphal's faith becomes unfounded in Kierkegaard's prophetic philosophy. Put succinctly, this faith can be described as unfounding because it consistently resists the help of reason to "legitimize" itself, thereby making it tenable to society. It resists, in other words, a systematization that can be defended (and co-opted) by apologetics. Within this faith is an acceptance of human finitism: we humans are not God and our reasoning is not only finite but also all too human, with hidden motives of self-autonomy and mastering the other. Westphal eventually highlights these aspects in his philosophy of religion, and he repeatedly returns to revelation's dual charge of being the source of faith and the command of faith toward discipleship. Faith permeates his entire thought—his is a phenomenology of faith, after all—but the question persists: what kind of faith does Westphal aspire to hold?

We have partially answered that question, revealing that it is a Kierkeg-aardian faith that refutes a Hegelian understanding of the role of religion within the self and society. It is deeply personal but also deeply motivated toward helping society, particularly one's neighbor. It is also deeply Protes-tant, specifically Lutheran. From what we have seen, there is no sense that one can reason toward faith (as argued, for example, in Catholicism) or that one can logically defend faith.[113] Apologetics are seen as antifaith even! Westphal eventually softens his anti-apologetical stance to allow for apol-ogetics to mean a sort of explanation rather than a defense. However, for now, even though his current anti-apologetical stance never explicitly severs all philosophical-theological dialogue that is not specifically aligned with Kierkegaard, it does put a strain on how ecumenical one can be with West-phal's work. This may cause friction with Christians who seek to engage those outside the faith. Westphal's concept of faith, based almost entirely on the reception and recognition of revelation (and later, a Levinasian experi-ence of revelation through ethical action), directly challenges that discourse by accusing it of trying to wrestle with the God of faith, an attempt to tie God down to human reason.

To my mind, this is not unlike Jacob's wrestling with the angel of the Lord in Genesis 32:22 31. In that story, Jacob wrestles with an angel through-out the night, never winning but holding his own. Jacob left that struggle renamed Israel, meaning (depending on the translation) "one who wrestles with God." He also left with a new sense of mission in God's unfolding re-lationship with God's chosen people and the outside world. It seems to me no small connection that the newly named Israel is the son of Isaac and the grandson of Abraham; he is a direct descendent of the Akedah story him-self. There is a connection, in other words, with the faith to which Abraham willing assented and the struggle Israel has with the God of that faith. One is the genesis of faith while the other is the exodus of faith that moves beyond the internal, familial struggle and toward the outside world. This struggle will partially culminate with the founding of Israel, a place for God's people in the world that was fought for and defended.

Like Jacob's night-long wrestling with the angel of the Lord, there is a reason for apologetics, and giving a strident defense of faith is necessary not just for outsiders but for believers as well (it is also a very biblical prac-tice, as seen 1 Peter 3:15).[114] The Abrahamic faiths are wrought with stories of struggle toward understanding, of defending the faith while also trying to make (all-too-human) sense of it. Westphal's anti-apologetical faith is not a direct affront to this struggle—despite his concerns against reason he still holds that it can aid faith toward understanding—but he does cut off and mire the practice of an effective defense of the faith, potentially isolating faith from the outside world.[115]

Part of this is by design for Westphal, as he wants to maintain that faith is a miracle, given by God as a phenomenon originating from revelation. Perhaps he is right to argue that without revelation there would be no faith for humans to hold, that God and God alone is the source of faith. Human reason then wrestles with God to seek an understanding of the commandments that lay within God's revealing. Through this line of argumentation, Westphal would make a good Barthian, and in *Transcendence and Self-Transcendence* he examines Barth's account of revelation. There, one can see a more mature and developed Westphal who attempts to align Barthian revelation with an understanding of God that blends the apophatic, cataphatic, and analogous traditions to make God known and unknown to human reason.[116] From this concept of God and revelation, he returns to Kierkegaard (as well as to Levinas) to explore its inherent ethical imperative. In our present discussion, however, one finds Westphal's unfounding faith containing a mystical element where faith is miraculous and is received as a gift solely from God. I would challenge Westphal to consider that mystics and theologians are not adversaries and that both can worship at the same altar.[117] Both can recite the same creeds and sit at the same table of fellowship. Both can give the same blessing and take of the same bread.

The dialogue that might happen at that table would be difficult to transcribe, to be sure, and the miracle of faith (or, to use a Catholic-laden term, the mysteries of faith) would never be fully settled or completely argued. However, looking at Kierkegaard's two Johanneses, perhaps the unresolved tension between the mystic and theologian can be fruitful and eschew any attempt at absolute understanding. Perhaps believers do not need a definitive source of faith through revelation, and maybe human reason can lead one to faith. Perhaps believers do not need a definitive defense of faith and maybe one can leave some things unresolved, devoted to mystery. Perhaps the miracle exists within the fellowship of the mystic and theologian, within the tension where, when two or more are gathered in the name of the Lord, the Lord appears in their midst (Matthew 18:20).

NOTES

1. See chapter 6 of this book. See also *HFM*, particularly "Hegel, Hinduism, and Freedom," and 85, 135–148. For his most comprehensive take on Husserlian phenomenology, see Merold Westphal, "Phenomenologies and Religious Truth," in *Phenomenology of Truth Proper to Religion*, ed. Daniel Guerriere (Albany: SUNY Press 1990), 105–125; and Westphal, "The Second Great Revolution in Phenomenology," *Journal of Speculative Philosophy* 26, no. 2 (2012): 333–347. Also, Westphal essentially breaks down Levinas's critique of Husserl and employs it as a foundational critique throughout *LKD*.

2. See Merold Westphal, "Kierkegaard, a Kind-of Postmodernist," in *International Kierkegaard Commentary: Concluding Unscientific Postscript to 'Philosophical Fragments,'* ed. Robert L. Perkins (Macon, GA: Mercer University Press, 1997), 53–72; Westphal, "Levinas, Kierkegaard, and the Theological Task," *Modern Theology* 8, no. 3 (July 1992): 241–261; Westphal, "Kierkegaard and Hegel," in *The Cambridge Companion to Kierkegaard*, ed. Alistair Hannay and Gordon Daniel Marino (Cambridge: Cambridge University Press, 1997), 120; Westphal, *Kierkegaard's Critique of Reason and Society* (Macon, GA: Mercer University Press, 1987), 120–126. Regarding Marx, Nietzsche, and Kierkegaard, see *OCOT*, "Positive Postmodernism as Radical Hermeneutics" and "Deconstruction and Christian Cultural Theory: An Essay on Appropriation."

3. *LKD*, 138–147.

4. See J. Aaron Simmons and David Wood, eds., *Kierkegaard and Levinas: Ethics, Politics, and Religion* (Bloomington: Indiana University Press, 2008), Simmons and Wood are mainly responding to Westphal (5–7). See also C. Stephen Evans's contribution to Westphal's *Festschrift: Gazing through a Prism Darkly*, 35–45.

5. For more, see chapters 6 and 7 of this book.

6. C. Stephen Evans, *Kierkegaard on Faith and the Self* (Waco, TX: Baylor University Press, 2006), 3–4.

7. Westphal calls Kierkegaard and Nietzsche the "unfounding fathers of a postmodernism that is nervous about all father imagery"; hence the use of the neologism *unfounding*. Merold Westphal, "Postmodernism and Religious Reflection," *International Journal of Religion* 38 (1995): 134.

8. Regarding his articles and chapters in volumes, *Fear and Trembling* is typically a background reference. As an overview, see Westphal, "Levinas, Kierkegaard, and the Theological Task"; Westphal, "Commanded Love and Moral Autonomy: The Kierkegaard-Habermas Debate," *Ethical Perspectives* 5, no. 2 (1998): 263–276; Westphal, "The Importance of Overcoming Metaphysics for the Life of Faith," *Modern Theology* 23, no. 2 (April 2007): 253–278; Westphal, "Abraham and Sacrifice," *Neue Zeitschrift für Systematische Theologie und Religionsphilosophie* 50 (2008): 318–352.

9. See *KCF*, chapters 1–6. Each chapter corresponds to an aspect of faith in *Fear and Trembling*, such as faith as a task word, faith as an epistemic command, and so on. Since our exploration is primarily focused on what Westphal discovers through Kierkegaard, not his scholarship on Kierkegaard proper, we focus primarily on the texts that he wrote early in his career, footnoting *KCF*.

10. See *KCRS*, vii–viii.

11. Using pseudonyms helps create a space between Kierkegaard's works. Westphal, as we will see, thinks this is because each pseudonym engages in dialogue with the others. See Merold Westphal, "Johannes and Johannes: Kierkegaard and Difference," in *International Kierkegaard Commentary: Philosophical Fragments and Johannes Climacus*, ed. Robert L. Perkins (Macon, GA: Mercer University Press, 1994), 13–32.

12. Regarding Westphal's later work, note that he does not agree with Levinas's reading of *Fear and Trembling*. Levinas thinks that the Akedah is about sacrifice, yet for Westphal, De Silentio accepts the premise that it is solely about faith. Levinas levies three critiques against De Silentio: first, he overlooks that the Akedah is the sacrificial premise; second, he overlooks that Abraham did not complete the sacrifice; third, he fails to incorporate Abraham's involvement in the Sodom and Gomorrah story, where Levinas argues that "Abraham is fully aware of his nothingness and mortality." Emmanuel Levinas, *Proper Names*, trans. M. B. Smith (Stanford, CA: Stanford University Press, 1996), 66–74.

Westphal argues that Levinas misreads *Fear and Trembling*. Later, Westphal employs this misreading to open a dialogue between Levinas and Kierkegaard. See Westphal, "Abraham and Sacrifice," 321–327; *LKD*, introduction and chap. 1; Westphal, "The Many Faces of Levinas as a Reader of Kierkegaard," in *Kierkegaard and Levinas: Ethics, Politics, and Religion* (Bloomington, IN: Indiana University Press, 2008), 21–40.

13. Kierkegaard, *Fear and Trembling*, 6–8.

14. Ibid., 7. This is also a subtle dig at Hegelians who attempt to demonstrate that art, religion, and philosophy each grasp and present the same content in different yet complementary ways but never contradicting each other.

15. *TST*, 203.

16. Ibid.

17. Ibid.

18. Ibid. Westphal covers how faith in this mode can become a "one way covenant" with God in *SF*, 44–54, 115–119, 176–177.

19. *TST*, 203. Emphasis is mine. Westphal quotes Hegel from *Lectures on the Philosophy of Religion*, ed. Peter C. Hodgson (Berkeley: University of California Press, 1984–1987), 1:180, cf. 3:283. In a note, he further quotes Hegel to clarify that "in religion, the content of the idea appears in forms accessible to sense experience or understanding, because religion is the truth for everyone. . . . In religion the truth has been revealed as far as its content is concerned; but it is another matter for this content to be present in the form of the concept, of thinking, of the concept in speculative form."

20. Kierkegaard, *Fear and Trembling*, 41–47.

21. Ibid., 41–42.

22. Ibid., 43: "The knight, then, will recollect everything, but this recollection is precisely the pain, and yet in infinite resignation he is reconciled with existence."

23. Ibid., 44. See also *KCF*, chap. 2, 34–36.

24. Kierkegaard, *Fear and Trembling*, 46, De Silentio is paraphrasing Matthew 19:26; Mark 10:27 and 14:36, and Luke 8:27.

25. Kierkegaard, *Fear and Trembling*, 47.

26. Ibid., "Problema I."

27. Ibid., 60–64, 66, 68, 70.

28. Regarding madness, De Silentio refers back to the Platonic notion of divine madness. This contributes to his refutation that faith is subordinate to reason as *pistis* is to *doxa*.

29. *TST*, 207. Westphal never mentions that Hegel also utilizes a concept of moral law, or *Moralität*, in an abstract sense. Hegel, *Philosophy of Right*, §135 A, §139. Westphal repeatedly refers to Kierkegaard's teleological suspensions as suspensions of *Sittlichkeit*, rarely getting any major pushback from Kierkegaard scholars. However, as shown later, Henry Piper critiques Westphal for making Kierkegaard too Hegelian, but Westphal defends this by evidencing sections where Kierkegaard clearly meant *Sittlichkeit* when discussing the ethical. See Henry B. Piper, "Kierkegaard's Non-Dialectical Dialectic or That Kierkegaard Is Not Hegelian,"

International Philosophical Quarterly 44, no. 4 (December 2004): 497–518; Merold Westphal, "Kierkegaard's Religiousness C: A Defense," *International Philosophical Quarterly* 44, no. 4 (December 2004): 535–548.

I agree with Westphal: even though Hegel does make a distinction between *Sittlichkeit* (laws, customs, morality of mores) and *Moralität* (abstract right, Morality with a capital *M*), Kierkegaard's critique of Hegel primarily focuses on the outcome of the concretely ethical, *Sittlichkeit*. For Westphal's part, he repeatedly argues that Kierkegaard is only speaking of *Sittlichkeit*. It is curious, however, that Westphal does not further explain why Kierkegaard's corpus does not address Hegelian *Moralität*. I think this is because, first, Westphal reads Kierkegaard's concept of faith as an ideology critique primarily (if not only) against a concept of right that is concretized in social interaction—basically, morality can become an ideology only once it is enacted through a concrete ethical system of rights and duties (*Sittlichkeit*). Second, for Kierkegaard an abstract morality can belong only to God, and any human understanding of morality must accept that it is subordinate to God and God's law.

It is interesting that Westphal's critique against Levinas's reading of *Fear and Trembling* comes from this distinction between *Moralität* and *Sittlichkeit*. Levinas interprets the Akedah as a meditation on sacrifice, believing that Kierkegaard misses this point by extrapolating a faulty notion of God's relation to ethics from the story: "Thus, [Kierkegaard] describes the encounter with God as a subjectivity rising to the religious level: God above the ethical order!" Levinas, *Proper Names*, 74. Westphal finds that Levinas does not understand that Kierkegaard's teleological suspension of the ethical is a suspension of *Sittlichkeit* and not *Moralität*. Westphal, "Many Faces of Levinas as a Reader of Kierkegaard," 34–36.

30. See *GTPD*, 35–39.

31. Westphal, "Kierkegaard and Hegel," 101–102. For Kierkegaard's analogy, see *Concluding Unscientific Postscript*, 105.

32. Westphal, "Kierkegaard and Hegel," 102.

33. With a nod to Stephen N. Dunning, Westphal states that to justify reading Kierkegaard through a Hegelian structural analysis, "we only need to notice that triadic [i.e., Hegelian] structures as such would not compromise the positions normally attributed to Kierkegaard and his pseudonyms over against Hegel. Climacus, for example, insists that his own presentation is dialectical and rejects only the notion that it is a speculative dialectic, one that can be brought to closure." Westphal, "Kierkegaard and Hegel," 103.

34. Ibid., 107.

35. Ibid., 106.

36. Ibid., 106–107.

37. Ibid., 108

38. Ibid., 109. Westphal's Hegelian reading of Kierkegaard has contributed to the debate on Kierkegaard's critique of Christendom and his reception of Hegel. See Jon Stewart, *Kierkegaard's Relations to Hegel Reconsidered* (Cambridge: Cambridge University Press, 2003). Westphal was a juror for Stewart's doctoral dissertation (the impetus to this book), and he is cited in the latter sections of the text (at pages 312 and 621). Obviously, Steward does not base his thinking solely on Westphal's reading of Kierkegaard; raising it here helps contextualize Westphal's work in light of his peers. Stewart argues that misunderstanding Kierkegaard as anti-Hegelian ignores Kierkegaard's appreciation of Hegel while obscuring Kierkegaard's primary target: Christendom and Danish Hegelians. Stewart develops this thesis differently than Westphal, but for our purposes, Westphal's thinking is rather similar: Kierkegaard often takes Hegel's concepts (*Sittlichkeit*, *Aufhebung*, the dialectic) and subverts their original usage, turning them into critiques against Christendom and Danish Hegelianism.

39. Kierkegaard, *Fear and Trembling*, 55

40. Westphal, "Kierkegaard and Hegel," 109. Westphal also makes this claim throughout *KCF*; see, for example, 43, 94.

41. Westphal, "Kierkegaard and Hegel," 110.

42. Kierkegaard, *Fear and Trembling*, 70.

43. Westphal, "Kierkegaard and Hegel," 110. Westphal also defends this thesis in "Johannes and Johannes," 19.

44. *LKD*, 39.

45. Mark C. Taylor also sees the anti-Hegelian structure in *Fear and Trembling*, though he does not directly move toward Judge William to interpret it. See Mark C. Taylor, *Journeys to Selfhood: Hegel & Kierkegaard* (Berkeley: University of California Press 2000), 253–258.

46. For more on Kierkegaard and Regine Olsen, see Alastair Hannay and Gordon Daniel, *The Cambridge Companion to Kierkegaard* (Cambridge: Cambridge University Press, 1998), 3–4, 274–275, 283.

47. Alastair Hannay, *Kierkegaard* (London: Routledge Press, 1999), 63.

48. It is beyond our scope to delve further. For more, see Stewart, *Kierkegaard's Relations to Hegel Reconsidered*, 310–321. Westphal also relies heavily on Stewart's argument throughout *KCF*, situating Danish Hegelians as the primary target for Kierkegaard. See *KCF*, chap. 1.

49. *LKD*, 39. See also *KCF*, chap. 5.

50. *LKD*, 37. He is quoting from Kierkegaard, *Fear and Trembling*, 17, 35–36, 46.

51. This may provoke the question of the how of revelation, meaning, how does it occur without mediation? If it is something immediate, does it not fall into the Hegelian distinction of the universal and undetermined? Westphal addresses this through the notion of second immediacy in "Kierkegaard and the Role of Reflection in Second Immediacy," in *Immediacy and Reflection in Kierkegaard's Thought*, ed. Paul Cruysberghs, Johan Taels, and Karl Verstrynge (Leuven: Leuven University Press, 2003), 159–180.

52. *LKD*, 39–41; Westphal, "Johannes and Johannes," 13–15. In both texts, Westphal refers to Plato's *Meno* as both Platonic (*LKD*, 39) and Socratic ("Johannes and Johannes," 13). His reference to either depends on how Kierkegaard referenced it, but for the sake of clarity, I simply refer to it as Platonic throughout the present text. Additionally, see *KCF*, chap. 5, 96–100. Chapter 6 essentially details Climacus's argument that faith is a reception of divine revelation; he explains the Platonic theory, and its anti-Hegelianism, on 124–133.

53. Kierkegaard, *Philosophical Fragments*, 12: "Not even Socrates would be capable of giving [truth] to me, no more than the coachman is capable of pulling the horse's load, even though he may help the horse do it by means of the whip." More exactly, at page 14, Climacus states concerning the teacher: "If the teacher is to be the occasion that reminds the learner, he cannot assist him to recollect that he actually does know the truth, for the learner is indeed untruth. . . . Consequently, in this way, precisely by reminding [the learner of his untruth], the teacher thrusts the learner away, except that by being turned in upon himself in this manner the learner does not discover that he previously knew truth but discovers his untruth. To this act of consciousness, the Socratic principle applies: the teacher is only an occasion, whoever he may be, even if he is a god, because I discover my own untruth only by myself, because only when *I* discover it is it discovered, not before, even though the whole world knew it."

54. *LKD*, 42.

55. Kierkegaard, *Philosophical Fragments*, p. 43.

56. Westphal, "Johannes and Johannes," 18. In *KCF*, 143, Westphal also addresses this question.

57. Westphal, "Johannes and Johannes," 18. A and B stand for each Johannes's perspective in regard to revelation and faith; it is also a sly nod to Kierkegaard's *Either/Or*.

58. Ibid. "I want to suggest," Westphal explicitly states, "that Johannes Climacus [in *Philosophical Fragments*] is trying to work out the epistemological ramifications of the critical social theory presented implicitly in the Abraham story as told by Johannes de Silentio."

59. Ibid., 20.

60. Ibid. The ellipses are Westphal's.

61. Ibid.

62. Ibid., 21.

63. See also *HFM*, 147. Westphal implores that skeptics of the "faith as critical theory" should try the following experiment: First, take notice that if you, as a religious person of Christian faith, ever pledge allegiance to a country that your fidelity to that country can only be "relative and never absolute," excepting the moment when your country finds its completion in the eschatological Kingdom of God. Second, if you take this notice to heart, then every time you pledge allegiance to your country you must make a habit to always "cross your fingers as a sign of your conditional commitment." Third, you must especially do this on memorial days for wars and veterans, especially when you're among "God-and-country flag waving patriots" and you must make sure that they see your expression of conditionality and, when they do, make sure they know "that you're doing it because Kierkegaard has reminded you that your country is human, all too human, and that it is not worthy of unconditional allegiance." From Westphal, "Johannes and Johannes," 21.

64. *SF*, 213.

65. Pope Francis proclaims, "The current financial crisis can make us overlook the fact that it originated in a profound human crisis: the denial of the primacy of the human person! We have created new idols. The worship of the ancient golden calf (cf. Exodus 32:1–35) has returned in a new and ruthless guise in the idolatry of money and the dictatorship of an impersonal economy lacking a truly human purpose. The worldwide crisis affecting finance and the economy lays bare their imbalances and, above all, their lack of real concern for human beings; man is reduced to one of his needs alone: consumption." Pope Francis, *Evangelii Gaudium* (The Joy of the Gospel), November 26, 2013, http://www.vatican.va/holy_father/francesco/apost_exhortations /documents/papa-francesco_esortazione-ap_20131124_evangelii-gaudium_en.html#No_to _the_new_idolatry_of_money, §55.

66. Westphal, "Johannes and Johannes," 21.

67. Ibid., 21.

68. Ibid.

69. Ibid., 23. In summarizing Lessing's claim, Westphal states, "Kierkegaard would not be happy with [Lessing's] idea that human reason contains an *a priori* knowledge of God that is so ultimate and definitive that nothing that God could possibly do in history could affect it."

70. Ibid.

71. Ibid. See also *KCF*, chap. 10, where Westphal argues that Climacus's concept of faith as a leap is partially derived from Lessing. The chapter delves into the ways Kierkegaard appropriates Lessing to develop his concept of the leap.

72. In chapter 9 of *KCF*, "Faith as the Passionate Appropriation of an Objective Uncertainty," Westphal teases out this argument in Climacus's writings, showing how objective uncertainty relates to truth's subjectivity, which I argue can be called Kierkegaard's unfounding faith. The chapter is an account of Kierkegaard's argument that "existence is a system—for God, but it cannot be a system for any existing spirit. System and conclusiveness correspond to

each other, but existence is the very opposite." *KCF,* 167, quoted from *Concluding Unscientific Postscript,* 1:118.

73. Westphal, "Johannes and Johannes," 26

74. Ibid., 28.

75. Ibid.

76. See especially chapter 6.

77. *KCRS,* viii.

78. Ibid., 20

79. Ibid.

80. Ibid.

81. Ibid.

82. Ibid.

83. Ibid., 21. Westphal defines this term on page 22: "social groups [which] make themselves legitimate through the propagation of belief systems in which the established order is justified." In short, social groups, especially religions, help build and maintain order and also get to determine what does and does not count as reason.

84. Ibid., 21–22. Westphal quotes Kierkegaard from *Training in Christianity,* trans. Walter Lowrie (New York: Harper & Row, 1962), 69, and *On Authority and Revelation: The Book on Adler,* trans. Walter Lowrie (New York: Harper & Row, 1966), 60.

85. *OCOT,* 145.

86. Since Westphal refers to "we," to mean Christian believers in *Kierkegaard's Critique of Reason and Society,* our exploration takes on this character to clearly present Westphal's thought. *We* in the succeeding paragraphs should be understood as "us Christian believers."

87. Westphal addresses a potential objection of how God can "speak" without mediation through the concept of mediated immediacy, or second immediacy, in "Kierkegaard and the Role of Reflection in Second Immediacy," his contribution to *Immediacy and Reflection in Kierkegaard's Thought,* 159–180.

88. *KCRS,* 22. He is taking Kierkegaard's Judases comment from *The Sickness unto Death,* vol. 19 of *Kierkegaard's Writings,* ed. and trans. Howard Hong and Edna Hong (Princeton, NJ: Princeton University Press, 1980), 87; and *Training in Christianity,* trans. Walter Lowrie (London: Oxford University Press, 1941), 32.

89. *KCRS,* 22–23.

90. Ibid., 23.

91. See chapters 4, 6, and 9 on how this antiapologetical stance in Westphal's postmodern critiques of religion. For Westphal, this form of apologetics becomes another way of creating metaphysical constructions that too tightly wraps God and faith into the security of humanity's reason. It becomes the thirty pieces of metaphysical security to a Judas-like apologetics that betrays Christ and Christianity.

92. *KCRS,* 25.

93. Ibid., 24. Westphal quotes from Søren Kierkegaard, *For Self Examination,* in *For Self Examination and Judge for Yourselves!,* trans. Walter Lowrie (Princeton, NJ: Princeton University Press, 1941), 101.

94. Westphal references Kierkegaard in this chapter of *KCRS,* "Kierkegaard and the Logic of Insanity," simply as Kierkegaard, not citing any of his pseudonyms. This is because he primarily references texts in Kierkegaard's second authorship, penned in his own name: *On Authority and Revelation, Training in Christianity,* and *Sickness unto Death.* Westphal also references *Søren Kierkegaard's Journals and Papers,* a collection of Kierkegaard's personal writings. Though he references *Fear and Trembling, Philosophical Fragments,* and *Concluding Unscientific*

Postscript, he does so in relation to these self-authored works to show that Kierkegaard's logic of insanity spans across his works.

95. Westphal quotes from *Phaedrus,* trans. R. Hackforth (Cambridge: Cambridge University Press, 1952).

96. *KCRS,* 86.

97. See ibid., 86–88. Westphal plainly states that this is a modern enterprise, highlighting how "when it is said that 'modern man' finds the incarnation incredible, [Kierkegaard] acknowledges the sociological fact, but not without pausing to ask who 'modern man' may be." Ibid., 86. Throughout these pages, the essential point becomes clear that Kierkegaard is levying a charge against modernity and humanity's attempt to "sanitize" faith through reason, or just doing away with biblical faith altogether. This Kierkegaard makes the same argument throughout his works, particularly *Fear and Trembling* and *Concluding Unscientific Postscript.*

98. *KCRS,* 89. Westphal wrote about this distinction in Kant early in his career. See Merold Westphal, "In Defense of the Thing in Itself," *Kant Studien* 59, no. 1 (1968): 118–141. So far, we have yet to delve into Westphal's debt to Kant. This debt is deeply hidden in his work and often rises as a general Kantianism that he references but never exclusively explores. In chapter 6 we explore this in more detail. Here, I acknowledge this debt and regretfully accept that we cannot delve further into it because of its hiddenness. For the purpose of deconstructing (or perhaps psychoanalyzing) Westphal's work, it may prove valuable. But for reviewing Westphal's overall thought, it proves distracting and daunting given that he does not address this debt thoroughly enough.

99. See Immanuel Kant, *Critique of Pure Reason,* ed. and trans. Paul Guyer and Allan Wood (Cambridge: Cambridge University Press, 1998), 687–690; A824, B852–A831, B859. Additionally, see R. Z. Friedman's work on the relationship between Kant's limits of human reason and Kierkegaard's concept of faith: "Kant and Kierkegaard: The Limits of Reason and the Cunning of Faith," *International Journal for Philosophy of Religion* 19, nos. 1–2 (1986): 3–22.

100. *KCRS,* 89.

101. Ibid.

102. It should be noted that Westphal first explored this through his critique of Husserlian phenomenology through Nietzsche in his "Nietzsche and the Phenomenological Ideal," *Monist,* 60, no. 2 (April 1977): 278–288. I highlight his critique in *KCRS* because, in this work, Westphal finds not only a critique but also a possible solution to the critique. Within Kierkegaard, in other words, Westphal is able to move beyond a mere description of the problem toward a prescription by highlighting the prophetic nature of Kierkegaard's thought. This finitism will practically become the theme of chapter 5, where we explore how it permeates Westphal's postmodern thought.

103. *TST,* 34. Emphasis is mine. Westphal quotes from Martin Heidegger, *Identity and Difference,* trans. Joan Stambaugh (New York: Harper & Row, 1969), 56.

104. *TST,* 35.

105. Regarding the Heidegger quote above, Westphal repeatedly quotes *Identity and Difference* (55–56) when discussing onto-theology. For more examples see *OCOT,* 30, 258, 282, 286. Also, Westphal quotes Paul from 1 Corinthians 1:20, and references Heidegger's essay "The Way Back into the Ground of Metaphysics" from *Existentialism from Dostoevsky to Sartre,* 2nd expanded ed., ed. Walter Kaufmann (New York: New American Library, 1975), 276. Westphal finds that Heidegger often quotes this to summarize his critique of theology as a scientific discipline.

106. *KCRS,* 92–93.

107. Ibid., 92. See also *KCF*, chap. 10. Within *Kierkegaard's Concept of Faith*, Westphal teases out this issue further by situating Lessing's contribution to Kierkegaard's leap of faith while showing ways in which Kierkegaard critiqued Lessing (see especially 199–206).

108. *KCRS*, 92.

109. Again, this goes back to Kierkegaard's concept of revelation as found in *Philosophical Fragments*, 46–47, 87–88, 182–183, and 217.

110. *KCRS*, 93. Emphasis is mine.

111. *KCRS*, 93–94. "Nothing here is introduced," Westphal reminds us, "to free the situation from the objective uncertainty natural to the doubly limited human understanding. Neither sensible certainty nor rational self-evidence enters the scene to provide guarantees against the possibility of being mistaken or an absolute veto against alternatives."

112. Ibid., 95.

113. See chapter 6 of this volume. Concerning a Catholic position, see Norman Tanner and Giuseppe Alberigo, eds., *Decrees of the Ecumenical Councils* (Washington, DC: Georgetown University Press, 1990), 804–806; Henry Denzinger, ed., *The Sources of Catholic Dogma* (Freiburg: Herder & Co., 1954), nos. 1789–1791. See also Pius X, *Pascendi Dominici Gregis*, September 8, 1907, http://www.vatican.va/holy_father/pius_x/encyclicals/documents/hf_p-x_enc_19070908_pascendi-dominici-gregis_en.html, secs. 3, 5–7, 22.

114. 1 Peter 3:15: "Always be ready to give an explanation to anyone who asks you for a reason for your hope" (NAB). Other translations, such as the New Revised Standard Version, argue that this is best rendered as "Always be ready to make your defense to anyone who demands from you an accounting for the hope that is in you." In both translations, and in supporting stories within Acts (especially Acts 17:16–34), one can see a need for an openness to give an account for one's faith to those outside the church, however that church is construed.

115. One can read Westphal's work *God, Guilt, and Death* as an antiapologetical apologetics in that the question he seeks to answer is why religion matters to the world. He gives a phenomenological account as to why religion is so prevalent in the world and centers his analysis on a description of religious practices that seek to ease the pains of death and guilt. It can be read apologetically in that religion matters on a sociological level. Yet this is a rather weak apologetics since it never attempts to defend that the content of religion is actually true, that the beliefs of the believing soul are more than social constructs to deal with death and guilt. I find that the work is not so much an apologetics but an attempt at understanding how religion functions within the life of the believing soul and that it should not be read as apologetical.

116. See chapter 6.

117. Some can be a bit of both even, as seen with Meister Eckhart, to pick one example among many.

5. RELIGIOUSNESS

The Expression of Faith

The previous chapter partially answered the question of the type of faith Westphal holds by finding it to be Kierkegaardian and wholly dependent on revelation, and thus resists any reasonable foundation to ground itself. However, this was only a partial answer since it merely addresses how one assents to, or otherwise accepts, faith. Holding or enacting that faith through discipleship is the decisive step and what follows will continue our investigation by describing how, exactly, faith is opposed to sin and how this opposition, once enacted and lived, becomes an ideology critique.

We begin with the epistemological question proposed at the end of the previous chapter: How is faith opposed to sin and not reason? Furthermore, how is sin an epistemological category?

After answering this, we explore how Westphal's Kierkegaardian and epistemological relationship between faith and sin solidifies faith as ideology critique by emphasizing faith's political nature. This will lead us to an inquiry into Kierkegaard's Religiousness C, a hidden and final stage in his theory of stages that Westphal discovers and develops as a mode of discipleship. Establishing how Religiousness C explains the ethical ramifications of faith deepens our study of Westphal's Kierkegaardian writings by exploring how they influence his work as a whole. Our final, concluding section reviews what I call Westphal's third concept of revelation, which is based on his dialogue between Levinas and Kierkegaard and is mainly concerned with the ethical task that revelation requires. What is unveiled in this final section is how theological Westphal's concepts of revelation are and how they command all Christians, and especially theologians, to become liberation theologians whose focus is always on the least of us: the widow, orphan and stranger.

RIGHT REASON, SIN, AND THE "ANTIFAITH"
EPISTEMOLOGICAL CATEGORY

Westphal ends *Kierkegaard's Critique of Reason and Society* on how "Kierkegaard combined a Lutheran understanding of the noetic effects of sin with the essential insights of the sociology of knowledge to produce a theologically grounded critique of society."[1] Through this Lutheran understanding of sin, Westphal seeks to deepen and enrich his previous argument that Kierkegaard, via Johannes Climacus, is a critical theorist who sees that "ideology critique is an intellectual enterprise that concerns itself with religion only from the perspective of hostile unbelief."[2] Faith over and against sin posing as reason again comes to the forefront.

Westphal's investigation takes shape as an argument for faith as an ideology critique that focuses on the sinfulness found within ideologies that choose human understanding over divine revelation. Faith, as the believing soul's acceptance of God's revelation, stands "beyond the moral dichotomy of egoism and altruism," which he finds are the means by which ideologies try to compartmentalize human action.[3] Contra ideology, faith opens up "the religious dichotomy of obedience and rebellion, faith and offense" by moving the self beyond a "social, this-worldly dimension [toward the] . . . tradition of inward, spiritual self-examination."[4] Yet again, Westphal emphasizes the political nature of faith, arguing that politics and faith have always been inextricably intertwined.[5]

Westphal unpacks his argument by describing how Luther's concept of sin influences Climacus and how both are Pauline in nature. Similar to tagging Judge William as Hegelian, Westphal infers that Johannes Climacus is Lutheran whether he knows it or not. He argues that Climacus's epistemological concept of sin appropriates Martin Luther's understanding of the "noetic effects" of the Fall in Genesis: because of humanity's fall from grace, its reasoning is "a blockhead and a dunce."[6] This aligns Luther's critique of Roman Catholic theology to Kierkegaard's critique of Hegel, since both are criticizing an overreach in their adversaries' concept of reason and their hubristic trust in worldly thinking over godly faith.[7] Truth for both Luther and Kierkegaard is divinely given, not acquired by humanity's sinful reasoning.[8]

Westphal then establishes both Kierkegaard and Luther's concept of sin as Pauline since it heavily emphasizes embodiment: one cannot reason without the body, and the body's mortal and finite nature cripples all abstract, inward thinking, however infinite this thinking claims to be. Thinking and acting are connected, and since all acts are finite and sinful, it follows that one's thinking is sinful. For example, one commits adultery not just through the physical act of lust but also by lusting in one's heart (Matthew 5:28). Accordingly, sin reaches its apotheosis not in acts but whenever the self claims to be autonomous, or free, "in relation to God's sovereignty. Thus reason as an expression of the flesh is human thought uninformed by, and independent of, the Word and Spirit of God."[9] In essence, this is a reading of Luther's doctrine of total depravity, where, after the Fall, humanity becomes blinded by its own sin and is completely and utterly estranged from God because of its selfish nature. The self, in its total depravity, can be reached only by the loving grace of God in and through revelation.[10] Therefore, proper reason is steeped in faith and informed by Scripture and revelation, in contradistinction to a reason that is offended by Scripture and, in Westphal's words, "flees from God through sin."[11]

Having established Climacus's Lutheran inclinations, Westphal then explicates Climacus's overview of revelation and our 'condition,' or ability to recognize revelation when it is given to us by God.[12] Revelation, here, is a message coming from outside the self but recognized from within (through the given condition of recognizing truth as truth).[13] Sin, then, is something that originates entirely within the self. Sin and evil are seen as anything but divine given the depravity of humanity, thereby making it a matter of original sin and concupiscence.

Westphal is adding onto the Lutheran concept of sin within Climacus's works by revealing that its historical legacy comes from Augustine. Thus, all three—Climacus, Luther, and Augustine—understand sin as a foundational condition of error brought on by the Fall.[14] The lens through which Kierkegaard reads Augustine, in other words, is Lutheran. Furthering this connection and the idea of sin is an epistemological category, Westphal employs the Augustinian notion that evil is the deprivation of good, and that sin originates from humanity's inability not to sin (concupiscence).[15] Sin, consequently, is the self's refusal to accept revelation, choosing rather to go at it alone and proceed as if its lone reasoning were the arbiter of everything. The sinful self cannot accept either's essential paradoxes, hence it is offended by faith and revelation. Sinful reason, divorced of faith, can respond only yes and no to revelation's paradoxes. Moreover, it cannot fully assent to its own yes or no, therefore never completely grasping the meaning and content found in revelation that faith is able to do. Divorced and unable to accept these paradoxes, sinful reason creates its own version of knowledge and understanding of the world.

Expanding on this, Westphal lays out the schema of the "three expressions of the Paradox" found in *Concluding Unscientific Postscript*: the initial expression, the essential expression, and the decisive expression.[16] The initial expression is a "metaphysical expression" of the inward contemplation of God as God, as a paradox to human understanding. This becomes the essential expression, which is "metaphysically confessional" because it can grasp the revealed concept of an incarnate God: "not simply the Eternal, but the Eternal in time that is paradoxical to (finite) human understanding."[17] In the final, decisive expression, the paradox becomes "personally confessional" in that, by assenting to the "God on the cross who is offensive to (sinful) human understanding," one accepts the Incarnation as an account of the paradox that breaches sin through God's (i.e., Christ's) suffering and death on the cross. From this account, it also becomes the atonement for the "suffering and death" caused by sin.[18] The paradox, therefore, finds its apotheosis through the life, death, and resurrection of Jesus Christ. According to Westphal:

> We pass from the finitude of a human understanding that has conceptual problems with God . . . to the sinfulness of a human understanding that has existential problems with the notions that Christ dies for our sins. This is the point at which the Paradox moves from absurdity to offense, at which it becomes possible to understand how Luther could see human reason as an expression of the flesh. For this is the point at which repentance is an indispensable condition for hearing the Christian story of God's love as good news.[19]

The Incarnation as the paradox is not manifest only conceptually but existentially as well. The fact that it concerns God becoming human makes this paradox a real, existential transgression to our everyday reasoning. Because the self is mortal and the self's reasoning finite, and the paradox is immortal and its reason infinite, the aggressor of this offending action is not the paradox but the limits of reason and the self that tries to master what it cannot understand. Westphal explains:

If death is more bitter than wormwood for mortals, how much more bitter
for an *immortal*. But this is death on a cross, and the paradox is that he who
dies as one who is guilty is in fact the only one who is *innocent*. That the immortal should die is puzzling enough, but that the innocent should die for
the guilty, the just for the unjust, that is more than puzzling. The difference
between mortal and immortal is immediately *aufgehoben* in the difference
between the guilty and the innocent.[20]

Starting from an Augustinian or Lutheran foundation of humanity's perpet-
ual state of error (original sin), Climacus does not maintain that the Teacher
(i.e., God, or Christ in the Incarnation) is indifferent or, even worse, an offending agent toward humanity but that it is humanity that feels offended
by the Teacher because it has encountered something that it does not understand.[21] In a violent reaction toward this incomprehension, humanity
condemns the Teacher as guilty even though it is the Teacher who is purely
innocent. Indeed, the Teacher is the only one who can even be considered
innocent. The Teacher's ability to accept this undeserved condemnation,
and even die for it (as an immortal), further confounds humanity since the
failings of mortality have been taken up by the Teacher.[22]

For Westphal, this is essentially a Pauline argument concerning the
limits of human reason, where it is inextricably drawn to its own boundaries in trying to "discover something that thought cannot think."[23] Human
reason is drawn "like a moth to the flame" as Westphal remarks, toward the
edges of its own understanding.[24]

Westphal sees an underlying Kantian critique of reason throughout
Climacus's texts (and perhaps the works of Kierkegaard as a whole). Perhaps
this could be said for any philosopher who came after Kant, and especially
for Hegel and Hegel's critics, among whom Kierkegaard situates himself.
Yet Westphal employs it here to highlight how Climacus is distinct from,
and critical of, Kant. He concludes that both are essentially dealing with
the concept of God, but that, unlike Kant, Climacus's concept of reason and
its limits toward understanding the existence of God do not rest on conditions for understanding but on the fact that God is wholly other.[25] "Reason
cannot think what is wholly other than itself," Westphal proclaims, noting
that, in Pauline fashion, the paradox of God comes not from a finite account
of our reasoning but from the fruit of our sinful nature.[26] God and humanity's difference, as absolute, "cannot be accounted for on the basis of what
man derives from . . . God, for in so far they are akin. Their unlikeness must

therefore be explained by what man derives from himself, or by what he has brought upon his head."[27] What humanity has brought upon itself is sin.

God is 'wholly other' and therefore faith in God, as sin's antithesis, is not only a turn away from one's fallen nature but also a turn toward God; faith is "the alternative to offense" and an offended consciousness.[28] Quoting Luther, Westphal argues that this turn away from self-legitimating reason toward a "right reason," or the "reason of faith," makes it an ideology critique.[29] As an ideology critique, Westphal's concept of a faithful reasoning is one where a hidden inward faith necessarily implies an outward ethical reaction, faith becomes a response to the sinful actions of humanity that are guided by a reason that authorizes such behavior.

This concept within Climacus's *Philosophical Fragments* is developed further in *Concluding Unscientific Postscript*, when he explains the stages of the life of faith in the ethical and religious stages (called Religiousness A and B, respectively), and is finalized in Kierkegaard's second authorship.[30] Westphal, for his part, sees that there is a hidden third stage latent in Kierkegaard's text that can be seen only when one takes into account Kierkegaard's later works. This Religiousness C is revealed in the self becoming a contemporary of Christ through loving God with all one's heart and, thus, loving one's neighbor.

Before moving on, let us take a look back. We have just covered the theoretical foundations behind the hidden inwardness and the outward expression of faith, showing the necessary ethical action required by faith. That faith implies or requires an ethics clarifies how its antithesis is sin, not reason. Additionally, we have explored how faith as ideology critique exposes the underlying sinfulness of human reason's desire to proceed on its own without expressing allegiance to God through revelation. Going back to a familiar refrain, faith as ideology critique continually asks society, "What does your religion, your response to faith, justify? Is your faith utterly dependent on God and God's revelation or is it all too human and focused on your own desire for autonomy?"

In response, the believing soul must use reason to better understand how faith can be enacted in life, how reason can be in service to faith and revelation, not against it. How one can prevent one's wits from getting the best of him or her in service of one's own selfishness. This also illuminates Westphal's antiapologetical stance in that the believing soul requires no reasonable defense for faith, since what stands on the other side is sin and accordingly death. Jerusalem needs Athens not for authority but for better understanding its expression in everyday life.

Religiousness C: The Expression of Faith in the Life of Christ

Westphal discovered what he calls Religiousness C by noticing that there are not only connections between Kierkegaard's pseudonymous authors (Johannes De Silentio and Johannes Climacus, Climacus and Anti-Climacus, and so on) but also with the works directly penned by Kierkegaard in his later, so-called second authorship period. Westphal follows a similar line of reasoning that he has presented all throughout work on Kierkegaard: that Kierkegaard's second authorship is a continuation and refinement of themes and concepts presented implicitly and explicitly throughout his pseudonymous writings, contrary to others who argue that there is a break between them.[31] By connecting all of Kierkegaard's works as an internal dialogue, Westphal believes the second authorship can be read as Kierkegaard's final word concerning faith as ideology critique.[32] To unpack this, we must begin by understanding how Westphal reads Kierkegaard's oeuvre as an internal dialogue, particularly through Kierkegaard's theory of stages.

Kierkegaard develops his theory of stages as a way of explaining how one passes through different understandings of itself and others—moves through passages of existence—in becoming a true and authentic self. These stages are the aesthetic, ethical, and religious, with the religious stage divided into Religiousness A and Religiousness B. According to Westphal, Religiousness B contains a hidden stage, only implicitly stated, called Religiousness C, which elevates the self to becoming contemporaneous with Christ, the object of adoration in Religiousness B.

Westphal understands the theory of stages as an answer to the question "What is the good life?" or "Where is true happiness found?"[33] Within the aesthetic stage, one answers this question "without reference to good and evil"; thus, it is best described as preethical and oriented toward pleasure seeking. It can also be described as hedonistic. Moreover, its pleasure seeking is preethical in the sense that it is primarily concerned with self-gratification since it gives into immediate desires without considering any consequences. In *Either/Or*, for example, the author of "The Seducer's Diary" writes that "what is glorious and divine about esthetics is that it is associated only with the beautiful: essentially it deals only with *belles lettres* and the fair sex."[34] Hence, the aesthete is solely focused on the immediacy of the moment with little to no reflection beyond pleasure.[35]

Eventually, the aesthete grows tired of pleasure seeking and immediate gratification. To move beyond this consumption of 'good things,' the aesthete begins to contemplate 'What is the good?' or 'Why is this good? What makes it so?' From its contemplation, the aesthete passes onto the ethical stage where he reflects upon his desires, asking which actions are good and bad and which actions can best bring about a happy life. This reflection makes the now ethicist self-aware of the mediation between him and society. Whereas the aesthetic stage "embodies a philosophy of self-choice," the ethical stage, according to Westphal, contrasts self-choice "in relation to the difference between good and evil, or as [Judge William in *Either/Or*] puts it, an *absolute* choice of the self in its *eternal* validity."[36]

Westphal emphasizes that the notions of absolute and eternal that Kierkegaard is using come from Hegel, and Hegel's use of the term essentially stems from Aristotle. In other words, Westphal is pointing out how Kierkegaard develops his theory of the stages through and against a Hegelian construct, and he is using an Aristotelian terminology as a bridge between his stages and Hegelianism. Westphal clarifies this connection by stating that, for Hegel, it "is always a matter of *Sittlichkeit*. . . . The right and the good are to be found, not abstractly in a rational principle but *concretely* within one's social order, which is, for each individual, the essential mediator of the absolute and eternal."[37] The ethicist distinctly embodies this concretely socialized ethic since his reflection on the good life, and the subjugation of his impulse towards immediate gratification, is always socially mediated.

Westphal sees this subjugation of desire within the ethical as an *Aufhebung* since (aesthetic) self-choice is not abolished but is taken up by the ethical and reconstituted in a process of mediation and socialization. There is still self-choice, but it is now defined in terms of duty toward "the laws, customs, practices, and institutions of a people" (*Sittlichkeit*).[38] Judge William, particularly in his "First Letter to A" in *Either/Or Part 2*, serves as the Hegelian par excellence and, as such, gives us a prime example of how the ethical can be understood as *Sittlichkeit* and how it is also an *Aufhebung*. Here, the good Judge wishes to show A how "romantic love can be united with and exist in marriage, indeed that marriage is its true transfiguration."[39] Like any good authority figure, he just wants to show the young and passionate how righteous and loving marriage can be for the soul. Romantic love is thus seen as erotic and wild; it controls the lovers, the aesthetes, as it were, and not the other way around. It is only within the bond of marriage (society's mandated place for sex) that romantic love can find a fruitful and rightful place. Consequently, sex and sexual desire are rectified in marriage, a socially mediated construct.

The Seducer, on the other hand, answers only to his own desires. One day, however, he might grow up and get married, just like God and society intended. That is, one day he will answer to his society and settle down. However, is this what God intended? Marriage may make the ethicist happy, as far as sex is concerned, but does it fulfill all of one's desires, or is there perhaps a higher purpose or calling? It is from these reflections that expose the ethicist toward the religious stages, Religiousness A and B.

Let us call to mind what Kierkegaard intends when he discusses 'the religious' before we progress. Additionally, we should also recall how the religious functions in relation to *Sittlichkeit*. For Kierkegaard (via De Silentio's *Fear and Trembling*), the religious involves a teleological suspension of the ethical in faith. Westphal argues that this is a teleological suspension of *Sittlichkeit* in the name of answering the call of faith.[40] Thus, one can see the religious stage as a double *Aufhebung*: the aesthetic is *aufgehoben* in the ethical stage, and the ethical is *aufgehoben* in the religious stage. "What makes any stage the 'next' one in relation to some other stage," for Westphal, "is not some normal pattern of psychological development or some necessity of conceptual entailment but the value judgment that makes one stage the proper sphere for relativizing the other."[41] In other words, each of these stages should be treated as concentric, such that each one overlaps with, or is inhabited by, another.[42]

The religious stage does not merely signify a completion of the two antecedent stages. Instead, it is subdivided into two separate realms called Religiousness A and Religiousness B. In response to the question "What is the good life?" or "Where is true happiness found?" the ethicist, in Religiousness A, is turned inward toward a subjective, self-contemplation, thus becoming a religious self. This movement toward subjective contemplation sets the religious self toward a search for truth from within himself. From this inward speculation, the religious self recognizes that he is situated within history—within society, and space and time—but from his inward speculation he begins to try to see himself from outside this history, to see *sub specie aeternitatis*, or from a God's-eye point of view.[43]

In Religiousness A, the religious self's inward reflection seeks a deeper meaning to life; Truth—with a capital *T*—and it begins with interior, inward speculation.[44] *It is subjective*, in other words, consequently rejecting the notion that there is a Truth that exists as objective fact. However, it is not as if all objective things disappear to the religious self—he recognizes that he exists in the world and that other things exist. He is not caught up in a Cartesian tailspin. Rather, he recognizes that existence, particularly his own, is a matter of becoming and understanding himself from *within himself*, and then relating this truth to the outside world. In regard to the concept of truth, to the object of thinking, he recognizes how abstract and subjective it is and how this relates to his own existence.

Once the religious self has this epiphany he can no longer think of truth as existing outside of himself, as an objective fact, and that it is "a chimera of abstraction, and truly only a longing on the part of creation [i.e., of the self], not because truth is not so, but because the knower is one who exists and thus, as long as he exists, truth cannot be so for him."[45] In other words, truth can no longer be self-evident for the religious self because he recognizes his inextricable relationship with truth: both he and his concept of truth are in an intertwined, constant state of becoming. Since he is constantly becoming, his notion of truth is also constantly becoming and evolving. Therefore, he can no longer consider truth an objective fact to which he can appeal in times of crisis or angst. Here, Climacus is not saying that truth no longer exists; only that it is no longer *guaranteed*. It is no longer an objective fact, something to be acquired or used like a talisman. The expression "what is true is true whether you believe it or not" thus has no meaning to the religious self.

As Climacus explains, this inwardness can contemplate truth only in such a way that objectivity vanishes. It consequently becomes a purely immanent method of reflection since its focus is inward, with nothing to which it can transcend. Moreover, in regard to the question "What is the good life?" or "Where is true happiness found?" this thinking shows itself to be *purely abstract*. In its deep inwardness, this form of thinking cannot prescribe any objective acts or intentions. Its ethics can never leave the realm of theory.

Trapped in the purely theoretical, when tasked with the question of where to begin thinking about the good life, the religious self can answer only, "With pure being." Accordingly, inward subjectivity is open to religious understanding because it seeks an inward, abstract origin. Yet it also seeks how one must begin to think of the good life by contemplating how the religious self understands himself before he moves toward understanding others. Climacus argues that Socrates is the paradigm for Religiousness

A given his concern for the question of existence over speculative reasoning. This is especially so, for Westphal, since the absolute good within the question "What is the good life?" variously accounts for the idea, the eternal, or God.

In contrast, where Religiousness A is the religiousness of immanence, Religiousness B is the religiousness of transcendence. For Climacus, this means that Religiousness B is specifically understood as Christianity, since it is the "religion of the dialectical and of transcendence."[46] Like the stages before it, Religiousness A is taken up into Religiousness B in an *Aufhebung* or teleological suspension where the inward reflection of Religiousness A meets the "paradoxically dialectical" nature of Christianity.[47] The notion of paradox, however, is nothing new to Religiousness A. As Westphal notes:

> Christianity, as Religiousness B, is more radically paradoxical, for the eternal itself has become paradoxical as the insertion of God in time. In this way the task of relating absolutely to the absolute becomes even more strenuous, for human reason is overwhelmed, even offended, by the claim that Jesus is fully human and fully divine.[48]

Within Religiousness B one can directly see what role Kierkegaard's critique of reason plays in the stages on life's way, at least for Westphal. The religious self in Religiousness A in a Hegelian fashion attempts to understand the world *sub specie aeternitatis*. There is a quasi-dialectical form of reasoning here, since the religious self is trying to reconcile aspects of his consciousness by trying to step out of that consciousness, making judgments as if they were universal and eternal truths. However, that dialectical form of reasoning never truly moves outside of itself: it never has to completely encounter the radical paradox, nay, the *offensive* paradox, of revelation and its expression of God. Its faith is purely theoretical and never actualized.

Religiousness B, however, experiences the dialectic in an outward expression, with little to no aid from reason, such that one cannot comfort oneself or feel at ease. Hence, *fear and trembling*. The leap of faith is a scary one, and although Climacus acknowledges that one must pass through moments of inward reflection (via Religiousness A) to reach Lessing's "broad, ugly ditch," one can make that outward movement into Religiousness B only through an act of will. Hence, Religiousness B's answer to the question "What is the good life?" according to Climacus:

> So when the eternal happiness, it being the absolute [*telos*], is absolutely his only comfort, and when his relation to it is reduced to its minimum

through existential taking to heart, by reason of guilt-consciousness being the relation of repulsion and wanting constantly to take this [*telos*] away from him, and this minimum and this possibility are nevertheless absolutely more to him than everything else, then it is fitting to begin with the dialectical. It will, when he is in this state, give rise to a pathos that is still higher. But one does not prepare oneself to become aware of Christianity by reading books, or by world-historical surveys; one does it by deepening oneself in existing. Any other propaedeutic must eo ipso end in a misunderstanding, for Christianity is an existence-communication; it would beg to kindly be excused from being understood; it is not understanding what Christianity is that is difficult, but being and becoming a Christian.[49]

The hidden inwardness of Religiousness A cannot lead to authentic Christianity because authentic Christianity cannot be understood through reflection; it must be expressed and lived, as one finds in Religiousness B. For most scholars, this is the final step of Kierkegaard's theory of stages. However, for Westphal, Religiousness B is no easy charge. It is wrought with fear and trembling, and to live this life of faith as a task of a lifetime is to live a life of continual discipleship. Reason's role in one's life, therefore, is that of discipleship, of taking the ideology critique found within faith's acceptance of revelation (its commands and promises) and living such a faith—daily. These sentiments, according to Westphal, are found in Kierkegaard's second authorship and they compose a Religiousness C, where the self, in the attempt to become (or be) Christian, takes up the cross with Christ in a lifetime of discipleship.

Westphal's first published mention of Religiousness C comes in "Kierkegaard's Teleological Suspension of Religiousness B," where he examines the incredible difficulty of the final teleological suspension of the ethical (*Sittlichkeit*, or social reasoning) in Religiousness B.[50] This teleological suspension is exceedingly difficult for the self, and Westphal thinks that Religiousness B does not go far enough, "for there is nothing about the gods of Religiousness A and B to keep them from being the echo of our social mores, the legitimizing servant of the Established Order, while the God of Religiousness C is essentially a danger to every Establish Order."[51] There is still a tinge of Hegelian abstraction in Religiousness B, Westphal claims: while Religiousness B holds Christ as the paradox in the *Postscript*, in Kierkegaard's *Training in Christianity, For Self Examination, Judge for Yourself*, and *Works of Love*, he shows us that Christ is more than an intellectual riddle but is "the Pattern or the Paradigm. As Paradox Christ is to be believed; as Pattern or

Paradigm he is to be imitated."[52] Christ, as the Paradigm, affects our lives in three different ways: through offense, objectivity, and outwardness.

Offense, as seen earlier, comes from an Augustinian conceptualization of sin in which faith becomes a response to one's prideful nature. It offends the self insofar as it reminds him that he is a fallen and finite creature who, in attempt to become like god, continually fails. This attempt, however, fashions God in service of one's own "esthetic project," thus permitting "lots of God-talk while leaving us [i.e., Christians] free to collectively preside over our own goodness without any real interference."[53] Religiousness A, Westphal finds, produces such God-talk in which indeed the Christian community's own ingenuity gets the best of it and, despite its higher intentions, that talk often produces a god that legitimates the community's own *Sittlichkeit*.[54]

Religiousness B responds to this ideological construction by attempting "to be honest about the nature of biblical faith" and by recognizing that "the object of faith" is to be offensive toward this ideology.[55] Moreover, it must never forget that this offense is the core to Christianity and that the Incarnation, God in the flesh, is the direct response to Religiousness A. Religiousness A's speculative nature, however, is not obliterated, but taken up, teleologically suspended (Westphal unswervingly calls it *aufgehoben*) within Religiousness B's humble faith. This faith thus becomes "doubly supernatural," according to Westphal, since "the incarnation is itself a miracle, and the faith by which I acknowledge it is also a miracle."[56] A miracle signified by the leap required to have such faith.

However, this miracle of the leap of faith in Religiousness B is not self-maintaining and requires continual discipleship. Continual discipleship is required because faith almost becomes too offensive in the absence of evidence or proof and our desire for "epistemic autonomy," to preside over what Christians call truth. Discipleship plays the roles of penance and renewal, like a penitential rite that calls to mind one's sins before continuing on with the liturgy.

This discipleship must go beyond prayer and worship, however, and must move to loving action in the life of faith. Without this, Religiousness B is liable to become a "second negotiated compromise" in that it remains merely a theological contemplation, in this case, of the Paradox, for the leap to sustain itself.[57] In this way, Religiousness B begins to sound more like a bargain with God, Christians give God "epistemic autonomy" and add the motto "under God" to their coins, their state seals and their pledges, but in exchange keep their "ethical autonomy." For Westphal, Christians do this when they try to "restrict the divine voice, which is not the echo of our human voice (transcendence), to the area of metaphysics (and the liturgical celebration of that metaphysics once a week or so), the God of bargains might be good enough to leave the social order to be run by us [Christians] the rest of the time (immanence). This is precisely the project that Religiousness C shows Religiousness B to be, at least in Christendom."[58]

Faith, however, is not a bargain but a task of a lifetime: there is a continual striving to be *Christ-ian*, Christ-like. Religiousness C is the emulation of Christ, becoming Christ-like through discipleship. It is an imitation that requires more than just mastering doctrine. It is a continually striving life that is "a threat to the established order" that enacts the words and life of Christ.[59] Westphal claims that the self embodies the prophetic voice (i.e., a hermeneutics of prophecy) in Religiousness C by imitating Christ's life and words through daily living. Following Christ offends one's attempt at self-legitimization within a social order; the Christian places himself with the lowly and the suffering. It is one thing to read the Beatitudes, but another to continually strive for them. "Only Religiousness C knows the offense of lowliness," Westphal remarks, "only Religiousness C knows how to rejoice in those avoidable sufferings" that happen in imitating Christ and offending human nature and reasoning.[60]

One can see how Westphal's hermeneutics of suspicion, the prophetic voice, fits into his completed understanding of Kierkegaardian faith. Religiousness C's faith becomes a critique of ideology since it reveals that what passes for the good life throughout Kierkegaard's theory of stages is desperately inept, save for perhaps Religiousness B (albeit briefly). These stages are all too tinged with humanity's desire for autonomy and mastery; they are all too focused on the self.

Religiousness C's critique "rudely interrupts the Marxian suggestion that religion always functions to legitimize the status quo."[61] But Marx, Westphal continues, "will wonder whether such a critique is not entirely utopian and thus ideological [itself]."[62] Marx would have a point given that the knight of hidden inwardness is somewhat preoccupied with an internal and personal contemplation of the Paradox. Indeed, as Westphal has noted in the preface to *Kierkegaard's Critique of Reason and Society*, critics have jumped on this characterization of Kierkegaard's thinking, leading to the misrepresentation of him as an individualist with indifference to the outside world, holding it with only "relative importance."[63] As we have seen, Westphal's research aims to refute this claim against Kierkegaard, and while Religiousness B does hold itself guilty to the charge (at least for Westphal), it finds its existential completion (and thus its exoneration) in Religiousness C.

Moving from offense to objectivity, the second of three claims he makes for Religiousness C, Westphal emphasizes outward political concern through the self's imitation of Christ as the Paradigm. In clarifying what he means by objectivity, Westphal states that it pertains to a certain "aloofness" found in those who, "to preside over their lives and to be fully in charge of every situation, find it useful always to remain above the fray."[64] This aloofness separates the self from the world by extracting one's subjectivity from the equation and by objectively seeing the world *sub specie aeternitatis*. In response, Religiousness B contrasts faith as uncertain, "that Christ can only be believed, never known."[65] Faith, according to Climacus, is categorized not as something knowable, but only as an acceptance of an objective uncertainty "maintained through appropriation in the most passionate inwardness."[66] There is risk involved in the faith of Religiousness B, but in C that risk moves from an epistemic uncertainty into action: one's faith must produce works (James 2:14–26) in the practice of imitating Christ. According to Westphal, Kierkegaard pointedly reveals this in *Works of Love*.

Works of Love is a touchstone text for Westphal; it is where he finds Kierkegaard's "most eloquent account of neighborly love as welcoming the stranger, the widow, the orphan, and the poor."[67] Kierkegaard's neighborly love centers on an extended reflection on the commandment "You shall love your neighbor as yourself," and he emphasizes this love's commanded nature and its relation to God's divine law. What is of particular interest for Westphal, and for Kierkegaard, is that this form of love is written as a part of the Law—Jesus proclaims that it is the greatest commandment—and consequently it becomes a foundation for living an ethical, good life.[68] However, contrary to the social order, which also can show appreciation for the neighbor (even if it often fails to do so in action) and constitutes laws to that effect, it is the how and why one enacts this divinely commanded neighborly love that make it so important. This is also why faithfully following this commanded love resists objectification.[69]

Kierkegaard is quick to point out that this source must come from God and that God compels the Christian to love the neighbor from deep within. Westphal elaborates on this, noting that other forms of love, such as friendship and erotic love, "grow from preferences based on natural inclination and are actually a form of self-love."[70] These are self-interested loves since they come from one's own inward interests and desires (e.g., for companionship). In contrast, neighborly love, in and of itself, can only be commanded since it fulfills no self-interest. Connecting *Works of Love* to Kierkegaard's first authorship, Westphal notes that "in the language of *Fragments*, love of one's neighbor cannot be recollected but only revealed. In the language of *Postscript*, it cannot be grounded in speculation but only in ethical-religious subjectivity."[71] Additionally, and this will eventually play out in his future work in phenomenology, Westphal sees that this is a primary issue taken up by Levinas and his ethics as first philosophy.

Regarding objectivity, one can again see epistemic risk within neighborly love. For one, the self cannot ground this love, and more to the point, neighborly love may even run against one's self-interest. When you choose to love your neighbor as yourself, you put his or her needs above your own, which could have dire consequences to your personal wealth, social standing, ambition, and even your own life. It's not all volunteer soup kitchens and building homes for Habitat for Humanity on a Saturday. In answering the call to love your neighbor, you may have to make some major life choices and personal sacrifices.

Religiousness B recognizes this, Westphal claims, and often tries to mitigate the risks involved in fulfilling this commandment. Doctrine, in this manner, objectifies the nature of neighborly love by placidly securing it as a form of charity and almsgiving or, even worse, fashioning it into merely an abstract discipline. Westphal believes that neighborly love is much more radical than that: "The attempt by Religiousness B to make Christianity into a doctrine" restricts "the offense of faith to epistemic matters," which is just another way of legitimating Christendom.[72] "Christianity as doctrine," Westphal concludes, "is Christendom's defense against Christ as Pattern [or Christ as Paradigm], a way of reducing the price at which Christian consolation can be bought."[73]

This is not to say that doctrine is unnecessary; rather, doctrine must be guided by this principle of neighborly love and must be in the service of discipleship.[74] Far too often, Westphal elaborates, doctrine and discipleship become separated, often through apologetics or by making doctrine a particularly academic matter. Biblical scholarship is a key example for Westphal, where many scholars have become adept as interpreters of the Bible—critiquing its origins and historicity (calling to my mind the historical Jesus debates in certain scholastic circles)—but they far too often cease to be followers. This is a case of objectivity being a "separation of words from deeds," and while objectification does not only rest in the academy, it does present a strong example of the aloofness toward faith and toward the Word of God. Religiousness B, for Westphal, is liable to lapse into this aloofness, which is why he sees a final stage of religiousness in Kierkegaard.[75]

Religiousness C, however, does not seek to end academic research in theology but rather seeks to ensure that it always aids discipleship and always imitates Christ. Religiousness C demands that theologians (and all Christians) continually ask, reflect, and pray: "Are we following Christ and Christ's teachings? Are we bringing about a greater sense of discipleship in our works and deeds?" These questions are part of imitating Christ and are part not only of what it means to do theology, for Westphal, but also of what it means to become a self.

This brings us back to Westphal's prophetic task for philosophy and the task of liberation for theology. Speaking on the role of theology, Westphal states that "all theology should be liberation theology, a guide to the practice of overcoming oppression in all its forms."[76] To me, this comes directly from his reading of Kierkegaard's Religiousness C. This can be seen in the fact that he cites the exact same passages within Kierkegaard's second authorship, particularly *Works of Love*, and presents the same conclusions. However, he does not cite them as examples of Religiousness C but instead relates them to Levinas's phenomenological account of ethics as first philosophy to provide a contemporary argument for neighborly love as the primary motivator for theology.

One can see this concept of Religiousness C underlying Westphal's critiques of theologies that do not adhere to overcoming oppression or do not take the neighborly love commandment seriously. These theologies fall into three disparate forms of ideology or objectification: "overt espousal," where they "explicitly justify practices as slavery, apartheid," et cetera; and "vague generality," where notions such as the love of neighbor become abstracted and lame, where "a theology that is capable of calling racism a sin, but [is] incapable of identifying apartheid as a racism" and thus creates a "comfortable theology." Last, theology becomes a "dualistic hermeneutics" when it sifts the world into opposing categories (such as sacred and profane) and then, "by opposing evil on one side of the great divide . . . they permit themselves to remain totally silent about the evils on the other side."[77] For the rest of "Levinas, Kierkegaard, and the Theological Task," Westphal argues for ways that Levinas and Kierkegaard's thought allays these theological tendencies.

For our present purposes, though, note that the three critiques against theology sound exactly like the critiques Religiousness C has against Religiousness B's tendency toward objectivity. Furthermore, note that there is a place for doctrine, for both Westphal and Kierkegaard (as well, one might add in a broader sense, for Levinas), and that place is at home within neighborly love, especially in service of the widow, orphan, and stranger.

Moving on to outwardness, Westphal's third category of Religiousness C, one's service to the other, is an enactment of faith; as an enactment, it often involves suffering. It often embodies the first two categories, offense and objectivity, creating problems for the established order. Religious suffering is not so much a matter of dying or martyrdom as much as it is living joyously and humbly in faith through an ethical and religious inwardness that does not turn inward toward the self to ease or alleviate its suffering. Rather, it moves outward, toward a voluntary yet necessary suffering. Accordingly outward suffering becomes an essential expression of faith not merely being epistemic but also ethical. The inward struggle of faith is manifest in the outward struggle, where the "contemporaneity" with Christ is achieved "not only in the movement from knowledge to belief, but more basically in the movement from word to deed."[78]

This sense of suffering emanates from the idea that the self constantly tries to avoid or otherwise master suffering. Suffering is a humiliating experience, Westphal notes, and Christendom often tries to ignore or explain away this humiliation through its triumphalism and self-exaltation. However, "the church triumphant is the triumph of the spirit of the scribes and Pharisees over [the] apostolic spirit."[79] It has deified its achievements as God's glory, as God's established order. It has replaced the spirit and teachings of Christ as servant and sufferer for the world with Christendoom as God's ruling power over the world. Religiousness C continually critiques this Pharisaic attempt by accepting its humiliation and suffering because of its faith. Through accepting suffering as a part of one's faith, and through continuously expressing one's faith in the love of neighbor, the self disestablishes, or subverts, Christendom.[80] It causes offense, and it expresses faith in service of the other.

Suffering, here, is primarily understood through service. Westphal clarifies this in *Becoming a Self*, where he situates Religiousness C within the love of neighbor and its appeal toward alterity. Westphal states that "this outwardness involves an essential relation with my neighbor that challenges my self-love. . . . [I]t involves an essential relation to the established order that challenges that order's ultimacy."[81] Westphal finds that this challenge reveals that the "Christian faith is *aufgehoben* in the call to a discipleship which imitates the life of Christ on earth" and can be expressed only as Religiousness C.

However, many disagree with Westphal's rather Hegelian reading of Kierkegaard and his attempt to connect all of Kierkegaard's writings through the singular theme found in Religiousness C. Two scholars in particular, Jack Mulder Jr. and Henry Piper, quite pointedly express this, causing Westphal to respond and defend his concept of Religiousness C. Piper's critique deals primarily with Westphal's particular Hegelian reading of Kierkegaard, and Mulder's questions the concept of Religiousness C. We will briefly explore Mulder's critiques and Westphal's defense to better understand how Westphal fits into the prevailing Kierkegaardian scholarship.[82]

Mulder's critique of Religiousness C initially touches on Kierkegaard's shifting conceptions of the teleological suspension of the ethical in *Fear and Trembling* and Kierkegaard's subsequent works. Mulder's examination of the teleological suspension of the ethical follows a tradition of scholarship that follows the belief that Kierkegaard actually corrects the teleological suspension in these later works. Moreover, contrary to Westphal, Mulder believes that Kierkegaard even distances himself from his early formulation of the teleological suspension, especially within his second authorship and journals.[83] At the risk of oversimplifying, the prevailing scholarship argues that Kierkegaard noticed that the teleological suspension of the ethical may only lead toward inward contemplation since the ethical is suspended in an inwardness that is not just *Sittlichkeit*, but also of the contemplation of the good, or a Socratic and Kantian morality. Kierkegaard recognizes this error, the argument goes, and he eventually changes the teleological suspension, particularly in *Concluding Unscientific Postscript*.

Mulder, agreeing with Westphal, refutes this claim by citing a passage in *Works of Love* that reaffirms the teleological suspension in *Fear and Trembling*.[84] Although Westphal and he agree that the ethical that is suspended can be equated to *Sittlichkeit*, and that Kierkegaard affirms this in his second authorship, Mulder parts ways with Westphal on the matter of where this teleological suspension happens. Mulder argues that the teleological suspension of the ethical, as read in *Fear and Trembling*, becomes taken up within what Climacus calls Religiousness A in *Concluding Unscientific Postscript*. In doing so, Kierkegaard evolves his understanding of the teleological suspension since the suspension within Religiousness B fulfills the suspension of A through the Paradox of faith: there is joy at the end of the knight of infinite resignation's journey through a faith that fulfills the prior suspension. Although each suspension can be compared, Mulder argues, this does not mean that they are one and the same. Thus, it becomes the case that Abraham in *Fear and Trembling* is not the same as Socrates in *Concluding Unscientific Postscript*, contrary to Westphal's reading. Mulder states that, "in seeing Socrates as an exemplar of the teleological suspension of the ethical, we already are recognizing that one who commits the teleological suspension of the ethical has not *eo ipso* become the knight of faith. Something more is needed, and this is faith, the ability to come back to the finite with joy,"[85] something that Abraham explicitly is able to do but that Socrates cannot, something that can happen in Religiousness B but not A. "This would imply," he concludes, "that the dialectic would not finish until after the teleological suspension."[86] Hence in *Concluding Unscientific Postscript*, Kierkegaard founds Religiousness B.

Pushing the teleological suspension of the ethical into a Religiousness C is a movement too far for Mulder. He claims that it severs "the relation to the god in time at Religiousness B," since the dialectical nature of the hidden inwardness and outer expression (which should be understood as equal movements faith requires to be real) are seen as merely hypothetical and nonreal, according to Religiousness C.[87] In other words, since Westphal calls this merely a contemplation of outward expression, he severs the dialectic that creates Religiousness B in the first place. No dialectic between inwardness and outwardness, no Religiousness B. No Religiousness B, no Religiousness C. Westphal undercuts the whole project by moving it too far. Therefore, Mulder finds that Religiousness C is "misleading" and "superfluous" since the teleological suspension in Religiousness A, caught within Religiousness B, already accomplishes what Westphal is trying to argue and what the second authorship fleshes out.[88] True, Kierkegaard emphasizes an outward, ethical love of neighbor in his second authorship, but to make it a double *Aufhebung* of the previous two religious stages is at best redundant and at worst separates the dialectic seen in B, which is to say it renders B useless.

In response, Westphal first reestablishes that the teleological suspension of the ethical indeed concerns *Sittlichkeit*, something that Mulder, departing from Evans, recognizes. Westphal rejects that the teleological suspension changes in Kierkegaard's writings and for evidence they both cite *Works of Love*'s emphasis on God's law being above humanity's laws and customs.[89] From here, he goes on to defend Religiousness C through an account of what is lacking in Religiousness A and B, namely, an ethical paradigm for living faith as a task.

He agrees that a teleological suspension of the ethical, as seen with Socrates, is necessary for and in Religiousness A. However, what Mulder misses, according to Westphal, is that this suspension can be completed only in Religiousness C. In this sense, the suspension in Religiousness A is necessary for "authentic religion that is not Christian," and in Religiousness B, Kierkegaard focuses on his primary objective of describing an authentic Christian religion that he distinguishes from Christendom and biblical faith.[90] For this purpose, Kierkegaard takes up the authentic religion found within Religiousness A and places it in the Paradox of Christ in Religiousness B. However, Westphal claims, Religiousness B provides no ethics as it "focuses on the epistemic paradox of faith in the God in time and, so far as ethics is concerned, gives us [at] best such formal notions as subjectivity, the *how,* and appropriation, which as such have no specifically Christian content and which are applied in *Postscript* to *belief* in the Incarnation rather than to *behavior* in the mode of *imitatio Christi.*"[91] *Works of Love,* however, does provide us with a paradigm of "Christian ethics" that repudiates and surpasses *Sittlichkeit.*

Religiousness C fulfills this lack of an ethical paradigm within Religiousness B. It also negates the other claim by Mulder that Religiousness C is superfluous. This is especially so given the abstract nature of the God relation in Religiousness B, which Westphal argues needs to be intensified and supplemented if it is to be expressed beyond a "(monastic or bourgeois) outwardness."[92] Citing Kierkegaard's journals and papers, Westphal argues that this is *Works of Love*'s primary thesis and, since it continues Kierkegaard's patterns of thought as seen within his first authorship, it is necessary to understand the previous formulations (the stages, Religiousness A and B) in light of Kierkegaard's second authorship.[93]

After rebuffing these two claims, Westphal addresses Mulder's final objection, which centers on the "religious resistance" found in the teleological suspension and Westphal's assertion that it is only in Religiousness C where this is overcome.[94] Again, as we shall see, Westphal defends his concept of a Religiousness C from an omission in Religiousness B.

Mulder's objection essentially focuses on his contention that "the teleological suspension is the crucial step of resignation that is necessary before faith can occur."[95] Westphal quickly counters that this is a faulty understanding of when the teleological suspension happens: "as presented in *Fear and Trembling*, the teleological suspension of the ethical is simultaneous with faith, neither prior nor subsequent. Faith just *is* the teleological suspension of the ethical in the sense that there is no faith without it."[96] Moreover, as seen in *Either/Or*, "it is with a faith that necessarily includes the teleological suspension of the ethical that the religious stage is defined in distinction from the ethical."[97] And yet when faith is understood in our society, it is often understood through a piety that rests on a *Sittlichkeit* by which the pious and holy are those who follow the laws and customs best. They are saints of law and order.

Westphal argues that Kierkegaard's saints are those who maintain a tension between their faith and their *Sittlichkeit*, concerning their behavior at least. Religiousness B all too easily succumbs to the temptations of dissolving this tension between one's *Sittlichkeit* and one's faith, given its "abstractness . . . along with the fact that it distinguishes itself from Religiousness A by virtue of specifically Christian elements."[98] These historical and cultural artifacts can so easily be assumed into Christendom and its metanarrative (the prevailing *Sittlichkeit* of Kierkegaard's time—and ours, for that matter). Thus, a religious resistance to this temptation is needed, and this is where Westphal situates Religiousness C.

Westphal defends his position throughout by noticing a lack within Kierkegaard's first authorship and then pointing out where the second authorship fills those gaps. This is especially clear when he addresses Piper's main critique against Religiousness C, that Kierkegaard's *Upbuilding Discourses* from 1843 to 1845 emphasizes a "'non-dialectical dialectic' in which difference and tension prevail over mediation and resolution," which runs counter to the completion that Westphal sees in Religiousness C.[99] Defending his reading, Westphal asserts "that there is nothing specifically Christian" in those discourses and that "if one wants an account of what is involved in becoming a Christian one must go beyond the *Upbuilding Discourses* on which Piper draws just as one must go beyond Religiousness B as presented by Climacus."[100] This, Westphal claims, is where Religiousness C comes enters the picture.

Conclusions on Kierkegaard: Toward Levinas and Liberation Theology

Thus far we have explored Westphal's reading of Religiousness C in light of Kierkegaard's theory of stages. Westphal concludes that Religiousness

C is the final move in Kierkegaard's critique of reason and society since it builds off his previously established concept of faith. It moves from faith as an individual, willing act (à la Abraham and the hidden inwardness of Religiousness A and B) toward a concrete, outward act of loving God and the neighbor as one loves oneself. In our exploration we have done a great deal of spadework exploring not only Westphal's writing but Kierkegaard's as well. Yet where does it leave us? What can we gather from Westphal's Kierkegaardian scholarship?

Our exploration has revealed that, in his early Kierkegaard scholarship, Westphal discovers the primary motivation for most of his philosophy of religion. In these works he finds his voice not only as a philosopher but also as a theologian. Kierkegaard gives Westphal a way to understand faith and how faith can serve as an unfounding source for a Christ-like (Christ-ian) witness to the world. Kierkegaard's critique of society and Christendom presses upon the all-too-human wound that is sin, and faith serves as the divine salve to heal that wound. Moreover, faith is not only a healing salve but also the therapy that moves the patient from critical condition to stable. The belief of faith is the initial care, and the act of faith is the continual rehabilitation of the patient. Reason is the medicinal prescription aiding rehabilitation.

The next chapter explores how this faith is central to Westphal's thinking and how he articulates it through a postmodern context. Westphal finds that the postmodern critique of society aligns quite well with Kierkegaard's critique of Christendom, and he appropriates both to articulate how the believing soul can become a better believer. Both critiques aid the believing soul to accept that its faith is the task of a lifetime. This is the core of his dialogue between Levinas and Kierkegaard. We have briefly summarized how this dialogue compels Westphal to state that all theology should be focused on liberation and on the preferential option toward the outcast. He develops Kierkegaard's Religiousness C and Levinas's ethics as first philosophy to argue how the self should always focus on the other, that one is *commanded* to lift the other above oneself in loving service to God through revelation. Westphal articulates this as a liberation theology, an articulation that he will eventually distance himself from but that is nonetheless revealing. Even though he omits "Levinas, Kierkegaard, and the Theological Task" from his book *Levinas and Kierkegaard in Dialogue,* stating that it was "more a research agenda than anything else," I believe that it is essential to understanding the book since it reveals the underlying impetus to better understand faith as a task and the concept of revelation that is needed for such a faith.[101] Through his scholarly account of Levinas and Kierkegaard, he makes the case for a phenomenology that opens the believing soul toward the world in service of that world.[102] In the book's sixth chapter, for example, Westphal explores how the heteronomy of self, other, and God creates a responsibility. This responsibility, even though it can be nontheistically understood, also relates to how the believing soul grasps and follows revelation. Westphal accepts that Levinas understands that responsibility "is born with the incursion of the Other into my very identity," but he also reads this responsibility from a theological, biblical perspective where "the law comes from a radically transcendent God" who is above and beyond "the self-legislation of human reason."[103] Whether it is inscribed in the Law or in the face, it always points toward the same self-abnegation and preferential option, and its inscription, however written, can lead the believing soul in faith seeking understanding. Within both, a preferential option for the other is imposed upon the self.

Westphal often emphasizes Kierkegaard's account of revelation over Levinas's obligation toward the other, as seen in his critique of Levinas's concept of God,[104] but it is clear that, within both, he is attempting to articulate something that he finds as truth, however subjective: becoming a self means accepting an epistemic uncertainty (faith, for Kierkegaard; the face of the other, for Levinas) and obligating oneself toward the other in service of making that uncertainty concrete.

When considering its implications, this concept of epistemic uncertainty makes the theological mind wonder about doctrine and the nature of theology. Westphal's critique against a certain kind of apologetics has already been well documented in this chapter and the last, but the extension of this to a suspicion of doctrine is a matter for concern. It reveals a more Lutheran approach to doctrine in that it wishes to proceed from faith solely on an account of revelation (*sola scriptura*, one might argue) and not on humanity's account of tradition, which entails a intertwined relationship of human reason and revelation. Westphal's account of revelation, here, has become threefold: it can be maieutic, a mediated immediacy, or it can be through the encounter of the other.

Westphal's concern against doctrine also points toward a somewhat anticreedal position in that there is a (Kierkegaardian) worry against a creeping Christendom when someone professes and codifies his or her beliefs into propositions and statements. Recall Westphal's remark against

Religiousness B: "Christianity as doctrine is Christendom's defense against Christ as Pattern, a way of reducing the price at which Christian consolation can be bought."[105] Say the magic words, Christendom yelps, and Jesus is your friend and salvation your reward—living those magic words, Kierkegaard mocks, is much, much harder. I can see why Westphal follows Kierkegaard in arguing against these abuses of doctrine, but I also fear that he is dismissing (or diminishing) the concept of doctrine mainly because it has been often misused throughout history.[106] He might be throwing the baby out with the bathwater, so to speak.

In Westphal's defense, it should be remembered that he does find a place for doctrine—situated along the path of faith seeking understanding—but it is subordinate to one's personal belief. It has very little at stake in the journey of faith since, if the believing soul finds that she must defy doctrine to fulfill her loving obligation to her neighbor, then she must do so. This stems from Kierkegaard's articulation of the subjectivity of truth and his worry about any objective fact being named as Truth. Although I am not ready to fight over the infallibility of the pope with Westphal, I find disconcerting this negation of objective truth—and thus the foundation of doctrine; it actually does a disservice to our understanding of God, even. When Westphal claims that there is no objective truth in the world, I wonder if he is constraining God. With this account of revelation, aren't Christians still putting God in a box just like they do within Christendom? To be sure, it is a different box, but it nonetheless limits what God can and cannot do.

I see this doctrinal strain in how he articulates the love commandment through a quasi-Kantian, "conditions of possibility" style of love. Westphal articulates that Religiousness C should be focused on loving the neighbor as one loves oneself. Sure, loving our neighbor should be our primary, Christlike objective, but the question arises: Whose love? Which neighbor? Would loving a slave be whipping her for insubordination (Colossians 3:22; Ephesians 6:5)? Or would loving a slave be to free her (Exodus 21:2; 1 Corinthians 7:21)? Are slaves even our neighbors?

Answering this question, Westphal would immediately point toward reason aiding faith in seeking understanding. For him this is what seeking is all about: reasoning about how to best enact the love commandment toward the neighbor, how to correct our all-too-human tendency to co-opt God (and the neighbor, for that matter) to do our own bidding. Furthermore, he also acknowledges that Truth can be manifest in the world, as seen through Christ as the Paradox and Paradigm. I can see how he answers this question, but I still cannot follow him fully, since these critiques are just as subjective as one's concept of revelation and truth. Even myself and my atheist friend can agree that Jesus was a historical person, but that he is the Incarnation is still an internal matter of recognition. I fear this leads toward a "truthiness" mentality, where it is true because you believe it is true, not because it is objective fact. In *Overcoming Onto-Theology*, he will try to defend postmodernism against the "anything goes" brush with which it is often painted, and he will also try to establish that history and tradition are not only meaningful but, following Gadamer, also the only ways in which we can interpret our world. If this is so, and this is further explored in the next chapter, then I must hold onto the belief that some of the discoveries humanity has made within, through, and by revelation via the aid of reason and the Holy Spirit can rise to the level of doctrine. Some things that people do not accept may still be true even if they are unacceptable. Some things we come to realize are true only after a long, painful process. Westphal's development of Kierkegaard's paradox within Christ answers this somewhat, but he limits this only to the Incarnation, as if God's revelation within the objective world ended there. This causes some concern for me.

Doctrine extends beyond the Incarnation and is indeed often cause for our recognition of the meaning of the Incarnation. For example, doctrine proclaims what revelation is, not just in the texts, but that the texts themselves are artifacts of revelation. In his concluding interview with Putt in *Gazing through a Prism Darkly*, Westphal concedes that the biblical canon is more or less a closed question; noting that certain parts are up for discussion (e.g., the Apocrypha) and that biblical exegesis can also shed light on how texts were formed (e.g., the several additions to the book of Isaiah), yet "it isn't the case that the Epistle of James is sometimes part of the Bible and sometimes not part of the Bible."[107] However, how does one come to know these texts as a canon or, more pointedly, as sacred Scripture? The answer lies within doctrine, however one construes the term, which defines what is Scripture and what is not. Moreover, doctrine is formed by tradition and human reason.

To delve further into such arguments goes beyond our scope into historical-biblical scholarship. I raise the point merely to suggest that perhaps doctrine is too narrowly defined in Westphal's thought and, perhaps by extension, in Kierkegaard's. If one is to believe that faith is a hidden inwardness, steeped in the self's recognition of God's revelation and then expressed in an outwardness, then one must accept that this outwardness—either in works of love or in writings of love—concretely manifests itself in the world. If this is so, then one can point toward objective, historical (sometimes written) moments that reveal the inwardness of that love. If that is the case, then perhaps there is a claim that doctrines—and the rational justification of those doctrines (i.e., apologetics)—have a place within Christianity.

Yet Westphal is not entirely wrong to be worried about doctrine or to be concerned with human reason's all-too-often misuse of doctrine. There have been far too many atrocities carried out in the name of God and God's love to not be worried and concerned. However, perhaps one should not be so wary of doctrine such that it is equated with Christendom. Perhaps, in doctrine, one can find particular cures for his or her own particular wounds. If one is to be open to the inward paradox of faith, as seen through Christ and revelation, then one must be open to the idea that this paradox can express itself outside of oneself, in others and in the world through God and the Holy Spirit. One must be open to revelation existing in a shared tradition or a shared covenant between God and God's people. Perhaps that paradox even extends to the church's embodying of both the battlefield and the hospital, where wounded sinners meet their divine physician whose nurses are wounded sinners also.

NOTES

1. *KCRS*, 105. See also *KCF*, 26–36 on Kierkegaard and Lutheranism; as well as 30–32 on Kierkegaard and Pietism. Our focus here is on Kierkegaard and Lutheranism since this is Westphal's main appropriation.

2. *KCRS*, 105.

3. Ibid.

4. Ibid.

5. Ibid., 106. Since *KCRS* is about gaining insights *through* Kierkegaard rather than a scholarly examination of his work (viii), these sentiments pertain to Westphal's thinking.

6. Ibid., 105.

7. Ibid., 107 Westphal mainly draws this from *Philosophical Fragments*, 53–54, and *Concluding Unscientific Postscript*, trans. David F. Swenson and Walter Lowrie (Princeton, NJ: Princeton University Press, 1941), 327–328. In *Fragments*, Climacus's notion of the paradox confounds reason, turning "the understanding [into] a clod and a dunce who at best can say 'yes' and 'no' to the same thing, which is not good theology"; this is an offense—a sin—to good theology. *Philosophical Fragments*, 53. Westphal follows his argument concerning Climacus's Lutheran view of reason and sin by looking at subjectivity and truth in *Concluding Unscientific Postscript*, noting the relationship between pathos and the inwardness of faith. *KCF* covers the same argument about Climacus's understanding of sin in chapter 7.

8. *KCRS*, 107.

9. Ibid., 107–108.

10. For the doctrine of total depravity, see Jaroslav Pelikan and Walter A. Hansen, eds., *Luther's Works* (St. Louis, MO: Concordia, 1963–1964), 26:174–175, 27:53, 12:323, 12:341–342, 26:33–34, 26:340–41. Westphal cites these sections. See also *The Heidelberg Catechism*, question 8, Center for Reformed Theology and Apologetics, http://www.reformed.org/docu ments/index.html?mainframe=http://www.reformed.org/documents/heidelberg.html; *Formula Concordiae of 1576*, article 1, Christian Classics Ethereal Library of Calvin College, http:// www.ccel.org/ccel/schaff/creeds3.iii.iv.html; Peter C. Hodgson and Robert H. King, eds., "Sin and Evil," in *Christian Theology: An Introduction to its Traditions and Tasks* (Minneapolis: Fortress Press, 1994), 194–221; John Webster, *Barth's Moral Theology* (New York: T&T Clark, 1998), 72–75.

11. *KCRS*, 108.

12. Ibid., 109–110.

13. See Kierkegaard, *Philosophical Fragments*, 11–15.

14. *KCRS*, 110.

15. Ibid. He cites Augustine's *Confessions*, 4:15, 5:10, 7:3, 8:10, and 9:4, never giving any specific edition.

16. *KCRS*, 111.

17. Ibid.

18. Ibid. Westphal does not give any exact page numbers or references for these descriptions in *Concluding Unscientific Postscript*. This is perhaps because the self's relation to the Paradox and the subjectivity of truth within the self is a theme spread throughout the *Postscript* and perhaps its main thesis. However, for a pertinent section of *Postscript*, see 168–176, 325–361, 440–465. See also Kierkegaard, *Postscript*, 168–170, for the initial expression; 171, for the essential expression; and 174–176, for the decisive expression.

In *BS*, Westphal details these expressions their relation to Kierkegaard's concept of hidden inwardness on 156–175. While the two are interrelated, in *BS* he does this in relation to Climacus's concept of pathos and not paradox. He also further explores Kierkegaard's concept of the paradox in chapter 8 of *KCF*.

19. *KCRS*, 111.

20. Ibid., 113. The concept of the Teacher is an allusion to Socrates in *The Meno*. See Kierkegaard, *Philosophical Fragments*, 27–32.

21. Kierkegaard, *Philosophical Fragments*, 28. Climacus allegorically states: "The god wants to be his teacher, and the god's concern is to bring about equality. If this cannot be brought about the love becomes unhappy and the instruction meaningless, for they are unable to understand each other. We probably think that this may be a matter of indifference to the god, since he does not need the learner, but we forget—or rather, alas, we demonstrate—how far we are from understanding him; we forget that he does indeed love the learner."

22. Ibid., 31–32. Climacus muses that the only way that the god could do such a thing as to take the lowly form of humanity's servant: "In order for unity to be effected, the god must become like this one. He will appear, therefore, as the equal of the lowliest persons . . . the god will appear in the form of a *servant*."

23. *KCRS*, 113. Westphal quotes Climacus's opening lines to "The Absolute Paradox," which mockingly refer to Kant's *Critique of Pure Reason*, where Kant argues (in the preface of the A edition) that "human reason has this peculiar fate that in one species of its knowledge it is burdened by questions which, as prescribed by the very nature of reason itself, it is not able to ignore, but which, as transcending all its powers, it is also not able to answer." Westphal cites

from this version. See Immanuel Kant, *Critique of Pure Reason*, trans. Norman Kent Smith (London: Macmillan, 1929), 7/A vii.

24. *KCRS*, 113.

25. Westphal draws from *Philosophical Fragments*, 39–41. For Kierkegaard's Climacus, one cannot use these conditions to prove God's existence since, as the necessity for all existence, God's essence necessarily includes existence. He demonstrates this by explaining the difference between Napoleon and his works, given that someone else could have performed Napoleon's works, noting this "is why I cannot reason from the works to existence" of Napoleon. However, God's existence is an affront to this form of reasoning, given that "between the god and his works there is an absolute relation. God is not a name but a concept, and perhaps because of that his *essentia involvit existentiam* [essence involves existence]."

26. *KCRS*, 114.

27. Ibid. Westphal quotes from Kierkegaard, *Philosophical Fragments*, 46–47.

28. *KCRS*, 108

29. Ibid. Westphal is quoting from Pelikan and Hansen, *Luther's Works*, 26:194, 26:323, 26:262.

30. Kierkegaard's second authorship has become a standard assumption among Kierkegaard scholars. The term denotes a change in writing style shortly after the "Corsair Affair" in which the *Corsair*, a Danish satirical magazine, began to increasingly mock Kierkegaard's works after having previously praised them (and with Kierkegaard contributing to the magazine as well). The works that are included in the second authorship are authored by Kierkegaard himself with no pseudonyms and are shorter than his previous ones, save for *Works of Love*, which is generally considered the most important text of the second authorship. Other texts included in the second authorship are *Two Ages: A Literary Review, Upbuilding Discourses in Various Spirits, Phister as Captain Scipio*, and *The Crisis and a Crisis in the Life of an Actress*. For more information, see Howard Hong and Edna Hong, "Historical Introduction," in *Works of Love*, by Søren Kierkegaard (Princeton, NJ: Princeton University Press, 1995), ix–xvi; M. Jamie Ferreira, *Blackwell's Great Minds: Kierkegaard* (Oxford: Blackwell, 2009), 122–146.

31. In *GTPD*, C. Stephen Evans agrees "with critics that much of the emphasis on outward action that is seen in Kierkegaard's later writings is already present, implicitly and sometimes explicitly, in Kierkegaard's earlier work; however, ultimately that does not undermine but confirms the point Westphal is trying to make, which is that being a follower of Christ, one who 'lives contemporaneously' with Christ and thus comes into conflict with the established order, is precisely the final goal of the whole authorship" (*GTPD*, 36).

32. In chapter 13 of *KCF*, Westphal explores ways in which Anti-Climacus points toward a Religiousness C. His concept of Religiousness C does not change in this text but attempts to support it by citing a non–second authorship text. He merely points toward its potential development, noting that Anti-Climacus elaborates on the faith as an offense and that Christ, as both the Paradox and the Paradigm, must not just be contemplated but followed as a role model for the task of faith (261–266). We stick to how Westphal develops his concept of Religiousness C earlier in his career to show chronologically his intellectual development.

33. *BS*, 22.

34. Søren Kierkegaard, *Either/Or Book I*, trans. Howard Hong and Edna Hong (Princeton, NJ: Princeton University Press, 1987), 1:396.

35. *BS*, 22–23. Remember that reason is also a matter of the flesh. Thus, pleasure seeking encompasses art, music, literature, and even religiously oriented themes such as Christ's passion where he is portrayed as a tragic hero.

36. Ibid., 24; Westphal quotes from *Either/Or*, 2:166–69, 178, 188–90, 214–19, 223–24.

37. *BS*, 24. Emphasis is mine.

38. Ibid., 24–25. The construct of marriage also happens to be the primary stage of Hegel's theory of *Sittlichkeit*, where marriage "ennobles" the esthetic pleasure seeking. *EO*, 2:61; cf. *EO*, 21, 30, 57.

39. Kierkegaard, *Either/Or*, 2:31. See also *BS*, 25; Ferreira, *Blackwell's Great Minds*, 21–23.

40. Westphal summarizes this in *BS*, 25–28.

41. Ibid., 25–26.

42. See Kierkegaard, *Works of Love*, 467.

43. Westphal frequently uses *sub specie aeternati* instead of its original formulation, and he attributes this to Spinoza. I use the original formulation to avoid confusion for those not familiar with Westphal's style but who are familiar with the concept. See *KCF*, 191, esp. 191n14.

44. See *KCF*, chap. 11. Although *KCF* and *BS* more step-by-step guides through Climacus's texts, Westphal's other Kierkegaardian scholarship reveals how he found these arguments and illuminates his appropriation of them.

45. Kierkegaard, *Concluding Unscientific Postscript*, 165. See also 465–467, where Climacus formulates this into Religiousness A "for the sake of brevity."

46. *BS*, 175.

47. Kierkegaard, *Concluding Unscientific Postscript*, 465–470.

48. Merold Westphal, "Søren Kierkegaard," *Encyclopedia Britannica Online*, http://www .britannica.com/EBchecked/topic/317503/Soren-Kierkegaard/271899/Three-dimensions-of -the-religious-life. I include this quotation from the encyclopedia to highlight that Westphal is so convinced that Religiousness C is within Kierkegaard's writing that he places it in the most basic of texts, no longer leaving it up to debate.

49. Kierkegaard, *Concluding Unscientific Postscript*, 468.

50. Merold Westphal, "Kierkegaard's Teleological Suspension of Religiousness B," in *Foundations of Kierkegaard's Vision of Community*, ed. George Connell and C. Stephen Evans (London: Humanities Press, 1992), 110–129. This is our foundational text for understanding Religiousness C. I also use *BS*, "Beyond Postscript: The Teleological Suspension of Hidden Inwardness in Religiousness C"; Merold Westphal, "Kierkegaard's Religiousness C: A Defense," *International Philosophical Quarterly* 44, no. 4 (December 2004): 535–548; and see C. Stephen Evan's contribution to *GTPD* and B. Keith Putt's concluding interview with Westphal himself.

51. Westphal, "Kierkegaard's Teleological Suspension of Religiousness B," 114.

52. Ibid., 115. Here, Westphal does not mention *Works of Love* but does in later texts. See *BS*, 195, 197; Westphal, "Kierkegaard's Religiousness C," 536, 538–539.

53. Westphal, "Kierkegaard's Teleological Suspension of Religiousness B," 115.

54. Ibid. "With help from Plato" and his notion of recollection, Westphal summarizes, "Religiousness A can filter out all those putative divine voices that do not echo the voice of the people. As the Postscript's account of resignation, suffering, and guilt shows us, Religiousness A is capable of intense subjectivity. But the epistemological immanence in which it operates blurs the distinction between . . . the voice of the people and the voice of God (Reason)" (116).

55. Ibid.

56. Ibid.

57. Ibid.

58. Ibid.

59. Ibid., 117.

60. Ibid.

61. *BS,* 194.

62. Ibid., 195.

63. Ibid.

64. Westphal, "Kierkegaard's Teleological Suspension of Religiousness B," 118.

65. Ibid.

66. Kierkegaard, *Concluding Unscientific Postscript,* 171.

67. Merold Westphal, "Levinas, Kierkegaard, and the Theological Task," *Modern Theology* 8, no. 3 (July 1992): 252. For more on his estimation of this text, see *GTPD,* 164–166, 191–193.

68. Westphal utilizes this aspect of *Works of Love* throughout his writings. For prime examples, see *LKD,* 54–56; *BS,* 195–196; Westphal, "Levinas, Kierkegaard, and the Theological Task," 252–253. Also, Westphal notes in *BS,* 195, that this commandment did not originate with Jesus but was a reference to Leviticus 19:18. He takes special notice in connecting this commandment both to Abraham, the exemplar of faith for De Silentio, and to Jesus.

69. Kierkegaard, *Works of Love,* 11–15; *BS,* 196. In "Kierkegaard's Religiousness C," 536, Westphal also places this passage alongside 1 John 4:20–21, adding another layer to his understanding of the relation between faith and works.

70. *BS,* 196.

71. Ibid.

72. Westphal, "Kierkegaard's Teleological Suspension of Religiousness B," 119.

73. Ibid., 120.

74. Concerning apologetics, Westphal makes it emphatically clear that "doctrine should define discipleship rather than defend against it." Ibid., 119.

75. Ibid., 121.

76. Westphal, "Levinas, Kierkegaard, and the Theological Task," 246.

77. Ibid., 251.

78. Westphal, "Kierkegaard's Teleological Suspension of Religiousness B," 124–125.

79. Ibid., 124.

80. Westphal directly links this suffering to joy throughout this article, using the apostle Peter's joyous acceptance of his suffering on behalf of spreading the Gospel (Acts 5) as a foil to express how the Christian's suffering is also joyful (110, 124). For Westphal, calling suffering on behalf of God joyful emphasizes that the sufferer does not begrudgingly accept suffering but rather does so with elation. Suffering thus changes from an act of torture to an act of faith in Christ, becoming a cause for celebration.

81. *BS,* 197.

82. Jack Mulder Jr., "Re-Radicalizing Kierkegaard: An Alternative to Religiousness C in Light of an Investigation into the Teleological Suspension of the Ethical," *Continental Philosophy Review* 53 (2002): 303–324; Henry B. Piper, "Kierkegaard's Non-Dialectical Dialectic or That Kierkegaard Is Not Hegelian," *International Philosophical Quarterly* 44, no. 4 (December 2004): 497–518; Westphal, "Kierkegaard's Religiousness C," 535–548.

83. C. Stephen Evans's and Edward F. Mooney's Kierkegaardian scholarship becomes central to this debate. Mulder, "Re-Radicalizing Kierkegaard," 305–307, Westphal, "Kierkegaard's Religiousness C," 537–539. For a robust debate on this topic, which is cited heavily by all three authors, see George B. Connell and C. Stephen Evans, eds., *Foundations of Kierkegaard's Vision of Community: Religion, Ethics and Politics in Kierkegaard* (Atlantic Highlands, NJ: Humanities Press, 1992), which includes a chapter by Mooney and Westphal's general argument for Religiousness C. See also Edward F. Mooney, *Knights of Resignation: Reading Kierkegaard's Fear and Trembling* (Albany: SUNY Press, 1991), 71–88; C. Stephen Evans, "Faith as the *Telos* of Morality:

A Reading of *Fear and Trembling*," in *International Kierkegaard Commentary: Fear and Trembling and Repetition*, ed. Robert L. Perkins (Macon, GA: Mercer University Press, 1993), 9–27.

Concerning Piper's critique of his overly Hegelian reading, Westphal quickly dismisses these claims by citing instances where Kierkegaard's "authors" either take on Hegelian personae (i.e., Judge William) or utilize Hegelian concepts such as *Sittlichkeit* and *Aufhebung*. Westphal, "Kierkegaard's Religiousness C," 546–548. Since this concern has been addressed throughout this chapter, I refrain from rehashing them. Suffice it to say that both Piper and Westphal agree that Kierkegaard obliquely uses Hegelian concepts, but Piper finds Westphal skewing the ratio between Kierkegaard's appropriation and negation of Hegel.

84. Westphal, "Kierkegaard's Religiousness C," 538; Mulder, "Re-radicalizing Kierkegaard," 310. The quotes in question are from Kierkegaard, *Works of Love*, 126, 441: "It is God who has placed love in the human being, and it is God who in every case will determine what is love," and "Neither is it human judgment as such that it is to determine what sacrifice is, because God is to determine this, and human judgment is valid only when it judges in accordance with God's Judgment. God's requirement is that love shall be self-sacrifice, but how this is to be interpreted more specifically in the particular case, God, again, must determine."

85. Mulder, "Re-Radicalizing Kierkegaard," 312.

86. Ibid.

87. Ibid., 320.

88. Ibid.

89. Kierkegaard, *Works of Love*, 126, 441.

90. Westphal, "Kierkegaard's Religiousness C," 540.

91. Ibid.

92. Ibid., 542.

93. Ibid. Westphal quotes from the Hong translation of *Works of Love* (409), which has selections of Kierkegaard's *Journals and Papers*. He quotes from this passage often in his works when linking the second authorship's themes of Christ as paradigm to the theory of stages. In the section, Kierkegaard muses that the themes within *Upbuilding Discourses* (which focus on an ethical Christian life rooted in biblical faith and the *imitatio Christi*) has only reaffirmed his previous ideas, meaning within his pseudonymous authorship. From here, Kierkegaard gets the next theme of his book and its title: *Works of Love*.

94. Ibid., 542.

95. Mulder, "Re-radicalizing Kierkegaard," 305. Westphal also quotes this in "Kierkegaard's Religiousness C," 543.

96. Westphal, "Kierkegaard's Religiousness C," 543.

97. Ibid.

98. Ibid.

99. Ibid., 548.

100. Ibid.

101. *LKD*, 2.

102. He will eventually formulate this as a self-transcendence in the aptly titled *Transcendence and Self-Transcendence*.

103. *LKD*, 103.

104. Ibid., 47.

105. Westphal, "Kierkegaard's Teleological Suspension of Religiousness B," 120.

106. In chapter 9 I show how Westphal critiques Kearney for a similar offense. Kearney, Westphal argues, conceives of God without *esse*, or being, precisely because human selfishness has capitalized on God's being for its own legitimization (onto-theology, in this vein, is seen

as permission for war and destruction "in the name of God"). Westphal thinks that Kearney, in his attempts to find a God of peace, removes *esse* too easily. One can see Westphal's disdain for apologetics (and perhaps doctrine) as a similar charge: to make faith more "pure" to follow God's commandments, he removes apologetics and, by extension, the doctrinal statements that are based upon an apologetical foundation.

107. *GTPD*, 204. See also chapter 1 of this book.

6. FAITH SEEKING UNDERSTANDING

Westphal's Postmodernism

APPROPRIATING POSTMODERNISM, REVEALING REVELATION:
WESTPHAL'S FUNDAMENTAL THEOLOGY

Overcoming Onto-theology finds itself in two worlds: one that is suspicious of postmodern critique of religion and one whose appreciation of postmodern thought makes it suspicious of religion.[1] Speaking to both, Westphal situates the work as a primer for the Christian theist's endeavor into postmodern philosophy. The book's very first words set this trajectory:

> Some of the best philosophers whom I count among my friends are post-modernists. But they do not share my faith. Others of the best philosophers whom I count among my friends share my faith. But they are not postmodernists. . . . At varying degrees along the spectrum that runs from mildly allergic to wildly apoplectic, [these believing philosophers] are inclined to see postmodernism as nothing but warmed-over Nietzschean atheism . . . that leads ineluctably to moral nihilism. Anything goes.[2]

Westphal continues by siding with the postmodernists even though few share his faith. Citing postmodernity's suspicion of the Enlightenment project and subsequent critique of "science in the service of technology," Westphal finds himself often agreeing with postmodernists as he did with Freud, Marx, and Nietzsche in *Suspicion and Faith*.[3] Yet he asserts that the central critiques against religion made by postmodern philosophers can also be found in the Christian tradition, and through *Overcoming Onto-theology* he seeks to appropriate these postmodern themes for a Christian audience.[4]

"This appropriation," he argues, "is a recontextualization in which the themes in question are removed from the anti-Christian or atheistic settings that are the horizons of the postmodern philosophers and articulated within the framework of Christian/theistic assumptions that are, I claim, *their proper home*."[5] That is quite an audacious argument! That the ideas of these serious scholars—most of whom are majorly critical of Christianity—properly reside within Christianity is eyebrow raising. Yet it is also familiar to Westphal's thinking; he is essentially following the same pattern from *Suspicion and Faith*, in which he jokingly accused the masters of suspicion, particularly Marx,[6] of plagiarizing biblical sources. However, here he proclaims something much more piercing: that these critiques' proper home, the origin of their scholarship and their appropriate place in culture, is within Christianity. This makes his philosophy a fundamental theology and a very peculiar fundamental theology at that.[7]

It is a fundamental theology that evades an apologetics and is primarily interested in appropriating (or perhaps reoriginating) philosophical critique aiding in faith seeking understanding. I further articulate how his work reads as a fundamental theology in what follows by exploring Westphal's notion of faith in "faith seeking understanding," a motto that permeates all his postmodern work. I also switch from calling him a philosopher of religion, as he calls himself, to calling him a theologian. From a theological perspective, I show that Westphal's engagement with postmodernity is an appropriation for a Protestant theology crafted in light of his concepts of revelation. This ultimately leads to an exploration of his appropriation that trails a hermeneutical epistemology based on overcoming metaphysics. From there, we investigate Westphal's phenomenology and its emphasis on the believing soul's loving obligation to the widow, orphan, and stranger.

Fides: The Source of Westphal's Fundamental Theology

Westphal's thinking, considered as a fundamental theology, at first glance shows him giving an apologetics for postmodernity—making it palatable for Protestant sensibilities—but he then turns toward a serious discussion about how he sees these postmodern scholars echoing critiques made in the Judeo-Christian tradition, dating back to Amos, Elijah, and Nathan. Perhaps it initially seems to be merely a matter of "who made the argument first," but it runs deeper: Westphal is quietly making an argument about revelation, or at least is arguing from a perspective that presumes revelation.

Revelation, for Westphal and his Christian faith, pertains to God revealing God's self to humanity and, in that revealing, disclosing timeless truths about faith and how to live a faithful life, a task of a lifetime.[8] The postmodern critique of religion—with its suspicious forebears Freud, Marx, and Nietzsche—speaks to us from a contemporary perspective and its convergence with Christian thought only reveals how timeless and consistent these particular critiques are. They echo biblical revelation; for the Christian, they concern how to live and express one's faith. This perspective of revelation further exposes Westphal's thinking as a fundamental theology. As we have previously covered, Christians need these critiques alongside the Bible because their contemporary authors speak to our present conditions in ways that ancient authors cannot. Both work in tandem for the believing soul: Amos's writings, for example, show the timelessness of the critique (while linking it back to one's relationship to God), whereas Marx shows the timeliness of the critique (while linking it back to one's contemporary economic and political concerns).[9]

The notion that postmodern thought echoes biblical revelation finds its headwaters early with Westphal's philosophy. Philosophy matters to the believing soul, Westphal claims, because it places the believing soul into question. He explicitly shows this concern in his essay "Faith Seeking Understanding."[10] Easily his most personal contribution to the field, Westphal recounts how he fell in love with philosophy against his family's religious concerns and why he thinks philosophy matters to faith; it reads convincingly as a letter to his family as to why he chose this profession. He gives an autobiographical account of how he fell in love with philosophy by first describing how he came from a Christian community that viewed philosophy with even more distrust than the masters of suspicion viewed Christianity. Philosophy can be quite a "traumatic" and "violent" encounter to the young believer, as it was to Westphal's mother, whose college professor "shamelessly ridiculed religious believers" and "convinced her that the relation between faith and philosophical reason was an unqualified either/or."[11] Moreover, his own love for philosophy gave his family grave concerns about his prayer life and whether his service toward God as a philosopher could be fruitful:

> To their dying days, neither my father nor my mother was able to reconcile my philosophical vocation with the fact that I continued to profess the faith, to be active in the church, to pray, and to teach our children the faith.

Instead of rejoicing that there were Christian philosophers quite unlike the one who had almost cost her her faith, my mother comforted herself with Proverbs 22:6: "Train up a child in the way he should go, and when he is old he will not depart from it." She continued to hope that eventually I would abandon philosophy and come back to the true faith.[12]

This astonishing moment of candor helps us understand the underlying force in Westphal's thinking: he is always striving to craft a philosophy that can, in fact, be seen as Christian while also being philosophical. The unqualified either-or that was cemented into his mother's judgment of philosophy becomes the backdrop from which Westphal appropriates philosophy for theology: he wishes to show how philosophy can and does aid ones faith, not destroy it. I am not trying to psychoanalyze Westphal here. Rather, through his family's concerns, and his attempts to put them at ease, Westphal highlights the driving leitmotif throughout his work.[13] For the most part, this text has gone neglected, but it is important since it reveals a confessional aspect in Westphal's thinking, further pushing him into a theological discourse.

In the text, Westphal shows the need for philosophical reflection by highlighting the dangers of an unexamined faith. Confronted one day during his daily commute with a car's bumper sticker that reads "God said it; I believe it; that ends it," Westphal reflects on the sticker's brand of hermeneutics, which effectively terminates all conversation with regard to interpretation, including whether or not one has to interpret *anything* at all.[14] Fifteen years later, Westphal still shows this concern in *Whose Community? Which Interpretation?*, where he appropriates a Gadamerian hermeneutics for biblical interpretation, arguing against certain faith communities that contend that the Bible needs no interpretation. "I am reminded of an ad," Westphal recalls, "for a new translation of the Bible billed as so accurate and so clear that the publishers announce 'no interpretation needed.' The ad promotes 'the revolutionary translation that allows you to immediately understand exactly what the original writers mean.'"[15] Instances like these lead Westphal to be doubly concerned about hermeneutics and critical reflection.

Returning to "Faith Seeking Understanding" and the slogan on the bumper sticker, Westphal notes that "ironically, the quest for certainty that motivates this posture is anything but philosophically innocent."[16] By exposing the problems within this philosophical ignorance, Westphal finds that "philosophy could be faith seeking understanding" since it places the believer, like any reader of philosophical texts, into question.[17] Through his philosophical training, Westphal began to see "that the walls erected to keep 'us' safe could function as blinders, and that I [Westphal] didn't need to cling blindly to them lest I see something dangerous."[18] Westphal recounts his philosophical journey in the rest of the text, illuminating the relationship between his faith and his academic career. For our present study, however, what is astounding about this essay is how Westphal continually relates philosophy back to humanity's limited rational faculty—which he gathers from Kant, generically calling it a Kantian finitism—and his own need to be placed into question.[19] Whether it was his first philosophical love (Kant) or his primary influence (Kierkegaard), or even the topic of his dissertation (Hegel's *Phenomenology of Spirit*), Westphal is continually asking, in effect, "What does your faith legitimate?"[20] Thus, he is able to talk about how Kant opened a Pandora's box in which the "movement between faith's preunderstanding and philosophy's self-examination" can meet.[21] This would cause him to review his faith in a fashion where he would dispose himself "toward one philosophical theme or another," such as the hermeneutics of suspicion, which then "reacted [upon] my faith and caused me to reconstrue it."[22] This circular pattern allowed him to always keep his faith as the source of contemplation (the preunderstanding, as he calls it) while also seeking out new ways to critique and refine his faith. Faith seeking understanding, for Westphal, necessitates one to seek and take seriously honest critique (philosophical and otherwise), which may be hostile to faith for the sake of understanding. Lent, particularly an atheistic Lent, should never be comfortable:

> *If there is ultimately a theological rationale for my serious exploration of these powerful secular forms of finitism—variations, if you will, on a Kantian theme—it is clear that this is possible only where there is a willingness to be put in question.* However imperfect my practice of this willingness, I have come to see it as an essential ingredient in faith as a virtue. . . . Such faith includes the trust that in this process one's relation to God will be deepened rather than destroyed, and that has been my experience. I don't have the world on a string (or God in a box), as I did when I first came to philosophy. *But I am convinced that I understand both God and myself (and my faith) better because of these losses.* What Jesus said about finding our life through losing it has many meanings, one of which, in my experience, pertains to the life of the believer engaging in philosophical reflection. (Matt. 10:39, 16:25)[23]

This lengthy quote shows us three key ideas underlying Westphal's fundamental theology that we will continually revisit: First, Westphal's approach to philosophy never wavers from a foundation in faith and he is never afraid to pronounce the faith-laden context from which he comes. Second, Westphal links his faith to these philosophical (i.e., atheistic) critiques of religion; both are concerned with the fact that "we are not God" (i.e., finitism), and by being put into question, Christians practice a necessary humility.[24] Finally, this ability to be put into question is a matter of discipleship. Putting himself into question—losing himself, or losing the safety and security that a comfortable, unquestioning faith permits—has given him a stronger sense of faith and has made him a better Christian.

All three notions continually return throughout Westphal's work, and it is of no surprise that they first find fertile ground in a Kierkegaardian faith. Perhaps this is why Westphal recalls his encounter with Kierkegaard as providential.[25] Therefore, in what follows, we trace how his Kierkegaardian faith influences his understanding of philosophy, especially postmodernism. Correspondingly, we explore how Westphal continually returns to the idea that Nietzsche is at once a kindred spirit to Kierkegaard and his foil. Westphal finds a suspicion toward modernity in both, enough to make them postmodernists as well as existentialists, but he eventually sides with Kierkegaard as a return to faith after suspicious cross-examination.

Kierkegaard's work is defiantly Christian, and above all, he continually placed the Christian's faith into question, arguing that Christianity is a task of a lifetime and not something that is fulfilled easily. This is essential for Westphal's concept of faith. In *Kierkegaard's Critique of Reason and Society*, Westphal highlights this when discussing Kierkegaard's description of "the inventor of the notion of defending Christianity in Christendom as Judas No. 2 and the attempt to develop historically grounded apologetics as blasphemy."[26] Furthering his analysis, Westphal argues that Kierkegaard's critique "includes the Kantian theme of the finitude of human reason" and that Kierkegaard expands on Kant, recognizing the social component to human reason and thus, as if presaging Gadamer, how it is affected by history.[27] In light of this, Westphal argues that "the finitude and sinfulness of human reason" is integral to reason's historicity, making Kierkegaard's critique of reason a critique of ideology. Accordingly, the fact that one cannot argue to faith through reason convinces Kierkegaard "that the final result [of such an apologetics] is *corrupted Christianity*."[28] If one cannot rely on a logical defense of her faith, then she must be willing to accept it as beyond reason, even resembling a form of Socratic divine madness.[29] Faith is a task or process and not a proposition to which one reasons: one cannot have faith; one must practice faith.[30] Kierkegaard solidifies this in his theory of stages, and Westphal's argument for a hidden Religiousness C is an argument to move beyond the contemplation of the paradox of Christ toward fulfilling the love commandment in the name of Christ. Thus, the final understanding, in faith seeking understanding, is to be fulfilled via service to God through loving the neighbor.

Similar to the three notions described earlier, Westphal's adaptation of Kierkegaard's stages follows the triptych-like pattern that Westphal developed early in his philosophical career. First, through Kierkegaard's explicitly Christian context, Westphal finds an uncomfortable faith. Second, this faith compels one to resist the relief and certainty of reason (particularly the certainty provided by apologetics). Third, this faith is always already placed into question with the hope and anticipation of strengthening the believing soul's understanding of that faith, particularly through service. This is how Kierkegaard becomes the postmodern foundation to Westphal's fundamental theology. For Westphal, this type of suspicious faith offers evidence for the claim that Kierkegaard himself is postmodern and that his work provides a foundation for not only suspicion toward modernity but also for a positive postmodernism. While postmodernity covers many areas and themes, Westphal, in his own philosophy, primarily utilizes the term in relation to its critique of modernity. He does not understand postmodernity to be only a critique of modernity, but his appropriation often follows this line of thinking.[31] This is a crucial feature of Westphal's faith seeking understanding; it allows him to maintain a faith while intensely scrutinizing it. This scrutiny also unites Kierkegaard with his fellow existentialist Friedrich Nietzsche, both of whom play a balancing act for Westphal's project of appropriating postmodernity for Christianity.

Westphal begins to unpack this appropriation by explaining his understanding of postmodernity before moving toward how he appropriates it. His first step is acknowledging that who or what counts as postmodern varies but that it is often "defined with reference to modernity. But there are so many modernisms."[32] In this sense, postmodernity is not a movement beginning at a particular time in history, but a countermovement to modernity (or modernities). This characterization of postmodernity gives witness to the fact that we are still "moderns,"[33] according to Westphal, insofar as our economic, legal, and political structures (in addition to the moral and cultural constructs that undergird them) are still deeply grounded in what counts as modernity. The *post* in postmodernity is therefore a critique (or deconstruction, from a Derridean perspective) of modernity,[34] but it is never without modernity itself; it is never something completely, or even remotely, new.[35] For Westphal, this justifies his belief that Kierkegaard and Nietzsche are postmodernists.[36]

Westphal often refers to them as postmoderns since both have "graduated from being the founding fathers of existentialism to being the unfounding fathers of a postmodernism that is nervous about all father imagery."[37] Existentialism, for Westphal, is linked to postmodernity since it is a direct challenge to a metaphysical understanding of the world that, in the Enlightenment especially, attempts to see the world as an absolute whole; to see the world *sub specie aeternitatis.*[38] Kierkegaard's existentialism challenged a Hegelian holism in an "attempt to rescue Jerusalem from Athens," that is, an attempt to retrieve Christianity from Christendom.[39] Nietzsche, however, employed his existential critique to destroy both Jerusalem and Athens on the grounds that Christianity is mere Platonism and that both enslave the self.[40] In *Suspicion and Faith,* Westphal notes that "Nietzsche sees Reason as an ersatz god through whom modern secularism seeks to salvage as much of God as possible. Having directed suspicion toward religion and its works, he continues in the direction of what Habermas calls 'totalized critique' by subjecting Reason and Enlightenment to the same suspicion."[41] When postmodern authors assert that "the truth is that there is no Truth," Westphal sees them as following both Nietzsche and Kierkegaard in acknowledging how deeply situated we are in the world—how deeply embedded we are in the Socratic cave, as Westphal puts it—and how extricating ourselves from this circumstance is impossible. "We are always *in medias res,*" Westphal summarizes, "and can never stand at the Alpha or Omega point where Truth can be had."[42]

One can gather from his understanding of postmodernism and existentialism a pointed critique of the self's limitations—similar to the Kantian finitism that has been previously mentioned—but also a strong concept of original sin. Westphal thus calls these masters of suspicion "secular theologians of original sin."[43] Their suspicion toward our lack of access to the Truth parallels Kierkegaard's claims regarding humanity's fallen nature. For all involved, whether God exists is beside the point: the fact remains that "we are not God," nor could we attain a God-like all-encompassing knowledge. Where some opponents of postmodernism see the abandonment of the search for Truth as a rallying cry for anarchy and relativism, Westphal sees a profoundly religious sentiment: "If Nietzsche is right in [his understanding of] the will to power, then everything tends to absolutize it-self, to treat the world as its oyster, as the collective means to its own flour-ishing. In its content, monotheistic religion provides a powerful challenge to this tendency among human selves and societies."[44]

Westphal's remarks ring a familiar bell, but they are nevertheless as-tonishing given Nietzsche's view of monotheistic religion: how could any-one who wrote that "Christianity in particular should be dubbed a great treasure-chamber of ingenious consolations—such a store of refreshing, soothing, deadening drugs it has accumulated within itself" ever be used alongside Christianity?[45] For Westphal, Nietzsche's theological importance comes from his outsider perspective and his external critiques of theology and religion turns the actions of Christians and their professed beliefs against themselves. For Westphal, this outsider perspective is taken up into faith as a form of self-reflection, a Lenten reflection that moves the believer "from penance to penitence to repentance."[46] One can recognize a *West-phalian Aufhebung*, or appropriation, since Nietzsche's critique of religion is taken up into religion—via Kierkegaard no less, as detailed later—in the process of reflection and discipleship.[47]

Westphal's *Aufhebung* of Nietzsche can be seen in "Nietzsche as a Theo-logical Resource," the final chapter in *Overcoming Onto-theology*. Here, he recounts Nietzsche's version of the "hermeneutics of finitude," but then he surprisingly aligns it with the writings of Paul, noting that Nietzsche's per-spectivism echoes a sentiment of "how badly we want to see reality face-to-face, [but] we only see 'in a mirror, dimly,' even 'in a riddle' (1 Cor. 13:12). So [Nietzsche] speaks of truth as 'linguistic legislation,' as 'customary meta-phors,' and as 'illusions about which one has forgotten that this is what they are.'"[48] Establishing Nietzsche's critique as running parallel to the Chris-tian prophetic tradition, via Paul, already sublimates Nietzsche's critique into the tradition itself. However, this appears to be as far as Westphal can take Nietzsche in that he immediately returns to Kierkegaard's similar re-marks about how "existence itself is a system—for God, but it cannot be a system for any existing spirit."[49] For Westphal, a hermeneutics of finitude and suspicion makes Nietzsche a great diagnostician, but one must look elsewhere for a remedy.[50] Similarly, Westphal remarks that a hermeneutics of suspicion, and likewise a postmodernism solely focused on critique, will lead only to despair.[51]

Kierkegaard, however, leads one out of despair through his critique of Christendom and his concept of faith. In *Overcoming Onto-theology*'s chapter

"Positive Postmodernism as Radical Hermeneutics," Westphal again aligns Nietzsche with Kierkegaard, but this time he elevates Kierkegaard's faith above Nietzsche's critique, creating a positive postmodernism that moves beyond a mere critique of reason and modernity toward a concept of society (an "up building" of society, if you will) based on faith seeking understanding. In what he admittedly calls a "sketch argument" in need of development, Westphal cites Nietzsche's commentary on the Dionysian faith in *Thus Spoke Zarathustra*, which finds Nietzsche hopelessly writing: "In the end, one only experiences oneself."[52] Thus, while revealing modernity's allergy toward alterity (hence, the eternal return of the same), Nietzsche also reveals his own aversion to alterity: "Nietzsche remains . . . more the child than the enemy of modernity, not just in the passages cited, but throughout his writings. For they are the quest for a form of autonomy far more extensive than anything modernity ever dreamed of."[53]

This is a puzzling claim in its density and needs some unpacking. For one, there is a conflation of exposing an aversion to alterity and stating that one is always averse to alterity. Moreover, Westphal never explains the way in which *Nietzsche himself* shows such an aversion in his writings. Given Nietzsche's writing style, which, like that of Kierkegaard, crosses genres and voices, in addition to his reception throughout scholarship, Westphal's argument is rather underdeveloped. One might wish that Westphal had devoted a singular text to this argument. However, for our present scope, what is important is what Westphal states when he contrasts Nietzsche with Kierkegaard and argues that Kierkegaard's "authorship is a sustained attempt to spell out the conditions of the possibility of encountering the genuinely other."[54] Westphal quickly notes that Kierkegaard's famous individualism, unlike Nietzsche's, is not the final word but is "penultimate," since "it seeks to expose the crowd (Nietzsche's herd) as a strategy for collectively warding off any truly other, in order to open the essentially relational self . . . to the thoroughgoing otherness of God and the other."[55] By welcoming the other and God, Westphal claims that Kierkegaard is "more *radically* postmodern than Nietzsche."[56] Hence, Westphal's postmodern critique of faith and reason always leads back to faith.

Following the three notions laid out here, Kierkegaard's radically postmodern thought deepens Westphal's understanding of faithful discipleship: beginning with faith, the believing soul opens herself to postmodern critique laced with a hermeneutics of suspicion, putting herself into question. This reminds her that we humans are all too human and that our lofty

Truth claims can never achieve their aims of absolute knowledge. From there, postmodern critique leads her to understand faith from a perspective that does not require absolute knowledge but absolute discipleship and love toward the other. In this way, Westphal's appropriation of postmodernism follows a similar pattern of self-critique and discipleship that he himself discovered through his own faith seeking understanding. This paradigm is the foundation of what I call Westphal's fundamental theology: it sets out the parameters of how faith dialogues with reason and establishes why it is necessary to hold such a dialogue. Since he always begins with faith, this dialogue primarily functions as an appropriation, or a Westphalian *Aufhebung* in which religious critique (as seen through reason) is taken up by faith in the service of seeking understanding. One thing to note about his use of suspicion, here, is that he has begun to develop it as an appropriation for a theological project. In his earlier scholarship, Westphal often discussed a hermeneutics of prophecy, as we reviewed earlier. In his postmodern writings, however, he transitions to merely calling it a hermeneutics of suspicion, perhaps because this hermeneutics is more self-critical and focuses on an inward self-critique. However, it still contains a sense of prophecy, in the religious sense, because it is inspired by faith and is used to correct (and thereby better understand) faith.

QUAERENS: Westphal's Epistemological Hermeneutics

Westphal's appraisal of the failure of the Enlightenment project rests on its desire for complete understanding and absolute Truth, as explained earlier. Not surprisingly, Westphal targets Hegel's philosophy as a prime example, thereby making Kierkegaard into an advocate against the Enlightenment project. Additionally, he brings Nietzsche into the fold to create a dual critique against both the temples of reason and basilicas of Christendom, as he often calls them. To complete this critique, however, Westphal eventually employs another duo—Gadamer and Derrida—to explain how one moves from critique to prescription. As disciples of Heidegger,[57] both present different paths of hermeneutical theory at the end of metaphysics. In what follows, we explore those paths by first understanding how the critique of metaphysics marks an end to the absolutization of truth. From there, we explore Westphal's appropriation of Gadamer, whose hermeneutics, he argues, are just as radical as Derrida's deconstruction while also maintaining a connection with tradition and history.

Westphal contends that metaphysics, as a "project of rendering the whole of reality intelligible to human understanding," is the clockwork behind an epistemic tradition that the Enlightenment inherited.[58] Including Aristotle and Hegel as the high-water marks of this tradition, Westphal agrees with the postmodern attempt to abolish this faulty project. While he continually articulates this abolishment through Heidegger's critique of onto-theology, later in his career he situates this in a Kantian framework, a framework I think was the impetus for his exploration of Heidegger all along. This is because his work on Heidegger's onto-theological critique of metaphysics recalls Westphal's Kantian finitism while showing the same pattern of faith seeking understanding. It thus is our entry into Westphal's understanding of onto-theology.

In "The Importance of Overcoming Metaphysics for a Life of Faith," Westphal explains this Kantian foundation through Kant's *Critique of Pure Reason* along with Kant's later work, *Religion within the Limits of Reason Alone*. Focusing on those two works, Westphal develops three theses: metaphysics is impossible, metaphysics is not necessary, and metaphysics is dangerous.[59] The first thesis aligns smoothly with the Kantian finitism described earlier,[60] and therefore is assumed. His second and third theses, however, reveal Westphal's distinctive interpretation of Kant's analysis of the possibility of knowledge and his famous denial of knowledge to allow room for faith; therefore, we focus on these.

Westphal argues his second thesis by exploring the need for evidence to believe in God, noting that Kant says it is necessary "that one should convince oneself" in order to have belief, but that it is not necessary "that [God's] existence should be demonstrated," effectively distinguishing speculative and practical reason.[61] Westphal then demonstrates how this distinction allows room for belief in God's existence within speculative reason, but as a means of knowledge, God's existence is a priori, as seen from within practical reason, and thus passes "beyond the limits of all possible experience."[62] For Westphal, the result is that God's existence, as logically prior to all existence and therefore beyond experience, consequently requires no scientific or demonstrative proof. What Westphal is demonstrating is that a metaphysical proof for God's existence can be avoided altogether by focusing on how Kant limits theoretical knowledge, eschewing the appropriate need for rational proof via metaphysics. Thus, he quotes Kant at length from *The Critique of Pure Reason* (the brackets are Westphal's own commentary):

Reason has, in respect of its practical employment, *the right* [emphasis added] to postulate what in the field of mere speculation it can have no kind of right to assume without sufficient proof... in the practical sphere reason *has rights of possession* [emphasis added], of which it *does not require to offer proof* [metaphysics is not necessary], and of which, in fact, "it could not supply proof [metaphysics is impossible]."[63]

Westphal goes on to develop in Kant's work two possibilities for understanding God without metaphysics, but what is important at present is that Westphal's anti-metaphysical posture, along with his lifelong appreciation for Kant's finitism and critique of metaphysics, is connected to his issues with apologetics, or at least a negative apologetics that attempts to rationally defend faith, that is, to use reason to defend the unreasonable.[64] If the apologeticist is Judas for Westphal, as mentioned earlier, then perhaps metaphysics is his thirty pieces of silver: Judas has betrayed the Godhead for a measure of metaphysical security that leads only to despair.

This despair leads to danger, his third thesis against metaphysics. The primary danger of metaphysics, according to Westphal's reading of Kant, is its "dogmatism," whereby metaphysics effectively silences all dialogue as it seeks and claims its monopoly on Truth and all subsequent truth claims.[65] Westphal effectively claims that metaphysics is the metanarrative par excellence, as all dialogue about truth is sacrificed to a particular, assumedly universal Truth. More accurately, Westphal summarizes the danger of metaphysics to the life of faith as twofold:

Formally speaking, it consists in the arrogant claim of philosophical speculation to the highest tribunal by which all questions of right (*quid juris*) regarding our God talk are to be settled, without whose *Nihil Obstat* and *Imprimatur* our religious beliefs are to be considered mere opinion if not outright superstition. Substantively speaking, metaphysics is dangerous because when God has been reshaped to fit the Procrustean bed by which it defines rationality, what remains is both different from and less than the God of faith.[66]

In other words, Westphal argues how our metaphysics-laden thought threatens (if not severs) our relationship with God, as it is intrinsic to our own quest for the absolute, to become—like Adam and Lucifer before us— "like the Most High."[67] For Westphal, Kant's discovery of the problems and dangers of metaphysics is a watershed moment that eventually begets the hermeneutical turn in philosophy, our second "Copernican Revolution."[68]

To dramatize the seriousness of this point, Westphal even proclaims Kant to be the "Luther in the Church of Reason. Just as the earlier German had defended the priesthood of all believers against the monopoly claims of the Pope . . . so Kant opposes a populism of reason to the philosophical popes that make up the schools."[69] Continuing this tradition for Westphal is another German, Martin Heidegger.

Westphal raises Heidegger's critique of onto-theology often and with different emphases but always with the same refrain: Heidegger's critique is against a metaphysics that demands that God enter into its understanding merely to verify what it knows as Truth while playing the silent and distant role of approving what human thought deems as knowledge. We can see shades of a *nihil obstat* and *imprimatur* in this critique as well. Through onto-theology, Westphal argues that "philosophy makes the rules that God must play by" while humanity dictates how God can or should enter into the world; it bleeds the *mysterium tremendum et fascinans* from our relationship with God.[70] As only *causa sui*, this God leads to ideologies of self-legitimization.[71] Thus imprisoned, God becomes only a tool in our own will to power.[72] While Westphal acknowledges that there is more to Heidegger's onto-theological critique than this, his interests in onto-theology essentially center on this issue.

Westphal continually emphasizes this formulation of Heidegger's critique throughout his postmodern work. In several ways, it functions as a contemporary rendition of Kantian finitism, and as such, it marks where Westphal begins to formulate his hermeneutical epistemology.[73] For Westphal, the death of metaphysics and its quest for the absolute not only ends (or at least marks the frivolity of) at the Enlightenment project but also reveals the death of an epistemology born of this project, one that attempted to give legitimizing foundations for our knowledge. This, for his anti-postmodern friends, is where the cry of "anything goes" originates: if one has no absolute Truth, then how can one make any truth claims at all?[74]

Westphal answers this question through hermeneutics and, eventually, through a hermeneutical phenomenology. Westphal's main hermeneutical influence comes from Gadamer and his masterwork, *Truth and Method.*[75] To focus only on how Westphal goes from a critique of metaphysics to a hermeneutical phenomenology and what that transition means to his fundamental theology, we narrow our scope to how he appropriates Gadamer's hermeneutics. We first look at what Westphal's hermeneutics rejects and then how it expresses an existential epistemology.

Westphal's hermeneutics follows Gadamer in that it shuns any attempt at interpretation as a process of reconstructing and reexperiencing the author's original intent, which purportedly leads to one true (i.e., absolute) interpretation. Westphal rejects this under the charge that it fluctuates between psychologism and objectivism.[76] Regarding the claim of objectivism, Westphal points to this method of interpretation's need for having a "determinate and unchanging object (for which role the author's intention is a splendid candidate)" and its reliance on normativity through its need to validate itself via "determinate and unchanging . . . rules or canons."[77] When Westphal critiques these two principles, he yet again follows the theme of finitism, arguing that these principles reveal the impossibility of a complete interpretation.[78] In contradistinction to this normativity through methodology, Westphal points to the *ontological* nature of Gadamer's hermeneutics where ontology "signifies . . . that interpretation belongs as a fundamental feature to the being-in-the-world of the being that each of us is."[79] Westphal claims that seeing interpretation as a part of being-in-the-world—as one exists in the world, one is always already within the world—effectively radicalizes and deregionalizes hermeneutics.

This hermeneutics is radicalized in that it finds nothing can be outside of interpretation, thus revealing how one experiences and interprets the world simultaneously. Rather than explaining his hermeneutics as an evolution of the prevailing interpretive method, Westphal, following Caputo, casts it as radical to express its revolutionary character.[80] This new hermeneutical method shatters the superficiality and objectivism of previous interpretative methods—in *Whose Community? Which Interpretation?* Westphal notes how these previous hermeneutical methods treat the text as a dead letter, like "a cadaver handed over for autopsy."[81] By teasing out the underlying structures of both the text and one's interpretation of it, Westphal intends to avoid this outcome, moving toward a type of deconstruction in which the text itself is treated as dynamic and living within the self's interpretation of it.[82] The radical nature of this interpretive method therefore reveals how the text and the reader (and, to a certain degree, the author) are interrelated.

This leads to a deregionalization in that hermeneutics no longer exists above or outside of the interpreter's own existence; there is no longer an abstract, True interpretation to which one can strive. This allows for an embeddedness by which one acknowledges how deeply entrenched she always already is in the world, accepting that her interpretations (be it of literature or general experiences) are also implanted in the world. We are confined to our experiences, in other words, and our experiences help dictate our interpretations. Westphal capitalizes on this concept through Gadamer's historically-effected-consciousness (*wirkungsgeschichtliches Bewusstsein*), which establishes the foundation for Westphal's own hermeneutical phenomenology as well as his biblical hermeneutics in *Whose Community? Which Interpretation?*

What is interesting about his use of Gadamer is how it becomes the foundation for revitalizing tradition within a postmodern critique of faith. In Westphal's phenomenology, this is where he employs a hermeneutical-existential methodology and, consequently, where his use of phenomenology becomes less of a hermeneutical phenomenology and more an existential hermeneutics that occasionally touches upon phenomenology as a method.

Gadamer's account of historicity emphasizes tradition while also being radical since his version of the hermeneutical circle recognizes and embraces the prejudices and biases of the self—both products of being-in-the-world—as general "modes of pre-understanding that already have the form of judgment."[83] For Westphal, this rehabilitates tradition as it is "the primary source of prejudices without which understanding, including critical understanding, would not be possible."[84] Tradition, as a part of a people's embodiment, becomes the way in which they belong to each other and to their pre-judicial means of interpretation; as such, it becomes the means by which they judge and interpret the world. One could call this simply a historicity, but for Westphal it goes much deeper. Gadamer's emphasis on tradition does not just embed historicity into a particular affiliation (or set of prejudices and modes of understanding); it also opens an avenue to embedding revelation within history through the relation between revelation and (sacred) tradition.

This recovery of tradition in an hermeneutical framework is the Archimedean point for Westphal's postmodern thought: if the believing soul is going to follow Westphal's second step of critiquing faith to seek understanding, and hence lose faith to find faith, then there must be a possibility for her to find her way *back* to faith. Even though Gadamer's explanation of the role of tradition in the hermeneutical circle can stand as any historical situatedness and not Tradition, in a divinely revealed (i.e., Christian) understanding, for Westphal, it allows for a journey back to a biblical faith and religious practice. Moreover, it also allows for critique and refinement of that tradition, which is why Westphal calls it radical and how he believes it escapes both the cries of relativism (anything goes) and John Caputo's claim that Gadamerian hermeneutics are "reactionary," "too comforting," and signal a return to the Enlightenment project's search for absolutes.[85] However, one must remember that pointing back to historicity prevents an "anything goes" philosophy only because it follows a rubric set by history. The charge of relativism is not completely evaded since one could argue for an alternate understanding of historicity. Postcolonial and feminist thought are but two emerging disciplines that show how history—as an interpretation of events—is fluid and changeable. One might ask Westphal, "Whose history? Which tradition?"

Westphal, in his presumed reply, might argue that this is emphatically the point: history and tradition are malleable as society moves toward a better understanding of past actions and prejudices; society is continually (ideally) in a state of seeking better interpretations. One can see this presumed reply through his biblical scholarship that understands that interpretations can change.[86] History changes but still can be relied on for interpretation since it creates our preunderstanding; when things change (as with postcolonialism), our sense of history changes but not our appeal to history itself for interpreting those changes. Here, his attempt is to move away from a metaphysical or onto-theological foundation for interpretation by emphasizing how past events are interpreted in our being-in-the-world and how they influence the interpretation of current and future events. Interpretation becomes fluid yet not relative since interpretations are grounded in prior (interpreted) experiences.

The radicality of this argument returns again to Westphal's general finitism. By striking through the surface of interpretation to get at the heart of the matter, Gadamer recognizes that interpretation is "an infinite task which can never be complete."[87] Like faith, for Westphal, interpretation is a task of a lifetime since it can never be completed because it is embedded in the self's "conflicting a prioris, pre-understandings, [and] prejudices, which cannot be added together to give us an increasingly determinate and stable common object [or common interpretation of an object]."[88] Commonality, or a mutually shared interpretation, is important but not necessary: even within ourselves we hold competing preunderstandings, prejudices, and so on, which are often irreconcilable yet nevertheless brought together to create an understanding, an interpretation.[89] For Caputo (via Derrida), breaking down these fusions of horizons (Horizontenverschmelzungen) is an essential aspect of deconstruction.[90] For Westphal (via Gadamer), it is an essential aspect for recontextualizing tradition and interpretation in a religious perspective. Moreover, this is how postmodern philosophy echoes—even plagiarizes—Christian revelation.

According to Westphal, this recontextualization happens only by accepting one's finite grasp on knowledge and dependence on historicity and tradition for interpretation. Westphal's main point, one could say, is this: We are not God . . . and that's OK! For us, the world will never be completely intelligible, and to attempt to make it so is to become a second Judas, the blasphemer who trades in his salvation for thirty pieces of metaphysical security, leading only to despair. Notably, this is the entire message of Christian revelation and salvation, and, sounding much like Martin Luther, Westphal makes this abundantly clear at the closing of his essay on Gadamer and Derrida:

> But for the Christian it is God who is Absolute and Infinite, not us; nor does our knowledge lose its relativity and its finitude by being about God, any more than we become purple by thinking about grapes. Just as we are not saved by good works morally speaking, we are not saved by good works epistemologically speaking, by attaining to a knowledge of God and of God's will that is adequate (in the philosophical sense of the term *adequatio intellectus et rei*) to its intended object. It's OK to see in a mirror dimly, or if you prefer the King James here, to see in a glass darkly. Just as God's ways are not ours, so God's thoughts are not ours. As theists, Kant and Kierkegaard remind us of this biblical truth.[91]

Behold again the refrain of a general finitism and losing one's faith to gain it. Moreover, this quote echoes Kierkegaard's proclamation that "existence itself is a system—for God, but it cannot be a system for any existing spirit."[92] One can also see the concept of total depravity emerging in his hermeneutics: throughout its intellectual history, humanity has often tried to hold a complete, objective understanding of the world; it has tried to be "like the most High," having forgotten about its own fallenness. Biblical revelation continually reminds Westphal of this through the prophets of the Old Testament, the Gospels of Jesus, and the Epistles in the New Testament. Through a Lutheran lens, Westphal wants us to accept our finite (sinful) nature and acknowledge that we can never obtain this complete knowledge, and with his appropriation of Kant and Kierkegaard, and eventually Heidegger and Gadamer, he wants us to be continually aware of our finitude when we interpret objects and when we acquire and use what stands for knowledge. That is, he wants us to be aware of our finitude at all times. Westphal's philosophical project therefore adheres to a Lutheran anthropology and a quasi-Lutheran hermeneutics.[93] His hermeneutics recognize human-ity's fallen nature and that God has given us timeless yet timely correctives, first articulated through Scripture and revelation (i.e., biblical truth), then echoed throughout history in human thought. Interpretation, as a general part of one's existence, becomes a task of a lifetime. This is integral to West-phal's concept of faith as a task of a lifetime and his concept of faith seeking understanding: both require constant vigilance and renewal as the believ-ing soul habitually forgets the finite nature of her thought.

Before we move on, let us review the many movements of Westphal's project we have covered. Westphal's philosophy is best read as a fundamen-tal theology since he always begins from a position of faith that engages in dialogue with philosophy (reason) in a process of better understanding and practicing that faith. In practice, this involves three steps: First, the believ-ing soul should firmly express (or confess) her faith and should acknowledge that this is the context from whence she comes. Second, she should seek a critique of this faith-laden context since she habitually forgets that she is not God and is finite. Finally, she should accept this critique as a matter of dis-cipleship to strengthen and to learn how to daily enact her faith. Westphal's goal throughout his scholarship is to cultivate these movements by focusing on philosophical critique. He finds that the critique of onto-theology aligns itself with biblical truth since both criticize the self's all-too-human desire for mastery or autonomy through acquiring a complete, objective knowl-edge (Truth). In refutation of this habitual attempt, one can turn to Scrip-ture or to philosophical critique, but either way one must be in a continual state of awareness and renewal: faith is the task of a lifetime.

This awareness and renewal is what led Westphal to write *Suspicion and Faith* as a means of correcting religious praxis gone astray. However, in an interesting turn, he calls this work a sequel to *God, Guilt, and Death,* his existential phenomenology of religion.[94] In *God, Guilt, and Death* he is ask-ing what the existential meaning of religion is, and in *Suspicion and Faith* he transitions from questioning that meaning to correcting its praxis.[95] We can see that Westphal connects a phenomenological description of religion with a corrective, prescriptive guidance of religious practice. This sets him apart from a strictly philosophical exploration of the meaning of religion and the comprehension of a possible God, placing him into a fundamental theo-logical discourse. Although he uses philosophical tools, he firmly embeds his project in a concept of Christianity that he hopes to explain and guide. This inevitably leads him to articulate an ethics founded on revelation and developed through Levinas and Kierkegaard. In our next section, we explore Westphal's use of phenomenology as the keystone of his thinking, looking specifically at how he founds it on a hermeneutics that allows for a prescriptive phenomenology and how this ends in the ethical encounter with the other, which is the culmination of Westphal's faith seeking understanding.

INTELLECTUM: WESTPHAL'S HERMENEUTICAL PHENOMENOLOGY

Westphal's engagement with phenomenology occurs early in his philosophical career and he never wavers from his initial conviction that phenomenology must be more than a purely descriptive, philosophical science. In his first three publications solely dedicated to phenomenology, Westphal is highly programmatic and does not actually use phenomenology to make distinctions and arguments; rather, he gives prescriptions for the use of phenomenology in philosophy and theology.[96] These initial prescriptions stem from the idea that the discipline of philosophy must be more than descriptive, that it cannot rest at making distinctions upon distinctions regarding how one thinks and acts in the world. It must be motivated toward a common good.

Permeating through his entire understanding of philosophy is the notion that the discipline should be a force of change; philosophical reflection must lead to an ethics. As we covered before, he levies this concern against Hegel's purely descriptive philosophy by arguing, "The time has come for understanding the world to become the guide for changing it . . . belief in the ability of the rational to actualize itself may well take the form of hearing the call to do whatever one can to assist in the actualization. Philosophy becomes political action."[97] Accordingly, hermeneutical phenomenology allows Westphal the possibility to express how political action can be rightly formed. Thus, phenomenology becomes a means to an end for Westphal, a way he can articulate and explore the possibilities of philosophical-political action. Moreover, these possibilities always stem from a faith that can be fulfilled only in an ethics, the ultimate aspect of his faith seeking understanding and the focal point of all theology.

Westphal's phenomenology attempts to move beyond Husserl since his view of Husserlian phenomenology is aligned with his views of modernity and the Enlightenment project; namely, that both represent a desire to create a True science, akin to the pursuit of absolute knowledge.[98] Rather bluntly, he finds that the Husserlian project rests on a "pipe dream," since philosophy as rigorous science fails in the same manner as the Hegelian project in that both wish to accomplish an impossible epistemology.[99] Eventually, this leads to his binding of Levinas and Kierkegaard through their respective critiques of Husserl and Hegel.[100] To simplify these movements in Westphal's thinking, we will briefly treat Westphal's critique of Husserl and address it only so as to understand how it motivates his hermeneutical phenomenology.

From his first publication to his most recent, Westphal's critique against Husserlian phenomenology has been remarkably consistent: he wants the phenomenologist to take a hermeneutics of suspicion seriously, and he wonders whether the discipline can survive as a proposed rigorous science if one takes such a suspicion to heart. Through Nietzsche, he critiques humanity's self-deception, which leads him to believe that the Husserlian phenomenologist must ask himself regarding such an account "whether his phenomenology can continue to be a philosophy of consciousness," or whether it must adapt its goals to a hermeneutical methodology that wholeheartedly accepts Nietzsche's critique.[101] Continuing with Nietzsche's suspicion of human self-interest and corruption, Westphal casts doubt on the viability of a transcendental phenomenology by noting that, no matter how well one tries to see him- or herself honestly, one will never be able to reveal one's true self.[102] Nietzsche's critique stands in contrast to "the transcendental psychology which Husserl sought to develop in that it refuses to take consciousness at its word, but rather treats it as a mask, a surface which conceals more than it reveals."[103] Yet again, one can see a finitism arising within Westphal's critique.

Westphal further develops this line of reasoning throughout his work. In advocating for a prophetic philosophy of religion, Westphal concedes that a "phenomenology of religion," as it stands, "is a descriptive enterprise;" meaning that its task is to describe religious phenomena and experience from a point of bracketing out truth claims about God's existence.[104] For Westphal, this is not an entirely bad methodology, and he uses it in *God, Guilt and Death* (from Merleau-Ponty and Ricoeur, not Husserl) to get at the existential meaning of religion.[105] However, what he finds problematic about this descriptive exercise is that it does not move toward the prescriptive and does not allow a space from which the believing soul can speak. At the heart of his concern is "whether a discipline [i.e., phenomenology of religion] with such a discrepancy between methodology and subject matter could still be called scientific. . . . [M]y concern is whether such a discipline can serve as spiritual medicine in the crisis of our time."[106] Again, one can see shades of his critique against Hegel's purely descriptive philosophy. In the Husserlian model, however, he finds something more sterile since this methodology cuts itself off from the soul of religion, that is, the praxis of religion: "What reason do we have to think that a scientific phenomenology of religion (assuming it to be possible in some sense) would have any healing words to address to the specifically religious crisis of our time, since it has so assiduously cut itself off from religious involvement in order to give us disinterested descriptions?"[107]

In response to this question, Westphal suggests a prophetic model that takes into consideration that "there are . . . characteristics of prophetic speech that philosophers of religion might well seek to imitate. I have in mind particularly its character as *personal, untimely, political,* and *eschatological.*"[108] It is this pivot from a critique of Husserlian phenomenology to a prophetic phenomenology of religion that defines Westphal's entire project.

Against this Husserlian model Westphal embraces Paul Ricoeur's methodology and Levinas's phenomenological ethics. In Ricoeur, it seems that Westphal has found a foothold on a phenomenology that takes the believing soul's faith seriously while also keeping a hermeneutics of suspicion intact to aid and guide that believing soul.[109] Westphal's reading of Ricoeur connects his hermeneutics to a phenomenological description of religion, primarily through the notion that understanding the world is a matter of interpretation, not intuition.[110] Furthermore, this interpretation always already takes place in a hermeneutical circle, as Westphal argues using Gadamer's work. This further solidifies the link between Westphal's hermeneutics and phenomenology, in which one must be aware of her own prejudices and, following Nietzsche, her own self-deceptions before entering into phenomenology.[111] Westphal appropriates from Ricoeur a way to reject Husserl's phenomenology to formulate a phenomenological understanding through hermeneutics.[112] For example, he sees in Ricoeur a way to thoughtfully approach Scripture's importance to the believing soul and to philosophically express that importance to others. Ricoeur, Westphal notes, does not see religious texts as merely for the religious—much like how the religious critiques of the masters are for both the religious and the nonreligious. In this way, Westphal sees Ricoeur's project as a continuation of the Aristotelian quest for the good life in which (following Kant) one inevitably passes through religion.[113] Ricoeur's thought is a marriage of sorts, for Westphal, between philosophical-critical thinking and religious thinking, as both aid each other in the search for the good life:

The phenomenological and philosophical tasks that we have seen him distinguish . . . are blended together. On the one hand we have the description of a religious account of the normative "sieve" through which any account of the good life must pass; on the other hand, and at the same time, Ricoeur's wager is that reflection on biblical texts will "give rise to philosophical thinking," in other words, will guide us to truth about who we are and how we should live, whether or not we are believing, practicing Jews or Christians.[114]

Given what we have covered, it is difficult to discern from such a statement whether Westphal finds a foundation for his philosophical-theological project in Ricoeur or whether he reads Ricoeur through his own project.[115] What is clear, however, is that in Ricoeur, Westphal sees a willing ally to argue that philosophy can keep its discipline and embrace an account of the religious believing soul while striving toward the good life. The question remains, however, as to what the good life is for the believing soul (and for Westphal).

Westphal focuses much of his concern for the good life (and his prescriptive phenomenology) on the accounts of revelation he reads through Levinas and Kierkegaard. Revelation, in a Levinasian sense, happens when the "horizontal" nature of the self's relationship with the other (i.e., the object of my intentions) renders a verticality, where verticality is a spatial metaphor in which one's world opens up to a greater sense of existence. These moments are rare, to be sure, but for Westphal they point to why, exactly, the other matters to us from an experiential perspective, to why we cannot have to account for only ourselves. Westphal sees Levinas's ethics as first philosophy as a way to express what happens when one ethically enacts faith: how the Lord, in effect, becomes present when one lives his or her faith among others. The good life, from this account of revelation, is understood through one's obligation to the other and its benevolent consequences for the self. From Kierkegaard, Westphal sees that God, through revelation, has commanded us to love the neighbor, following a similar trajectory to Levinas. In this way, Westphal presents an understanding of faith that begins and ends with revelation: the revelation of God's self commands us to love the other and, in doing so, gives us a greater understanding of God. Revelation begins and ends faith seeking understanding.

In what follows, we explore how he appropriates from both Levinas and Kierkegaard an account of revelation that promises and commands. To simplify his reading of these authors, we emphasize two important concepts:

First, revelation can be seen as a phenomenological event that has major implications for the relationship between self and other. Second, this relationship further emphasizes the ethical obligation found within the event of revelation, explaining that revelation upends the self's desire for autonomy and mastery in service of the other. We explore this primarily through Levinas, but on this final note, we will see how Westphal brings Kierkegaard into the dialogue to show how revelation's upending of the self begins with faith.[116]

Regarding revelation as a phenomenological event, Levinas asks whether society has "been duped by morality," and whether reason has been reconstituted to be a handmaiden to violence.[117] Formulating his response, Levinas focuses on the issue of transcendence and the self. He begins by inverting the relationship between ethics and ontology by arguing that a Heideggerian ontology is totalizing in nature and holds a tendency toward violence. By positing ethics, rather than ontology, as first philosophy, the self's response to the other either opens the self toward an infinite transcendence or, conversely, closes the self from transcendence through the self's totalization and utilization of the other. Westphal states that Levinas's intentions in reversing the places of ethics and ontology are twofold: First, Levinas wants to preserve the connection between metaphysics and transcendence, and he believes that what we usually call Western metaphysics has largely been an attempt to eliminate or at least domesticate transcendence. Second, Levinas believes that giving primacy to the category of being has played a major role in this project that has turned reason into the ally of war. Being is epistemologically problematic insofar as being is understood as that which gives itself to human understanding to be thought, making human horizons the measure of meaning and truth. Being is ethically problematic since, as *conatus essendi*, it is the measureless self-assertion of the same over against any other—natural, human, or divine.[118]

Levinas expresses these claims through ethics, arguing that violence toward the other dehumanizes not only the other but also the self. Conversely, when the self recognizes the other as another self, the face of this other self expresses an absolute otherness. It is something that is recognizable but also entirely different. This otherness, through its difference to the self, opens the self to a possible self-transcendence toward infinity (or an infinite number of possibilities, an infinite transcendence) while simultaneously preventing any relativization of the other's selfhood or reducing of the other self to a means toward an end.[119] The face of an other therefore becomes an incarnation of infinity because it presents (the possibility of) infinity to the self. Westphal's capitalization of the Levinasian metaphor of the face emphasizes how the face of an other overflows with an absolute otherness that tears away from the self any motivation toward using or possessing the other. In the face of an other, one can see not only one's own humanity but also all of humanity: "It is face-to-face with the other that I experience the claim that puts my project of being the center of the world in question. The immediacy of the ethical relation is not that of intuitionism, for I am not gazing at an object or proposition but am the one looked at, spoken to. This is the infinity of another person incarnate in a face."[120] However, I press Westphal to be careful with the term *incarnation* in Levinas's work, as the face does not become the possibilities of infinity but rather points toward them. It is a *disincarnation*: while it represents a possibility of infinity, the face of an other does not become this possibility in and of itself. It only points to such a possibility and does not become this possibility. This concern aside, Westphal uses this concept of infinity within the face to explore a concept of radical alterity that may be seen in the self-other relationship, which leads to a responsibility and obligation within that relationship.

This responsibility can be seen as an obligation and understood through ethics: the self finds its ability to endure existence through interrupting (the totalizing) self-desire through the shared mutuality of respect seen within the self-other relationship, as well as for the self living for the other.[121] Moreover, because the face of the other can be understood as an (dis)incarnation of infinity, the obligation to the other becomes limitless as well. In this way, the claims put onto the self by the other are not only horizontal in the face-to-face but also radically above the self. This is represented in a double asymmetry where one is obligated to the face before oneself as well as obligated to all faces, especially toward the most vulnerable of all faces as seen in the widow, orphan, and stranger. This rends the self's understanding of the world, revealing an infinity to the self through its self-emptying and self-surpassing obligation.

It is through this revealing that any access to an infinite transcendence occurs for the self and thus where any access to God or what may be called God. Through the face-to-face, infinity expresses itself—in person, as it were—or, channeling Plato and Aristotle, καθαυτό, meaning through or by means of itself.[122] As Levinas puts it in *Totality and Infinity*, "The face of the other at each moment destroys and overflows the plastic image it leaves me. . . . It does not manifest itself by these qualities, but καθαυτό, it expresses itself."[123] What Levinas is appealing to is the notion that the infinite can reveal itself through the finite and, in this case, the privileged instance of the face. The singular, finite self is rent by the infinite possibilities found within the face of the other. This is a firsthand experience that the self can experience only through the other. The issue is one of epistemic immediacy, and what is revealed in the face. In this experience, part and whole are inseparable but distinguishable. The face, and the infinity seen through the face, are neither representations of the whole nor functioning parts in an ontological metaphysics of presence. They exist relationally to each other such that the part (the face of the other) opens the self to a greater other. There is a transition, in other words, which begins with the face-to-face encounter that may lead to a larger encounter with a greater Other (infinity, or what may be called God). For Levinas, this opening to a greater other is part and parcel of revelation, which can be experienced only through a relational, mutual engagement between the self and another self. Going back to ethics as first philosophy, everything is understood by us in its engagement with us, and this relationship is expressed, καθαυτό, in the radical alterity of the face.

It is this moment of revelation that, for Westphal, connects Levinas with Kierkegaard. This is also where he expands and details his third account of revelation: a revelation that occurs through the self's encounter with an other. Starting with Levinas's initial ambition to establish ethics over ontology, what one gathers from Levinas's phenomenology is an emphasis on the points at which an event occurs that cuts through all what Westphal calls a priori constructs, the "already saids," or conditions of possible experience; this leaves one with only the transcendence of the event in the face-to-face encounter itself. On this point, Westphal notes the connection with Kierkegaard, who is also concerned with the moments that cut through our well-reasoned understanding of the world. While Levinas is concerned with the way Heideggerian ontology totalizes, Kierkegaard fights a similar battle concerning the Hegelian notions of reason and autonomy. Both of these men are concerned with a moment of transcendence that cannot be rationalized but must be enacted.

Westphal summarizes this point by stating that "the claim [being made by both men] is rather that there is an exception to the sovereignty of these *a priori*'s, an immediacy that cuts through them, traumatically calling us (along with these defenses, for that is how both Levinas and Kierkegaard view them) into question and taking us hostage. The exception is the immediacy called revelation."[124] Looking at Kierkegaard, we can see this notion of immediacy cutting through everything in its path through *Fear and Trembling*, where the immediacy of Abraham's encounter with God (where *immediacy* means "beyond human horizons," not the so-called mediated word of God from which God speaks) compels him to act in a way that can be understood only through the discourse of faith and the notion of the knight of faith. This encounter comes by way of a command and voice of God that voice breaches all forms of mediation between Abraham and the world.[125]

Westphal's reading of *Fear and Trembling* rests on the notion that Abraham must teleologically suspend *Sittlichkeit* (the ethical) to follow God's commandment to sacrifice Isaac, as we have previously seen. Moreover, Westphal reads Kierkegaard's pseudonyms Johannes De Silentio and Johannes Climacus as a dialogue: De Silentio argues that revelation, seen as God's commandment to humanity, should supersede all humanly conceived ethics, and thus it functions as an ideology critique. Climacus argues that revelation is a maieutic process of recollection and recognition where the self internally comes to accept and recognize a revelation that is outside of itself.[126] Westphal situates these two forms of revelation beside Levinas's concept of revelation that relies on the self's obligation to the other. "Just as revelation for Levinas is immediate," Westphal concludes, "that is independent of [a priori] conditions, so for Climacus revelation means not merely that the teacher presents the learner with some knowledge not already possessed, but most importantly, also the condition for recognizing it as truth. Only when the teacher gives the truth in this double sense does the relation to the teacher become essential."[127] For Westphal, this shows how both Levinas and Kierkegaard require revelation to be independent of the self, yet also require the self's participation either in recognizing revelation or in following what is commanded through revelation. What is commanded, for both men, is an obligation to the other.[128]

Through the self's acknowledgment that what has been received is in fact revelation, the self also acknowledges the obligations in the content of said revelation. Revelation becomes, then, an epistemic command that opens the self to a greater understanding through action. Revelation becomes the source and the commanded task within faith; it requires discipleship, in other words. This discipleship, or obligation, becomes the final movement of faith seeking understanding and the reason it is a task of a lifetime: for the self to receive faith, the self must accept an account of revelation, and to accept that account, the self must enact the commandments found in revelation through the self's encounters in the world. Understanding the revelation event that spurs faith requires enacting that faith daily, at all times, in an asymptotic search for understanding the mysteries of revelation which initially stirs the self to become a believing soul.

Conclusion: Westphal's Pastoral, Fundamental Theology

Because it hinges upon first recognizing revelation—and thus begins with faith—and then seeking an understanding of that faith through discipleship and obedience to revelation, Westphal's philosophy is better understood as a theology. However, I do not argue this to denounce fundamental theology, or to take a swipe at Westphal himself. By calling him a fundamental theologian, I am merely trying to situate Westphal in his proper home, just as he did with the atheistic critiques of certain postmodern authors and the masters of suspicion. By placing him in fundamental theology—a genre discourse and academic discipline that heavily relies on the appropriation of outside disciplines for an internal, Christian dialogue—my hope is to find Westphal a place where his philosophy and theology can thrive and do some sorely needed good work. Westphal wants to correct faith through seeking understanding, so what better place to do so than from the pews of the church?

This does not mean that his work has no philosophical import—quite the contrary. He approaches his philosophical interlocutors with honesty and appreciation. However, his disdain for a logical defense of faith often leans on a presupposition of faith. Even though he establishes and articulates that the beginning of faith is accepting revelation, he evades a philosophical defense of this unfoundation. That creates tension for him as a philosopher of religion, particularly in a postmodern context that is critical of all presuppositions that refuse to be scrutinized.[129] Furthermore, some may find that his appropriation of postmodern thought is an abuse of his sources, particularly when it comes to how they sometime seem to be moving like chess pieces across his work: move Kant to A4, which sets up Heidegger's move to F6, which opens Kierkegaard to attack at H3. Checkmate, onto-theology.

One can see this throughout our review of his work, which reveals a confounding philosophical strategy imparted by Westphal in which he attempts to argue his points through several sources rather than articulate them through a simplified and singular voice. Perhaps this strategy is related to a Protestant, *sola scriptura* ethos that seeks to find understanding primarily (and sometimes only) through the Bible. Theological inquiry into belief within this tradition begins (and often ends) with the Bible. Moreover, proving one's point through Scripture is essential because Scripture in and of itself holds the classic wisdom revealed by God through his prophets and, ultimately, through Jesus and his disciples. The dangers of proof texting Scripture to make one's point, however, are very real in this tradition, and an overreliance on interpretation or a sheer determination to make one's point certain can lead to disastrous, sinful, and violent conclusions. This concern corresponds to Westphal's motivation to write a book on biblical interpretation, which is one of my primary reasons for seeing a connection between this tradition and his own philosophical methodology of appropriation. Westphal sticks to his sources, in other words, just like his faith tradition. While this is an oversimplification of a complex relationship, I believe it reveals a truth in the way Westphal thinks.[130] On the one hand, he draws on texts (and shifting them about on the chessboard) to get to a point or to accomplish a greater understanding of faith, while on the other hand, he is not fully willing to abandon a more philosophical, scholarly account of reading them for their own sake. This tension is exhibited in his desire to carve a niche in philosophy for the prophetic: when one moves from making distinctions and descriptions (philosophy's primary task, according to Hegel and Husserl) to making prophetic prescriptions, there will inevitably be a loss of academic fidelity to one's sources and the philosophical distinctions they make.

Some may wish to levy the charge of proof texting against Westphal's appropriation, since he sometimes fails to read his sources in their own context or with enough breadth. The Continental tradition in which Westphal situates himself often devotes an almost slavish work ethic to critically understand the sources of that tradition; Derrida's *Speech and Phenomena,* for example, is a text that explores only one, singular aspect of Husserl's project and never tries to deviate or extrapolate from that aspect to make a larger case about Husserl's work or philosophy in general. In several ways, it is an exhausting, analytical text. It is only after such formative exercises that Derrida begins to explore the greater import of his discoveries in Husserl's work. Against this example, Westphal might reply that he himself performed a similar tutelage of Hegel and Kierkegaard in his early research. However, what marks a great distinction between the two is that Derrida eventually articulates his discoveries through his own voice, quoting sources when they enlighten an argument but never appropriating or otherwise basing his arguments solely on those sources.

Appropriation, in contradistinction to the Derridean example, is West-phal's modus operandi. Because of this, the philosopher might critique Westphal's postmodern work for playing too fast and loose with its sources. That is a fair charge given how quickly he moves between them, how he often uses sources to make a point. However, from a theological point of view, which as an academic discipline seeks to use human reason as an aid to comprehending faith and revelation, this is not a lack of rigor. Rather, it is pastoral, and pastoral theology has its own sort of rigor. Pastoral theology employs what is at humanity's disposal—that is, our own traditions of reason in tandem with our own recognized sense of God's revelation, however finite—to make the human condition better, to aid in crafting faith and belief. Westphal's work emerges as pastoral in the sense that he never forgets the human (all-too-human) condition, that even at his most cerebral he is still concerned with the task of faith, and that he continually attempts to formulate prescriptions for those within the church pews. This can be seen through the fact that three of his works (*Inflation, the Gospel, and Poortalk, Suspicion and Faith,* and *Whose Community? Which Interpretation*) are directly addressed to everyday churchgoers.

Importantly, rigor also exists in theology and especially in pastoral theology. Westphal's rigor is simply adhering to a different body of principles and methodologies, which is why it is necessary to distinguish between theological and philosophical discourses. Like philosophy, theology applies great emphasis on reading one's sources carefully and with an hermeneutical methodology that does not distort or misuse the ideas and notions in the text in question. However, one aspect that separates a theological discourse from a philosophical one is that theology does not take as its primary foundation methodologies that formulate reasonable arguments and conclusions. Westphal, with his critique of reason and metaphysics, follows a theological line by which all reasonable arguments and conclusions must submit to something that cannot be reasonably understood: namely, the ineffability of God. One's faith, through praxis, embodies this submission. Reason, therefore, is employed by the faithful in seeking understanding of this submission to God; thereby making God relatable and somewhat understandable while also remaining a mystery (i.e., one can come to know God but not completely). Westphal's theological rigor, therefore, is one based on fidelity to expressions of faith as seen through submission or acceptance of revelation and how one employs faith (i.e., praxis) in daily life. Rigor, here, is not based on methodology; rather, it is based on a fidelity to revelation and the praxis of faith. In service of this rigor, Westphal appropriates freely from philosophy to better understand these principles of faith. This is explored in the following chapter.

In conclusion, situating Westphal in his proper home in fundamental theology enhances his pastoral significance. It also reveals that his appropriation functions in a context that seeks to aid the believing soul, not in a context that is overly concerned with philosophical distinctions pertaining to understanding the nature of reason itself. Faith seeking understanding, as the backbone of Westphal's entire thought, effectively reveals and solidifies this fundamental-theological discourse at nearly every turn. Westphal the philosopher, then, is revealed to be more pastoral than philosophical. This is as it should be. He has based his entire philosophical career, after all, on St. Anselm's motto.

NOTES

1. As are several of his books, *OCOT* is cobbled together from published articles, with Westphal picking the ones that best represent his overarching arguments.

2. *OCOT*, ix. Immediately after this characterization, Westphal quickly dismisses the idea that postmodernity adheres to an "anything goes" philosophy. See also *OCOT*, 177–180.

3. Ibid., x.

4. Ibid., xi. Nietzsche, Heidegger, Derrida, Foucault, Lyotard, and Richard Rorty are specifically mentioned.

5. Ibid., xi. Emphasis is mine.

6. *SF*, 203, 213.

7. As mentioned in the introduction to this volume, fundamental theology, like postmodernism, has many definitions. For the sake of simplicity, fundamental theology is understood as a theological discipline operating through two movements. First is an inward, reflective exploration of the foundations of Christianity as a faith based on God's revelation. In this movement, fundamental theology seeks to understand Christianity's reception of revelation through Scripture and tradition. Second, it operates through an outward, dialogical exploration of understanding revelation (and subsequently doctrine) by engaging sources and disciplines that do not adhere to revelation as a basic principle. While this outward engagement often holds an apologetical line (and indeed fundamental theology has its historical roots in apologetics), it need not always be concerned with a rational defense. I situate Westphal as a fundamental theologian through this latter, outward movement: he does not give an apologetical defense of Christianity or revelation; rather, he seeks to better understand both through

an outward, philosophical engagement with postmodern thought. See Jean-Yves Lacoste, ed., *Encyclopedia of Christian Theology* (London: Routledge, 2005), 593–599.

8. See chapter 5 of this volume. In *KCRS* (88–94) Westphal expands on Kierkegaard's concept of revelation. See also Merold Westphal, "Johannes and Johannes: Kierkegaard and Difference," in *International Kierkegaard Commentary*, ed. Robert L. Perkins (Macon, GA: Mercer University Press, 1994), 13–46. In *TST* (142–177), Westphal turns to Barth's concept of revelation for his final chapter on how to speak about God before pivoting again to Kierkegaard's concept of faith as a task of a lifetime.

9. See chapter 1. See also *SF*, 213.

10. Merold Westphal, "Faith Seeking Understanding," in *God and the Philosophers*, ed. Thomas V. Morris (Oxford: Oxford University Press, 1994), 215–226.

11. Ibid., 16.

12. Ibid., 217.

13. This was the theme of this section of the text itself. See ibid., 215–216, where Westphal explains how he fell in love with philosophy as a discipline.

14. Ibid., 217.

15. *WCWI*, 18. In the note, Westphal states that he was first made aware of this ad by James K. A. Smith and that Smith himself wrote about the ad in his work *The Fall of Interpretation: Philosophical Foundations for a Creational Hermeneutic* (Downers Grove, IL: Intervarsity Press, 2000), 39. Smith, a philosopher of religion, is no stranger to the sort of conservative theological pushback that Westphal highlights; Smith's own work often deals with similar themes and issues. In addition to *The Fall of Interpretation,* he is the series editor for Westphal's *WCWI*. Smith's inaugural work in that series, *Who's Afraid of Postmodernism?* argues, on behalf of the forthcoming books in the series (Westphal's included), for a more open dialogue between conservative Protestant Christians and postmodernity.

16. Westphal, "Faith Seeking Understanding," 217.

17. Ibid.

18. Ibid., 218.

19. Again, an interesting aspect of Westphal's writing is its underlying Kantianism. Westphal often remarks that an aspect of this or that philosopher's work is Kantian, or resonates with Kantian finitism, but he typically leaves it as a presumption that the reader acknowledges where and how it is. Rarely does he write about Kant himself, save for brief sections in articles, and he specifically devotes major attention to Kant in only three articles and one chapter in *OCOT* ("Christian Philosophers and the Copernican Revolution"). The best sustained explanation of Kantianism permeating through his postmodern thought, which we review in the next section, is the following: Merold Westphal, "The Importance of Overcoming Metaphysics for the Life of Faith," *Modern Theology* 23, no. 2 (April 2007): 253–278; Westphal, "In Defense of the Thing in Itself," *Kant-Studien* 59, no. 1 (1968): 18–41; and Westphal, "Post-Kantian Reflections on the Importance of Hermeneutics," in *Disciplining Hermeneutics: Interpretation in Christian Perspectives*, ed. Roger Lundin (Grand Rapids, MI: Eerdmans, 1997), 57–66. See also Westphal, "Temporality and Finitism in Hartshorne's Theism," *Review of Metaphysics* 29 (March 1966): 550–564; *KCRS*, 4–6, 72–74, 88–90, 112–114; John Caputo, "Methodological Postmodernism: On Merold Westphal's *Overcoming Onto-Theology*," *Faith and Philosophy* 22, no. 3 (July 2005): 285–288. In the last article, Caputo effectively situates the underlying Kantianism in Westphal's work, particularly his hermeneutics.

20. This question is especially expressed in his early Hegel scholarship. See chapter 2. See also *HFM*, 135–148.

21. Westphal, "Faith Seeking Understanding," 221.

22. Ibid., 220.

23. Ibid., 221. The emphasis is mine. "Secular forms of finitism" refers to philosophical inquiries that are motivated by unbelief. On this page he explicitly mentions "Nietzsche's perspectivism, Heidegger's hermeneutical circle, and Derrida's deconstruction" as examples.

24. This is a quote Westphal is fond of using; see, for example, *OCOT*, 171–172, 187–196.

25. Westphal, "Faith Seeking Understanding," 221. See also *KCRS*, vii–viii.

26. *KCRS*, 22. The apologeticist as Judas and blasphemer! It is a wonder that neither Kierkegaard nor Westphal goes on to compare him with Peter's denial of Christ for the trifecta!

27. Ibid.

28. Ibid. Westphal is basing his remarks on *Sickness unto Death* and *Training in Christianity*. For more, see chapter 5 of this volume.

29. *KCRS*, 89. I cover this in detail throughout chapter 4.

30. In *KCF*, Westphal will make this the theme and message of the work itself. "Faith is a task word," he argues throughout. See 19, 22, 26, 64, 131, 255.

31. For an example of Westphal's broader sense of the postmodern, see James Marsh, John Caputo, and Merold Westphal, eds., *Modernity and Its Discontents* (New York: Fordham University Press, 1992), 128–161.

32. *OCOT*, 77. By so many modernisms he refers to artistic and literary movements in addition to philosophical movements.

33. *HFM*, vii.

34. See *OCOT*, 223–228; Merold Westphal, "Postmodernism and Religious Reflection," *International Journal of Religion* 38 (1995): 132–134.

35. *OCOT*, 79–81.

36. Ibid., 82.

37. Westphal, "Postmodernism and Religious Reflection," 134.

38. *OCOT*, 82, 132–135; Westphal, "Postmodernism and Religious Reflection," 133–135. Westphal originally quotes this Latin phrase as *sub specie aeterni*; I replaced it here with the original quote for ease.

39. Westphal, "Postmodernism and Religious Reflection," 134.

40. Ibid., 134. He quotes Nietzsche from *Beyond Good and Evil*, trans. Walter Kaufman (New York: Random House, 1966), preface.

41. *SF*, 226.

42. *OCOT*, 81.

43. See, for example, *SF*, 77, 230, 288.

44. *OCOT*, 288. See also "Nietzsche and the Phenomenological Ideal," 281, for an earlier version of this argument.

45. Friedrich Nietzsche, *On the Genealogy of Morals*, trans. Samuel Horace (New York: Dover Publications, 2003), essay 3, sec. 17, p. 94.

46. *SF*, 4.

47. For more on the Westphalian *Aufhebung*, see chapter 1.

48. *OCOT*, 290. Westphal quotes Nietzsche from *The Portable Nietzsche*, trans. Walter Kaufmann (New York: Viking Press, 1954), 44–47.

49. *OCOT*, 291.

50. This final chapter of *OCOT* follows a similar argument established in the final chapter of *SF*, "In Conclusion: The Dangers of Suspicion," 283.

51. *OCOT*, 141: "Such a discipline," Westphal contends, "may be good for our spiritual health, but by itself it is like a diet of nothing but ex-lax" in that it helps purge and purify ourselves of waste "but it satisfies no spiritual hunger."

52. Ibid., 145. Westphal gives only an in-text citation for the quote, but see also Friedrich Nietzsche, *Thus Spoke Zarathustra*, trans. Adrian Del Caro, ed. Adrian Del Caro and Robert Pippin (Cambridge: Cambridge University Press, 2006), 121.

53. *OCOT*, 145. See also ibid., 233–234, where Westphal argues that, by letting "Zarathustra's credo [goes] unchallenged, Nietzsche shows that he more nearly belongs to the onto-theological tradition than to its overcoming. To use language to which I shall return, Nietzsche is a Neoplatonist in the grips of ontological xenophobia."

54. Ibid., 145.

55. Ibid.

56. Ibid., 146.

57. Ibid., 156–158.

58. Ibid., 4.

59. Westphal, "Importance of Overcoming Metaphysics for the Life of Faith," 254–257.

60. In "Importance of Overcoming Metaphysics," Westphal devotes only a paragraph to this thesis, presuming that readers can easily gather this conclusion from their own knowledge of Kant (254).

61. Ibid., 254–255, he is quoting Kant from *The Only Possible Argument in Support of a Demonstration of the Existence of God*, in *Theoretical Philosophy, 1755–1770*, trans. David Waldorf and Ralf Meerbote (Cambridge: Cambridge University Press, 1992), 201. Further down, he solidifies this quote with *Critique of Pure Reason*, B xxi–xxii.

62. Ibid., 255. Westphal is quoting from *Critique of Pure Reason*, B xxi–xxi.

63. Ibid. Westphal is quoting from *Critique of Pure Reason*, A 776 = B 804.

64. At this point, it is worthy to note that not all consider Westphal antiapologetical. In *Reexamining Deconstruction and Determinate Religion*, Simmons and Minister explore a dialogue between Caputo and Westphal concerning "religion with religion." In that dialogue Simmons situates Westphal as an apologeticist in the sense that Westphal's work articulates and defends a positive apologetics that argues on behalf of the faith: "Ultimately," Simmons writes, "I find Westphal's philosophy to itself serve as a postmodern, Christian apologetics. He consistently demonstrates that being a postmodernist does not require abandoning the specific claims of one's historical religious tradition . . . even though it might cause us to rethink how those claims are affirmed and appropriated" (42). Simmons continues this argument with a parallel exploration of Justin Martyr's philosophical apologetics in which Christian truth claims are defended as both a defense on behalf of those truth claims and a method of clarifying and understanding them—a fundamental theology of sorts. In what I have argued, Westphal does, in fact, succeed as an apologeticist as Simmons portrays him, and in the following chapter I argue that *Transcendence and Self-Transcendence* works as a form of apologetics. However, as I have shown through Westphal's Kierkegaard scholarship, there is uneasiness in his thought concerning a philosophical defense of Christianity in the traditional vein of apologetics, where one can reason toward a faith and defend that faith without the presupposition of revelation. See J. Aaron Simmons and Stephen Minister, eds., *Reexamining Deconstruction and Determinate Religion* (Pittsburg, PA: Duquesne University Press, 2012), 24–60. Note that Westphal and Caputo respond to these claims in the final chapters of this book, and Westphal admits that he is "allergic" to the term *apologetics* (251).

65. Westphal, "Importance of Overcoming Metaphysics for the Life of Faith," 255.

66. Ibid., 259.

67. *OCOT*, 55. In the essay "Hermeneutics as Epistemology," Westphal effectively makes the same argument as above, albeit through Heidegger's critique.

68. This is another term Westphal is fond of repeating. See *OCOT*, chap. 8.

69. Westphal, "Importance of Overcoming Metaphysics for the Life of Faith," 257.

70. *TST,* 34–37.

71. See *OCOT,* 156–158, 205–207, 273–275. See also *TST,* 36, 148.

72. *TST,* 21. "The task of God is to make science possible," Westphal concludes, "and metaphysics will treat any God who shirks this responsibility as an illegal immigrant in the brave new world of modernity."

73. To see the many formulations of Heidegger's critique—variations on a theme if you will—see *OCOT,* 2–6, 30–34, 51–55, 119–122 (these sections relate Heidegger to Kant), 80–84, 231–235, 257–261, 264–266, 275–276, 288–286; *TST,* chap. 1 (Heidegger's critique is the essential foundation of the rest of the text); *LKD,* 13–14, 31–33 (via Levinas), 58–62, 138–139; Westphal, "Importance of Overcoming Metaphysics for the Life of Faith," 260–265; Westphal, "Whose Philosophy? Which Religion? Reflections on Reason as Faith," in *Transcendence in Philosophy and Religion,* ed. James Falconer (Bloomington, IN: Indiana University Press, 2003), 15–17; Westphal, "Onto-Theo-Logical Straw: Reflections on Presence and Absence," in *Postmodernism and Christian Philosophy,* ed. Roman T. Ciapalo (Washington, DC: Catholic University Press, 1997), 264–267. These are but a few of the many instances of Westphal's use of Heidegger's critique. What is most interesting is that in many of these texts, Westphal uses Heidegger as a foundation, or launching pad, for his own considerations of the limits of reason in the life of faith.

74. *OCOT,* 47–48.

75. Aligned with his biblical metaphor of Father Adam (Heidegger) and his feuding sons (Derrida and Gadamer), Westphal continually presents Heidegger as an instigator of the hermeneutical turn in Continental philosophy and will often enter into a Derridean version of hermeneutical theory to explain the hermeneutical turn, only to eventually critique Derrida in favor of a Gadamerian hermeneutics. This is often the core issue in his debates with John Caputo (See *OCOT* 135–138, "Gadamer and Derrida as Equally Radical," for a typical response by Westphal to Caputo and his Derridean radical hermeneutics). See also *OCOT,* 157–171 for Westphal's most thorough examination of Derrida's hermeneutics. For more on Caputo and Westphal, see chapter 8.

76. In *WCWI,* Westphal sets the two methods apart as "romantic hermeneutics" to be avoided. In their place he posits a Gadamerian hermeneutical method. See 29–34 (for summary), 35–56 (in detail). See also *OCOT,* 115, 133–135, 149–154.

77. *OCOT,* 150. This relates to his concern of the violence of canonicity and normativity. See chapter 1 of this book.

78. *OCOT,* 152–155. Westphal's references again point to a general Kantianism.

79. Ibid., 151.

80. Westphal more than likely is indebted for his own use of the term *radical* to Caputo's use in *Radical Hermeneutics.* Westphal continually cites Caputo and this book, directly addressing it at times (*OCOT,* 130), and Caputo's elevation of Derrida's deconstruction of Gadamer's hermeneutical theory is what causes Westphal to defend Gadamer as being equally radical as Derrida (135–138).

81. *WCWI,* 68. Westphal is quoting André LaCocque and Paul Ricoeur, *Thinking Biblically: Exegetical and Hermeneutical Studies,* trans. David Pellauer (Chicago: University of Chicago Press, 1998), xii.

82. *OCOT,* 130.

83. Ibid., 66. See also *WCWI,* 69–74.

84. *OCOT,* 67. This evokes Heidegger's concept of preontological understanding. For there to be any such discipline as ontology at all, Dasein must be familiar with being. That is, before making being into a theme of speculative science, Dasein is acquainted with being. Indeed, it is

this very acquaintance with being that leads Heidegger to take Dasein as the first central being to be investigated before investigating being itself. Dasein's basic, daily happening (or event-ing) comports our being in the moment and interpreting that moment in and through prior experiences. Dasein is understood as "ontico-ontologically prior" to understanding and can never be grasped immediately yet it is always adjoining us to the world and others—"*Dasein* is not only close to us—even that which is closest: we *are* it, each of us, we ourselves." Westphal, following Gadamer, is emphasizing the process in which those experiences help us interpret and understand current and future experiences. See Martin Heidegger, *Being and Time*, trans. John Macquarie and Edward Robinson (Oxford: Blackwell, 2001), 36–38, ¶5, 16–17.

85. *OCOT*, 68, 157. In a response to Caputo, Westphal quips: "Where is the excessive comfort in this unflinching acknowledgement of reason's inability to become self-sufficient by escaping the hermeneutical circle?" (70).

86. See *GTPD*, 204–205; *WCWI*, 78–82.

87. *OCOT*, 158: "[Following Heidegger,] Gadamer has seen the radical implications of Schleiermacher's recognition that the infinite whole(s) in terms of which the parts must be interpreted set for interpretation an infinite task that it can never complete."

88. Ibid.

89. Although Westphal does not, one could find the psychological term of cognitive dissonance as an example of when competing prejudices and pre-understandings are irreconcilable yet still arrive at an interpretation.

90. *OCOT*, 163–171.

91. Ibid., 172.

92. Ibid., 291.

93. See also Merold Westphal, "The Phenomenology of Guilt and the Theology of Forgiveness," in *Crosscurrents in Phenomenology*, ed. Ronald Bruzina and Bruce Wilshire (The Hague: Martinus Nijhoff, 1978), 231–261, esp. 234–236.

94. *SF*, xiii.

95. Ibid.

96. See "Nietzsche and the Phenomenological Ideal," *Monist* 60 (April 1977), 278–288; "Prolegomena to Any Future Philosophy of Religion Which Will Be Able to Come Forth as Prophecy," *International Journal for Philosophy of Religion* 6 (Fall 1973): 129–150 (reprinted in *KCRS*; I cite hereafter from *KCRS*); "The Phenomenology of Guilt and the Theology of Forgiveness," 231–261.

97. *HFM*, 89.

98. *OCOT*, 62. This notion arises nearly every time Westphal discusses phenomenology. For the most thorough explanation of Westphal's take on Husserl and phenomenology, see Westphal, "Phenomenologies and Religious Truth," in *Phenomenology of Truth Proper to Religion*, ed. Daniel Guerriere (New York: SUNY Press 1990), 105–125; and Westphal, "The Second Great Revolution in Phenomenology," *Journal of Speculative Philosophy* 26, no. 2 (2012): 333–347. For supporting examples, see also, in order of relevance, *OCOT*, 20, 32–37, 54–56, 62; "The Importance of Overcoming Metaphysics for the Life of Faith," 265–266 (where Westphal highlights Marion's attempts at a post-Heideggerian or post-Husserlian phenomenology as a phenomenology with which Westphal himself agrees); "Whose Philosophy? Which Religion?"; "Nietzsche and the Phenomenological Ideal," 278–288; *GGD*, 1–23; "Levinas, Kierkegaard, and the Theological Task," *Modern Theology* 8, no. 3 (July 1992): 242, 249, 254; *LKD*, 1–6, 13–15, 17–22. Note that "Levinas, Kierkegaard, and the Theological Task" is incorporated in the same cited sections of *LKD*. Westphal, "Ricoeur's Hermeneutical Phenomenology of Religion," in *Reading Ricoeur*, ed. David Kaplan (New York: SUNY Press, 2008), 109–119; *KCRS*, 1–4, 6–8,

11–13; "Vision and Voice: Phenomenology and Theology in the Work of Jean-Luc Marion," *International Journal of Philosophy of Religion* 60 (2006): 118–119; Merold Westphal, "The Welcome Wound: Emerging from the *il y a* Otherwise," *Continental Philosophy Review* 40 (2007): 222–225; Westphal, "Prereflective Cogito as Contaminated Opacity," *Southern Journal of Philosophy* 45 (2007): 157–160; Westphal, "Postmodernism and Ethics: The Case of Caputo," in *A Passion for the Impossible: John D. Caputo in Focus*, ed. Mark Dooley (New York: SUNY Press 2003), 163.

99. *OCOT*, 62.

100. Westphal sees Levinas's critique as against Husserl and Heidegger, but he often traces Levinas's Heideggerian critique back to Husserl's phenomenology. See *LKD*, 15–22.

101. Westphal, "Nietzsche and the Phenomenological Ideal," 278.

102. Ibid., 279. Here, Westphal quotes both Jeremiah 17:9 and Nietzsche's *Schopenhauer as Educator*, sec. 1. His explanation of Nietzsche's critique is mainly a reformulation of similar critiques previously covered.

103. Westphal, "Nietzsche and the Phenomenological Ideal," 279.

104. *KCRS*, 3: "Phenomenology of religion discusses God," Westphal summarizes, "but it does so by describing various forms of belief in God rather than debating the truth of these beliefs."

105. *GGD*, 2–11.

106. *KCRS*, 11. This entire chapter is very useful for understanding Westphal's prescriptive phenomenology, as he makes a distinction between the Greek objectivity in philosophy and the Hebraic tradition of prophecy. See also chapter 1 of this volume and "The Canon as Flexible, Normative Fact," *Monist* 76, no. 4 (October 1993): 436–449.

107. *KCRS*, 11. Westphal is continuing his argument that the Husserlian project, like the Enlightenment's attempt to obtain absolute knowledge, is tentative at best.

108. Ibid., 12.

109. See chapter 9, where I treat this subject in greater detail.

110. "Ricoeur's Hermeneutical Phenomenology of Religion," 109–114, gives the best explanation for the transition from a transcendental phenomenology to a hermeneutical phenomenology. At the beginning of the article, Westphal makes such a transition clear, concerning Husserl's principle of all principles, he writes: "This attempt to make evidence, presentation, showing, and so on, a matter of intuition is the Cartesian Husserl speaking. By contrast, the hermeneutical claim is that what is given to intuition, strictly speaking, underdetermines our perception or understanding. . . . This is why Gadamer can say that "understanding is not merely reproductive but always a productive activity as well" (109–110). Westphal quotes Gadamer from *Truth and Method*, 296. See also Westphal, "Second Great Revolution in Phenomenology," 333–347.

111. Recall that Westphal attempts to perform this dual action through *GGD* and its sequel, *SF*.

112. Interestingly, Ricoeur himself never rejected a Husserlian phenomenology. See his appraisal of Husserl in *Memory, History, and Forgetting*, trans. Kathleen Blamey and David Pellauer (Chicago: University of Chicago Press, 2004), esp. 31–36.

113. Westphal, "Ricoeur's Hermeneutical Phenomenology of Religion," 113, 115. "Through his notion of philosophy as a kind of faith seeking understanding," Westphal summarizes, "[Ricoeur] will preserve as much of these 'modern' ideals as he can in a 'postmodern' context. The believing soul and the theologian . . . affirm the world of the sacred texts of their tradition as the actual, the real, and they treat the texts in question as authoritative. The philosopher,

as such, does not, but rather can be described, where the symbol gives rise to thought, as one *deeply indebted* to these texts but *not deeply committed* to them" (115, emphasis Westphal's).

114. Westphal, "Ricoeur's Hermeneutical Phenomenology of Religion," 119; Westphal is quoting Ricoeur from *Oneself as Another*, 172, and *Thinking Biblically*, xvi, respectively.

115. My wager is on the latter. See chapter 9.

116. I have diminished our exploration on Kierkegaard's role in Westphal's concept of revelation because we have already studied it in detail in chapters 4 and 5.

117. Emmanuel Levinas, *Totality and Infinity*, trans. Alphonso Lingus (Pittsburgh, PA: Duquesne University Press, 1969), 21. One can see that Westphal's capitalization of this query by Levinas directly aligns with his appropriation of onto-theology and his disdain for metaphysics.

118. *LKD*, 26.

119. Levinas, *Totality and Infinity*, 39, 47, 194–200.

120. *LKD*, 29.

121. Ibid., 146–148.

122. Ibid., 50–52. Note that καθαυτό expresses how the other becomes a means to reveal and open the possibilities of infinity, not an actualization of infinite possibilities, furthering the problem with calling the other an incarnation of infinity. Καθαυτό should be read as *in per se*, as an icon, not as an actualization of infinity itself.

123. Ibid., 50–51.

124. Ibid., 37.

125. Ibid. He quotes from *Fear and Trembling*, 17, 35–36, 46. See also chapter 4.

126. Internally, here, means that the self holds the conditions of possibility for recognizing revelation. Westphal articulates this through the concept of faith.

127. *LKD*, 42. See also ibid., 37–42.

128. See ibid., chap. 4 and, 55–57; Westphal, "Levinas, Kierkegaard, and the Theological Task," 252–258.

129. Westphal himself avoids apologetics and its metaphysical thirty pieces of silver.

130. See, for instance, Putt's concluding interview with Westphal in *GTPD*, 181–208.

7. INTERMEDIARY CONCLUSIONS
The Believing Soul's Self-Transcendence

My attempt thus far has been to craft Westphal's intellectual narrative, and what I have found is that Westphal's narrative is heavily theological. In fact, Westphal is so theological that I argue he is best read within this discourse, which is perhaps his proper home. The previous chapters have focused on how Westphal shapes his thinking and how it tacitly develops into a theology that appropriates philosophical reasoning to minister and guide the life of faith. Furthermore, his articulation of faith as a task of a lifetime, which compels the believing soul to continually enact the love commandment, has convinced me that his thinking involves pastoral elements alongside its fundamental-theological development.

In what follows we complete our intellectual history by assessing what, exactly, Westphal aims to teach the believing soul—what does the believing soul learn from reading Westphal? This question is answered in *Transcendence and Self-Transcendence*. Westphal situates the text as a response to Heidegger's onto-theological critique of metaphysics, giving it a more in-depth reading than he did in *Overcoming Onto-theology*. Through this prism, Westphal first presents how not to think about God through a dialogue among Heidegger, Spinoza, and Hegel. Once he has 'cleared the table' of bad God-talk, so to speak, he then inquires into how one can possibly speak about God through a dialogue among Augustine, Aquinas, Pseudo-Dionysius, and Karl Barth. From this possible way of speaking about God, Westphal extrapolates the possibility of having faith in God through a now-familiar dialogue between Levinas and Kierkegaard. These three dialogues touch on our previous exploration of his work, and *Transcendence and Self-Transcendence,* one could say, connects the many plot points Westphal has unveiled throughout his prolific writing and thus deserves a thorough examination before we move onto engaging Westphal's thinking with John Caputo and Richard Kearney.

Onto-theology and the Need for Self-Transcendence

Westphal begins *Transcendence and Self-Transcendence* with a story concerning Methodists and their theology, or lack thereof, which he claims is mostly based on the tenets "God is nice" and "We should be nice too."[1] For him, this contextualizes his need to present a different approach to theology. Specifically, he wishes to break through what could be construed as wishy-washy God-talk that amounts to very little substance; theologies resembling a "very thin soup" that neither nourishes nor fulfills believing souls.[2] Responding to these malnourishing theologies, Westphal presents this work with two goals: one is pastoral and seeks to give a theology that does, in fact, feed and fulfill the believing soul and one that is, surprisingly, apologetical in nature.[3] Given this surprising pivot in his thinking regarding apologetics, we shall begin by unpacking Westphal's apologetical intentions.

The nature of Westphal's apologetics here is atypical, and it does not seek to provide any arguments regarding the plausibility of God's existence. Rather, his use of the term is something of an appropriation that uses the original impetus of apologetics to defend religion and subverts it to explain religion without actually arguing for the plausibility of religious belief. He wants to make religion possible, not inevitable, the latter of which he believes might fall into ideology.[4] He does this by first removing onto-theological concepts of God (i.e., bad God-talk) and then presenting a discourse that articulates what God is while also not limiting God to those constructs. Once he establishes ways belief in God can be thoughtfully articulated, he then expresses to the nonbeliever the importance of this belief: how this faith compels the believing soul toward loving action.

Consequently, *Transcendence and Self-Transcendence* can be read as an extension of *God, Guilt, and Death* and *Suspicion and Faith. God, Guilt, and Death* establishes the existential meaning of religion for the believing soul through a phenomenological description of its intersubjective meaning in society. Following this description, *Suspicion and Faith* proceeds by describing how suspicion and critique can correct religion, how faith can remain focused on God's love and not on the believing soul's personal gain. Neither *God, Guilt, and Death* nor *Suspicion and Faith* are traditionally apologetical texts; rather, they run against the apologetical grain by explaining how belief happens and/or (should) function within the life of faith. Recall that Westphal's faith resists a reasonable foundation (contra traditional apologetics), and within *Transcendence and Self-Transcendence*, he accordingly attempts something of a high-wire act: he wants to maintain his stance against traditional apologetics while flirting with a quasi-apologetics by giving an explanation or description of faith that never posits a reasonable defense of that faith. At the heart of this act is a concern against epistemic certainty, a certainty that finds itself articulated in onto-theology and, more often than not, defended in traditional apologetics.

Reading *God, Guilt, and Death* and *Suspicion and Faith* as tandem works reveals that there is an intellectual gap between them, a question concerning the epistemic nature of belief and its contents. In what sort of God does the believing soul believe? Or, conversely, in what sort of God should the believing soul *not* believe? More exactly, the gap exists between understanding religion and its importance to faith communities (*GGD*), and how God can become distorted to the point where those faith communities need to practice "atheism for Lent" to rectify those distortions (*SF*). For Westphal, *Transcendence and Self-Transcendence* fills this gap through exploring the ways in which belief in God goes astray (as seen through the critique of onto-theology) and how it can be set aright (as seen through his exploration of proper God-talk in the second part). In the end, he connects *Transcendence and Self-Transcendence* to *Suspicion and Faith*'s attempt to aid and correct faith through *Transcendence*'s third section, where he argues that one's faith compels a loving obligation to the other; by loving the other as one's self, the believing soul opens a self-transcendence that deepens the understanding of God through transcendence. Westphal has thus crafted a trilogy that explores the meaning of religion, its possibilities, and the need for religious believers to practice self-critique in order to (re)gain these possibilities.

Transcendence and Self-Transcendence therefore begins by giving a proper explanation and critique of the role God plays in society through religion. However, the role he wishes to highlight is a negative one that fashions God as a tool for the self's mastery over the other and is best described through Heidegger's critique of onto-theology. Westphal's first chapter sketches out Heidegger's critique of metaphysics in a broad context, expanding upon his prior writings by showing how this critique extends beyond God-talk toward metaphysics itself. Here, he gives a much clearer and more thorough reading of Heidegger to criticize a type of epistemic certainty that takes its cues from a God or God-like *prima causa* that enables human reason to become the arbiter of all things. This extensive critique of metaphysics reveals that onto-theology, for Westphal, is a thoroughly *human* problem, not a problem with God's self or God's role in human thinking. It is not God who is at fault in onto-theology (nor is theology as a discipline, for that matter) but, rather, it is human thinking that is at fault, thus crafting a clear distinction between human reasoning and God.[5] Westphal, here, is setting up his eventual argument that belief in a theistic God is plausible in spite of (and, even with the aid of) onto-theology, since this critique focuses on how human reason fails to fully understand its limits; it habitually takes its perspectival concept of the world (and God) as the whole or absolute. In many ways, as seen below, Westphal's reading of onto-theology follows the Lutheran concept of total depravity.

Yet Westphal is not reading Heidegger's work as anthropology. Rather, Westphal is attempting to separate God from human thought and understanding through Heidegger. Onto-theology, in a pastoral sense, thus lends itself to be read through the guise of human sin, our own personal faults.[6] In an apologetical sense, this opens onto-theology to be read through a conceptual manner in which God is still a viable and understandable entity to human understanding since it is not a critique of God's existence, merely a critique of human understanding.[7]

Within this framework, Westphal notes that the theology within onto-theology emphasizes that theology concerns itself with "first philosophy," which entails a discipline of comprehending existence and being.[8] Rather than initially reading "onto-theo-logy" as three concepts enjoined through a metaphysics that renders the notion of being into a science, Westphal is emphasizing its importance to theology.

After reading onto-theology first as theology, Westphal then breaks down onto-theology into its traditionally understood parts: *onto*, being; *theos*, the highest being that gives existence (beingness), and *logos*, the science of understanding existence. Onto-theo-logy, then, is the science of the highest being which causes all other beings to exist.[9] Reading it first as "onto-*theology*," that is, as a theology, then as "onto-theo-logy," allows for Westphal to further distinguish the nature in which the critique focuses on human reason's attempts to render God for its own purposes. Westphal is moving the critique into the realm of theology, in other words, to highlight its relationship to sin and the fallen nature of human reasoning. This move also reveals a need for transcendence and a way for God to enter into our lives, which becomes his primary critique of Spinoza's pantheism, and a need to construct this transcendence outside of human understanding, which becomes his primary critique of Hegel. Although it is rather obvious that onto-theology is a critique of atheisms and pantheisms, in addition to theisms, Westphal highlights these two thinkers to posit the notion that there is a need, or lack, within human understanding that cannot be overcome through reason alone. Transcendence, here, becomes a way to open the self to fulfilling that need. Self-transcendence will become the way in which he explains how the self can become open to this.

Constructing onto-theology in this manner sharpens it as a critique of our all-too-human desire to make the world intelligible, leading toward our mastery and domination over that world. At its core it is suspicious of human self-legitimization and self-autonomy: "All forms of onto-theology have a common purpose. Each puts God, whether it be the Unmoved Mover, or Nature, or Spirit, or the Market to work as the keystone of a metaphysical theory designed to render the whole of reality intelligible to philosophical reflection."[10]

In Westphal's example of the market, he sees how onto-theology continues after secularization; whatever becomes the ground of our metaphysical thinking takes the place of God while functioning in just the same way. This is why he chooses to dialogue with Spinoza since Westphal believes that Spinoza's pantheistic formulation of God as *deus sive natura* (God or nature, where the *or* denotes a synonymous relationship) resembles a contemporary secularity that tries to hold onto religious sentiment while still being thoroughly secular.[11]

Whether or not one calls it God, the ground of thought maintains the role of aiding one's intelligibility of the world all the while giving one tacit approval to manage and control that world. Elaborating on this critique, Westphal points to three specific aspects latent in onto-theology: onto-theology is calculative thinking, it is representational thinking, and it is bad theology.[12]

Onto-theology as calculative thinking, following Heidegger, can be seen in our forgetfulness of the questioning of being itself when we think.

Being, in other words, is forgotten as some sort of given that does not need to be explained. Once the question of being is forgotten, or presupposed, the quest for understanding beings themselves can begin: no longer concerned about "why there is," the scientist can then begin to explore "what there is," which in and of itself is not problematic. The critique, here, is not against an epistemology that attempts to understand beings. Rather, it is a critique that there is also a latent assumption (hidden behind the forgetfulness) of what being actually is, which thus guides the scientist's results. The forgetfulness of why there is, then, reinforces assumptions that make science possible. By exposing these assumptions as onto-theological, one can see that an over-riding factor in them is to render being as calculative—that is quantifiable, determinate, and *testable*—which can then be understood through human reason. "As a method of objectivizing beings by calculation," Westphal summarizes, quoting Heidegger, "it is the condition, imposed by the will to will [Heidegger's phrase for Nietzsche's will to power], through which the will to will secures its own sovereignty." Moreover, "The truth of science 'is merely the truth about beings. Metaphysics is the history of *this* truth.'"[13] God, or whatever stands as ground for this metaphysics, has the sole task of making "science possible," and any God that does not allow for that possibility will be exchanged for a more approving God.[14] This results in scientific-calculative reasoning becoming the only path to knowledge. Moreover, once-transcendent concepts like nature and knowledge become understood only by their worth as utilities and/or resources.

Because these concepts are understood as valuable only with respect to a desired end, Westphal claims that onto-theology has fallen into representational thinking, where "there is nothing except representing subjects and represented objects," where "to be is to be represented" by a self, as another self's object.[15] This highlights one of the more dangerous aspects of onto-theology in that scientific-calculative and representational thinking can render beings only as objects toward an end. Representational thinking, in other words, can lead to a disregard of the selfhood (or personhood) of others, leaving only what they represent to the subject or self: *my* teacher, *my* garbage man, *my* employee, and so on. Thinking of others in relation to oneself is not always bad, as one can understand an other only in relation to oneself. However, the utilitarian nature of representational thinking can often become the primary, or only, way of understanding an other. The critique, then, settles on the nature in which the other becomes a composite of the self's understanding in service to itself. Westphal focuses this aspect of onto-theology on Heidegger's notion that transforming subjects into representational subjects furthers the scientific process of understanding and making the world intelligible. This follows a logic of understanding that orders representational subjects into definitions, or concepts, which can be researched and explained, quoting Heidegger, Westphal elaborates:

> Knowing, as research, *calls whatever is be account* with regard to the way in which and the extent to which it lets itself be put at the disposal of representation. Research has disposal over anything that is when it can either calculate it in its future course in advance or verify a calculation about it as past. . . . Nature and history become the objects of a representing that explains.[16]

Representational thinking formulates objects through a principle of reason that shapes "whatever is to account" to the knowing subject to "explain every fact or event and to justify every truth claim. The principle as the demand that reasons be given constitutes a 'jurisdiction' that encompasses all beings, including the Highest Being, God."[17] Representational thinking touches on our prior discourse on concept of totalization, which Westphal appropriates from Levinas, where the other is no longer seen as a self, as a face, but as an object to be used toward an end: the self becomes totalized—that is, completely understood—only as what it represents.

The onto-theological embrace of scientific-calculative and representational thinking reveals the human desire for epistemic certainty, which is especially seen in the role onto-theological thinking plays in modernity and modern philosophy. "Modernity begins with a bad case of epistemic anxiety," Westphal summarizes, as a part of the "modern turn to the (human) subject" in early modern philosophy, especially within Cartesian philosophy.[18] Continuing, Westphal notes:

> As the will to power, [modernity's] values all concern its own security. In this mode its highest epistemic value is truth, but only secure truth, guaranteed truth, certain truth. Looking for something that can be its own self-grounding certainty and the basis for all other certainty, Descartes discovers the *ego cogito*. It is not merely thinker or knower in relation to what is thought or known. It is subject, *subjectum, hypokeimenon*, that which is most basic.[19]

Latent in this certainty is a move to place everything in relation to the self or subject, or, in a broader sense, to human understanding. Humanity becomes the sole arbiter of all things, and the individual self, participating in this arbitration, becomes judge and magistrate of all things in relation to itself.[20] This directly relates to our prior exploration of Westphal's general (Kantian) finitism, yet again he is concerned with a mode of thinking that attempts absolute understanding. In the previous chapter I remarked that this finitism touched on a desire to continually be placed into questioning; reminding us that "we are not God" and that human understanding has certain limits.[21] There I argued that Westphal employed this questioning as a part of a fundamental theology that focused on the epistemic uncertainty articulated within an unfounding faith, that faith is not a reasonable, foundational truth to hold onto but an act of will that resists all foundations. Westphal's faith is unfounding primarily because of this resistance. As one can see in *Transcendence and Self-Transcendence,* this concern emerges through not just a theological component but also a philosophical one, in that Westphal charges human anxiety's issues with uncertainty as a cause for a metaphysics that provides certainty. It is theological in the sense that many believing souls use this certainty as the primary constant found in God; it is philosophical in the sense that a theistic God is not necessary to supply this foundational certainty, the market or nature (Spinoza), or some sense of human subjectivity (Hegel), can serve as this God.

Through Spinoza and Hegel, Westphal argues that alternative understandings of God remain within a similar onto-theology, albeit with differing consequences. He highlights their pantheistic constructions not only to follow contemporary scholarship but also to indicate how *theos*, as a part of onto-theology, encapsulates secular concepts that 'replace' God as ground. He is, in other words, indicting them with the same offense. In the Heidegger chapter, and indeed throughout some of his other works, Westphal has critiqued a theistic conception of onto-theology.[22] With these two chapters then, he wishes, in effect, to exonerate traditional monotheism and lay the charge of onto-theology on human reason as a whole. Once more, this points back to a particular view of human sin and how human reason, devoid of faith, can fall into sinfulness.

Concerning Spinoza, Westphal focuses on his a-theistic or pantheistic understanding of God that avoids any transcendence. Beginning with *deus sive natura*, Westphal notes the interchangeable characteristic of God and nature in his philosophy.[23] What matters for us is that Westphal articulates Spinoza's pantheistic a-theism as a naturalistic, immanent account where what stands for God can be understood by and through physical reality.

Gone is the once transcendent concept of God that is wholly other and what arrives in God's place can be described thus:

> There is only one substance, God. It exists necessarily and is the infinite cause of all finite things, which are its modes. Whereas substance exists in itself and is conceived through itself, modes exist in God, are conceived through God. Causally speaking, they occur necessarily through the laws of God's nature; logically speaking, they follow necessarily from God's essence. In all of these ways, substance and its modes can be distinguished.... [Spinoza's] distinction between God and the world of finite things is not like others'; it is not the distinction between a creator substance and created substances.[24]

From this formulation of Spinoza's God, Westphal is questioning purely immanent account of the world (or in a theological sense, of creation) and its implications. In effect, he is asking, "If accounts of God as transcendent and wholly other often lead to onto-theology, what if there is only immanence?" His reply points out the deterministic nature of this immanent account; that is, if "God thinks," it is because modes of God such as humans or birds think, in accordance with the laws of God and nature.[25] Thus, "to say that God is a thinking being is simply to say that nature produces finite minds."[26] This makes God impersonal, which means that God ultimately has no *telos*, no divine purpose.[27]

The lack of purpose thus limits God's interaction with the world; there are no miracles with this God. Spinoza has cleared away all the attributes that make a traditionally theistic God transcendent, leaving an ethos in society that attempts to uphold "the impersonal laws of nature [as] the ultimate fact of the universe . . . both in sophisticated theories and common sense. One could say that pantheism, in substance if not in name, is the secular faith of the world we live in," especially for those few who wish to uphold this materialism while still maintaining a vague sense of religiosity.[28] From here, one can again see a similar concern for a form of reasoning that attempts to go at it alone without the aid of faith.

It is no surprise, then, that Westphal capitalizes on Spinoza's use of the principle of sufficient reason, "as the demand that everything be rendered intelligible through the giving of reasons or explanations . . . reasons would not be demanded of us if we could not give them."[29] With this reading of Spinoza, Westphal pivots from a description of Spinoza's philosophy to a contrasting dialogue with theistic accounts of God that maintain transcendence. Meant primarily as an objection against Spinoza, Westphal critiques

Spinoza's immanent philosophy through highlighting the elements miss-ing in his account, an argument from absence rather than a straightforward critique against Spinoza.[30] Even though this may not be the proper way to refute Spinoza (one may prefer a more outright dissection, which Westphal briefly gives in certain sections),[31] this fits Westphal's theological narrative of appropriation. He does not so much wish to refute Spinoza, which would in itself take a book-length discussion, but, rather, to craft an argument in support of a theistic God. More exactly, he wishes to appropriate from Spi-noza a contrasting argument (not a supporting one) that reveals how a purely immanent construction of the world appears to lack a basic connection with human experience, an experience he claims requires self-transcendence. Re-member that Westphal is trying to make the claim that onto-theology reveals that humans need a concept of transcendence, by God, and that we cannot make the world intelligible merely through reason, thereby carving out space for faith and self-transcendence that opens the self to this transcendence. By providing an onto-theological framework and a Spinozist counterexample, Westphal claims that there is a place for divine mystery and revelation within the world, and self-transcendence allows the self to experience this. Self-transcendence, in this sense, is not so much defined by Westphal but hinted at: facing an awe-inspiring, ineffable moment that cannot be explained by reference to causality or the principle of sufficient reason.

This, to be sure, is not a pure description of self-transcendence. For Westphal, giving one would defeat the point of self-transcendence as he be-lieves that this should remain open to a multitude of possibilities. Rather, he describes certain kinds of self-transcendences and how others might emerge. In the introduction, Westphal hinted at this construction through evoking differing kinds of mysticism, nothing that these experiences resist a complete definition.[32] Here, with Spinoza, he displays it quite openly for the first time within the book itself: "to grant either mystery or revelation would be to grant that we are neither the apex nor the center of the cognitive world, but are oriented toward a reality and toward a knowing that are not at our disposal, epistemically speaking."[33] Humans are not at the zenith of the world, there is a divine mystery beyond us, and through Spinoza, West-phal reveals what we are missing when we remove this mystery from our understanding. Through Hegel, however, Westphal moves toward what can be called an abuse of God and self-transcendence.

Westphal claims that Hegel's pantheism focuses not on nature but on the subject, that Hegel's pantheism of the human spirit is a progression toward absolute understanding.[34] He critiques Hegel for attempting to articulate humanity's quest for complete knowing in and through history, and for trying to understand reality as the progressive accomplishment of the Absolute Spirit. Indeed, Westphal's concern here largely remains the same as in *Hegel, Freedom, and Modernity* and in related texts. That concern focuses on the hubris of such an attempt—recall the dancer who leapt so high he thought he could fly—by showing that grounding the self in thought itself is equally problematic as grounding the self in nature or an onto-theological theism.[35] Westphal, in a sort of refrain, continues his critique that we cannot go at it alone, that we need a transcendence which becomes available through self-transcendence.[36]

Hegel's concept of spirit enables and enacts itself through human understanding in history, developing toward an absolute knowing in which finite human understanding (*Verstand*) transforms itself into absolute reason (*Vernunft*), ultimately leading to what can be called Truth.[37] For Hegel, to put it rather succinctly, there is a self-actualizing idea latent in human reason; it is an idea within human reason that proceeds toward absolute understanding. It is not something to achieve or to strive for; it is something that achieves itself as the historical *telos* of human reasoning. This is how Hegel, for Westphal, can call God the absolute person while not claiming God to be a particular, distinct entity. Rather, the human self becomes deified through its self-actualizing quest for understanding.[38]

Ultimately, this quest for understanding falls victim to Heidegger's critique of science.[39] For Westphal, Hegel's self-grounding subject follows the Cartesian problem since it specifically posits the self as the arbiter of all things. This allows Westphal to argue that Hegel's philosophy falls into scientific-calculative thinking and representational thinking, where others are seen through their relation to the subject/self. Pointing back to his prior critique of Hegel's elevation of *Sittlichkeit*, Westphal also notes that onto-theological pantheism has society—the collective human will—as its highpoint. *Sittlichkeit*, here, follows the pattern of actualization in that the self is not just devoted to the other as another self, but to one's local society, then to one's state, and, ultimately, to world history.[40] This recalls our prior exploration of Hegel's politics, where Westphal explains that Hegel's theory of freedom moves from recognition of the self to another self and then builds toward society in its increasingly conglomerate iterations. What is lost here, for Westphal, is that individual selves lose their selfhood, thus becoming representative selves within a historical Spirit and used as a means to an (absolute) end.[41] There is, in short, a lack of ethics in this onto-theological construction. The self becomes a representative self (along with its representative objects) in the process of becoming something that is more than human, as it were, progressing beyond the self toward some absolute spirit. Just like the very thin soup of Methodism, Hegel's philosophy neither fulfills nor nourishes.

Reviewing the overall project of *Transcendence and Self-Transcendence*, Westphal's appropriation of these three authors has attempted to reveal onto-theology as a means through which we can understand our finite reasoning, a concern of his that can be traced throughout all of his works. This is not just a privation, as in stating what we cannot know, but it is also positive claim about how we can accept what little we can know once we've acknowledged what we cannot. By making a case for transcendence as a viable option in response to onto-theology, Westphal ultimately wants to rest on a faith that accepts its finite nature through its dependence on a God it can never fully comprehend. In what follows, we further explore this case, noting how these appropriations follow familiar themes within Westphal's thinking.

Self-Transcendence and Theism: An Argument

Westphal begins making his case for a belief in a theistic God by laying an Augustinian foundation that God is incomprehensible and yet humanity still has access to God through worship and prayer. Elaborating, Westphal compares Augustine to Wittgenstein, arguing that the unknowability of God happens through the prism of language, whereas Augustine's theory of language "affirms a hiddenness over sheer presence in our knowledge of God" that extends even to how consciousness understands the world, allowing for a certain concealment—an ignorance of the complete comprehensibility of things—to the world and to God.[42] From this ignorance, Augustine claims that knowing God is to seek God through worship and prayer, continually asking "what then, is the God I worship?"[43] As well as "what do I love when I love my God?"[44]

Westphal then transitions to a dialogue between Pseudo-Dionysius and Thomas Aquinas to show how something tangentially can be said of God. He situates his chapter on Aquinas through a basic assertion that postmodernity can be described as a "generalized apophatics," especially so for deconstruction.[45] However, what if one wishes nevertheless to move beyond silence towards speaking? By placing his argument in what he calls an epistemic transcendence, he believes that the self may begin to speak about God without falling into onto-theology. In describing this speech, he draws on Aquinas's analogy of being, or *analogia entis,* to illustrate how it is possible to speak of a highest being through the process of concealment and unconcealment. With this process, it is acceptable to state "God is Love," for example, but only if it is understood that God is not love qua love and rather is analogously understood as (and through) love.

Westphal argues that apophatic theology can address the life of faith through a simultaneous, dialectical mode of negative theology, where negative theology and positive theology work in a creative tension of revealing and concealing.[46] This tension works through a process of what Pseudo-Dionysius called a "dissimilar similarity," where knowledge of God "is *simultaneously* a similarity to be affirmed and a dissimilarity to be negated" because the positive statements concerning God are "always unfitting" but also are used "not unfittingly."[47] This means that the process of attributing something to God (what God is) cannot be separated from the process of denying something about God (what God is not). Hence, while positive statements about God are imperfect, a corresponding and imperfect negative statement about God counters that imperfection, thereby mitigating both statements by acknowledging their imperfection but allowing for an account concerning whom God is to be made. In short, our God-talk should always be understood as uncovering a truth about God while never becoming the sole truth about God. Therefore one can say that, in the vein of Aristotle, God is the prime mover as long as it is understood that God is more than just the prime mover. Importantly, Westphal adds that this mode of speaking, like deconstruction, is a process, not a metaphysics or system, and as such it cannot give any special advice concerning where it will (or should) lead the believer. It is a *method* for understanding, not a definable understanding or concept itself, and consequently does not have any fixed truths or statements.[48]

In both Pseudo-Dionysius and Aquinas, Westphal sees concealment and unconcealment as a form of dialectic. In Aquinas, this dialectic develops the notion that "God must be deemed unknowable . . . to assume the required transcendence, while [at the same time] allowing us to have some notion of what it is humans are referring to in addressing 'the Holy One,' 'our Father,' or 'Allah Akbar'" and that the "articulating of this dialectical tension" is the task of philosophical theology.[49] For Aquinas, this articulation is done through the *analogia entis.* Like Augustine before him, Aquinas's classical theism accepts that the human intellect cannot fully comprehend God, but he also argues that humanity can come to know God through the concept of *adaequatio rei et intellectus*, or Aquinas's argument for how one can obtain knowledge and understanding.[50]

This possibility of speaking about God is Westphal's main appropriation of Aquinas and Pseudo-Dionysius in *Transcendence and Self-Transcendence*. Therefore, we refrain from going into further detail as to how he explains and describes the *analogia entis* since Westphal primarily uses its basic function to be able to express something about God through analogy. Note, however, that in this three-part dialogue, this technique of understanding God is rooted in praxis for Westphal. He finds, in sum, that the Augustinian seeking out of an incomprehensible God is pursued through prayer and worship which, aligned with the God-talk of *via negativa* and *analogia entis*, removes the believing soul from the center of reality, allowing for a self-transcendence to occur that reveals epistemic knowledge about God through God's transcendence. Therefore, overcoming onto-theology is a process, an act of self-transcendence that opens the believer up to God.[51] Previously he explained how onto-theology reveals the need for self-transcendence through his critique of Spinoza and Hegel. Here, he makes the argument for this self-transcendence through the epistemic uncertainty that allows us to speak about God while knowing that our speech can never be complete.

This process of speaking about God has its roots in Scripture, is seen through its use in religious traditions, and, as such, touches on his prior work in *God, Guilt, and Death*, where he described how religion operates within the believing soul's life. Here, he connects this with religion's construal of God, emphasizing the praxis of religious belief in one's life. In effect, one can see that both are intertwined. Regarding onto-theology, one might say that the symptoms of onto-theological thinking can be seen in how one goes about putting that thinking into practice to find existential meaning and certainty. With his dialogue among Augustine, Pseudo-Dionysius, and Aquinas, Westphal corrects this through explaining what happens when one avoids onto-theological thinking by continually practicing a faith that constantly decenters the self (self-transcendence) in search of a transcendent God. Moreover, he establishes a line of reasoning in which overcoming onto-theology can be found in religious praxis and he holds the Christian Scriptures and the hermeneutical tradition based upon those Scriptures as a primary example.[52]

On the matter of Scripture, Westphal raises Karl Barth's analogy of faith to appropriate a concept of revelation that finds the self dependent on a God that speaks. Westphal describes Barth as antimodern (not postmodern) since he is against theologies that "sought to make the human subject the ground and basis for our knowledge of God."[53] Hence, Barth articulates a concept of revelation that can be appropriated as a response to onto-theology.[54] This form of revelation resists becoming the self's ground because it is accepted by a concept of faith that eschews the desire for epistemic certainty. Moreover, by accepting revelation as the unconcealment of God's self to humanity, revelation is also acknowledged to be limited in nature; revelation thus serves no function of legitimating God for a metaphysical system for the self. On this latter account, Westphal appropriates a Barthian critique of religion and theology that reads the Bible as a book that empowers the reader with a certain kind of truth by virtue of the fact that its theology can better understand revelation than others. This critique attacks the nature in which certain theologies wield the Bible as an authoritative weapon. Likewise, Westphal appropriates Barth to claim that theologies of this sort hold their own sense of reason and Scriptural interpretation over and above the content and revelation found within Scripture,[55] thereby making them the exact types of theologies or theisms that Heidegger critiques through onto-theology.[56] Barth and Heidegger, in other words, are concerned about the same problem within human reasoning.

Regarding *Transcendence and Self-Transcendence*'s pastoral intent, this concept of revelation allows Westphal to show the believing soul how a faith that is dependent on revelation resists a concept of ground since it accepts that revelation is not the ultimate concept of God; that revelation is not truth itself but a questioning and critique against what we come to think of as grounding Truth. By placing the believer into question, revelation reminds the believer of her own finitude. "In announcing the limitation of the known world by another that is unknown," Westphal quotes from Barth's *Epistle to the Romans*, "the Gospel does not enter into competition with the many attempts to disclose within the known world some more or less unknown and higher form of existence and to make it accessible to men."[57] In this process, revelation aids and corrects believing souls by reminding them of their fallen nature and that they need to accept a faith that opens them to God, and thus rejects theologies that attempt to utilize a concept of God for selfish gain. This concept of Barthian revelation connects well with Westphal's prior use of the hermeneutics of suspicion, particularly in *Suspicion and Faith* and *Overcoming Onto-theology.* In both, Westphal attempted to appropriate a suspicion of religious praxis in the process of aiding the believing soul in the life of faith.[58] In the previous chapter, I connected this suspicion with Westphal's faith seeking understanding, and in *Transcendence and Self-Transcendence* we can see that Westphal is now linking Barth with these masters of the hermeneutics of suspicion, since Barth is just as critical of religion and religion's abuses as they are.[59]

Connecting Barth's critique of religious praxis and religious belief in the Bible to the critique of onto-theology also buttresses Westphal's atypical, quasi-apologetical argument in *Transcendence and Self-Transcendence.* Here, the intent is to show the nonbeliever how critiques within revelation often mirror (and in some cases, are much more strident) than those outside of religious thinking. This concept of revelation, in a way, presages Heidegger's critique of onto-theology, for Westphal. Furthermore, his Barthian appropriation claims that Scripture can be understood as an authority for knowing about God, but by not making revelation itself the ground of thought, he opens up a dialogue between faith and reason as a way not to slip into onto-theology. Faith accepts revelation and reason, and reason in turn accepts this faith and guides it toward understanding revelation.

He still founds his phenomenology on the primacy of *faith* in the existence of God and not in a rational exercise that justifies this faith—no proof of God's existence can adequately overcome onto-theology or fill the believer with a sense of awe and wonder. This also establishes a link to Kierkegaard through its concept of faith in revelation. However, before touching on this link, Westphal first engages with Levinas. He chooses to begin with Levinas to connect the themes of transcendence he has established in the previous section with Levinas's ethics as first philosophy, showing how a heteronomous relationship is also necessary for transcendence.[60] Self-transcendence thus requires an other in addition to the Wholly Other, God. From this, Westphal will conclude his project layering a Kierkegaardian faith on top of his argument for a need for transcendence and a need for epistemic uncertainty. Like before, this faith is an unfounding one based on the Paradox of Christ and one in which the willing act of faith requires a heteronomous relationship. Thus Westphal engages both thinkers to establish that praxis is the foundation of religious faith, returning to his argument that a self-transcendence, a decentering, opens the self to transcendence with God through the other. This fusion of the paradox of faith and the ethical obligation of that faith is the Archimedean point for Westphal: to say something about God, we must enter into fellowship with the other (i.e., God's creation), and through that fellowship we are opened up to the ultimate Other, God.

In summary, Westphal's argument throughout the text ends where his prior work ended: with a praxis-based concept of faith that helps the believer overcome onto-theology through a revelation that can be experienced through enacting the love commandment. Namely, according to Westphal, you acknowledge your sinful (onto-theological) nature and overcome this by loving God above all things and loving the neighbor as much as you love yourself. In *Transcendence and Self-Transcendence*, Westphal gives this notion a postmodern framework through a dialogue with Heidegger's critique of onto-theology, but it is not postmodern merely because it engages Heidegger. Rather, it is postmodern because it holds modernity as the contemporary onto-theological framework to overcome. Additionally, one could say that the work is premodern in the sense that Westphal retrieves a theistic sense of understanding God through Augustine, Aquinas, and Pseudo-Dionysius. If one were to be somewhat anachronistic, one could add Barth to this premodern mix as he also retrieves an Augustinian line of argumentation.[61] What matters for us to answer the question "What can the believing soul learn from reading Westphal?" We can see that *Transcendence and Self-Transcendence* formulates Westphal's assorted writings into a digestible whole where the finitude of human reason is articulated through a contemporary problem and the argument for transcendence is retrieved through a tradition that has always concerned itself with the finite, fallen nature of humanity. In response to this finitude, Westphal articulates the same prescription he made in his prior work: when the believing soul bases her faith on revelation she can seek to disabuse herself of the illusion that she can fully understand the world (have absolute knowledge) by continually reminding herself that she is not God and that her highest task is to love God above all else and love the neighbor as herself. In a sense, there is nothing new in this work, but it does articulate Westphal's thinking as a whole, and thus is his most important text.

Conclusion: Caught in the *Aufhebung* of Transcendence

Although Westphal utilizes Levinas and Kierkegaard in the same way that he did in *Levinas and Kierkegaard in Dialogue* and in adjacent articles, what changes in *Transcendence and Self-Transcendence* is that Westphal fashions them into a Hegelian structure. Westphal hints at this structure only in the conclusion of the text, but it is a key for understanding how he uses onto-theology and for how he understands not only faith but also the believing soul.[62] Written almost as if he discovered the "strikingly Hegelian character" of the work only after he had written it, Westphal notes that the work indeed moves from "the abstract to the concrete"; that is, it moves from an abstract critique of thought (onto-theology) to a praxis-based concept of thinking (faith). Notice the dialectical nature of the work: the onto-theological thinking in part 1 stands as a sort of antithesis to the theistic, non-onto-theological concepts of God from part 2. In this way, both get taken up in an *Aufhebung* in the part 3.[63] I find that this *Aufhebung* is not a true one in the Hegelian sense, but rather is a *Westphalian Aufhebung* because the onto-theology of part 1 never negates anything within his arguments for theism in part 2 or elsewhere.[64] Instead, its purpose stands as a reminder of the dangers of human reason when it tries to shun a faith that is solely dependent on God and God's revelation. As a result, there is an eschatological nature to this *Westphalian Aufhebung*: the believing soul escapes onto-theology not so much by passing through onto-theology (as one would in a Hegelian *Aufhebung*) to get to God, but the believing soul can overcome onto-theology without even entering into it. Since onto-theology is equated to sin, because it is sin and not reason that opposes faith, one can draw a connection between salvation and non-onto-theological thinking.[65] God and revelation are the focal points for both salvation and non-onto-theological thinking. This occurs in the revelation of God becoming flesh through Christ who saves the believing soul from the effects of sin, and her belief in this miracle (in and through revelation) opens her to a self-transcendence that can avoid onto-theological thinking. In the following chapter, I explore this concept in greater detail since I think that it is imperative for understanding Westphal's use of onto-theology and that this Hegelian structure is overlooked by many, including John Caputo. Caputo, as we shall see, misreads Westphal's process of overcoming onto-theology since he does not see the Hegelian nature of Westphal's faith.

Notes

1. *TST*, 1.
2. Ibid.
3. Ibid., 2.

4. "Inevitable" touches on Kant's dictum about morality inevitably leading toward religion, but as we have seen with Westphal's use of Kant, inevitability here opens the questions: Whose morality? Which religion? See chapter 6 of this volume. See also Merold Westphal, Merold, "Whose Philosophy? Which Religion?" in *Transcendence in Philosophy and Religion*, ed. James Falconer (Bloomington: Indiana University Press, 2003), 2–7.

5. *TST*, 16.

6. Recall that Westphal, through Kierkegaard, finds that it is sin, not reason, that is against faith. In the pastoral sense mentioned earlier, one could read into Westphal's concept of ontotheology a reason steeped in sin that attempts to go at it alone. This turns reason into an enabler of the self's autonomy, which leads, more often than not, to the self's mastery of the other in a will to power.

7. Westphal still holds himself to be a theist as he has throughout his work. Ibid., 2.

8. Ibid., 17.

9. Ibid., 18.

10. Ibid.

11. Ibid., 52–53.

12. Ibid., 18.

13. Ibid., 21. Westphal is quoting Heidegger from *What Is Metaphysics?*, 194, 258, from Walter Kaufmann, ed., *Existentialism from Dostoevsky to Sartre* (New York: New American Library, 1975).

14. *TST*, 21.

15. Ibid., 29.

16. Ibid. Emphasis is Westphal's. He is quoting Heidegger from "The Age of the World Picture," in *The Question Concerning Technology and Other Essays*, trans. William Lovitt (New York: Harper & Row, 1977).

17. *TST*, 29.

18. Ibid., 30. Westphal gives a much more in-depth analysis of modernity's anxiety on pages 28–31. Since his explanation of modernity's epistemic anxiety is nothing novel, I only give a summarization here.

19. Ibid., 30. Westphal is referencing Heidegger from "The Word of Nietzsche: 'God is Dead,' from *The Question Concerning Technology and Other Essays*, 82–85, 88, 100.

20. *TST*, 31.

21. See also *OCOT*, 171–172, 187–196.

22. See Merold Westphal, "The Importance of Overcoming Metaphysics for the Life of Faith," *Modern Theology* 23, no. 2 (April 2007): 253–278.

23. *TST*, 41–47.

24. Ibid., 47.

25. Ibid., 49–50.

26. Ibid., 50.

27. In *TST*, 50, Westphal clarifies this by stating that, for Spinoza, "the very notion of a divine purpose is a human fiction and prejudice that arises from our ignorance of the true causation of things, our consciousness of our own appetites, our interpretation of our own behavior in terms of final causes, and finally, our projection of this purposiveness onto God." He gathers this from Spinoza's *Ethics*, 1 App II/78–80, from Edwin Curley, ed. and trans., *A Spinoza Reader* (Princeton, NJ: Princeton University Press, 1994).

28. *TST*, 53.

29. Ibid. 53–54.

30. See, for example, ibid., 60–63.

31. See ibid., 54–58, in which Westphal critiques Spinoza's ethics.

32. Ibid., 3–6.

33. Ibid., 60, and 65.

34. Westphal begins by giving a lengthy account of Hegel's reading of Spinoza, revealing how both pantheisms are interrelated. Ultimately, for Westphal, they are interrelated through their onto-theological construction of human reason's grounding within itself, either by Spinoza's use of the principle of sufficient reason (53–55, 64–65) or by Hegel's attempt at absolute understanding (67–72, 74).

35. See chapters 3 and 4 of this volume. See also *KCRS*, 89; Merold Westphal, "Kierkegaard and Hegel," in *The Cambridge Companion to Kierkegaard* (Cambridge: Cambridge University Press, 1997), 101–102.

36. *TST*, 75–78.

37. Ibid., 77–79.

38. Ibid., 79–83.

39. Ibid., 89.

40. Ibid., 87.

41. Ibid., 87–88.

42. In ibid., 95, "For Augustine, the inner word or word of the heart belongs to no natural language, but is derived from the direct presence of sense or intellect to its appropriate object. The secondary, outer word, which does belong to some human language, is arbitrarily assigned to the inner word simply for the purpose of communication. And just to assure us he has read his Derrida carefully, Augustine insists on the secondary character of writing. The written word is a sign of the outer, spoken word (which remains such when we silently think it); only this latter is a sign 'of the things we are thinking of.'" Westphal quotes Augustine from *Confessions*, trans. R. S. Pine-Coffin (Baltimore: Penguin, 1961), XV, 19.

43. *TST*, 96. Westphal quotes Augustine from *Confessions*, I, 4.

44. *TST*, 97, Westphal quotes Augustine from *Confessions*, X, 6.

45. *TST*, 115–116. He gathers this from John Caputo.

46. The terms *negative theology*, *apophatic theology*, and *via negativa* are interchangeable for Westphal.

47. *TST*, 116. Emphasis is Westphal's. Westphal quotes Pseudo-Dionysius from *The Celestial Hierarchy* in *Pseudo-Dionysius: The Complete Works*, trans. Colm Luibheid (New York: Paulist Press, 1987), 150/141A, 151–52/144B

48. *TST*, 116–117.

49. Ibid., 122, Westphal quotes a summary of Aquinas from David B. Burrell, C.S.C., in *Knowing the Unknowable God: Ibn-Sina, Maimonides, Aquinas* (Notre Dame, IN: University of Notre Dame Press, 1986), 2

50. *TST*, 131.

51. *OCOT*, 30–31. For a more detailed explanation, see also *TST*, 177–191.

52. *TST*, 164–174.

53. Ibid., 143.

54. Westphal goes into great detail in explaining Barth's critique of metaphysics, which Westphal reads as a critique aligned with onto-theology. See ibid., 144–147.

55. Ibid., 144, 147, 152, 154.

56. Ibid., 19, 21, 25, 34–38 (for Heidegger), and 143–145, 146–147, 149, 152–153, 156, 157–161 (for Barth).

57. Ibid., 150 Westphal quotes Karl Barth from *The Epistle to the Romans*, trans. Edwyn C. Hoskyns (Oxford: Oxford University Press, 1933, 1968), 35.

58. See Merold Westphal, "Levinas, Kierkegaard, and the Theological Task," *Modern Theology*, 8, no. 3 (July): 251; this is also explored throughout *SF*. See also Merold Westphal, "Taking Suspicion Seriously: The Religious Uses of Modern Atheism," *Faith and Philosophy* 4 (January 1987).

59. *TST*, 148.

60. Ibid., 178–180.

61. Ibid., 143.

62. Ibid.

63. Ibid., 228.

64. See chapter 2 of this volume

65. In chapter 5, I covered how Westphal uses Kierkegaard's critique of reason to establish this connection. In *Transcendence and Self-Transcendence*, Westphal only makes this connection tangentially through Barth (154–158) and in relation to God's grace through revelation. In both *Transcendence and Self-Transcendence* and his Kierkegaardian work, the concept of total depravity emerges as a way for articulating sin and human finitude.

8. RADICAL ESCHATOLOGY

Westphal, Caputo, and Onto-theology

How Radical Do We Need to Be?

It is impossible to speak of Merold Westphal's academic contributions without including the lengthy (and lifelong) debates he has held with John Caputo. Truly, the debates between Westphal and Caputo (also frequently involving Richard Kearney) have dominated Continental philosophy of religion in North America for quite some time, and stories of their witty jousting at conferences and symposia are familiar to many. One such account has been transcribed in *Modernity and Its Discontents*, where Westphal and Caputo, along with James Marsh, hold a roundtable discussion exploring topics ranging from the issue of transcendence in postmodern thought to what counts as 'radical' hermeneutics.[1]

The issue of what is radical in postmodernism is central to their debates concerning hermeneutics and philosophy of religion, and a persistent question for them is how far should one take deconstruction and (broadly) a postmodern hermeneutics.[2] This discussion pops up throughout *Overcoming Onto-Theology*, where Westphal defends Gadamer as being equally as radical as Derrida, the primary source of Caputo's thinking. Westphal contends that Caputo's critique of Gadamer as "reactionary" and "too comforting" misses the equally radical nature of Gadamer's notion of historical-effected consciousness (*wirkungsgeschichtliches Bewusstsein*).[3] Westphal contends that Caputo's Derridean deconstruction lacks a solid footing in that its disdain for religion, or "thick theology," for the sake of preventing violence is too abstract and opaque.[4] As are the Methodists he mentions in the preface to *Transcendence and Self-Transcendence*, Caputo's account of religion is weak and thus malnourishing soup for Westphal.[5]

This discussion concerning the radical is furthered through Caputo's review of *Overcoming Onto-Theology*, where he accepts Westphal's reading of Derrida as fair and even a defense of Derrida to those who call him a relativist.[6] However, after these kind remarks, Caputo critiques Westphal's understanding of Derrida's atheism (or what passes as such) and his lack of nerve regarding how far one should go in appropriating postmodern thought within Christianity:

> My chief objection concerning *Overcoming Onto-Theology* is that it turns on a classical and classically Greek metaphysical distinction between an epistemological self and a noumenal world (and hence between epistemology and some sort of ontology). So I would like to press Westphal a little harder in the direction of what I might call a more robust postmodernism, or what I usually call a more radical hermeneutics, where these distinctions are not so settled.[7]

While the issue of hermeneutics becomes pivotal in their discussions, the essential question becomes "Just how radical do we need to be?"[8] In many cases, each has proclaimed the other's hermeneutics as wanting, as Westphal states:

> I once suggested that [Caputo] write a prequel to his two books on radical hermeneutics. . . . I suggested that he might call it *Not So Very Damn Radical Hermeneutics*. In vintage form, he responded that it would not be necessary, since I had already written that book myself, namely . . . *Overcoming Onto-Theology*. Now he has graciously responded to my thought as expressed in *Transcendence and Self-Transcendence*, once again suggesting that my thought is insufficiently radical.[9]

In Simmons and Minister's book, *Reexamining Deconstruction and Determinate Religion*, Westphal and Caputo revisit this debate concerning hermeneutics by focusing on the attempt of Simmons and Minister (among others) to explore the degree to which deconstruction, and the concept of religion without religion, can function within a Christian belief system. This work, along with B. Keith Putt's text "Friends and Strangers/Poets and Rabbis: Negotiating a 'Capuphalian' Philosophy of Religion," seeks to explore how Westphal's thinking can function in dialogue with Caputo's own. Putt is correct in calling projects of this sort "Capuphalian."[10] These two works, along with Christina Gschwandtner's text *Postmodern Apologetics?*

Arguments for God in Contemporary Philosophy, cover a great deal of ground concerning the reception of Westphal and Caputo's thought within what I would call the second generation of Continental philosophy of religion in North America, that is, the generation after Westphal, Caputo, and Kearney.[11] What I would like to contribute to this discussion, and what I believe is most relevant to Westphal's thinking, is the issue Caputo takes with Westphal's *Transcendence and Self-Transcendence*, namely that he sees it as insufficiently radical.

I find that this critique of Westphal, fixated on onto-theology, is essential for understanding how his philosophy is best read as fundamental theology. I contend that, by seeing Westphal as a theologian and not a philosopher, the task has changed, and along with it the stakes as well: Westphal's theistic truth claims can be posited within a theological discourse that can accept and take up postmodern critique, so as to direct it and challenge it, while still remaining situated in a Christian tradition. Westphal's style of thought is one of appropriation: he takes up a concept, such as a hermeneutics of suspicion, and places it within his own Christian context. By fully accepting this context, and consequently making the shift from a philosophical to a theological discourse, he can acknowledge that his appropriation of these concepts do not directly address the author's original concerns but are placed in service of Westphal's Christian faith. This is not to say that philosophy and Christianity are irreconcilable; it is to argue that Westphal's ultimate concern is not philosophical but theological: his goal is to better understand the Christian faith in a postmodern context, and he employs philosophy to do so. This theological paradigm also further reveals the pastoral dimension of his work, which I address in the conclusion of this chapter.

Caputo's critique of Westphal's overcoming of onto-theology helps reveal this theological concern as it points out the eschatological nature of Westphal's theology. Westphal is dependent on revelation within his work, and, as one can see with his appropriation of *Aufhebung*, his thinking deeply involves concepts or subjects being taken up within a higher order (canceled but not negated in a traditional Hegelian fashion) that culminates in a transcendence with God. Caputo's critique hints at how Westphal's theism is dependent on an eschatology to make his philosophy work, and accordingly, one begins to notice the theological foundation of Westphal's work. As shown within Caputo's critique of *Overcoming Onto-Theology*, Westphal's thinking culminates in a future eternity, hinting at an eschatological moment when the concerns of onto-theology are alleviated:

The upshot of Merold Westphal's postmodern delimination of onto-theology is that, when all is said and done, we are free to believe everything that onto-theological arguments, in all their clumsy woodenness and misplaced absoluteness, were getting at. We are perfectly free to believe in the God of metaphysical theology: that God is an infinite eternal omnipotent omniscient creator of heaven and earth. Onto-theology is overcome by being postponed and chided for being so precipitous, presumptuous and impatient to shuffle off these finite, mortal and temporal coals. *What onto-theology is talking about comes true in eternity, but here in time we should make more modest proposals.* Postmodernism is the methodological requirement of the day, enjoining epistemological modesty and hermeneutical patience, *but at the end of days,* when this methodological veil is lifted, classical metaphysical theology steps on the stage, wholly unable to suppress a bit of an 'I told you so' smirk on its face.[12]

Caputo finds that Westphal's appropriation of postmodernism is mainly a contemporary formulation of an epistemic humility that accepts that 'we are not God.' Yet while Caputo's postmodernism asks, "Can we ever believe in the existence of a God?" Westphal is content to stymie the question of God's existence for the sake of giving the believing soul room to thrive in a postmodern context. "Westphal's epistemological or methodological appropriation of postmodernism proves too much," Caputo claims, pointing at how it stops just short of a true embrace of a postmodern suspicion and critique of the truth claims of traditional theism.[13] Westphal happily accepts that humanity does not have access to the Truth, or that we see through a glass, darkly, but he still holds to the Kierkegaardian principle that this does not entail that there is no Truth. Rather, it is accessible only to God: "Existence is a system—for God, but it cannot be a system for any existing spirit."[14] Westphal is not ready to abandon his theism for the sake of committing to a concept of postmodernity that Caputo claims is more radical. In fact, Westphal sees his work as radical precisely because he formulates postmodernity through a theistic lens: he sees how a determinate, "thick theology" can remain viable even after the death of metaphysics.[15]

CENTER OF GRAVITY: WESTPHAL'S 'ONTO-THEO-LOGICO-CENTRISM' IN *TRANSCENDENCE AND SELF-TRANSCENDENCE*

Before entering into Caputo's critique, it is important to summarize Westphal's process of overcoming onto-theology in *Transcendence and Self-Transcendence,* since it will remind us of what, exactly, Caputo is critiquing. Westphal presents his argument in three parts: part 1 explains the critique of onto-theology and how he utilizes this critique against what one could say is 'bad God-talk,' where God becomes a metaphysical tool for the all too human quest for self-autonomy. He directly engages Heidegger's critique in *Identity and Difference* and in *Being in Time*. From there, he explores Spinoza's and Hegel's pantheism to show how there is a need for a concept of transcendence in our thinking (contra Spinoza) and how the notion of absolute understanding, even with a sense of transcendence, is problematic as it continues—even masks—the quest for self-autonomy (contra Hegel). Humanity, as seen through the critique of metaphysics in Heidegger and the formulations of Spinoza and Hegel, perpetually attempts to develop an understanding of the world in which humanity is always at the controls. God thus becomes "the keystone of a metaphysical theory designed to render the whole of reality intelligible to [human] philosophical reflection."[16] This philosophical reflection, Westphal continues, is the beginning of making the world subject to human self-interest and mastery. Metaphysics, then, can be seen as humanity's selfishness, by which we try to make the world bend to our will, our will to power.

In part 2 Westphal tries to explicate a theistic account of God that avoids metaphysical onto-theology. He does this through an engagement with three premodern thinkers—Pseudo-Dionysius, Augustine, and Aquinas—and with Karl Barth, who at best can be called antimodern. Through this engagement Westphal formulates a way to comprehend God through what God is not (Augustine, Pseudo-Dionysius, a *via negativa*) and how God can be understood through asymmetrical analogy (Pseudo-Dionysius, Aquinas, the *analogia entis*). Finally, he shows how revelation, God revealing God's self to humanity, opens us to an understanding and dialogue with God even though we can never fully comprehend God or God's revelation (Barth, the *analogia fidei*). This dialogue allows Westphal to claim that a theistic account of God is tenable without onto-theological thinking and that it is possible to know of God, to experience God's involvement in the world (i.e., revelation), in spite of human selfishness. In this formula, Westphal sets up human sin as a primary obstacle for understanding God, as seen through Barth's concept of total depravity, and he relates sin to onto-theological thinking.[17] Once he has established a way not to understand God (which indeed informs the ways one can understand God), Westphal then turns to a phenomenological concept of revelation and how that possibly allows us to experience and understand God, albeit finitely and imperfectly. We see in Westphal's engagement with premodern thinkers that the human, reflective process of understanding God can function as an access point to conceptualizing God. Nevertheless, he eventually focuses on God's revelation to humanity as the primary mode of conceiving God, since it is at once God revealing God's self as well as a manner in which faith becomes a task and not a proposition.

Part 3 sees Westphal working somewhat inversely to metaphysics: he first teases out a nontheological encounter with God and revelation through Levinas's conception of ethics as first philosophy. This is meant to show how a concept of God and revelation can exist without theological presuppositions.[18] Then he lays a theological foundation underneath this phenomenological account through Kierkegaard's concept of faith as a task of a lifetime. With both Levinas and Kierkegaard, Westphal finds a way to understand how a believing soul arrives at faith through the experience of creation and how one is compelled by that faith to live a (faithful) life within creation through commanded revelation. The prior God-talk from parts 1 and 2 find their *telos*—their faith and purpose, basically—through the dialogue in part 3. As we shall see, this is an important aspect that I think Caputo's critique misses.

In his essay "What Is Merold Westphal's Critique of Onto-theology Criticizing?" Caputo dissects Westphal's *Transcendence and Self-Transcendence* by showing that while it does allow for some form of self-transcendence and decentering of the self, it still holds to a greater center, and therefore does not actually overcome the problem of onto-theology.[19] Caputo bases this critique on the Derridean line of thought, the thrust of which is that, although removing the self as the center of thought is good, the fact that there is still a center grounding the self means that onto-theology is still in play. Caputo even suggests that the critique of onto-theology be called a critique of "onto-theo-logico-centrism," arguing that Westphal falls into a familiar trap of basing his idea around a center that grounds thought.[20]

Setting up this critique, Caputo describes Westphal's overcoming of onto-theology as a dual-track process by which, "on the one hand, the transcending of the self [is seen] as an autonomous self and self-centered agency, and on the other hand, the transcendence of God, the irreducible alterity of God, [is seen as] beyond the confinements and constructions by which we humans seek to contain God's being."[21] One track sees a self-surpassing transcendence, whereas the other track, together with this self-surpassing, opens the self to a greater transcendence in and through the divine. Basically, the self overcomes itself through the other to find God. "The more

God's transcendence is respected," Caputo summarizes, "the more decentered and self-transcendent the self becomes."[22] On this account, Caputo settles Westphal into the postmodern debates concerning the decentered self and onto-theology. Moreover, he notices in Westphal's part 2 a particular version of "a ladder of ascent" that passes through three stages to understand the transcendence of God.[23] This is where Westphal's theism comes into play: after the 'bad God-talk' of part 1, Westphal describes the transcendence of God, which becomes understood through the task of faith in light of revelation, the essential point of part 3. These stages display human reason grappling epistemically to understand that which it seeks to find in transcendence. One could say that this ladder of ascent in part 2 is the foundation (or the actual tracks, in Caputo's metaphor) that Westphal establishes for the movements of the self in self-transcendence in order to find God's transcendence.

Regarding what onto-theology is and why it matters for God-talk, Caputo offers his own reading of Heidegger, noting the circular nature of onto-theology:

> 'Ontotheologic' is a circle or circulatory system in which Being serves as the ground of entities, and entities return the favor and serve conversely as the ground of Being. That is to say, Being is the common ground of everything that is, that which they all have in common, their common base, ground, or support, even while the First Entity (God) is the causal ground of other entities, thereby setting in motion the distribution of Being among entities, so that entities may have Being at all. Both Being and entities play crucial but complementary roles within the circulatory system of onto-theology.[24]

As a matter of circular reason, onto-theology, for Caputo, characterizes the ways in which human reasoning justifies itself through its own logic (or reasoning). He broadens this point through Derrida, whom Caputo sees as articulating how onto-theology is problematic because it focuses on a center of thinking that grounds thought; the *theo* in *onto-theo-logy*. Thus onto-theology "is a critique of the Center and of any possible 'centrism,' be it God or anything else."[25] This problem with a center is that God—or what stands for God in secular onto-theologies—is unquestionable, and thus "undeconstructionable": in the vein of onto-theology understood as circular reasoning, God is something that begins and ends the circular nature of thinking and thus is impermeable to inquiring into its own foundation.[26] As Caputo argues:

What is being criticized [by Derrida] is confidence in the Center itself and the protection it affords, the confidence that there is a Center that holds firm and encompasses all. [Derrida] describes a situation in which we are more radically de-centered, de-centered not because we are merely fallen and finite while the Center itself is infinite, holy and incomprehensible to our finite minds and wills, but because the Center itself is in question.[27]

Derrida follows the same critique of Heidegger: metaphysics is always problematic in its attempt to ground thought. However, Derrida reformulates this critique by questioning the seeking of ground or a foundation itself. The fact that a ground is sought becomes the object of a critique of metaphysics, not what functions as the ground. Caputo sees Westphal's attempt to articulate a theistic God beyond onto-theology as continuing this pattern, and therefore he does not overcome onto-theology.

Capitalizing on this Derridean formulation, Caputo places equal emphasis on all three aspects of onto-theo-logy, yet he begins the deconstruction (not the overcoming) of this term from the middle. One has to be aware of beingness (*onto-*) in relation to being, but also the center of gravity for which God represents within being (*theo-*) and the subsequent rationalism that formulates both into concepts that can be understood and thus exploited in human reasoning (*-logy*). "It is only when all three ingredients," Caputo summarizes, "in [onto-theology] are given their due weight that we can come to grips with this critique in its distinctive sense."[28] In the case of overcoming onto-theology, then, one must move beyond a center (*theo-*), as it is essential to both the *onto-* and the *-logy* in *onto-theo-logy*; it is the tie that binds the expression.

Considering Westphal's argument in *Transcendence and Self-Transcendence*, Caputo acknowledges that emphasizing the decentered subject is indeed a primary step toward overcoming onto-theology, but the fact that Westphal wants us to become more God-centered through our decentering (the second track, as he formulates it above) does not rid us of seeking a center, as the center itself is the objectionable concept. If we are to understand that "the critique of ontotheology is a confession of a lack of proper, determinate, and fixed names for what we love or desire," then we must maintain an "open-endedness" toward where that love and desire points.[29] Westphal, positing a theistic God beyond onto-theology—in spite of his clever use of the *via negativa*, *analogia entis*, and *analogia fidei*—fails to be radically open ended. He still holds to a center, however fuzzy he wants to make it.

For Caputo, being (radically) postmodern is to be more open to the possibility of what transcendence might mean to the self-transcending and decentered subject. Westphal, in Caputo's reading of *Transcendence and Self-Transcendence*, stops short of being sufficiently radically open to be willing to let go of a theistic God. I find that if one were to read Westphal in this way, one would rightly side with Caputo, since Westphal maintains a center and thus does not overcome onto-theology. It would seem as if Westphal is continuing what Caputo criticized in *Overcoming Onto-Theology*: he wants to believe in the God of metaphysical theology, albeit postponing the metaphysics until eternity. At the end of days, Westphal's (metaphysical) God may still smirk and say, "I told you so." However, although Caputo's critique is valid, I think he has ignored the Hegelian nature of Westphal's *Transcendence and Self-Transcendence*—and perhaps Westphal's use of onto-theology in general—when he formulates it along a dual-track process. The tracks Caputo uses are surely metaphorical, but I contend that the concept of decentering the self to find a greater center is a misreading of Westphal's argument. In that work, Westphal does not see either as tracks, as it were, but rather self-transcendence is *taken up* in transcendence via what I call a Westphalian *Aufhebung*; there is no movement of the self out of the center to experience the transcendence of God.[30] Rather, God's transcendence takes up the self-transcendent self through one's faith and obedience to revelation. Sin, as understood through onto-theology, is canceled in this dual transcendence through both the act of the self and the act of God. It is a dual transcendence, and thus it requires participation of both God and the self. However, it is the self who is being taken up into the higher order of God since one's self-surpassing transcendence opens oneself to God and to being taken up. Within this process, what is being negated is the individual's sinful nature.

Caputo is entirely correct to highlight the 'eternal' (or what I call, the eschatological) nature of this argument, but he is wrong to articulate it as he does, since his reading entails that, within the experience of decentering, the self becomes cognizant of the greatness of a larger center—as if the self slides away to gain a greater perspective of the whole. Instead, I believe that Westphal's argument of self-transcendence, which pertains to a decentered subject in a philosophical sense, is better seen theologically and, more pointedly, eschatologically: the self's self-transcendence is the process by which God takes one up through a transcendence that cancels the sinfulness of the self, particularly the noetic effects of sin (onto-theology), and lifts the self up into a higher purpose.[31] This higher purpose on earth is serving God through commanded revelation (particularly the love commandment), but it discovers its finality in an eschatological movement when God takes up the world in divine reconciliation. Caputo has a valid claim: for Westphal, the right for humanity to pronounce metaphysical truth claims is postponed here on the earth, and postmodernism becomes the contemporary articulation of this postponement. However, Westphal sees a future when this might not be the case. Existence is still a system for God, and faith is still only a task, but it anticipates a future eschaton. Westphal is indeed writing a thick theology.

RAPTURED BY THE SPIRIT: WESTPHAL'S ESCHATOLOGICAL *AUFHEBUNG*

After closely reading *Transcendence and Self-Transcendence*, one is surprised by how easy it is to misread the text as a straightforward argument explaining what God is not, and then what God is, and finally how we come to know God. In this fashion, it could be read almost like a long-winded sermon that chides believing souls in the pews with their foolish God-talk, then builds them up with a positive concept of God and concludes with an *Ite, missa est*, or blessing: "Go forth and sin no more! Follow God's commandments and you shall inherit the Kingdom!"

While there is something true to this understanding, one misreads Westphal if they see his argument as straightforward. As mentioned in the last chapter, he reveals that this is a misreading, surprisingly, in the conclusion of the work, when he remarks at the "strikingly Hegelian character" of the text, particularly in its method.[32] From this admission, he notes how his work follows the Hegelian structure of moving from an abstract notion (onto-theology, in Westphal's case) toward a "concrete particularity" (i.e., understanding of revelation and faith).[33] Furthermore, he explains that the text could be read backward, from part 3 to part 1.[34] Understanding this Hegelian character thus becomes the lens through which one should read the text.

Westphal articulates that this Hegelian structure reconstitutes a concept into a more complex whole, and as such, it follows what Hegel calls an *Aufhebung*, or what Kierkegaard articulates as a teleological suspension. As mentioned before, Westphal sees the concepts of *Aufhebung* and teleological suspension as synonymous, albeit with some small differences between them. For Westphal, Hegel's term relies on Aristotelian logic dictating a progress from "the atomic and abstract to the contextual and concrete" in the name of finding a presuppositionless science. Kierkegaard, however, holds "no such pretentions" and seeks to show how the "conceptual, teleological necessities" that constitute thinking "require relativizing and recontextualizing one stage within another" in relation to an "ultimate *telos*" which, in addition to being the end (hence, ultimate), also guides the suspensions (hence, *telos*).[35] While he sides with Kierkegaard's formulation over Hegel's own, Westphal has always been keen on describing both as identical—indeed, he admits that he treats them as such in this text.[36] Regardless of his agreement with Kierkegaard, Westphal admits that "the basic Hegelian structure remains," and hence one can get a greater understanding of the whole by looking at how the whole comprises the appropriative movements that begin at the atomic and end in the concrete. This becomes, essentially, a Hegelian form of mereology in which a reverse dialectic is employed to gather a greater understanding of how the whole comprises smaller parts by appropriation. However, contra Hegel, Westphal's understanding of this appropriation requires no outright negation of A when it is appropriated into B to become C.[37] Instead, it is 'canceled' via recontextualization: its intention, or *telos*, is suspended in the higher *telos* of C. This is what makes Westphal's *Aufhebung* similar to the teleological suspension within Kierkegaard and it is why I contend that it is an appropriation, a Westphalian *Aufhebung*.

In relation to *Transcendence and Self-Transcendence*, this appropriation of *Aufhebung* means that one has to read the text in full and then work backward. Therefore, part 1 is taken up by part 2 and both are taken up in part 3. Caputo was correct that there is a ladder of ascent in Westphal, but it is not seen in his understanding of *theos*. Rather, the ladder of ascent is an *Aufhebung*, or teleological suspension, in which each part is taken up by the next and is finalized in a *telos* that points to how the ethical and religious concepts in part 3 open the believing soul to God's transcendence, a transcendence understood through part 2 and part 1. This reveals how Westphal's thinking holds to the principle of an ultimate *telos*, an eschatological *telos*, in which the self-transcendent self is completely taken up in transcendence by God.

We can see these *Aufhebungen* in the conclusion, where Westphal explains how, throughout the work, he has tried to describe three types of transcendence: ethico-religious, epistemic, and cosmological. Beginning with his understanding of ethical and religious transcendence (part 3), he emphasizes that the call to faith comes from "welcoming the voice by trusting the promises and obeying the commands it hears from on high. From on high!"[38] The call to faith from the voice from on high (God) is revelation that promises and commands the believing soul to action. The promise, I contend, is eschatological; the command is how faith becomes the task of a lifetime in partial fulfillment of this promise: one does not overcome onto-theology simply by accepting revelation. Rather, one is always already overcoming onto-theology through accepting and living the commandments. Westphal lends himself to this reading when he talks about the "voice of transcendence" by which the self is transformed through the commandment of loving the neighbor, to whom the self is related but also distinct.[39] This functions as a decentering of the self in which the self places the other as the subject and thus stands in relation to the other as its object. This in turn allows for both selves, as it were, to be taken up and to become "part of something greater than either my own *conatus essendi* or our life world—namely the Kingdom of God, a game plan in which I become myself by serving rather than being served."[40]

Note the distinctly biblical connotation here, which I find follows the Gospel of Matthew and can be seen in the Sermon on the Mount, particularly Matthew 5:1–48. In the Beatitudes, Jesus pronounces who shall inherit the Kingdom, mainly those who faithfully work in service for the sake of mercy and to bring about peace (Matt. 5:5–9). Following this, Jesus instructs the crowd that his life and teaching are not meant to abolish the Law but to fulfill it: "But whoever keeps and teaches [the Law, the commandments] he shall be called great in the kingdom of heaven. For I say to you that unless your righteousness surpasses that of the scribes and Pharisees, you will not enter the kingdom of heaven" (Matt. 5:19b–20). The sermon continues by broadly explicating how one can follow this path of righteousness through personal relationships with others, particularly focusing on one's humble and faithful service to the other in loving mercy (Matt. 5:21–48). Traditionally, most biblical scholars do not see the Sermon on the Mount as an eschatological sermon but point to Matthew 24–25 as fulfilling that function instead. I mention it here to emphasize the dual nature of revelation that I see in Westphal's writing: the sermon points to the promise and command of revelation, and that promise is both being fulfilled through obedience to the commandments of revelation but is also yet to come. It is somewhat paradoxical in nature in that one brings about the Kingdom here on the earth while also working for the future Kingdom. This recalls

Westphal's description of Kierkegaard's faith over and against Christendom where he says: "Another way to put this point, is that we will all be Hegelians in heaven. But on earth . . . that is the question Kierkegaard wants us to ponder."[41] The problem with Christendom (as a product of onto-theology) is that it wants to make an earthly kingdom of heaven; a Tower of Babel–like structure invented out of sheer will to power. The believing soul must recognize this as a folly yet also know that it can experience the future Kingdom to come (i.e., God's heavenly Kingdom) through a loving fulfillment of the commandments. Thus, the believing soul does not abandon the eschatological ideal of God's greater transcendence; rather, through service, the believing soul begins to experience the Kingdom by enacting faith with a hope for the future.

When taken as a whole, one can see the relation between the works of faith and the revelation that has commanded those works; a revelation that has also promised a future that is experienced here on the earth but also is yet to come. In many ways, this sermon, as well as Westphal's *Transcendence and Self-Transcendence*, point to a partially realized eschatology where the works done here on earth bring about the Kingdom of heaven but are not yet completely satisfactory: the Kingdom is brought about on Earth and yet also promised in the future. For Westphal's part, the ethical and religious transcendence that occurs through obeying commanded revelation entails a future promise, a promise by which the believing soul is taken up by God's transcendence into a higher order.

From this understanding of ethical and religious transcendence, Westphal turns to another aspect of transcendence—namely, how one can come to know God through this promise and command, which he calls epistemic transcendence. This is where parts 2 and 1 enter into the picture, respectively. One can come to know God (part 2) through a faith that obeys the promise and command of revelation. Epistemic transcendence uncovers the mystery of God revealing God's self within the ethical and religious aspects of transcendence. Epistemic transcendence indicates that the notion of loving the neighbor reveals an understanding of God (revelation) that at once allows one to experience God in transcendence but does not delimit God to merely what one experiences. Experience, here, is understood as encountering God in and through revelation (via self-transcendence), and that encounter allows one to speak of God even though what one can say is only partial; this experience is veiled and so one can speak only of what she encounters as if she were looking through a glass, darkly. In this way, the ethical aspect of self-transcendence opens us to an epistemic path to knowing God. One could say you get to know Jesus through imitating him; the more you follow his teachings, the more you understand them, and thus the greater your relationship with Jesus. The same could be said of following the God of the prophets, the Lord who brought the people of Israel out of the desert. This also entails a superiority of ethics over and above all: "What have traditionally been called the 'moral' attributes of God need to have priority over the 'metaphysical' attributes."[42] Onto-theology, then, becomes an aspect of our thinking when this priority is reversed and we allow our metaphysics, or what stands in place of metaphysics in our postmodern age, to guide our morality.

This is also true for Westphal's final aspect of transcendence, what he calls a cosmological transcendence, in which God is understood as "the Creator, maker of heaven and earth" and one gathers other traditional attributes of God.[43] This aspect of transcendence directly relates to part 1, where Westphal defends and refines the concept of theism in contrast to onto-theology and the pantheisms of Spinoza and Hegel. His chief concern with cosmological transcendence again refers back to the ethical and religious transcendence in that the truth these cosmological attributes hint at what is necessary to come to know God (in epistemic transcendence), and they must never detract from the ethical and moral imperative contained in revelation. Westphal notes how a cosmological transcendence is taken up by both an epistemic and an ethical and religious transcendence in the final sentence of the text itself: "Where divine transcendence is preserved in its deepest sense, the affirmation of God as Creator is not merely the attribution of a certain structure to the cosmos but above all the *commitment of oneself to a life of grateful striving.*"[44] Thus, what is understood as the cosmological transcendence of God, and what one can know of God, must be understood through a faith that is the task of a lifetime. This faith is dependent on God's revelation to us, which can be understood nontheologically—that is, ethically—through Levinas. However, more important, it can be understood through the religious concept of revelation, which promises and commands the faithful self to a grateful striving to bring about the Kingdom of heaven, here on earth, while looking forward to the true Kingdom yet to come. There is indeed an *Ite, missa est* in Westphal's thinking, and it blesses the believing soul to enact faith in order to better understand what commands and promises of that faith.

Philosophically, this might be a contentious proposition, as revelation becomes the seeking for a grounding of revelation: when one follows the command of revelation, one seeks the promise of revelation and thus to better know the source (i.e., center, or God) from whence revelation came. Westphal's project, as a philosophy, runs into the problem that Caputo has raised: it has postponed its metaphysical, onto-theological propositions for a future eternity and here on earth has made the more modest proposal of living in faith and not seeking absolute knowledge. Yet when looking through a theological lens, a lens that particularly equates the noetic effects of sin to onto-theology, one can see that Westphal has written something quite profound: he has written a radical eschatology that explains that sin, which cannot be overcome here on earth, can be canceled in God's transcendence, but only through the believing soul's attempts to continually overcome (or avoid) sin, which she does through enacting her faith daily and constantly. Transcendence, then, becomes salvation, and while there is no complete salvation on earth—the believing soul still has the mark of sin and will lapse into sin—she can strive for a daily overcoming of her sin through aspiring to self-transcendence. She aspires to this through living for the other, following the commandments given by revelation, hoping for the future promise of a day when she no longer has to strive but is fulfilled by being taken up by God. Thus, Westphal has articulated something as radical as Caputo's full-on embrace of postmodern hermeneutics: he has articulated a theology that holds sin and its noetic effects as a principle for understanding the human condition.[45] In light of this, Westphal outlines a way for the believing soul to strive to overcome this sin through critiquing what she might initially think is God in order to find truer relationship with God and to fulfill God's commandments, a task that entails a future promise when she shall overcome her own sin. Akin to Meister Eckhart, Westphal has prayed for God to rid himself of God, but, in doing so, he has found this prayer to be a task of a lifetime that can be performed only through loving and serving the other.

We Shall Overcome: Radical Eschatology's Pastoral and Theological Implications

In the essay "Overcoming Onto-Theology," Westphal recalls a story of how singing the spiritual "O Mary, Don't You Weep" at a conference brought to mind Heidegger's critique and how startled he was to see that he and his fellow attendees were at that moment overcoming onto-theology.[46] While Heidegger's critique famously argues that "before the *causa sui*, no man can neither fall to his knees in awe nor can he play music and dance before this God," Westphal found himself in front of such a God before whom he could sing and dance—or clap anyway—as he was "before the God who drownded [sic] Pharaoh's army" in the salvation of Israel; that is, a God who is not the *causa sui*.[47] The essay goes on to detail how Heidegger's critique is adroitly pointed at those metaphysical theologies which turn God into a *causa sui* for their own selfish gain and how, in spite of those theologies, for Westphal there still stood a God before whom he could sing and dance. The essay is rather audacious in that, with a scant twenty-eight pages, he claims that onto-theology is overcome! An onto-theology, that is, that has been the focal point for philosophy and fundamental theology for nearly eighty years, yet he immediately sees its overcoming through a song. *Transcendence and Self-Transcendence* stands as a work that attempts to explain this overcoming in greater detail, but for Westphal the matter was somewhat simple: a lived faith—as experienced in that faith's worshipful hymns—overcomes onto-theology because it opens the believing soul to the love of God through the believing soul's love for God and the other:

> This love, this trust, this relationship—these are the *practice* for the sake of which it was necessary to deny theory. This is not to abolish theology. It is to see that theology's task is to serve this life of faith, not the ideals of knowledge as defined by the philosophical traditions Heidegger variously calls calculative-representational thinking, metaphysics, and onto-theology.[48]

Praxis is integral to this process, and in *Transcendence and Self-Transcendence*, this praxis gets its proper explication through part 3 of the work, and specifically through Westphal's articulation of ethical and religious transcendence. It is from this praxis that theology—both as moral theology and as fundamental or systematic theology—gets its charge to aid and support the praxis of faith. Parts 2 and 1 of *Transcendence and Self-Transcendence* further explicate how this type of theology is meted out. This is where I contend that Westphal's thought is pastoral: he is fleshing out the ethical and moral implications of theology in light of a postmodern critique of metaphysics and traditional understandings of God. While I doubt Westphal's *Transcendence and Self-Transcendence* would make for good Sunday-school reading, he has written many other works for laypersons and the Sunday-school crowd—as we have covered—and his more academic works present the theories that guide and support those pastoral works. They work in tandem to create a robust, thick theology.

Westphal, read as a theologian, has therefore created an oeuvre that has much more in common with Karl Barth than with his contemporaries: by not abandoning his theism for the sake of postmodernity and its critiques—and instead appropriating postmodernity to better understand his theism—Westphal has positioned himself as a point of contact between the church(es) and the philosophical academy.[49] However, two questions remain concerning the theological implications of reading his work as a voice for these churches: first, there is the question of the Holy Spirit's role in this transcendence; second, there is still the issue of fideism in his work.

There seems to be something of a neo-Pelagianism in his thinking, where the believing soul, once informed by revelation, can bring about her own transcendence with God; the self can bring about the transcendence of God through creating her own self-transcendence. If one reads his work as a radical eschatology, then one can see a self-made character latent in the argument where the believing soul may be able to bring about her own salvation through good works. I do not believe this was Westphal's intent, and truly he would argue that the Holy Spirit works within the life of faith through guiding the self to revelation and helping the self receive revelation. Moreover, his work often relies on the fact that even though the self's actions help bring about her own self-transcendence (ethical and religious transcendence), this does not entail that transcendence will magically be present; not every loving encounter with one's neighbor will be transcendent. If this were the case, then ethics would be magic: one could call God forth simply by doing good works! However, the issue of special divine action—how God interacts and interrupts the world in contemporary, real time—needs to be more thoroughly fleshed out in Westphal's thinking. In other words, throughout his oeuvre we have gained an understanding of God and Jesus (as Paradox and Paradigm), but the role of the Holy Spirit has yet to be explicated. As he has described his own work as a philosophical understanding of faith as the task of a lifetime, I do not hold this charge as an oversight on Westphal's part. It is merely that more work needs to be done to fully understand how the theory behind his thinking functions with other aspects of theology.

This leads to the second issue of *fideism*. In *Kierkegaard's Critique of Reason and Society*, Westphal argues that Kierkegaard's faith is not *fideist* since its opposite is sin and not reason. Reason, understood as a social epistemology, becomes sinful when it renounces faith or attempts to neuter faith in the process of making it "reasonable" or comprehensible to human understanding.[50] Conversely, reason becomes an aid to faith when it is used to guide faith to understanding.

In *Transcendence and Self-Transcendence*, one can see Westphal employing these principles when he argues that God's moral attributes must never be subjugated to so-called metaphysical attributes (i.e., those known through reason). Additionally, one comes to an understanding of God only by first enacting a religious and epistemic transcendence through faithfully enacting the love commandment. Yet how is one capable of understanding the commitments involved in faithfully enacting the love commandment (and being cognizant of the promise and command of revelation) without first knowing those commitments? How is it, in other words, that the believing soul comes to believe without first being able to understand or comprehend said belief? Westphal would probably refer to Levinas's ethics as a philosophical understanding of these commitments, which brings about a (Kierkegaardian) understanding of their religious implications. Moreover, he might point to the fact that one might enter into a faith like Christianity with certain pretensions only to have them obliterated through the act of transcendence and self-transcendence, a shattering of expectations, as it were. Yet still, the fact that there are expectations and that one can come to understand—study, even—the religious implications of a self-transcendence means that at some point these aspects can be understood by reason alone.

On this point, Westphal might agree: one can understand religious and ethical transcendence, and all it entails, without the aid of faith. In fact, *Transcendence and Self-Transcendence* fulfills this, as he mentions that the book can work as a form of apologetics to the nonbeliever.[51] However, by placing faith as the primary (or even the only "true," or proper) mode of understanding transcendence, Westphal is showing that there is a gap between comprehending transcendence as an essential aspect of faith and comprehending it as a phenomenon of human experience that can be understood through reason (i.e., philosophically). Perhaps, as a theology, this gap is where the Holy Spirit dwells in the world: the self only comes to recognize the revelation that spurs faith through the Spirit's continual acting in the world. However, in a postmodern context, which is just as fearful of all gaps as it is of foundations, this might prove untenable for a philosophy of faith.

Despite these two issues, one should not dismiss Westphal's theology. It is indeed a potent articulation of how faith works in the life of the believing soul, and it opens his Protestant faith to be further explored and understood by those within and without the church. Additionally, his work is a strong, ecumenical dialogue partner with the Catholic Church over the issue of so-called faith versus works and the promise of salvation. In other words, on the issue of how our acts on earth affect our salvation and relationship to God. This was and is an important issue between a Lutheran understanding of salvation and a Catholic one, and Westphal's contribution to the discussion can be immediately seen in his notion that one does not have faith but rather *faiths*. It is a task word, for Westphal, and the issue of salvation can be seen in the concept of self-transcendence and transcendence. Merely believing in the God of Jesus Christ is not enough for Westphal. Rather, the believing soul plays a part in salvation (and eschatology) through a self-transcendence by following the command and promise of revelation. Christians are working to bring about the Kingdom here on earth while looking forward to a future heavenly Kingdom yet to come.

NOTES

1. John Caputo, James Marsh, and Merold Westphal, *Modernity and Its Discontents* (New York: Fordham University Press, 1992). The penultimate chapter sees Marsh, Caputo, and Westphal discuss these debates in a forum style and is a great example of these aforementioned repartees.

2. *OCOT*, 72, 130.

3. Ibid., 68, 157.

4. See, for example, J. Aaron Simmons and Stephen Minister, eds., *Reexamining Deconstruction and Determinate Religion* (Pittsburgh, PA: Duquesne University Press, 2012), 256, 259–260, 263–265. Westphal's objection to the role of agape and eros in religion, specifically on the debate of religion with(out) religion, points to a similar lack on Caputo's part as mentioned earlier: "But here is my problem: However interesting and compelling the 'continuity' of agape and eros might be, I simply cannot find anything in it that could not be affirmed by Derrida and Caputo and fitted into their religion without religion. The location of a higher (heavenly) eros in Plato and Augustine seems neutral. We might say that for Plato it fits into religion without religion and for Augustine it is part of his religion with religion" (264).

5. This lack of nourishment pushes their debate toward the question of ethics in postmodern philosophy of religion. See the multiessay dialogue in Mark Dooley, ed., *A Passion for the Impossible: John Caputo in Focus* (Albany: SUNY Press, 2003), chap. 7.

6. John Caputo, "Methodological Postmodernism: On Merold Westphal's *Overcoming Onto-theology*," *Faith and Philosophy* 22, no. 3 (July 2005): 290.

7. Ibid., 292.

8. In *Reexamining Deconstruction and Determinate Religion,* Bruce Ellis Benson poses the same question concerning Simmons's reading of Caputo and Westphal. Benson addresses Simmons's statement that Westphal is "as radical as one needs to be," noting that this question changes depending on what needs to be overcome through postmodernism: "Yet just how radical does one need to be to do whatever it is that is truly post-modern and get over exactly whatever it is we need to overcome and why it is so bad that it needs overcoming?" (61). This causes Benson to hold a suspicion toward the assumptions underlying the entire philosophical project that Westphal and Caputo are engaging in. One the one hand, Benson is open to being challenged by Caputo and Derrida, among others, concerning his theism. On the other hand, Benson is concerned that, if this challenging is taken far enough, it negates too much, leaving him with "this absolutely other God [who is] *simply not enough,*" a God who is just as distant and unworshipful as Heidegger's critique of onto-theological gods (66). The difference between his concern and ours is that Benson, for his part, focuses this critique on Caputo, where I focus this critique solely on Westphal.

9. *GTPD,* 173.

10. Clayton Crockett, B. Keith Putt, and Jeffrey Robbins, eds., *The Future of Continental Philosophy of Religion* (Bloomington: Indiana University Press, 2014), 34–45. Westphal and Caputo respond on 45–50 and 51–58, respectively.

11. See: Christina Gschwandtner, *Postmodern Apologetics? Arguments for God in Contemporary Philosophy* (New York: Fordham University Press, 2012). Gschwandtner's book gives superb summaries of the contemporary debates in Continental philosophy of religion while also placing the major thinkers, such as Caputo, Westphal, and Kearney, within those debates.

12. Caputo, "Methodological Postmodernism," 291–292. Emphasis is mine.

13. Ibid., 292.

14. Søren Kierkegaard, *Concluding Unscientific Postscript,* ed. and trans. Howard Hong and Edna Hong (Princeton, NJ: Princeton University Press, 1992), 1:118. Westphal is fond of using this phrase. See *OCOT,* 291; see also Simmons and Minister, *Reexamining Deconstruction,* 34, where Simmons explains Westphal's philosophy of religion with the use of this quote.

15. Concerning how Westphal sees his own work, this might be debatable. However, he clearly frames his thinking through his theism. See especially Merold Westphal, "Faith Seeking Understanding," in *God and the Philosophers,* ed. Thomas Morris (Oxford: Oxford University Press, 1994), 215–226. See also 215–225; *OCOT,* ix–xi; *GTPD,* 183–185; and *TST,* 6.

16. *TST,* 18.

17. Ibid., 146–149, 154–156, 160, 162–163, 215–218; see also 128.

18. In other texts, Westphal calls this an ethical suspension of the religious. See Westphal, "Levinas' Teleological Suspension of the Religious," in *Ethics as First Philosophy,* ed. Adriaan T. Peperzak (New York: Routledge, 1995), 151–160.

19. *GTPD,* 100–116. Whether Caputo's critique of Westphal is correct is not our primary concern, since we are exploring how it draws out the eschatological nature of Westphal's thinking. Therefore I will not comment, as much as possible, upon the veracity of Caputo's claims.

20. *GTPD,* 107.

21. Ibid.

22. Ibid.

23. Ibid. These three stages can be understood as *via negativa, analogia entis,* and *analogia fidei,* respectively.

24. *GTPD,* 102.

25. Ibid., 109.

26. Ibid., 111. Caputo: "the name of God [or what serves as God] touches upon a nerve in the human heart and suggests something 'undeconstructible.'"

27. Ibid., 109.

28. Ibid., 111.

29. Ibid., 114.

30. See chapter 2 of this volume.

31. On the issue of the noetic effects of sin, see Merold Westphal, *Kierkegaard's Critique of Reason and Society* (Macon, GA: Mercer University Press, 1987), 97, 105–115.

32. *TST,* 227. He does mention this concept in the introduction (9–11), but only briefly; it does not get his full attention until the conclusion.

33. Ibid., 227–228.

34. Ibid., 229. "Still, the basic Hegelian structure remains, making it possible to read the text backwards. This means seeing the parts in relation to the whole in which they are eventually placed rather than in their supposed self-sufficiency. They may well be essential parts or necessary conditions, but they are only parts and they are ordered within the whole by a *telos,* not automatically their own (though they can make it their own)."

35. See ibid., 228–229.

36. Ibid., 228. "The attentive reader," Westphal remarks, "will have noticed that I treat Kierkegaard's notion of teleological suspension as virtually synonymous with *Aufhebung.*" See chapter 2 of this volume.

37. Moreover, A does not have to be completely and symmetrically opposed to B, as in Hegel's understanding of determinate being, where indeterminate (pure) nothingness passes over indeterminate (pure) being and thus is negated, making determinate being and beings. See G. W. F. Hegel, *Science of Logic,* ed. and trans. George Di Giovanni (Cambridge: Cambridge University Press, 2010), 48, 59, 82. (SL 107; HW 5/114–EA).

38. *TST,* 229.

39. Ibid., 230.

40. Ibid.

41. Westphal, "Johannes and Johannes," 20. The ellipses are Westphal's own.

42. *TST,* 231.

43. Ibid.

44. Ibid.

45. While this can be seen as orthodox, or traditional, Christian theology, Westphal sees within orthodoxy and tradition something just as radical as Derridean deconstruction. After all, he has argued that Gadamer, along with his appeal to history and tradition, is as equally radical as Derrida. Perhaps, contrariwise, one could say that Caputo's radical hermeneutics is not as radical as it sets out to be—that it is as equally "ordinary" as Westphal's hermeneutics or that it is not-so-very-damn radical. Since both capitalize on the notion of radicality, and the nature of the discussion involving them follows suit, Westphal's eschatology can be seen as radical.

46. I quote the eponymous essay within *Overcoming Onto-theology,* not the entire book.

47. *OCOT,* 2. He quotes Martin Heidegger from *Identity and Difference,* trans. Joan Stambaugh (New York: Harper & Row, 1969), 72.

48. *OCOT,* 27. Emphasis is mine.

49. While Caputo's thought is not the primary subject of this chapter, and I have primarily used his critique to draw out Westphal's eschatology, there is an interesting parallel regarding the theological tendencies of each. Stephen Minister flips this charge against Caputo, showing how Caputo himself exhibits a movement toward theology within his work: "While I

completely agree with Caputo's condemnation of fundamentalism . . . what is significant is the fact that even Caputo's attempt at religious inclusivity cannot help but define itself through the exclusion of certain theological positions." Minister, *Reexamining Deconstruction and Determinate Religion*, 84.

50. See Westphal, *Kierkegaard's Critique of Reason and Society*, 21–23. Here, Westphal is drawing on Kierkegaard's concept of faith as a critique of *Sittlichkeit*.

51. *TST*, 2.

9. COMPARATIVE ESCHATOLOGY

Westphal's Theology, Kearney's Philosophy, and Ricoeurian Detours

WITHOUT CAPUTO: WESTPHAL IN DIALOGUE WITH KEARNEY

In the previous chapter, we discussed Merold Westphal's thought in light of his primary debate partner, John Caputo. As I argued, Westphal is almost always discussed alongside his friend Caputo as both represent different, opposing sides of various debates in Continental philosophy of religion in North America. On the one hand, Westphal argues for a 'thick theology'—a hearty soup—that provides a theistic, religious appropriation of postmodern thought to nourish the believing soul. On the other hand, Caputo analyses theism through a radical critique of religion's onto-theo-logico-centrism. Caputo's postmodernism declares that religion must be rethought—even to the point of abandoning much of what qualifies as religious—to proceed after what we have discovered about the nature of human thought. It often feels as if this debate holds an unqualified either-or: one must take a side and argue it to the hilt. For their parts, B. Keith Putt as well as J. Aaron Simmons and Stephen Minister have tried to reconcile this debate by showing how Westphal and Caputo's thought might coalesce either as a "Capuphalian" philosophy (Putt) or a return to religion with religion (Simmons and Minister).

I have only touched on this discussion in my exploration of Westphal because it appears to me that each thinker approaches philosophy and theology from irreconcilable positions. Westphal is an open theist who wants to appropriate postmodernity for aiding and guiding a particular brand of theism, whereas Caputo wants to do away with anything that can be construed as theism and utilizes postmodernity for its eradication. Contrariwise, I find that we have overlooked Westphal's true dialogue partner: Richard Kearney. Even though Westphal and Kearney have engaged each other, with Kearney contributing to Westphal's Festschrift and with Westphal intervening at conferences and colloquia dedicated to Kearney's work, an in-depth discussion of the convergences of their thought has been lacking.[1]

This is surprising, as I have found that reading Westphal alongside Kearney (and vice versa) reveals a profound discussion about hermeneutics and theism. Importantly, I find this to be a discussion, not a debate. Initially, one can see Westphal and Kearney as dialogue partners through the profound influence Paul Ricoeur has had on their work and their shared use of Scripture. However, as I intend to show, their primary intersection is in their eschatology and in how humanity plays a role in bringing about an eschatology here on earth while awaiting an eschatological moment yet to come. Both focus their thinking on the command and promise of God.

After exploring their intertwining debts to Ricoeur, I unpack this notion by first exploring Kearney's eschatology in *The God Who May Be* and how it challenges Westphal's own eschatology.[2] What also emerges from this discussion is a shaper distinction between philosophy and theology. To simplify our inquiry, I center on how each conceives of God after onto-theology, paying particular attention to their views on ontology and eschatology. Accordingly, this inquiry reveals how Westphal and Kearney, despite using Ricoeur's hermeneutical phenomenology, methodologically approach the question of God after onto-theology in strikingly different manners. Westphal's methodological approach reveals an eschatology that is heartily theistic, revealing its theological roots, whereas Kearney's method strictly follows hermeneutical-phenomenological description of a possible God beyond ontology, which is best read as a philosophy. These contrasting disciplines impose certain limitations on both thinkers, thus deepening the need to read each alongside the other for a more robust understanding of religion in a postmodern context.

In Accord: A Shared Use of Ricoeur

Richard Kearney's reading of Paul Ricoeur's hermeneutical phenomenology closely resembles Westphal's earlier use of him in *God, Guilt, and Death* and adjacent articles. Therefore, we will capitalize on this mutual understanding by using this text to provide a baseline for when Westphal eventually diverges into an appropriation of Ricoeur. From there, we then follow how Westphal develops his own project through this appropriation, and finally, we will return to Kearney to contrast how his use of Ricoeur remains consistent throughout his career. What emerges from this is a distinction between Westphal's theological discourse and Kearney's philosophical one.

Westphal is indebted to Ricoeur's hermeneutics of suspicion, and consequently, he owes much of his methodology to Ricoeur. This is especially seen in *God, Guilt, and Death* and *Suspicion and Faith*, two works that define the contours of Westphal's overall project. In those works, Westphal first employs Ricoeur's overall hermeneutical phenomenology to understand the existential meaning of religion and then he appropriates Ricoeur's hermeneutics of suspicion to understand the ways religion can be corrected when it fails to live up to this meaning. Recall that Westphal describes *Suspicion and Faith* as a sequel to *God, Guilt, and Death,* and that he situates *Transcendence and Self-Transcendence* as a work that can be read as a sort of bridge between the two, effectively forming a trilogy.[3] In doing so, Westphal reveals that his three most original works are methodologically based on Ricoeur's hermeneutics. Finally, if one were to extrapolate further and say that *Overcoming Onto-theology* contains a constellation of ideas that led to *Transcendence and Self-Transcendence*, one can clearly see the great impact of Paul Ricoeur on Westphal's entire thinking.[4] Even though Westphal gathers most of the content of his core ideas from other thinkers—namely, Kierkegaard—he does so through a methodology that is based on Ricoeur's own.

This reliance on Ricoeur for a methodology first arises in *God, Guilt, and Death*. Here, Westphal inquires into the value of religion by exploring the 'believing soul' and her journey through religion. He thereby attempts to describe the existential meaning of religion through how it shapes the believer's concept of guilt and death.[5] From the start, two immediate themes emerge: the concept of the believing soul and a phenomenological method distinct from Husserl's. Furthermore, recall that Westphal even appropriates the term *believing soul* from Ricoeur.[6] Additionally, he founds his project on Ricoeur's hermeneutical framework, especially Ricoeur's concept of the sympathetic imagination. Through this, Westphal is able to place his readers as close as possible to the religious believer to understand how she experiences her belief. Quoting Ricoeur, Westphal clarifies:

> The philosopher adopts provisionally the motivations and intentions of
> the believing soul. He does not 'feel' them in their first naiveté; he 're-feels'

them in a neutralized mode, in the mode of 'as if.' It is in this sense that phenomenology is a re-enactment in the sympathetic imagination.[7]

Through the sympathetic imagination, Westphal declares that his phenomenology maintains a purely descriptive line of reasoning that never 'explains' religious practice. Philosophically speaking, he claims that an 'explanation' attempts to interpret phenomena, yet, rather than describing what occurs, it tries to give causal reasons for why it occurs. Regarding religion, this tactic can either 'explain away' or 'explain into' what happens to the believing soul. In other words, it is liable to either use phenomena to prove or disprove religious belief. Description, in contrast, avoids this problem by accepting a sympathetic 'as-if' position within its observations by only interpreting phenomena or experience through the believing soul's own perspective (or as close as one can get to it). Hence, the phenomenologist stymies as much bias as possible toward or against religion from entering into her work.[8] While this may be stating the obvious for any phenomenologist, it matters for our exploration because Westphal eventually abandons this descriptive methodology for one that is more personally involved, one that is prophetic and prescriptive.

However, given that the phenomenologist is human (all too human), at least some degree of bias is inevitable.[9] Knowing this, Westphal also incorporates Ricoeur's hermeneutics of suspicion as foundational to this method. Using it here as Ricoeur does, Westphal's goal is to employ such a suspicion only to correct his bias and not the believer's praxis.[10] So, one could say that in the text, Westphal strictly follows a Ricoeurian methodology, similar to Kearney's, as we shall see. Moreover, through Ricoeur's suspicion Westphal discovers that it cuts both ways: against those who wish to breathe too much belief into philosophy of religion and against those who suffocate belief through their 'objectivity':

> Might not that pursuit of objectivity which limits itself to the phenomenal, observable, perhaps even to the testable domain be a fear of error which turns out to be a fear of truth? Is not a descriptive philosophy of religion methodologically prejudiced against its subject matter, just as much in its methodological theism as in its methodological atheism?[11]

Here, Westphal uses Ricoeur's suspicion to cast doubt upon a phenomenological enterprise that claims an atheistic-like detachment from religion in order to better understand its purpose. By acknowledging the flaw of objectivity within this methodology—thus proceeding beyond a Husserlian phenomenology—one can make room for the believing soul to speak. Conversely, to not go too far and fall into the opposing trap of being methodologically prejudiced on behalf of this soul, Westphal argues that one must "establish" a position "of detachment and disengagement," which maintains that "the descriptive attitude is not motivated by the desire to be rigorously scientific, but rather by a passion for self-understanding that is neither detached nor disengaged."[12] Hence, the phenomenologist stands alongside the believing soul, asking her questions in an attempt at 'refeeling' and 'reenactment,' but the phenomenologist cannot assume the role of the believing soul.

What is surprising about this is that this creates a middle way between being confessional and observational: Westphal wants to describe religion's value but not explain (i.e., defend) it to those who may reject religion. Westphal has, in effect, established an anti-apological position in a framework wholly indebted to Ricoeur.[13] This adds another layer of depth to his Kierkegaardian position against a certain kind of apologetics that attempts to defend faith through reason alone.[14]

Westphal elaborates upon this anti-apologetical stance in his 2008 essay "Ricoeur's Hermeneutical Phenomenology of Religion," where he gives his understanding of Ricoeur's hermeneutical turn against the Husserlian project of phenomenology as a rigorous science.[15] Westphal notes that Ricoeur's hermeneutics involves not just an arduous reading of texts, but includes "the whole domain of meaningful action. Thus a hermeneutical phenomenology of religion will concern itself with practices as well as paragraphs and pericopes."[16] Regarding phenomenology and apologetics, this means that, to understand the significance of religious texts, one must first explore their function in their religious tradition and then reflect on what those texts say about that religion: why they are authoritative, how are they interpreted, et cetera. Thus exploring a tradition requires one to bracket out both skeptical and apologetical perspectives to walk alongside the believing soul. Through this bracketing, Westphal's reading of Ricoeur opens a space for dialogue where religious texts and practices become open to believers and nonbelievers alike, offering possibilities of intersections between the masters of suspicion and the prophets, a bridge between philosophy and theology.

Phenomenologically speaking, this entails an inquiry beyond the texts themselves to proceed "towards [the text's] immanent sense and towards the world which it opens up and discloses."[17] As such, it requires a reen-actment in which the phenomenologist provisionally adopts the motiva-tions and intentions of the believing soul.[18] Westphal eventually places this provisional adoption as a hermeneutics of recovery, arguing that both an hermeneutics of recovery and suspicion work together to thwart any sort of presumed psychologisms from appearing while also revealing the phenom-enologist's biases or prejudices. Thus, taken as a whole, Westphal's reading of Ricoeur allows the phenomenologist to enter into the lifeworld of the be-liever without taking her place:

> Even if the phenomenologist is a believing soul, seeking to articulate the meaning of religious experience and belief, to describe the world in which the believing soul lives is not immediate experience, belief, and life. To write an essay on the phenomenology of prayer is not to pray. To describe confession is not to confess. So the phenomenology of religion is not the religious life itself, and the phenomenologist need not be a believing soul engaging in the beliefs and practices being described (though that may be helpful).[19]

Questions concerning the veracity of those religious truth claims are brack-eted out for the phenomenology to unfold. Written more than twenty years apart, this essay essentially redescribes his project in *God, Guilt, and Death* while tacitly revealing how his appropriation of Ricoeur allows him to write in both philosophical and theological contexts by removing the issue of apologetics.[20] Kierkegaard gives Westphal a Christian motive for being anti-apologetical by pitching sin instead of reason against faith. Ricoeur deepens this position by giving Westphal a philosophical motive to remove apologetics by developing a phenomenological inquiry into faith that does not concern itself with a logical defense of that faith.

This is why Westphal finds that Ricoeur evades Dominique Janicaud's critique, which "accuses a number of thinkers . . . of smuggling theology into philosophy in the guise of phenomenology."[21] For Westphal, Ricoeur outlines the possibilities of a religious life and one's possibility of accepting or rejecting such a life. Ricoeur, at least in his philosophical work, makes this a possibility since he tries to avoid crossing over to confessional writ-ing, crossing over to speaking on behalf of the believing soul.[22] He rigor-ously maintains a sympathetic imagination and nothing more. Westphal summarizes Ricoeur's supposed response to Janicaud thus: "Precisely in understanding a religious world as a possibility of my being I can choose not to dwell in it."[23] This harks back to Westphal's concern against a methodological theism versus a countering methodological atheism, where an atheistic detachment can evade truth just as easily as its counterpart. However, Westphal often chooses to dwell in the religious world, thus revealing that this argument somewhat sidesteps the concerns held by nonreligious phenomenologists (à la Janicaud) who attempt to understand phenomena from a detached, observational perspective. In *Suspicion and Faith,* for example, he undermines any concern against maintaining a possible choice not to dwell in the religious realm. One might ask, "How can I follow a phenomenological method that solely ascribes to a sympathetic imagination regarding the believing soul and then continue on to prescribe and alter the religious praxis of the believing soul? Am I not crossing a boundary, at least phenomenologically?"

The answer is yes. One is crossing a phenomenological boundary, and Westphal crosses this boundary often by directly inhabiting a confessional position when crafting his prophetic concept of philosophy as faith seeking understanding. As I have argued previously, this disposition is what lends Westphal to be read as a fundamental theologian rather than a philosopher of religion.[24] This is also what separates Westphal and Kearney: Westphal's work is heavily confessional, whereas Kearney maintains a deeper philosophical line of reasoning.

DIVERGENCE: WESTPHAL'S THEOLOGICAL READING OF RICOEUR

Suspicion and Faith has a different audience than the other two books in his trilogy. Rather than aiming for the academy, it aims for the pews and is meant to be read as a guide for faith seeking understanding through Lenten reflection. This follows the now-familiar path that Westphal takes where philosophical description must also open itself to change; it must allow a space for, following Westphal's prior terminology, the prophetic voice. Its description of the world, in other words, gives way to becoming a guide for changing it. Despite the change in audience, *Suspicion and Faith* maintains a Ricoeurian framework through employing a hermeneutics of suspicion against the hermeneutics of recovery performed in *God, Guilt, and Death.*[25] The transition from walking alongside the believer, however, has been augmented toward a confessional stance: the phenomenologist is now a believing soul, talking to his fellow congregates, showing how the prophets of their tradition are still at work and in conversation with atheists who echo (plagiarize even!) their own critiques against religion.[26] Westphal has shifted to a confessional point of view and has crossed the phenomenological line to a prescriptive theology.

Even though this crossing from philosophy (sympathetic and descriptive) to theology (confessional and prescriptive) can also be seen in *Overcoming Onto-theology* and *Transcendence and Self-Transcendence*, it becomes less obvious. However, this is not because Westphal has distanced himself from Ricoeur, but because he has built his own project on Ricoeur's thinking. One can see this in how Westphal situates *Overcoming Onto-theology* as a text that reads as apologetics in reverse: faced with the seeming irreconcilability of theism and postmodern Continental philosophy, Westphal presents ways a traditional theist can exist within this philosophical terrain. Instead of defending traditional theism against encroaching postmodernity, he actually defends postmodern thought against contemporary theism by showing how many of its characteristics run parallel to those found in Christianity, thereby creating a positive postmodernity.

If *Overcoming Onto-theology* does indeed propose a reverse apologetics to theism, then one of its essential arguments pertains to how a hermeneutics of suspicion is healthy for faith. Suspicion is not skepticism; it does not have to eradicate faith, nor does it demand a logical defense of faith. Given the similar use of Ricoeur's hermeneutics of suspicion in both works, one could say that *Suspicion and Faith* is intended for a lay audience, whereas *Overcoming Onto-theology* adapts and expands the sentiments of the former work for an academic audience. Throughout both, Westphal is rather consistent on the matter, albeit with more nuance and depth in the latter text.

Both texts, however, warn readers about making suspicion the final resting place for a faith seeking understanding. If taken as the ultimate move, such suspicion can become dangerous and leads to despair or nihilism.[27] This is where Westphal posits his own take on Ricoeur's work through an appropriation of suspicion into the life of faith, where such a hermeneutics is *aufgehoben* into a larger philosophy or theology.[28] This is what he calls positive postmodernism: the hermeneutics of suspicion is placed into a hermeneutical epistemology that is articulated through a Kierkegaardian faith.[29] What makes this positive is not merely its religiosity but that it is open to alterity and to otherness. Unlike Nietzsche, Kierkegaard's concept of faith concedes that its movement toward inwardness (i.e., the hidden inwardness of faith) is only penultimate and that there is a final movement toward the other, as in Westphal's reading of *Works of Love* and his concept of Religiousness C.[30] In his summary, Westphal distinguishes Nietzsche's suspicion to Kierkegaard's faith thus:

> By contrast, Kierkegaard, who knows as well as Nietzsche how easily professed virtues are really splendid vices, does not give up on compassion and neighborly love but seeks to show how their true form is essential to human flourishing. By virtue of his fundamental willingness to find that decentered selfhood that can experience the other as truly other, Kierkegaard has the basic moral resources needed for a critique of modernity's moral Cartesianism, the placing of the self, individual, and collective at the center, thereby making wealth and power, personal and national, the overriding goals of life. Like the Hebrew prophets before him and Levinas after him, Kierkegaard is a philosopher of *shalom* rather than of *polemos* [the latter being the primary designation for Nietzsche].[31]

What is interesting is that Westphal appropriates a hermeneutics of suspicion to articulate a postmodern, theistic faith that can incorporate Nietzsche while still keeping its core religious values intact. Moreover, this *Aufhebung* of suspicion into faith helps it maintain these values through discipleship! However, perhaps his ultimate appeal to Kierkegaard fits a bit too neatly into this argument. Yet, for now, what this shows is that Ricoeur's hermeneutics is *aufgehoben* in Westphal's concept of positive postmodernity, which doubles as his concept of contemporary faith.

Westphal elaborates on this faith in *Transcendence and Self-Transcendence*, adapting the same hermeneutical posture to argue how discipleship can bring oneself closer to God. In the previous chapter, I pointed out the ways this leads the text to be read eschatologically, and I articulated this through what I call a Westphalian *Aufhebung*, by which something is taken up but not outright negated by an opposing antithesis, and yet still reconstituted (or recontextualized) into the whole. While this is the language of Hegel, I contend that Westphal utilizes a particular understanding of Ricoeur's hermeneutics for his foundation. Ricoeur allows the believing soul to take suspicious critique seriously, and once she has explored this suspicion in-depth, she can appropriate from it helpful concepts without negating her own faith. Hence, the Westphalian *Aufhebung*: Nietzsche's atheism does not outright negate Christianity; rather, it helps cancel out ways the Christian faith can lapse into self-service. More directly, Nietzsche's atheism never negates Kierkegaard's theism; rather, it opens Kierkegaard's theism to be read as a social (or ideological) critique that reorients society.[32] This

234 · REASONING FROM FAITH

appropriation of Ricoeur gives the believing soul a space to speak, to listen, to critique, and to inform her discipleship. It also gives Westphal impetus to exploit different interpretations of texts:

> Paul Ricoeur describes his relation to his philosophical predecessors as reinterpretation and re-appropriation "thanks to a meaning potential left unexploited, even repressed" by traditional readings. I seek to appropriate unexploited and even repressed possibilities of secular postmodernism for the renewal of theism and its essential linkage to the renewal of theists.[33]

In the conclusion, Westphal describes his debt to Ricoeur and Gadamer for his hermeneutical phenomenology, specifically regarding their understanding that texts are "marked by particularity and [historical] contingency."[34] All of this is to say that Westphal's model of appropriation is directly influenced by what he sees as Ricoeur's own appropriations, such as with Husserl and Freud. Westphal's understanding of Ricoeur's style of appropriation thus permits him to take important ideas from disparate and possibly opposing thinkers (e.g., Barth and Aquinas, or Levinas and Kierkegaard) and then reconstitute those ideas into his project.

If Westphal's model of appropriation follows Ricoeur's own, however, one thing that differentiates them is how each uses appropriation to advance his philosophical-theological projects. Ricoeur's philosophy is deeply hermeneutical, but this is only (or at least, primarily) a detour toward a phenomenological understanding. In that vein, Ricoeur's phenomenology still rigorously maintains a restriction to how sources can be used and what phenomenology can or cannot say. Ricoeur, in other words, stays within the limitations of phenomenology whereas Westphal does not. This is why I eventually find that Westphal is a hermeneutical thinker exploring phenomenology rather than a hermeneutical phenomenologist.

Finally, where is the sympathetic imagination in Westphal's work after *God, Guilt, and Death*? For example, although he maintains that *Transcendence and Self-Transcendence* can be read by the believing soul and the nonbeliever alike, his text changes genres for each. For the believer, it has a "pastoral intention" and for the nonbeliever it has, surprisingly, "an apologetic intention."[35] No longer is his work sympathetic as it blatantly holds a confessional disposition. He is not allowing room for the believing soul to speak but is speaking on behalf of (and to) the believing soul. Moreover, note that the apologetical intention is that of explanation. He does not give a rational defense of faith so much as explain how faith can lead to self-transcendence and possibly transcendence. Further, the preface also declares that he explored these two notions of transcendence in *God, Guilt, and Death* but did not explore them in "strict correlation with each other as I am attempting here."[36] While that work described religion as not merely instrumental—as though it were a means to an end—in bringing about a sense of transcendence, Westphal left the relationship between the self and God, Wholly Other, unexamined. Perhaps this is because Westphal thinks that a description of religious transcendence, and the type of faith needed to bring about this experience, cannot adequately be interpreted. Perhaps it can come only from a testimonial reflection. For Westphal, the task of faith is essential to self-transcendence, and although a description can reveal ways the self enters into such a relationship, it cannot direct or inform it. Westphal's thinking, however, has continually sought to direct believing souls in this relationship. *Transcendence and Self-Transcendence*, as a pastoral work, advances this trajectory by clearing away 'bad God-talk' (onto-theology) and prescribing a path for the believing soul to experience divine transcendence. He does so entirely through a confessional perspective precisely because his Christianity informs his understanding of both transcendences:

> As a Christian, I believe that the church, for all its failings, is the best place to encounter transcendence and experience self-transcendence. But my phenomenological analysis will signify structures that might occur, *mutatis mutandis,* in relation to synagogue, church, mosque, temple, or none of the above, as in what Derrida calls 'religion without religion.'[37]

After he acknowledges other areas in which such transcendences can occur, his own Christian belief shades this ecumenical understanding. *Mutatis mutandis*, here, reveals that certain foundational structures in his thinking may need to be changed for this ecumenism to happen. This, in and of itself, is nothing revelatory. A hermeneutical thinker such as Westphal typically presents his biases and prejudices to readers for consideration. However, when one looks at how Richard Kearney situates his own prejudices in *The God Who May Be*, one sees an entirely different perspective:

> So how do I respond to the standard hermeneutic question: Where do you speak from? . . . Philosophically, I would say that I am speaking from a phenomenological perspective, endeavoring as far as possible to offer a *descriptive* account of such phenomena as *persona,* transfiguration, and desire, before crossing over to hermeneutic readings. . . . Religiously, I would say

that if I hail from a Catholic tradition, it is with this provisio [he continues, explaining his ethically informed sense of religiousness].... *But regardless of labels, I would like to think that the kind of reflections advanced in this book are vigorously ecumenical in terms of interfaith dialogue.*[38]

Kearney attempts to maintain the purely descriptive character of phenomenology, and more important, he describes his work along the lines of reflections on the subject of God rather than a direct, theological engagement with a particular (concept of) God, therefore rigorously maintaining an openness to other faith traditions. Whereas Westphal directly says that his work comes from a Christian perspective that might occur in other faiths, Kearney strictly employs a phenomenologically descriptive methodology that, in keeping with the original intent of the hermeneutics of suspicion, recognizes that Christianity influences his own perspective and that he will vigilantly try to be aware of this throughout the work. From both acknowledgments we can essentially distinguish each project: Westphal uses his biases and prejudices to advance a theological project, whereas Kearney attempts to advance a strictly phenomenological project while being cognizant that he cannot completely avoid his biases.

Detours and Possibilities: Kearney's Hermeneutical-Phenomenological Methodology

Kearney's understanding of Ricoeur follows Westphal's similar reading in *God, Guilt, and Death*, albeit with varying emphases. As such, Kearney would probably agree with Westphal's description of religious experience, or at least accept his methodological approach. It is only when Westphal adopts the role of the believing soul that their projects' methodology diverges. Therefore, for the sake of simplicity, my primary focus here is on how Kearney's use of Ricoeur differs from Westphal's later writings, and thus I do not completely review Kearney's reading of Ricoeur.[39] What I intend to show is how Kearney's fidelity to Ricoeur's hermeneutical phenomenology challenges Westphal's thinking and further reveals his project as theological.

Whereas Westphal is a hermeneutical thinker exploring phenomenology, Kearney is a thinker who begins in phenomenology and then employs hermeneutical detours to craft a stronger, descriptive understanding of the phenomena in question. The essential difference between Westphal and Kearney comes down to this disposition, but it can be broken down even further to how each reads Ricoeur's relationship to Husserl. As we have covered, Westphal has little faith in the Husserlian project. His reading of Ricoeur is shaded by this prejudice, seeing Ricoeur as an ally in support of his critique. Thus, Westphal takes a sharp hermeneutical turn presumably alongside of Ricoeur.[40] Westphal clearly understands that Ricoeur is deeply influenced by Husserl but he takes from Ricoeur a phenomenology that is, if not anti-Husserlian, then post-Husserlian. However, as the term *postmodernity* implies that modernity is still with us in some form (without modernity there could be no *post*-modernity), so Husserl remains very present in a post-Husserlian phenomenology. To put it somewhat churlishly, if Ricoeur takes the hermeneutical turn, he doesn't kick Husserl out of the car altogether.[41] It can seem as if that is the case for Westphal's reading.[42] Contrariwise, Husserl's standing in Ricoeur's work is something that Kearney takes more earnestly than Westphal does: Kearney's phenomenological analysis—via Ricoeur—is deeply situated in a Husserlian influenced phenomenology and he attempts to supplement it, not overcome it, through hermeneutical detours.[43]

This is clearly seen in *Strangers, Gods, and Monsters*, where Kearney presents a phenomenological project on otherness through a hermeneutical exploration of how otherness can turn on the fear and fascination of the divine and the monstrous. He proceeds by reading texts that present otherness in the extreme, that describe the monstrous and the divine. However, Kearney first and foremost maintains that this is a phenomenological project, albeit through a hermeneutical path that twists and turns with each examined text. Phenomenology, here, is necessary because, without it, the hermeneutical interpretations he attempts may fall in on themselves, collapsing like a house of cards.

Kearney shows this in the introduction, where he details the necessity of such a phenomenological methodology against a solely hermeneutical approach.[44] Here, he notes that those who see themselves as primarily hermeneutical, in somewhat of a "post-phenomenological" stance, fail to properly understand the self-other relationship, either through conflating both to the point that there is little to no difference between them or, conversely, "separating them so schematically that *no* relation at all is possible." The problem of proceeding without phenomenology, he continues, is the tendency:

> to externalize the category of alterity to the point that any contact with the self smacks of betrayal or contamination. The attempt to build hermeneutic

bridges between us and 'others'... should not, I will argue, be denounced as ontology, onto-theology or logo-centrism—that is to say, as some form of totalizing reduction bordering on violence. For such denunciation ultimately denies any form of dialogical inter-being between the self and other.[45]

Kearney is aware of how his own project, even within a phenomenological methodology, can fall into this collapse between the self and the other, and thus he employs a countermeasure of suspicion against his project.[46] As such, the work employs a phenomenological method throughout, with textual readings illuminating but not becoming the means by which he explains alterity; the texts themselves are matters of exploration but not, ipso facto, arguments for alterity unto themselves. Thus, there is little by way of appropriation, at least in the way texts are read, in Kearney's *Strangers, Gods, and Monsters*. However, methodologically, Kearney has appropriated aspects of Ricoeur's phenomenology (as well as, it should be mentioned, Levinas's). What matters to us is that Kearney, contra Westphal, has not conjoined or taken up these texts to make a hermeneutical point and has not placed his sources into dialogue. Rather, he presents a phenomenological project that utilizes these texts as descriptive markers that inform his phenomenology. Notice that I am using "into dialogue" here in the same way that Westphal often places chosen texts alongside others. His dialogues between two thinkers often work as a means of negating certain aspects of each's thought, taking them up in a Westphalian *Aufhebung*.

In Kearney's *Strangers, Gods and Monsters*, the concept of alterity, as described in his reading of certain texts, discloses the ways in which otherness is comprehended and 'dealt with' (to put it broadly) in various cultures, which speaks to a larger sense of the human comprehension of otherness. This differs from a typical Westphalian project in that Westphal, if he were interested in such a topic, would have attempted to hermeneutically establish a concept of otherness that gathers various textual readings into a larger whole. In doing so, he would, hypothetically, utilize a dialogue between Levinas and Kierkegaard to construct a quasi-phenomenological understanding of what, hermeneutically, he has appropriated. Phenomenology, in this imaginary construct, is not so much a methodology to be employed but an evolution of an existentialist style of philosophy.[47]

Kearney's thinking, in contradistinction, refuses to be anything but strictly phenomenological. Turning to *Anatheism*, published after *The God Who May Be*, one can see that this extends to even his most personal philosophical texts.[48] "Anatheism" is Kearney's term for the concept of returning "to God after God," as a space between atheism and theism, broadly speaking.[49] This exercise is very personal to Kearney, as one can see from how he employs his own experiences throughout the work and personally reflects on his various intellectual influences.[50] Justifying this personal approach and answering the question "Why not other texts or authors?" Kearney replies, "Because in each case I write of those who marked me most."[51] However, even though *Anatheism* emerges from a deeply personal background, in the project he refuses to advocate for any kind of "new religion" or particular "theology."[52] He instead advocates for a philosophical "wager" that posits a thought experiment concerning what one should do about the concept of God in light of what Christians, particularly in Western society, have collectively and personally experienced in such a traumatic century.[53] It is, in essence, remaining faithful to how Westphal defended Ricoeur's philosophical-religious reflections against Janicaud: Kearney is describing a concept of God and religious understanding in which one can choose or not choose to dwell. It is not his concern what one does, theologically, with his work. Rather, he wishes to describe and comprehend the possibilities of God in light of our present history.

Kearney draws his line between philosophy and theology on the possibility of claiming God's existence. The philosophical enterprise of reflecting on God can only point to openings and pathways for religious action; it cannot traverse those pathways. To do so is to take on a character or disposition that negates the entire project: by taking a path one has occluded oneself from taking others, and therefore one enters into a theological, or at least a confessional, discourse. Contrastingly, Westphal chooses a path in his writing, and while I have been somewhat critical of Westphal's undertaking, his choice is not without merit. In many ways it outshines Kearney's philosophy, as we shall see. In this section, we have explored how these divergent paths follow how each writer reads and utilizes the work of Paul Ricoeur, with Westphal's path being one of appropriation and Kearney's being one that remains, at least on a methodological level, more faithful to Ricoeur's own project. I have maintained that this demarcates a line between theology (Westphal) and philosophy (Kearney).

In the following section we explore how this line is followed throughout their work by contrasting Kearney's *The God Who May Be* with Westphal's theological eschatology. This comparison centers on the question of just how ontological do we need to be concerning our understanding of God.

Or, more pointedly, just how much being does God need to have for our faith? For Westphal and Kearney, this question breaks along a theological and philosophical divide in response to these questions. This divide is further defined by the hermeneutical approach each utilizes when engaging religious texts, and the truth claims that are either accepted or bracketed out in this engagement.

Persona: Kearney's Phenomenology in The God Who May Be

Kearney begins *The God Who May Be* by presenting a radical phenomenological framework that posits a description of God without the concept of being, or *esse*. Rather, he employs the concept of *persona*, which he claims is a better way of describing the self's relation to the other and, by extension, the relationship between the self and God. *Persona*, as a phenomenological concept, relates to how one can understand "the otherness of the other," where, "at a purely phenomenological level, *persona* is [or represents] all that in others exceeds my searching gaze, safeguarding their inimitable and unique singularity."[54] Latent in *persona* are the possibilities that the other holds beyond one's gaze or understanding. This indicates the ways the other's selfhood is beyond one's complete grasp. Kearney sees in the concept of *persona* multiple possibilities of understanding the other that may come to fruition through our relationship. Nevertheless, these new understandings do not place limits on future experiences that may deepen my comprehension of the other. From this, one can come to comprehend these possibilities as having an "eschatological aura" where the appearance of possibility "eludes but informs a person's actual presence here and now."[55] Kearney's concept, here, is following Levinas's phenomenology, particularly Levinasian Καθαυτό.[56]

Persona, in this framework, configures the other as something that is "present in absence, as both incarnate in flesh and transcendent in time"; that is, she is real and present, yet her otherness transcends this real-time experience and thus she cannot be completely grasped. Kearney goes on to buttress this concept by accepting its paradoxical nature as presencing-yet-absencing the other through the two extremes of "pure presence (thing)" and/or "pure absence (nothing)."[57] These two extremes either call forth an idol from the other, which can be totalized, or one sees the other as pure transcendence and wholly other, where the attempt to manifest this otherness creates an ideological construct. In preventing either extreme, and to accept this paradox, Kearney employs an as-if proviso, where "the other always appears to us *as-if* s/he were actually present," yet it acknowledges that what is present before us is not a complete presence or a total understanding of the other's selfhood.[58] In relation to God, who Kearney notes is not a self, this as-if proviso remains. He employs the as-if proviso to reveal how the *persona* of God presents-yet-absences himself to the human self. Kearney, here, is using Ricoeur's as-if proviso in the sympathetic imagination to proceed between the total acceptance and negation of the other's presencing, be it God or an other self. Kearney thus uses the as-if proviso to inform his concept of persona and to make sure it stays on a course between the two extremes; however, he also maintains Ricoeur's typical use of the as-if proviso to keep his project philosophical and as ecumenically open as possible.

This rather dense opening chapter lays the phenomenological foundation for Kearney's project. It shows how he intends to address the concerns of onto-theology and to consider God outside of a metaphysical structure.[59] *Persona*, for Kearney, is a stronger form of understanding God, as it denotes how God's appearance to humanity is a presence-yet-absence. In Levinasian fashion, these appearances inform the human self of God's self, yet this information is not complete. It also opens a relationship between the self and God and, within that relationship, myriad possible future experiences that deepen the self's understanding of God.[60] For Kearney, basing his phenomenology on *persona* reveals the *posse*, or possibility, which arises in this relationship. This is relational, and it does not require (and even rejects) an understanding of God as *esse*, or existence. Understanding God through existence, Kearney argues, is faulty since it builds a metaphysics, which he finds is a "recipe for war," as we shall see.[61]

Hermeneutics and Possible Truth Claims: Kearney's Biblical Detours

To describe how a relationship with God is possible, Kearney begins his first hermeneutical detour through the initial encounter between Yahweh and Moses. It is, for him, an exemplary account of how God's revelation commands and promises through a presencing that becomes more realized throughout the relationship between God and humanity. However, while dealing with the realm of possibility, Kearney maintains his hermeneutical wager and makes no statement as to whether or not this event actually occurred; that is, he has not made an actual truth claim concerning this moment of revelation.

From what we have covered, note how markedly different Kearney and Westphal's approaches to ontology are: Westphal's construction still perceives God as something related to being, whereas Kearney attempts to diminish the ontological aspect of God by working through a framework that describes God as possibility. When the two discussed this difference at the colloquium held for *Anatheism*, Kearney states that he does not hold a belief in God, "as a thing 'out there,' which we can describe phenomenologically" and, consequently, one must turn to hermeneutics to find an understanding of God.[62] This, of course, is a rather sharp reading of *esse* within ontology, and one that Westphal probably does not accept.[63] Yet still, one can see how Westphal's adherence to historical truth claims—that God has existed in human history—sets his project apart from Kearney's. Additionally, one can see that Kearney, by avoiding existential claims concerning God, presents a descriptive, philosophical project; one that takes the presumption of revelation as a mere possibility. Hence, he only describes how this could have occurred while not stating what occurred. Yet Westphal does more than 'possibilize' these occurrences and he attempts to understand God as a being after onto-theology. The question between the two men, essentially, is a question of just how much being does God need to have for our faith? This recalls the question between Westphal and Caputo: just how radical do we need to be?

Continuing in *The God Who May Be*, Kearney sees the biblical encounter of Moses and God in Exodus 3 as the beginning of God's eschatological promise, and thus a pivotal moment in humanity's experience of God's *posse*; God's *persona*, through the burning bush, initiates a relationship with Israel through an eschatological promise. Kearney only describes the possibility of an eschatological moment, thereby avoiding a proto-evangelical, historical unfolding; he is not staking a truth claim about salvation and God's role in salvation. He brackets out these concerns to hermeneutically explore the event's possible meaning and how it might reveal the ways our motivations bring about the kingdom of heaven, here on earth, and how they relate to a future eschatological promise. He is threading a needle, basically, trying to vigorously remain ecumenical and philosophical by steadfastly remaining in his hermeneutical-phenomenological framework. If he were to make a truth claim here, stating that this event actually happened, he might cross into the bounds of theology, positing that God has historically 'happened,' or existed within human history, raising questions concerning God's *esse* in historical-human time. Westphal, conversely, stakes his work on truth claims presented in biblical revelation and although he tries to remain philosophical, I argue that he 'fails.' This is where he enters into a theological discourse, and this 'failure' deepens the ontological divide between him and Kearney. Recall that, in *Overcoming Onto-theology*, he tries to explain how theism can thrive in a postmodern framework and that one can use postmodern critique without abandoning theism. One of the concerns that emerges from Kearney's reading of a God of *posse* is that it lacks a foundational relationship with humanity. Without situating God within an ontological framework, the problem becomes whether this hermeneutical concept of God is merely an interpretation of texts and not a lived, dynamic experience.

Kearney counters this by trying to reorient the conception of such a dynamic experience through a description of how the God-self relationship is freely given and participation in it is voluntary. His concern about the God of power and sovereignty, understood primarily through *esse*, is that it might overwhelm this free choice. He gives one example in the colloquium where, when the angel Gabriel comes to Mary to begin the Jesus narrative, Mary is free to choose to accept this gift from God. A God of power and sovereignty (a God of *potestas*, as Kearney calls it) might not give her this choice and perhaps would have overwhelmed her. Yet she freely participates.[64]

He initially develops this thesis in *The God Who May Be* though explaining Moses's free choice. Kearney describes how Moses's encounter with God's *persona* in the burning bush centers on Moses asking for God's name. God responds to this question with the statement: *"'ehyeh 'asher 'eheyeh,"* or, as Kearney notes from the New Jerusalem Bible, "I am who is," also typically translated as "Yahweh."[65] Kearney's hermeneutic thesis capitalizes on the name Yahweh to consider the possibility that it can be interpreted as "I am who may be," and hence the God who promises.[66] By clouding this name in a construction that resists translation, Kearney considers that God is revealing himself as the one who suffers alongside his people. Moreover, in refusing to give a direct name, God has repudiated all the ways "that [one could] seek to appropriate Him here and now as some thaumaturgical property. Instead, God keeps himself open for a future, allowing for a more radical translation of his nameless name as 'I am as I shall show myself.'"[67] In this way, God not only resists appropriation but also may be understood as "theophanic and performative."[68] Theophany relates to God's appearance through revelation and performance relates to the command latent in the name itself. As Kearney clarifies, the performative notion of the holy name of Yahweh further reveals how Moses and Israelites can come to a greater understanding of God by following his promise:

> In short, the nameless Name is not an *acquis* but a promissory note. Its self-disclosure is inextricably tied to Moses' commission to go and announce to his fellow Hebrews their liberation and redemption. "You shall know that I am Yahweh your God, who frees you from the burden of the Egyptians...." Henceforth, Yahweh is to be experienced as a saving-enabling-promising God, a God whose performance will bear out his pledges. As Psalm 138 makes clear, "You have made your promised word well above your name."[69]

For Kearney, this performative aspect of Yahweh, interrelated with the name's theophanic qualities, is what opens God to be understood as an eschatological, promising God. This continues his phenomenology of *persona*, as this disclosure allows humanity to experience God, in the here and now, while pointing to a futurity of experiences that may unfold as partial fulfillments of God's promises. This experience comes via a messianic temporality that is outside of human history. Furthermore, Kearney advances his phenomenological method to make a description of God's nature in an eschatological framework through human participation. This eschatological framework is dynamic since God commits himself to his people, "as pure gift," and one is free to choose to follow God. Elaborating on this relationship, Kearney states, "With the revelation of his Name, God says of himself something like 'with you Moses—and with Israel throughout history—I stand or fall!' Exodus 3 is the proclamation that God has invested the whole of himself in his emissary's history."[70] This reveals how God instigates a historical and eschatological relationship with his people who, by their own expression and action, are free to shape and change this relationship. History, however, is fashioned only as a hermeneutical concept. Kearney is still deeply situated within an as-if proviso, although here it takes on a different character and is more in line with Ricoeur's sympathetic imagination than the way he employed it to accept the paradox of *persona*. Additionally, freely participating in this eschatological relationship brings about these eschatological moments, or micro-eschatologies, by which this promise becomes present in the here and now yet also absences this promise by pointing to what is yet to come.[71]

Westphal's *Transcendence and Self-Transcendence* follows a similar path by which the self-transcendent act brings about the Kingdom here on earth, via God's transcendence, yet always points to the future Kingdom yet to come. Both thinkers employ Levinas for their concept of revelation where what is experienced rends the self to a futurity of experiences through the acts which bring about this initial encounter (self-transcendence, micro-eschatology). However, Kearney's view of revelation diverges through his emphasis on these events as possibilities. Furthermore, both employ Levinas's argument that the self's relation to the other is integral to revelation; however, through Kierkegaard, Westphal posits the notion that God has acted within history and has, on occasion, revealed himself to humanity outside the self-other relationship. Westphal, in other words, sees different types of revelation, or ways revelation can occur. Kearney's philosophy does not elaborate other forms of revelation, and although he uses singular moments of God revealing himself (e.g., the burning bush, Jesus as the Stranger in *Anatheism*), he adheres strictly to a phenomenological analysis.

Westphal's thought postulates a theistic God where this special divine action is immanently conceivable. Furthermore, Westphal's use of biblical stories diverges from Kearney's. Westphal accepts that "God's involvement in the production of those [i.e., biblical] texts is such that they are the Word of God," regardless of the human error that might occur in their writing.[72] Throughout all of his texts, Westphal's approach to the Bible is confessional. Even though he vacillates between walking alongside and directly speaking for the believing soul, he is always a believing soul himself, and this always already informs him. Consequently, he is never as devoutly phenomenological as Kearney, and his work is resultantly more theological.

Continuing with *The God Who May Be*, Kearney advances his phenomenological reading of eschatology through the transfiguration of Jesus on Mount Thabor, where Jesus reveals his dual nature. Linking this narrative to his concept of *persona*, Kearney notes that the Gospel writers used the term *preopen heteronym*, which "means literally 'his face was othered.' And yet he somehow remained *some* one, for he was *still recognized* as himself."[73] Simultaneously, Kearney presents the idea that Jesus' transfiguration continues the promise and command of Yahweh while deepening the relational comprehension between God and humanity; God is further revealing himself through the transfigured Christ while also continuing his promise. Kearney's hermeneutical phenomenology of *persona* thus describes how Jesus could be the God of Yahweh while also being Jesus-the-man.

Kearney further elaborates upon Jesus' dual nature by showing how Jesus, and the divine voice through which his otherness is announced, resists a totalization. Noting how Jesus' disciples wished to set up a temple cult, the voice intervenes and commands them to merely listen to Jesus. "In this manner," Kearney states, "the voice of transcendence speaks through Christ as divine *persona*, thereby arresting [their] idolatrous impulse . . . to fuse with [Jesus'] person or to possess him as a cult object."[74] This follows the presencing-absencing schema of a phenomenology of *persona*, where the disciples 'have' Jesus in their sights—they can see him and his divine otherness—but they cannot totalize his presence through a cult of idolatry. Jesus simultaneously remains recognized yet wholly other. Noting how this narrative testifies to the struggle of God's people, Kearney states that "the transfiguring *persona* signals the ultimate solidarity, indeed indissociability, of spirit and flesh."[75] God is still with God's people, either through Moses and the continuing story of the Israelites or through Jesus and his suffering along with his disciples.

Jesus' role in this solidarity, for Kearney, brings about a messianism where God not only participates in the deliverance of his people but also directly suffers for and with them, as with Jesus' crucifixion. The solidarity is deepened, the gift is better understood, and the human self's need for a transcendent otherness is further revealed.

Kearney's description of the self's desire for God—where the self's desire to be fulfilled by a something-otherness causes a searching and restlessness—effectively places the self in an ethical framework that helps bring about these eschatological moments.[76] It is similar, in many ways, to Westphal's concept of self-transcendence, primarily given how both thinkers situate these eschatological moments through an ethical encounter with the other that may bring about a greater Other, God. In Kearney's case, from this notion of desire comes the moment where God becomes 'possibilized:' the impossible can become possible by following and enacting God's promise. This enacted faith in the possibility of the impossible evinces the same trust that made the disciples see Jesus as both a man and wholly other.[77] Within this possible impossibility, the promise of God continues and is partially realized in the self's participatory relationship with God "until the Kingdom comes—and with it a new heaven and earth."[78] This happens in a messianic time that "supersedes the linear, causal time of history moving ineluctably from past to present to future."[79] Adding to this, Kearney retrieves from the prologue of the Gospel of John a concept that humanity has a familial relationship with God, where John states that humanity is both born of flesh and of blood, and as children of God. Humanity, according to Kearney's reading, thus holds an affiliation with God—humanity being born of God makes humanity interrelated with God, and one's participation in God's promise helps us comprehend this interrelationship.[80] Therefore, concerning messianic time, the self participates in bringing about the kingdom of heaven here, in historical time, while participating in the Kingdom through messianic time. The self's experience of God transcends historical, linear time to enter into messianic time, where the impossible is made possible.

This transcendence of historical time indicates that the desire for God is an affiliation to and with God, expressed through God's promise and command: what we desire is something impossible (a relation with the divine, who is wholly other), but it is made possible through God's promise that he will forever be with us—in solidarity with our cries and suffering as well as rejoicing in our moments of happiness. This dynamic promise is brought about here on earth through the command to participate with God in this solidarity, in the time of causality and history. God just does not 'come' and overflow us with his presence, rending open our sense of time or being. Rather, we must participate with God as God participates with us. The God who would just overflow humanity would be a God of power, a God of ontology or *esse*. Instead, our participation merges causal and messianic time through those moments when revelation makes the impossible possible. Instead of being dependent on *esse*, God's *posse* becomes realized (in linear time) through our participation with God's promise.

Kearney calls this 'possibilizing God,' where the teleological possibility in this relationship confronts us with a future that is unknown yet desired. He does so through a Derridean faith that places its hope on the "impossible-possibility" paradox where one hopes that something might happen in one's day-to-day lives that transcends 'ordinary' or 'normal' experiences of the possible—that is, that something miraculous might happen.[81] Since a thorough exploration of possibilizing God would take us beyond our scope, we will set aside Kearney's further explication of the impossible-possibility. However, what Kearney concludes from these readings is that a possible God, "understood as the eschatological may-be," can be seen as radically transcendent.[82] This possible God calls God's people into a relationship that eschatologically unfolds an understanding of 'the God who may be' while simultaneously revealing a deeper understanding of humanity.

If one were to follow along the lines of the Economic Trinity, this dynamic relationship could be seen as paracletic, where the Holy Spirit dwells with those who, gathered in God's name, work to bring about the Kingdom. Kearney, for his part, discusses a similar notion in the final chapter, where he reflects on the Trinity as "God-play" and the "poetics of the possible God."[83] Poetics, here hermeneutically retrieves a Trinitarian model in which the three divine actors are seen as players in creation, withdrawing their powers to allow creation to exist, to have an *esse*:

> My eschatological reading . . . sees the divine Creator as transfiguring our being into a can-be—a being capable of creating and recreating new meanings in our world—without determining the actual content of our creating or doing the actual creating for us. . . . In short, the divine *nous* [i.e. the plural form of the trinity, together yet distinct] transfigures out capacity *for* seeing into a capacity *of* seeing; it makes us *able-to-think* at the same time as it makes the world *think-able*.[84]

Kearney's eschatological reading sees an understanding of the Godhead as *posse*, where the best 'name' for God is one denoting possibility. Yahweh, as a name revealing God's persona, reveals God's *posse* through its use of 'may-be.' God, as the divine Creator, gives humanity a glimpse of himself through his eschatological promise, and Christ, as the "perfect 'Image' of God," gives people a transfigured 'face' that they can place alongside the name of Yahweh. However, as Jesus' face is transfigured, this image only gives us a glimpse, "through a glass darkly."[85] This prevents a totalization of God by preventing God's image and name from becoming an idol, where all one understands of God is all that one can see. One cannot fully comprehend the Lord of Creation through the image and face of Jesus; one can only deepen her relationship and comprehension of God's eschatological promise through Jesus. The Holy Spirit continues this promise through its ongoing relationship between God and his people. Here, the Holy Spirit works in these micro-eschatological moments, where God is present here on earth, and the impossible is made possible, by participating in the believer's life while also receding in order to make room for the believer's freedom of action. God, through his eschatological promise and as the Holy Spirit, is kenotic: God lets go of creation to allow it to exist, to be free and to participate in God's promise. Understood as play, this letting go opens a space for the self to experience the God of possibilities. An example Kearney gives of this letting go is the notion that we can only gain the Kingdom by losing it, namely "renouncing the illusion that we possess it here and now. If we think that we have the Kingdom, it can only be in the mode of the 'as if,' as imaginary, a play of images."[86]

This play of images is best understood, for Kearney, as "three distinct persons moving *toward* each other in a gesture of immanence and *away from* each other in a gesture of transcendence," where each at once join in play with creation while also distancing themselves to let creation be, as "an interplay of loving and letting go."[87] This hermeneutical model, then, can be seen as poetical and creative since it at once presences an understanding (through promise and command) yet still absences, leaving room for participation and interpretation of the possibilities within the encounter.

At first sight Kearney's notion of play and poetics seems to overcome some old difficulties, yet the same problem of ontology arises with a poetics of the possible since it does not see the encounter as factual. These are mere descriptions of what is *possible* in the relationship between the Godhead and humanity; they do not (and cannot) inquire into the factualness of the encounter itself. By now it is clear that this is the major break between Kearney and Westphal: it is the difference between proclaiming the possibilities of a relationship with God, and proclaiming the actualities that this relationship has occurred and continues to occur. What is not so clear are the implications of this break for each thinker and how it relates to the distinctions between philosophy and theology.

Sovereigns and Strangers: Why Couldn't the King Throw a Feast?

Returning to Kearney and Westphal's divergent uses of Ricoeur, we can see how Kearney is maintaining a vigorous, 'ecumenical' position by bracketing out any particular truth claims regarding the event of revelation. He brackets out issues of factual accuracy regarding the biblical narratives he uses, and more important, he thinks that he needs to do so. As a hermeneutical phenomenologist, his concern is not with the actuality that revelation has occurred, but that revelation might be possible and, if so, how that could be hermeneutically understood and phenomenologically described. He reaffirms his philosophical position by stating that he "is not a theologian" and his project is a "philosophical questioning" where he merely posits his own hermeneutical wager regarding the relationship between God and the self.[88] Kearney notes throughout that this philosophical questioning is an attempt is to explore whether theism or atheism is the "only way" to conceive of this relationship.[89] By describing God as *posse*, Kearney attempts to move beyond the atheism-theism binary toward how God might be thought of and experienced. However, by bracketing out the truth claims in the religious traditions he uses, he also might be bracketing out the promise and command of God; for how can God make such commands and promises without entering into humanity's state of existence and becoming a part of a people's tradition?

Kearney's answer, perhaps, is that God does not enter into causal-chronological time but instead that one enters into messianic time: one's causal history interrupts or trespasses into messianic time at the moment of revelation, where one's own *esse* enters into the realm of impossible possibilities; an inverted interruption of history. Although this is a 'possible' answer to the critique above, it still does not satisfy since all that we experience becomes a moment of our history and, as such, we must rely on an event that has occurred. Even when God is seen as *posse*, he still relies on some form of existence to manifest these micro-eschatologies to continue his promise and to fashion himself into the Son of Man who redeems and continues this eschatological promise.

This is where Westphal's theology primarily outshines Kearney's philosophy of religion. Westphal boldly stakes a claim that these things have occurred and thus one needs to consider them as historical events, to some degree. These events are a part of a living, historical tradition which informs his thinking and what he sees as his task of faith seeking understanding. Despite his concern for onto-theology, God's theistic existence, God's *esse*, is a necessary concept for understanding God. As such, he attempts to *explain* (and sometimes describe) theism in light of postmodern critique. Despite this critique, Westphal never wavers from an orthodox Christian faith in God.

At the colloquium for *Anatheism*, Westphal argues for the necessity of ontology and thus shows his orthodoxy. In response to Kearney's anatheism, which follows the same methodology and description of God within *The God Who May Be*, Westphal raises the question of God's sovereign nature. "[Kearney sees] God as a sovereign or a stranger," Westphal remarks, "why not, a sovereign-stranger? Sovereignty or hospitality, why couldn't the King throw a feast?"[90] He notes that if one reads the Bible as hermeneutical accounts of revelation, one cannot forget the fact that God acts, that God rewards and punishes, and that God gives and enforces laws:

> On [Kearney's] journey ... he wants us to travel lightly, and it seems to me that he wants us to travel too lightly. . . . He clearly wants us to abandon a sovereign God, and he talks about religion assuming too often the power of sovereignty resulting in theocracy. He talks about the sovereign power being too easily transferred in human agencies. And who could dispute that . . . history is full of instances of that kind. But it seems to me that the solution [to] that problem is not to abandon the sovereignty of God but to

complain about the human entities that deify themselves and do wicked things in the name of God.[91]

For Westphal, the critique of onto-theology should be read through humanity's perversion of God's sovereignty for its own gain; he sees onto-theology as revealing the ways humanity manufactures a metaphysics that can be wielded as a weapon against others. His response to onto-theology is not to do away with the power of God but to limit how that power can be understood—and thus co-opted—by human thought. Kearney agrees with Westphal's critique, acknowledging how the concept of God's sovereignty far too often becomes the cause for bloodletting. Having witnessed his family's distress after World War II and his native Ireland's religiously political civil war reminds him of this tendency.[92] However, Kearney departs from Westphal by regarding the issue of God's sovereignty as unnecessary and even dangerous. Kearney agrees with the critique that he wants to get rid of a sovereign God, wishing to replace it with a concept of a God "of the small things."[93]

Kearney argues that sovereignty is applied to God, specifically the "God of Platonism or [the] God of the philosophers," sovereignty becomes "the notion of a pure act that excludes any form of possibility." This is the construct of God as "unmoved and unmoving . . . of an indivisible God . . . who, when delegated to the powers of the world, becomes the one and indivisible emperor, becomes the one and indivisible sovereign king, and then one and indivisible sovereign state [which is] . . . a recipe for war."[94] For Kearney, this is bad politics as well as bad theology, it is helps construct an onto-theological metaphysics and it strips God's ability to love and to bring about justice.[95]

Conversely, Kearney shows how one can go beyond sovereignty in search of love and justice. As an example, he argues that sovereignty is what divided Ireland and the United Kingdom for almost three hundred years and that the impasse concerning which country could rightfully claim Northern Ireland was broken once both sides took the issue of sovereignty off the table: "Eventually someone said, 'let's get rid of sovereignty. Let's have a post-nationalist, a post-unionist situation where we forget about sovereignty."[96] And so the impossible became possible: the concept of joint sovereignty was accepted—"a contradiction in terms"—and "people in Northern Ireland could be Irish, or British, or both; and that meant going beyond the idea of sovereignty as one and indivisible."[97]

Furthermore, Kearney proclaims that "that the sovereign God and the sovereign nation-state have been a source of huge misinterpretation and huge violence.⁹⁸" This is why he embraces the God of *potentia* or *posse*, who is "the God of multiplicities and pluralities."⁹⁹ He elaborates by stating ways this God delegates and diminishes his authority through plurality, first with the three different angels visiting Abraham, and then through the Trinitarian pattern finds throughout the Bible. This reading sees a God who requires interaction and interpretation, a God of hermeneutics, which requires one to return to the tradition in order to look forward to future possibilities. For Kearney, the God of possibilities invites us to participate in making the impossible possible:

> [The power of] *potentia*, or *posse*: . . . for me, is [one of] invitation. It is the power of powerlessness. In the sense of what [Nicolas of] Cusanus called, 'divine *posse* is a child's cry in the street.' . . . It is a cry in the street, a cry in the wilderness that invites us to respond; to give *posse*, *esse*. To give flesh to the word. And if we don't say yes, it doesn't happen. There is no sovereign power here, no absolute power that can impose itself. So the invitation . . . [calls us] to say yes or no. And it's a God of desire, there's no God of desire in the sovereign being that has no possibility.¹⁰⁰

For Kearney, it is humanity that gives God ontology: it is our participation with God, in God's promise, which gives flesh to the Word, and thus to God. This is a free choice and our response determines revelation and how God unfolds his relationship to humanity: if Moses says no to the divine voice, then there is no Exodus. If Mary says no to Gabriel, then there is no Jesus. God kenotically relinquishes his power and Christians have become the inheritors of the Kingdom, a Kingdom whose king is no longer sovereign. Yet Westphal's question of whether God can be both sovereign and hospitable remains. Kearney's philosophical God follows an abnegation of God's *esse* where God is completely dependent on human interaction. Kearney's God holds a similar weakness to John Caputo's God, who reveals a similar dependence.¹⁰¹ Perhaps Westphal might claim that Kearney—like Caputo—has cooked a very thin soup, which neither nourishes nor fulfills the soul. For Westphal, one must express God in ontological terms, a God of *esse*, for how else is one to understand these moments of revelation which cannot be expressed in Levinasian, ethical terms? How is one to regard the Bible as true if we do not hold to some degree that these events actually occurred? His entire project rests on a faith that accepts God's revelation and even though it can be expressed in an ethical relationship, it still has to be open to the idea that God can simply 'be' without humanity, or that God can reveal himself in any and every possible way.

Westphal's three modes of revelation—ethical, maieutic, and/or mediated immediacy—follow this perspective.[102] The issue of sovereignty, for Westphal, ironically takes root with the suspicion that Kearney is stripping God of the possibility to appear on God's terms; as if hearing God through a child's cry in the street is the only way to hear God. This is why truth claims matter to Westphal: these claims do not limit God; rather, they express the myriad possibilities at God's disposal. God can come in a burning bush, or through the love of the neighbor, or he can come and bring about justice, or he can empty himself on the cross and abdicate his power. However, these claims do not prevent God from appearing in other fashions and ways. Moreover, a philosophy that uses these revelatory moments while bracketing out their historical particularity, their factualness, and how they are assembled within a particular tradition, fails to adequately express how a religious concept of God is possible. Indeed, it fails to even consider how it is feasible to follow such a God without these attachments. Kearney's project makes great philosophical strides toward describing certain aspects of God and revelation, and his kenotic description of human participation deepens our understanding of revelation's role in ethics and how God's promise might be conceived. Yet still, bracketing out all of the above in the name of removing a metaphysical, sovereign God raises concerns regarding how one can receive this God within one's tradition. How a does such a God exist in a shared history with God's people? How does one worship, pray, and dance before this God? Incarnation requires ontology; inscription requires truth claims.

Nevertheless, in defense of Kearney, one needs to remember his phenomenological methodology and what it can and cannot do. Kearney's phenomenology aims to be merely descriptive. It expressly endeavors to understand God between theism and atheism, so it will naturally not be fully in line with the tradition from which it gathers its texts. In other words, his philosophical project is decidedly different from a theological project which is situated within a tradition and, with that tradition, must accept certain matters of fact. Westphal's critiques are valid and sound as theological critiques. However, these critiques fail to take into account the limits of Kearney's discipline and the particular, defining goals of that discipline.

As Westphal stated earlier, to give a phenomenology of prayer is not to pray and to describe confession is not to confess. While Westphal crosses over into theology, and thus embraces the truth claims of that tradition, Kearney remains at the limits of his profession: he goes right to the edge of philosophy and peers over into theology, and merely describes what he sees. However, what he describes is not a part of theology, nor is it part of a tradition that comprises theology. This is where Westphal catches Kearney in a rub: his phenomenology, while attempting to remain within the contours of its methodology, fails to be completely descriptive by positing a different sort of God. His consideration of a 'different way' to conceive of God between atheism and theism fails to consider that the God of which he is speaking has already been spoken for. This is not to say, however, that Kearney cannot, or should not, present such a God. Rather, when he does, he is mindful of this God's purely philosophical nature and is aware that what he retrieves from his hermeneutical detours is never purely philosophical. They are embedded in and are composed by a particular tradition. His 'hermeneutical wager' partially recognizes this when it separates his work from the tradition and openly states that he is merely retrieving something out of this tradition. However, when he excises the essential characteristic of *esse* from his retrieval, his wager fails to ultimately retrieve anything and, rather, constructs something new and different. "How much ontology do we need?" thus becomes not just a question for how to understand God; it becomes a question for how we do theology and philosophy: how much can we retrieve of God from within particular traditions—and how much can we manipulate this retrieval—while remaining faithful to our methods and purposes? Can philosophy rightly take from theological discourses anything it wants in order to do philosophy, or should it be bound to the traditions from which it takes? Conversely, recall where I cautioned that some philosophers might charge Westphal with a lack of rigor when he appropriates freely from philosophical sources, arguing that Westphal does so to prescribe a particular theology, yet this did not absolve him of this lack of care in respecting his sources.[103] Here, one can see that this critique can cut both ways and that both theologians and philosophers might need to be more vigilant in respecting the particulars of their sources, especially when appropriating from different genre discourses.

This reveals the problem with losing a distinction between philosophy of religion and theology, and how thinkers far too often forget the discipline and aims that distinguish one from the other. Kearney's project cannot function as theology, and although Westphal's critique is correct, he primarily critiques a theological encroachment he sees within Kearney's use of his religious tradition.

Conclusion: Westphal, Kearney, and the Theological-Philosophical Divide

Throughout this chapter, and throughout this book, I have argued that there is a distinction between theology and philosophy. However, some may inquire why this distinction is even necessary. I find that this objection is overruled when one places Kearney and Westphal in discussion, since it shows how their methodologies (even though deeply rooted in the same influences) diverge and create two, fundamentally different projects; they start with the same principles and concerns, yet wind up in markedly different places. This is because one speaks as a philosopher and within a philosophical discourse, whereas the other (unknowingly, perhaps) speaks as a theologian within a theological discourse. This is also why I have chosen Kearney over Caputo as Westphal's true dialogue partner: Kearney and Westphal are more alike than they are different, yet their projects are distinctly separated through their intentions and purposes. Kearney, as a philosopher, is freer to explore conceptualizations of God outside of any particular tradition even while he hermeneutically retrieves aspects within particular traditions to do so. Westphal, however, is more theologically bound. His work is tied to a particular faith and he thinks and writes in light of that faith: for him it is always *faith* seeking understanding, and that faith has baggage. It has a tradition and has content to which he is obliged. Even though Westphal has proved that he could do otherwise (as one can see in *God, Guilt, and Death*), his obligation to the content and tradition from which his faith arises is a discernable and deliberate choice.

In conclusion, one can see these distinctions by how each thinker approaches the critique of onto-theology: Kearney wishes to disregard any sense of *esse* in God as metaphysical and thus harmful; Westphal wishes to see the critique of metaphysics as a purely of human concern that does not prevent God from having an *esse*; still, both present their findings in an eschatological framework. Philosophically, perhaps one could describe the self's relation to God without crossing into onto-theology. However, when this description becomes implemented within a tradition, that is, when it becomes more than a description, it takes on the issue of particularity and, with it, the concerns of ontology and metaphysics. A philosophical response may be to do away with ontology altogether, such as one might see in Kearney's possibilizing God and his understanding of messianic time. In contradistinction, theology may resort back to its tradition—to an exploration of sin and the human condition—and Westphal's project does just that by aligning the onto-theological critique with sin, particularly with the notion of concupiscence and sin. His overcoming of onto-theology follows a path of salvation, where faith in the promise and command of God leads to self-transcendence and, eventually, to one being taken up by God's transcendence. For Westphal, his project remains within a framework where this faith in God and revelation can be understood (I would contend, must be understood) within a Christian tradition. Kearney's project, contrariwise, retrieves from the Christian tradition but it evades from being understood through that tradition. It seeks to explore philosophical notions between theism and atheism, and it perceives that there is a way to do so outside of onto-theology; perhaps the impossibility of overcoming onto-theology is made possible through this 'between.' Yet even if it is possible, even if Kearney's may-be God solves this Gordian knot, it floats above any tradition without directly entering it.[104]

This is not to say that philosophy of religion is not important for believers; rather, it speaks to how philosophy approaches religion from a different angle. Kearney's contribution alone raises important questions concerning how placing God within an ontological framework can lead to God becoming co-opted for selfish gain, leading to a recipe for war. In response, Kearney's proposed wager invigorates the discussion about God's plurality and has spurred on a dialogue concerning the importance of concepts such as the Trinity and natural theology. In a philosophical vein, I appreciate how his fidelity to the hermeneutical-phenomenological method reveals the ways Westphal's work fails to be a proper phenomenology. Therefore, it presents a critique to Westphal regarding how he goes about appropriating his sources and how he uses philosophical methodologies for his own theological project. The critique cuts both ways, as I have mentioned, yet I have mainly focused on the theological side of this critique since we have previously explored various aspects of the philosophical side.

In the future, I hope that the philosophical-theological discussion will maintain its 'dash' so that it does not become a theosophical discussion in which these respective disciplines begin resembling some sort of metatheology, or metaphilosophy—even the thought of doing so sounds irresponsible. Yet still these disciplines can engage each other, highlighting differing aspects and understandings of God and humanity while still respecting their particular boundaries.

NOTES

1. See *GTPD*, "Between the Prophetic and Sacramental"; "Is There a God after God?," *Boston College Magazine*, http://frontrow.bc.edu/program/westphal. This is a video recording of a colloquium for Kearney's *Anatheism* with Westphal being an intervener. I refer to time signatures (e.g., min. 85) when citing it.

2. I have chosen *The God Who May Be* since it provides the phenomenological basis for Kearney's more recent works. For example, *Anatheism* largely stems from his eschatological 'may-be' God.

3. *SF*, xiii, *TST*, 3n5.

4. See chapter 6 in this volume.

5. *GGD*, xi–xiii. This notion also stems from Ricoeur's research into psychoanalysis, particularly in *Freud and Philosophy* and *The Symbolism of Evil*.

6. *GGD*, xi.

7. *GGD*, 11. He quotes from Paul Ricoeur, *The Symbolism of Evil*, trans. Emerson Buchanan (New York: Harper & Row, 1967), 10, 19.

8. *GGD*, 5–9.

9. Recall that, from Westphal's reading of Gadamer, bias is not always pejorative.

10. *GGD*, 20. This incorporation of a hermeneutics of suspicion directly relates to Westphal's first phenomenological text in which he uses Nietzsche to critique Husserlian phenomenology, which further reveals how Ricoeur's hermeneutics influences Westphal's phenomenology. See Westphal, "Nietzsche and the Phenomenological Ideal," *Monist* 60, no. 2 (April 1977): 278–288.

11. *GGD*, 21.

12. Ibid., 22.

13. Or, in the very least, it is a nonapologetical position.

14. See chapter 4 of this volume.

15. Merold Westphal, "Ricoeur's Hermeneutical Phenomenology of Religion," in *Reading Ricoeur*, trans. David Kaplan (Albany: SUNY Press, 2008), 109–127.

16. Ibid., 112.

17. Ibid. Westphal is quoting from Paul Ricoeur, *Hermeneutics and the Human Sciences*, ed. and trans. John B. Thompson (New York: Cambridge University Press, 1981), 47–53.

18. Westphal repeats this in "Ricoeur's Hermeneutical Phenomenology of Religion," 113.

19. Ibid., 114.

20. 'Tacitly' since Westphal does not outright explain this appropriation; if one reads the text with an eye on how Westphal uses hermeneutical phenomenology throughout his work, then one can clearly see that this is the case.

21. Westphal, "Ricoeur's Hermeneutical Phenomenology of Religion," 114.

22. Obviously, some of Ricoeur's work does not follow this strict model, such as certain essays in *Figuring the Sacred* (Minneapolis: Fortress Press, 1995) and *Thinking Biblically* (Chicago: University of Chicago Press, 2004). I am solely talking about Ricoeur's philosophical writings.

23. Westphal, "Ricoeur's Hermeneutical Phenomenology of Religion," 114.

24. Again, this is not a negative critique; placing Westphal into this discourse elevates the importance of his work.

25. *SF*, xiii–xv, 3–9.

26. Ibid., 144.

27. *OCOT*, 142. This echoes the final chapter of *SF*, "In Conclusion: The Dangers of Suspicion."

28. *OCOT*, 143: "I have in mind not to abandon these negations [in light of their dangers] through a desperate defense of realism . . . but their *Aufhebung*, their teleological suspension, their incorporation into a larger whole of which they are but parts, however crucial."

29. Ibid., 144–146. Westphal couples this suspicion with a so-called "hermeneutics of finitude" (138). This hermeneutics acknowledges the limited (finite) nature of human understanding and is the first step to entering into a hermeneutics of suspicion. Like recovering from addiction, the first step is recognizing the problem and the second is to create an environment that precludes temptation of relapsing.

30. See chapter 5 in this volume.

31. *OCOT*, 146.

32. See chapters 7 and 8.

33. *TST*, 7. Westphal quotes from Ricoeur, Paul, *Oneself as Another*, trans. Kathleen Blarney (Chicago: University of Chicago Press, 1992), 298.

34. *TST*, 227.

35. Ibid., 2. See chapter 7 for more on how he places this book into these genres.

36. *TST*, 3.

37. Ibid., 6.

38. Richard Kearney, *The God Who May Be* (Bloomington: Indiana University Press, 2001), 5–6. Emphasis is mine.

39. For a stronger understanding of Kearney's reading of Ricoeur, see his *On Paul Ricoeur* (London: Ashgate, 2004).

40. For more evidence, see Westphal, "Ricoeur's Hermeneutical Phenomenology of Religion," 109, 115–116, 118–119; Westphal, "Nietzsche and the Phenomenological Ideal," 278–277, 281.

41. Boyd Blundell's *Paul Ricoeur: Between Theology and Philosophy* does us a great service by showing how Ricoeur's other primary influence, his mentor and teacher Gabriel Marcel, balances out Ricoeur's philosophy, preventing it from diverting into a "spirit of abstraction" through Husserl. Husserl and Marcel, as cantilevering influences, allow Ricoeur to maintain a phenomenological methodology that acknowledges its limits while also engaging in a more existential-hermeneutical enterprise:

"The ease in which [Ricoeur] separates out the 'method' of phenomenology from the 'idealism' implies that it is phenomenology rather than hermeneutics that is undergoing the process of grafting [i.e. appropriation]. In this sense, Ricoeur's phenomenology was not a 'pure' phenomenology onto which hermeneutics was later grafted; rather, it was an existential phenomenology that developed into a hermeneutic phenomenology. Or . . . [to clarify] it was a phenomenological existentialism (in Marcel's sense of existentialism, which stresses the embodied, participating subject) that developed into a phenomenological hermeneutics. On this reading, hermeneutics was not grafted onto phenomenology, but rather the phenomenological method was *transplanted* from existentialism to hermeneutics. To cast it in terms of detour and return, Marcel's reflexive philosophy of existence was the original moment of belonging, Husserl's eidetic method was the distanciating detour, and the return to belonging was the enriched sense of belonging-to (*Zugehörigkeit*) and dependence-on (*Abhängigkeit*) characteristic of Gadamer's Hermeneutics. In Ricoeur, the three moments are held together in the pattern of detour and return that was derived from Marcel's practice of secondary reflection." Blundell, Boyd, *Ricoeur: Between Philosophy and Theology* (Bloomington: Indiana University Press, 2010), 65.

42. For more, see chapter 6. Recall that this position even extends to his reading of Levinas as a critic of Husserl, who was not a hermeneutical phenomenologist.

43. Kearney, *On Paul Ricoeur*, 15–17, 29–33.

44. Richard Kearney, *Strangers, Gods, and Monsters* (London: Routledge, 2003), 7, 9.

45. Ibid., 9.

46. Ibid., 10–14, 37. Kearney's use of the hermeneutics of suspicion is somewhat tacit but emerges through his considerations of the problems that might arise in his project.

47. By "existentialist style of philosophy," I mean an attempt to understand the self through things outside the self (the 'world' and the self's interaction with that world and with others within that world). The divide I am making between existentialism and phenomenology is based primarily on method: how one chooses to explore the self in relation to what is outside the self. On the issue of Westphal hypothetically involving Levinas and Kierkegaard, see how they are employed within *Transcendence and Self-Transcendence* to give a phenomenological construct to the implications of his previous two sections (on onto-theology and God-talk). See also "Levinas, Kierkegaard, and the Theological Task," where he utilizes the phenomenology of the two (recall that Westphal sees Kierkegaard as a proto-phenomenologist) to explain and prescribe the task of theology. Neither, as phenomenologists, is employed to disclose a meaning of theology in light of religiously understood phenomena. Rather, they are used more for their existential discoveries.

One can also see a similar process in *Levinas and Kierkegaard in Dialogue*, where each's thought is explored around concepts to arrive at insights derived from the convergences and divergences of their thought. It is almost like a chemist who proceeds by mixing two substances together to make a reaction. Although Westphal's dialogues, in this fashion, have produced great 'reactions,' the point I am making is how markedly different this process is from a more phenomenological (perhaps Husserlian) methodology.

48. I am not including his works of literature in this scenario.

49. Richard Kearney, *Anatheism* (New York: Columbia University Press, 2010), loc. 28.

50. Ibid., loc. 149.

51. Ibid., loc. 128.

52. Ibid., loc. 171.

53. Ibid., loc. L. 199, L. 173.

54. Kearney, *The God Who May Be*, 10.

55. Ibid., 10.

56. For more on Levinas, see chapter 6.

57. Kearney, *The God Who May Be*, 10–11.

58. Ibid., 10.

59. Ibid., 1–8.

60. Ibid., 15–18.

61. Kearney, "Is There a God after God?" mins. 82–85.

62. Ibid., min. 68.

63. Kearney spoke at the colloquium's end, and Westphal had no chance to respond.

64. Kearney, "Is There a God after God?" mins. 92–95.

65. Kearney, *The God Who May Be*, 21. Kearney, unless otherwise noted, quotes from the New Jerusalem Bible (New York: Doubleday, 1990).

66. Kearney, *The God Who May Be*, 22.

67. Ibid., 27.

68. Ibid., 28.

69. Ibid.

70. Ibid., 29.

71. For more on 'micro-eschatologies, see Richard Kearney, "Paul's Notion of Dunamis," in *St. Paul among the Philosophers*, ed. John Caputo (Bloomington: Indiana University Press, 2009).

72. *GTPD*, 205, 178.

73. Kearney, *The God Who May Be*, 40.

74. Ibid., 42.

75. Ibid., 51.

76. See, for example, ibid., 54–56, 60–62, 63–64, 67–69, 78–79. It should be noted that Kearney relies heavily on mystical encounters such as that of Nicolas of Cusa.

77. Kearney, *The God Who May Be*, 81. *Possiblized* is Kearney's neologism.

78. Ibid.

79. Ibid. Kearney calls this messianic time: "We cannot think of the time of the *persona* except as an immemorial beginning (before the beginning) or an unimaginable end (after the end). That is precisely its eschatological stature—the messianic achronicity which breaks open the continuous moment-by-moment time of everyday chronology" (17).

80. Ibid., 81: "The light shone in darkness . . . and to all those who received it was given the possibility of becoming children of God."

81. Ibid., 98–100.

82. Ibid., 100.

83. Ibid., 101–102. Poetics is derived from the Aristotelian term *nous poetikos* (*De Anima* 3.5), where the term suggests a 'making mind,' or a creativity, which Kearney sees in the possibilizing God.

84. Kearney, *The God Who May Be*, 102.

85. Ibid., 103.

86. Ibid., 108.

87. Ibid., 109.

88. Kearney, "Is There a God after God?" min. 76. The wager in *Anatheism* follows from the wager he poses in *The God Who May Be*. Additionally, Westphal and Kearney have exchanges regarding their approach to God after the critique of onto-theology in *GTPD* and in a retrospective work on Kearney's thought, *After God*. I chose to focus upon their exchanges at this colloquium since this is the one place where both Westphal and Kearney directly and thoroughly address each other's respective criticisms. See also *GTPD*, 139–150; 163–180; John Manoussakis, ed., *After God: Richard Kearney and the Religious Turn in Continental Philosophy* (New York: Fordham University Press, 2006), 39–54, 78–93; Westphal, "The God Who Will Be: Hermeneutics and the God of Promise," *Faith and Philosophy* 20, no. 3 (July 2003): 328–344.

89. Kearney, "Is There a God after God?" min. 80.

90. Ibid., min. 84. The following transcription is my own, Westphal and Kearney spoke extemporaneously and therefore some pauses and phrases have been omitted for clarity.

91. Westphal, in Kearney, "Is There a God after God?" mins. 37–40.

92. Kearney, "Is There a God after God?," mins. 72–75.

93. Ibid., mins. 94–96.

94. Ibid., min. 84.

95. Ibid., min. 85.
96. Ibid., min. 86.
97. Ibid., min. 87.
98. Ibid., min. 86.
99. Ibid., min. 88.
100. Ibid., mins. 88–90.
101. John Caputo, *The Weakness of God* (Bloomington: Indiana University Press, 2006). Caputo, much to his delight, notices the same. See his "Richard Kearney's Enthusiasm: A Philosophical Exploration on *The God Who May Be*," *Modern Theology* 18, no. 1 (2002): 87–94.
102. See chapter 4.
103. See chapter 6.
104. Importantly, Kearney himself argues that he does not intend to create a "new religion" or theology of his own. See Kearney, *Anatheism*, loc. 171.

CONCLUSION

Westphal as a Theologian and Why It Matters

As I mentioned in the introduction, when researching this book and speaking at both philosophical and theological conferences (mostly in Europe, but also in North America), I got mainly two reactions to Westphal's thinking: those who thought his work truly embraced Protestant Christianity and provided a pathway for Christians to seriously consider mostly secular critiques of religion (similar to his opening statements in *Overcoming Onto-Theology*), and those who found that his work did not pass the standard for rigorous philosophical thinking. Those in the latter camp, especially phenomenologists, charged that his appropriations did not adequately consider the original context and intentions of the text. However, once I began describing his work in a theological vein, and him as an academic who wishes to take thinkers like Nietzsche and present his critique to a Christian audience who can use it to reflect on their own faith, they began to appreciate the intent—and yes, the rigor—of his academic work. Of course, this is anecdotal, and it does not found my initial thesis of reading Westphal theologically, but it does inform it and helps clarify why reading Westphal in his proper discourse is essential to grasping the importance of his work.

However, by stating that Westphal is best read as a theologian, not a philosopher, I am not saying that theologians cannot do philosophy or that philosophers cannot do theology. Rather, I make this distinction to best situate Westphal's work, and possibly the works of others. I argue that when one writes an academic text that might cross the borders of these discourses, one must be aware that he or she is crossing a border, and that what lies on the other side of that border might have different audiences, goals, and methodologies to take into account. Theologians must be aware that the texts they appropriate are works within respective genres, and they must cross these borders by carefully adhering to the established traditions of those genres; theologians cannot appropriate freely to suit their own purposes. Philosophers must likewise be aware of this and must acknowledge that what they appropriate comes with strings attached, so to speak. They cannot easily snip those strings and merely call it an appropriation or recontextualization.

In Westphal's case, he reasons from faith, and he uses philosophy to better understand how faith can be enacted. Perhaps in line with Kierkegaard, he takes the Epistle of James seriously and proclaims that faith is a task and without enacting one's faith daily, that faith is dead. It is primarily because of this, and arguments I have explained throughout this book, that I think Westphal is best understood as a theologian. Philosophy, particularly phenomenology and Continental philosophy's emphasis on hermeneutics when engaging texts, requires a certain rigorous fidelity to a chosen method in order to make distinctions and better understand the issue in question. Accordingly, philosophers go about their work by presenting a method that holds certain presuppositions and has certain limitations. In our exploration of Westphal, I have shown that he often breaks this rule so that he can better understand the religious beliefs of his own Christian community and find better ways to enact those beliefs in day-to-day life. Westphal is not wrong in doing this; he is merely appropriating texts for a religious purpose, which is best understood as a theological purpose. St. Anselm's *fides quaerens intellectum* is not only Westphal's motto—it is theology's, and Westphal's work is more in line with this style of thinking than his contemporaries are, especially John Caputo and Richard Kearney.[1]

Philosophy and theology share borders, and each has its own respective traditions and ways of proceeding through thought, yet there are always points of contact between the two. In the previous chapter, I highlighted one of these points of contact over the issue of ontology, although there are doubtless many more. Perhaps further researching the borders of theology and philosophy—with an emphasis on a clear distinction between the two rather than an argument for blurring this border, as most current research is wont to do—will enhance the dialogue between philosophers and theologians. I envision such research as discovering ways that each respective discourse might serve as a potent critique of the other's findings. That philosophy might find insights in theological texts while also respecting such texts as a part of a religious tradition. That theology might find a proper critique of its systems, frameworks, and/or constructs through a rigorous, philosophical analysis. In this way, crossing the border from one discipline into another might work likes a customs office, where travelers declare what items they bring into one country as they travel or, upon return, declare what they have retrieved and are taking home. During such time, a thorough evaluation is held as to whether such transport is possible or if certain modifications or reductions might be necessary. The point of a customs office, to extend the metaphor, is not to prevent transportation or emigration or immigration; rather, it is to help facilitate such events and to make sure that such transactions have been thoroughly vetted and negotiated so as to respect the sovereignty of each country (or, in this case, discipline). In this vein, philosophers and theologians would declare what their intentions are once they engage in interdisciplinary work and would also, upon returning to their native discipline, further declare what they have retrieved from their bordering discipline. Doing so would help others follow their intellectual journey, and so allow for a thorough investigation of what has been appropriated and recontextualized, thus showing how the process has changed what has been appropriated. An example of this is how we traced Westphal's appropriation of Ricoeur's hermeneutical phenomenology and how, in his later work, Westphal begins to use it more as a hermeneutical heuristic and less as a phenomenological method.

However, before one could enter into such a customs office, a working definition of philosophy of religion and theology—and fundamental theology in particular—needs to be established in order to find the borders of each discipline. The definitions I have given are merely working definitions for our present study, and perhaps better ones may arise in future conversations between theologians and philosophers. Nonetheless, I defined fundamental theology as having two movements, the first of which is an inward and reflective examination of the foundations of Christianity as a faith tradition which is based on God's revelation. This inward movement seeks to further understand revelation through reasoning and examines how revelation has been received through the tradition as well as content of revelation itself. The second movement, which holds a heavier emphasis in contemporary fundamental theology for one reason or another, is an outward movement that dialogically explores an understanding of the content of revelation (and therefore also the reception of revelation through tradition) by engaging other disciplines that do not hold revelation as a basic, founding principle. Philosophy often is this other discipline. Importantly, philosophy does not adhere to revelation as its founding principle and consequently bases its discipline on the primacy of human reason. This primacy of reason is employed and articulated through the philosopher's chosen methodology. An analogy between theology and philosophy might be construed thus: as revelation is primary in fundamental theology, and its reception or development is seen through tradition, so is reason primary in philosophy of religion, and its reception or development is seen through methodology. Therefore, the basic foundation of philosophy of religion might be understood as adhering to the principles of reason, broadly construed and defined by the philosopher in question and articulated through that philosopher's chosen method. Within postmodern thought, which holds a heavy suspicion against any founding principles, scholars scrutinize how reason is employed in philosophizing (or thinking), with critiques such as onto-theology questioning not only the validity of metaphysics but also the notion of thought itself.

Consequently, postmodern philosophers of religion have begun to reconsider the theological tradition and its reflection on faith in revelation— something that surpasses reason—and this movement in the academy has been fashioned as a so-called turn to religion, or theological turn. Westphal and Kearney write within this theological turn, and in the course of examining their thought, I have highlighted how each privileges either revelation (Westphal) or reason (Kearney) in his thinking. Westphal's thought always gives primacy to faith (in revelation) over reason (and thus over method, as in his departure from a strict hermeneutical phenomenology). Kearney conversely gives reason primacy through his rigid employment of the hermeneutical-phenomenological method, retrieving from revelation only what he considers intellectually significant. Kearney never proclaims that revelation has occurred, only that within so-called sacred texts one might see a way to possibly conceive of God or a way out of onto-theology, a way out of questioning the notion of thought itself. This distinction becomes crucial when one begins to scrutinize the validity and soundness of their arguments, as each holds different founding principles and each must be judged accordingly. Westphal's thinking, as seen through our analysis of Caputo's critique, does not logically cohere to the philosophical problem of onto-theology. Kearney's thinking does not take the truth claims in the Christian tradition as factual, and hence he limits his thinking to being only a philosophical wager. Taking all of this into account, I find that it is primarily within their respective genre discourses and disciplines that each thinker might flourish.

The notion of reading Westphal as a fundamental theologian tightens when one remembers that Westphal considers himself a Christian philosopher and not a theologian. As we have seen, Westphal designates himself as a philosopher who allows his Christian beliefs to be scrutinized by philosophical critique. In light of this, Westphal not only emerges with a more refined understanding of his Christianity but also articulates a desire to carve a space for a hermeneutics of prophecy in philosophy. Yet the only way he can achieve such a prophetic voice is through appropriating sources that are not recontextualized via a particular method to further understand the topic in consideration; instead, they are recontextualized to achieve a particular end. Westphal, for example, appropriates the hermeneutics of suspicion solely to function as a critique of one's life of faith; after *God, Guilt, and Death* Westphal rarely refers to this sort of hermeneutics as a corrective device for hermeneutical phenomenology. Rather, he employs this hermeneutics to guide the believing soul's faith and to center theology on liberating the other. This highlights a latent consequence in theology: by working within a living tradition of believing souls and reflecting on the beliefs of those souls, theologians of all subdisciplines are inevitably bound to the praxis of faith. What further separates theology, and fundamental theology in particular, from philosophy is that it is dealing with a living faith that, according to our definition here, cannot divorce itself from revelation and the reception of that revelation within the life of the tradition of the Christian church. As a Christian philosopher, Westphal's house appears divided in terms of authority: can one rightly give equal primacy to faith in revelation and to reason? In some Christian contexts, this is not as divided as it may initially seem, since reason is essential in the process of one accepting revelation. In Westphal's case, especially regarding his eschewal of any reasonable foundation for the acceptance of revelation, this division becomes untenable. As we have seen, Westphal always gives primacy to faith, and philosophically, he is willing to abandon his methodology when he needs to employ his findings in a faith-based context.

Perhaps the problem here resides in what one considers philosophy and theology, especially in a mostly Protestant context that maintains a different understanding of reason than a Catholic context. Fundamental theology is often considered a Catholic academic endeavor that entails a belief in Sacred Tradition: that revelation can be reflected on and developed through the life and history of the church, and both actions can be apologetically explained. In a Protestant context—or more specifically, a Protestant context that leans more Lutheran than others—which often holds to a *sola scriptura* understanding of revelation, this style of religious reflection is unsustainable. Although there is ample research on the theological and intellectual divide between Catholics and Protestants, scholars have yet to examine how this divide might influence Continental postmodern thought, especially in terms of philosophy of religion and fundamental theology. By calling Westphal a fundamental theologian, I have presented a need to further understand how the distinction between philosophy of religion and fundamental theology is necessary in order to properly scrutinize the work of those who reside at either's borders. The next step after this distinction is perhaps to examine the plurality of discourses across these borders to reveal the multitude of voices, and possible divisions, that reside near them, one being that Protestants conceive of philosophy and the philosophical task differently than Catholics do. The results of such research might yield an interesting ecumenical dialogue based on the relationship of faith, reason, and human sin. When discussing the implications of reading Westphal's overcoming of onto-theology as a Protestant eschatology, I highlighted some possible avenues of fruitful discovery.

Now that we have a working definition of philosophy of religion and fundamental theology, and have seen why such definitions are necessary, a final word is needed as to how these bordering academic fields might welcome their neighbors. Philosophy needs theology's critique about philosophical formulations concerning the nature of thinking, as seen in the definition of postmodern philosophy of religion and the so-called theological turn. Likewise, theology needs philosophy's critique of theology's reflections on faith and revelation in order to gain new insights and methods for the future development of the religious traditions. I envision each neighboring discipline working as allies in the pursuit of understanding, whether that understanding begins with faith or with reason. The theological tradition is rife with great philosophers and interdisciplinary thinkers who have helped progress Christian thought throughout the centuries. Likewise, one could say that philosophical discourses have been enriched through their engagement of Christian (or other religious) texts and traditions, which have helped provide answers to the limits of reason and the intellectual condition of the self. Westphal is an exemplary case of why these borders need to be respected and why they also need to be opened: Westphal's work reads as theology, yet without philosophy and the intellectual critique it provides, his faith would be left unexamined and perhaps its content would be underdeveloped and immature. With a cooperation of both, Westphal grasps the content of his faith by understanding better ways to daily enact his faith. Reading Westphal and learning how he developed his thinking— both when strictly following his given methodology and when he strays to speak to his own faith community—thus shows us why we have academic borderlands while also proving why we should travel across those borders.

NOTE

1. More exactly, this is the motto of Roman Catholic theology, but it might also function for theology proper.

BIBLIOGRAPHY

Primary Bibliography of Merold Westphal

Texts that were not directly cited in this book are marked with an asterisk. I have included them to give Westphal's comprehensive bibliography and because many were consulted but not cited since they often restated ideas from other, more relevant texts.

Scholarly Contributions

Gregor, Brian. "Hermeneutics, Scripture & Faithful Philosophizing: An Interview with Merold Westphal." *Journal of Philosophy and Scripture* 4, no. 1 (2007): 26–40.*

Westphal, Merold. "A Dialectic of Dialecticians: Reflections on Hegel and Kierkegaard." *Clio* 13, no. 4 (Summer 1984): 415–424.*

———. "Abraham and Hegel." In *Kierkegaard's Fear and Trembling: Critical Appraisals,* edited by Robert L. Perkins, 62–80. Mobile: University of Alabama Press, 1983. (Reprinted in *KCRS*).*

———. "Abraham and Sacrifice." *Neue Zeitschrift für Systematische Theologie und Religionsphilosophie* 50 (2008): 318–330.

———. "Academic Excellence: Cliché or Humanizing Vision." *Thought* 63, no. 251 (December 1988): 348–357.*

———. "Against Unconditional Gifts." In *With Gifted Thinkers: Conversations with Caputo, Hart, Horner, Kearney, Keller, Rigby, Taylor, Wallace, Westphal,* edited by Mark Manolopoulos, 233–247. Bern: Peter Lang, 2009.*

———. "Appropriating Postmodernism." *ARC* 25 (1997): 73–84. (Reprinted in *OCOT*).*

———. "Aquinas and Onto-Theology." *American Catholic Philosophical Quarterly* 80, no. 2 (2006): 173–191.*

———. "Atheism for Lent." In *"God Is Dead" and I Don't Feel So Good Myself,* edited by Andrew David, Christopher Keller, and Jon Stanley, 67–78. Eugene, OR: Cascade Books, 2010.*

———. *Becoming a Self.* West Lafayette, IN: Purdue University Press, 1996.

————. "Becoming Real—With Style." In *Styles of Piety*, edited by S. Clark Buckner and Matthew Statler, 76–93. New York: Fordham University Press, 2005.*

————. "The Canon as Flexible, Normative Fact." *Monist* 76, no. 4 (October 1993): 436–449.

————. "The Cheating of Cratylus (Genitivus Subjectivus)." In *Modernity and Its Discontents*, edited by John Caputo, James Marsh, and Merold Westphal, 163–182. New York: Fordham University Press, 1992.

————. "Christian Philosophers and the Copernican Revolution." In *Christian Perspectives on Religious Knowledge*, edited by C. Stephen Evans and Merold Westphal, 161–179. Grand Rapids, MI: Eerdman's, 1993. (Reprinted in *OCOT*).*

————. "The Christian Uses of Secular Postmodernism." *Revista Portuguesa de Filosofia* 60 (2004): 845–869.*

————. "Climacus on Subjectivity and the System." In *Kierkegaard's Concluding Unscientific Postscript: A Critical Guide*, edited by Rick Anthony Fortas, 132–148. New York: Cambridge University Press, 2010.*

————. "Cogito and Conversion: A Phenomenology of Prayer as Pre-Reflective Presence." In *Phenomenology and the Understanding of Human Destiny*, edited by Stephen Skousgaard, 355–366. Washington, DC: University Press of America, 1991.*

————. "Commanded Love and Divine Transcendence in Kierkegaard and Levinas." In *The Face of the Other and the Trace of God: Essays on the Philosophy of Emmanuel Levinas*, edited by Jeffrey Bloechl, 200–233. New York: Fordham University Press, 2000. (Reprinted in *LKD*).*

————. "Commanded Love and Moral Autonomy: The Kierkegaard-Habermas Debate." *Kierkegaard Studies Yearbook* (1998): 1–22.

————. "Continental Philosophy of Religion." In *Oxford Handbook of Philosophy of Religion*, edited by William J. Wainwright, 472–493. New York: Oxford University Press, 2005.*

————. "Coping and Conversation: The Limits and Promise of Pragmatism." *Hedgehog Review* 3, no. 3 (Fall 2001): 73–92.*

————. "Deconstruction and Christian Cultural Theory: An Essay on Appropriation." In *Pledges of Jubilee*, edited by Lambert Zuidervaart and Henry Luttikhuizen, 107–125. Grand Rapids, MI: Eerdman's, 1995. (Reprinted in *OCOT*).*

————. "Derrida as Natural Law Theorist." *International Philosophical Quarterly* 34, no. 2 (June 1994): 247–252. (Reprinted in *OCOT*).*

————. "Dialectic and Intersubjectivity." *Owl of Minerva* 16, no. 1 (1984): 39–54. (Reprinted in *HFM*).

————. "Divine Excess: The God Who Comes After." In *The Religious*, edited by John Caputo, 258–276. London: Blackwell, 2002. (Reprinted in *OCOT*).*

————. "Divine Givenness and Self-Givenness in Kierkegaard." In *Kierkegaard as Phenomenologist: An Experiment*, edited by Jeffrey Hanson, 39–56. Evanston, IL: Northwestern University Press, 2010.*

———. "Donavan's Critique of Sittlichkeit." *Idealistic Studies* 15, no. 1 (January 1985): 1–17. (Reprinted in *HFM*).*

———. "The Emergence of Modern Philosophy of Religion." In *A Companion to Philosophy of Religion*, 2nd ed., edited by Charles Taliaferro, Paul Draper, and Philip L. Quinn, 133–140. Oxford: Wiley Blackwell, 2010.*

———. "The Empty Suitcase as Rainbow." In *Saintly Influence: Edith Wyschogrod and the Possibilities of Philosophy of Religion*, edited by Eric Boynton and Martin Kavka, 48–62. New York: Fordham University Press, 2009.*

———. "The End of Secular Thought?" In *Rethinking Secularization: Philosophy and the Prophecy of a Secular Age*, edited by Herbert DeVriese and Gary Gabor, 355–366. Newcastle, UK: Cambridge Scholars Publishers, 2009.*

———. "Existentialism and Environmental Ethics." In *The Environmental Crisis: The Ethical Dilemma*, edited by Edwin R. Squires, 77–89. Mancelona, MI: Ausable Trails Institute of Environmental Studies, 1982.*

———. "Faith as the Overcoming of Ontological Xenophobia." In *The Otherness of God*, edited by Orrin Summerell, 149–172. Charlottesville: University of Virginia Press, 1998. (Reprinted in *OCOT*).*

———. "Faith Seeking Understanding." In *God and the Philosophers*, edited by Thomas V. Morris, 215–226. New York: Oxford University Press, 1994.

———. "The Fonda Fallacy All Over Again." *Mississippi Review* 10, no. 1 (2004): n.p.*

———. "God as King: A Reply to Lewis Ford." *Christian Scholars Review* 1 (Summer 1971): 323–324.*

———. *God, Guilt, and Death*. Bloomington: Indiana University Press, 1984.

———. "The God Who Will Be: Hermeneutics and the God of Promise." *Faith and Philosophy* 20, no. 3 (July 2003): 328–344.

———. "Hegel (The Hermeneutics of 'Christian' Pantheism)." In *The Blackwell Companion to Modern Theology*, edited by Gareth Jones, 293–310. Oxford: Blackwell, 2004.*

———. "Hegel and Family Values." In *In the Socratic Tradition*, edited by Tziporah Kasachkoff, 209–213. Lanham, MD: Rowman and Littlefield, 1998.*

———. "Hegel and Husserl: Transcendental Phenomenology and the Revolution Yet Awaited." In *Critical and Dialectical Phenomenology*, edited by Don Welton and Hugh J. Silverman, 103–135. Albany: SUNY Press, 1987. (Reprinted in *HFM*).*

———. "Hegel and Gadamer." In *Hermeneutics and Modern Philosophy*, edited by Brice Wachterhaus, 65–86. Albany: SUNY Press, 1986. (Reprinted in *HFM*).*

———. "Hegel and Onto-Theology." *Bulletin of the Hegel Society of Great Britain* 41–42 (2000): 142–165.*

———. "Hegel and the Reformation." In *History and System: Hegel's Philosophy of History*, edited by Robert L. Perkins, 73–92. Albany: SUNY Press, 1984. (Reprinted in *HFM*).*

———. "Hegel between Spinoza and Derrida." In *Hegel's History of Philosophy: New Interpretations*, edited by David Duquette, 143–163. Albany: SUNY Press, 2002.*

———. *Hegel, Freedom, and Modernity*. Albany: SUNY Press, 1992.

———. "Hegel, Human Rights, and the Hungry." In *Hegel on Economics and Free-dom*, edited by William Maker, 209–228. Macon, GA: Mercer University Press, 1987. (Reprinted in *HFM*).*

———. "Hegel, Hinduism, and Freedom." *Owl of Minerva* 20, no. 2 (1989): 193–204. (Reprinted in *HFM*).*

———. "Hegel on Slavery, Independence, and Liberalism." *Cardozo Law Review* 10, nos. 5–6 (March–April 1989): 1563–1573.*

———. "Hegel, the Old Secularism, and the New Theocracy." Presidential address to the 1984 meeting of the Hegel Society of America. (Reprinted in *HFM*).*

———. "Hegel, Pannenberg, and Hermeneutics." *Man and World* 5 (August 1971): 276–293. (Reprinted in *HFM*).*

———. "Hegel, Tillich, and the Secular." *Journal of Religion* 52 (July 1972): 223–239. (Reprinted in *HFM*).*

———. "Hegel's Angst vor dem Sollen." *Owl of Minerva* 25, no. 2 (Spring 1994): 187–194.*

———. "Hegel's Phenomenology of Perception." In *The Phenomenology of Spirit Reader*, edited by John Stewart, 122–137. Albany: SUNY Press, 1997.*

———. "Hegel's Radical Idealism: Family and State as Ethical Communities." In *The State and Civil Society: Studies in Hegel's Political Philosophy*, edited by Zbigniew Pelcynski, 77–92. New York: Cambridge University Press, 1984. (Reprinted in *HFM*).*

———. "Hegel's Theory of Religious Knowledge." In *Beyond Epistemology: New Studies in the Philosophy of Hegel*, edited by F. G. Weiss, 30–57. The Hague: Springer, 1974. (Reprinted in *HFM*).*

———. "Hegel's Theory of the Concept." In *Art and Logic in Hegel's Philosophy*, edited by Warren Steinkraus, and Kenneth Schmitz, 103–119. Newark, NJ: Humanities Press International, 1980. (Reprinted in *HFM*).*

———. "Heidegger's 'Theologishe' Jugendschriften." *Research in Phenomenology* 27 (1997): 247–261. (Reprinted in *OCOT*).*

———. "Hermeneutical Finitude from Schleiermacher to Derrida." In *Between the Human and the Divine: Philosophical and Theological Hermeneutics*, edited by Andrzej Wiercinski, 50–65. Toronto: Hermeneutic Press, 2002.*

———. "Hermeneutics and Holiness." In *Analytic Theology: New Essays in the Philosophy of Theology*, edited by Oliver Crisp and Michael Rae, 265–279. New York: Oxford University Press, 2009.*

———. "Hermeneutics and the God of Promise." In *After God: Richard Kearney and the Religious Turn in Continental Philosophy*, edited by John Manoussakis, 78–94. New York: Fordham University Press, 2006.

———. "Hermeneutics as Epistemology." In *The Blackwell Guide to Epistemology*, edited by John Greco and Ernest Sosa, 415–435. Oxford: Blackwell, 1999. (Reprinted in *OCOT*).

———. *History and Truth in Hegel's Phenomenology*. 3rd ed. Bloomington: Indiana University Press, 1998.

———. "Idealism and/as Secularism." *New Mercersburg Review* 20 (Autumn 1996): 17–28.*

———. "The Importance of Mystery for the Life of Faith." *Faith and Philosophy* 24, no. 4 (October 2007): 367–384.*

———. "The Importance of Overcoming Metaphysics for the Life of Faith." *Modern Theology* 23, no. 2 (April 2007): 253–278.

———. "In Defense of the Thing in Itself." *Kant Studien* 59, no. 1 (1968): 118–141.

———. "In God We Trust: Biblical Interpretation and the Hermeneutics of Suspicion." In *The Hermeneutics of Charity: Interpretation, Selfhood, and Postmodern Faith*, edited by James K. A. Smith, Henry Isaac Venema, and James Olthuis, 98–108. Grand Rapids, MI: Brazos Press, 2004.*

———. "Intentionality and Transcendence." In *Subjectivity and Transcendence*, edited by Søren Overgaard and Ibsen Damgaard, 71–93. Tübingen: Mohr Siebeck, 2007. (Reprinted in *LKD*).*

———. "Inverted Intentionality: On Being Seen and Being Addressed." *Faith and Philosophy* 26, no. 3 (2009): 233–252.*

———. "Ibsen, Hegel, and Nietzsche." *Clio* 14, no. 4 (Summer 1985): 395–406.*

———. "Jaspers' Reception of Kierkegaard." In *Karl Jaspers on Philosophy of History and History of Philosophy*, edited by Joseph W. Koterski and Raymond Langley, 223–235. Amherst, NY: Humanity Books, 2003.*

———. "Johannes and Johannes: Kierkegaard and Difference." In *International Kierkegaard Commentary: Philosophical Fragments and Johannes Climacus*, edited by Robert L. Perkins, 13–32. Macon, GA: Mercer University Press, 1994.

———. "The Joy of Being Indebted: A Concluding Response." In *Gazing through a Prism Darkly: Reflections on Merold Westphal's Hermeneutical Epistemology*, edited by B. Keith Putt, 163–180. New York: Fordham University Press, 2009.

———. "Kenosis and Offense: A Kierkegaardian Look at Divine Transcendence." In *International Kierkegaard Commentary: Practice in Christianity*, edited by Robert L. Perkins, 19–46. Macon, GA: Mercer University Press, 2004.*

———. "Kierkegaard and German Idealism." In *The Routledge Companion to Nineteenth Century Philosophy*, edited by Dean Moyar, 347–376. New York: Routledge, 2010.*

———. "Kierkegaard's Psychology and Unconscious Despair." *International Kierkegaard Commentary: The Sickness unto Death*, edited by Robert L. Perkins, 39–66. Macon, GA: Mercer University Press, 1987.*

———. "Kierkegaard as a Prophetic Philosopher." *Christian Scholars Review* 7, nos. 22–23 (1997): 109–119. (Reprinted in *KCRS*).*

———. "Kierkegaard." In *A Companion to Continental Philosophy*, edited by Simon Critchley and Bill Schroeder, 128–138. Oxford: Blackwell, 1997.*

———. "Kierkegaard and Hegel." In *The Cambridge Companion to Kierkegaard*, edited by Alastair Hannay and Gordon D. Marino, 101–124. Cambridge: Cambridge University Press, 1997.

———. "Kierkegaard and the Anxiety of Authorship." *International Philosophical Quarterly* 34, no. 1 (March 1994): 5–22.*

———. "Kierkegaard and the Logic of Insanity." *Religious Studies* 7 (September 1971): 193–211. (Reprinted in *KCRS*).

———. "Kierkegaard and the Role of Reflection in Second Immediacy." In *Immediacy and Reflection in Kierkegaard's Thought*, edited by Paul Cruysberghs, Johan Taels, and Karl Verstrynge, 159–179. Leuven: University of Leuven Press, 2003.

———. "Kierkegaard as a Prophetic Philosopher." *Christian Scholar's Review* 22, no. 3 (1977): 109–118. (Reprinted in *KCRS*).*

———. "Kierkegaard on Language and Spirit." In *Language and Spirit*, edited by D. Z. Phillips and Mario von der Ruhr, 64–90. Hampshire, UK: Palgrave Macmillan, 2004.

———. "Kierkegaard, Socratic Irony, and Deconstruction." In *International Kierkegaard Commentary: The Concept of Irony*, edited by Robert L. Perkins, 365–390. Macon, GA: Mercer University Press, 2001.*

———. "Kierkegaard, Søren;" *From the Encyclopedia Britannica Online: Academic Edition*. 2007. http://www.britannica.com/EBchecked/topic/317503/Soren-Kierkegaard.

———. "Kierkegaard's Climacus: A Kind of Postmodernist." In *International Kierkegaard Commentary: Concluding Unscientific Postscript to Philosophical Fragments*, edited by Robert L. Perkins, 53–71. Macon, GA: Mercer University Press, 1997.

———. *Kierkegaard's Concept of Faith*. Grand Rapids, MI: Eerdman's, 2014.

———. *Kierkegaard's Critique of Reason and Society*. Macon, GA: Mercer University Press, 1987.

———. "Kierkegaard's Phenomenology of Faith as Suffering." In *Writing the Politics of Difference*, edited by Hugh Silverman, 55–71. Albany: SUNY Press, 1991.*

———. "Kierkegaard's Politics." *Thought* 55 (September 1980): 320–332. (Reprinted in *KCRS*).*

———. "Kierkegaard's Religiousness C: A Defense." *International Philosophical Quarterly* 44, no. 4/176 (December 2004): 535–548.

———. "Kierkegaard's Sociology." In *International Kierkegaard Commentary: Two Ages*, edited by Robert L. Perkins, 133–154. Macon, GA: Mercer University Press, 1984. (Reprinted in *KCRS*).*

———. "Kierkegaard's Teleological Suspension of Religiousness B." In *Foundations of Vision and Community*, edited by George Connell and C. Stephen Evans, 55–71. Atlantic Highlands, NJ: Humanities Press, 1991.

———. "L'autre critique Kierkegaardienne de Hegel." In *L'idéalisme allemand et la religion*, edited by Phillippe Soual and Miklos Vetö, 189–211. Paris: L'Harmattan, 2008.*

———. "Laughing at Hegel." *Owl of Minerva* 28, no. 1 (1996): 39–58. (Reprinted in *OCOT*).*

———. *Levinas and Kierkegaard in Dialogue*. Bloomington: Indiana University Press, 2008.

———. "Levinas and the Immediacy of the Face." *Faith and Philosophy* 9, no. 2 (October 1993): 486–502. (Reprinted in *LKD*).*

———. "Levinas and the 'Logic' of Solidarity," *Graduate Faculty Philosophy Journal* 20–21 (1998): 297–319. (Reprinted in *LKD*).*

———. "Levinas' Teleological Suspension of the Religious." In *Ethics as First Philosophy: The Significance of Levinas for Philosophy, Literature, and Religion*, edited by Adriaan Peperzak, 151–160. New York: Routledge, 1995. (Reprinted in *LKD*).*

———. "Levinas, Kierkegaard, and the Theological Task." *Modern Theology* 8, no. 3 (July 1992): 241–261. (Reprinted in *LKD*).

———. "The Many Faces of Levinas as a Reader of Kierkegaard." In *Kierkegaard and Levinas*, edited by J. Aaron Simmons and David Wood, 21–40. Bloomington: Indiana University Press, 2008.

———. "A Midrash of (and for) Hope." *Conversations on Jesuit Higher Education* 18 (Fall 2000): 16–24.*

———. "Nietzsche and the Phenomenological Ideal." *Monist* 60 (April 1977): 278–288.

———. "Nietzsche as a Theological Resource." *Modern Theology* 13, no. 2 (April 1997): 213–226. (Reprinted in *OCOT*).*

———. "Of Stories and Language." In *Christianity and the Postmodern Turn: Six Views*, edited by Myron B. Penner, 229–240. Grand Rapids, MI: Brazos, 2005.*

———. "On Thinking God as King." *Christian Scholar's Review* 1 (Fall 1970): 27–34.*

———. "Onto-theological Straw." In *Postmodernism and Christian Philosophy*, edited by Toman Ciapalo, 258–267. Mishawaka, IN: American Maritain Association, 1997.

———. "Onto-theology." In *Dictionary for Theological Interpretation of the Bible*, edited by Craig Bartholomew, Daniel Treier, and Kevin Vanhoozer, 546–549. Grand Rapids, MI: Baker Academic, 2005.*

———. "Onto-theology, Metanarrative, Perspectivism and the Gospel." *Perspectives* (April 2000): 6–10. (Reprinted in *OCOT*).*

———. "Orthodoxy and Inattention." *Reformed Journal* 30, no. 1 (January 1980): 13–15.*

———. "The Ostrich and the Boogeyman: Placing Postmodernism." *Christian Scholar's Review* 20, no. 2 (1990): 114–117.*

———. "Overcoming Onto-theology." In *God, The Gift, and Postmodernism*, edited by John Caputo and Michael Scanlon, 146–169. Bloomington: Indiana University Press, 1999. (Reprinted in *OCOT*).*

———. *Overcoming Onto-Theology*. New York: Fordham University Press, 2001.

———. "Paganism in Christendom." In *International Kierkegaard Commentary: Christian Discourses and the Crisis in the Life of an Actress*, edited by Robert L. Perkins, 13–33. Macon, GA: Mercer University Press, 2007.*

———. "Paranoia and Piety: Reflections on the Schreber Case." In *Psychoanalysis and Religion*, edited by Joseph H. Smith and Susan A. Handelman, 117–135. Baltimore: Johns Hopkins University Press, 1990. (Reprinted in *LKD*).*

———. "Participation and Kenosis: A List for Schindler." *Saint Anselm Journal* 3, no. 1 (Fall 2005), n.p. http://www.anselm.edu/library/SAJ/SAJindex.html.*

———. "Phenomenologies and Religious Truth." In *Phenomenology and the Truth Proper to Religion*, edited by Daniel Guerrière, 105–125. Albany: SUNY Press, 1990.

———. "Phenomenology and Existentialism." In *A Companion to Philosophy of Religion*, edited by Philip L. Quinn and Charles Taliaferro, 167–175. Oxford: Blackwell, 1997.*

———. "The Phenomenology of Guilt and the Theology of Forgiveness." In *Crosscurrents in Phenomenology*, edited by Ronald Bruzina and Bruce Wilshire, 231–61. The Hague: Springer, 1978.

———. "Phenomenology of Religion." In *The Routledge Companion to Philosophy of Religion*, edited by Chad Meister and Paul Copan, 661–671. London: Routledge, 2007.*

———. "Philosophy as Vision and as Critique." In *The Recovery of Philosophy in America: Essays in Honor of John Edwin Smith*, edited by Thomas P. Kasulis and Robert Cummings Neville, 183–200. Albany: SUNY Press, 1997.*

———. "Philosophy, Faith, and Personality Theory." In *Man and Mind: A Christian Theory of Personality*, edited by Thomas J. Burke, 111–131. Hillsdale, MI: Hillsdale College Press, 1987.*

———. "The Politics of Religious Pluralism." In *The Proceedings of the Twentieth World Congress of Philosophy: Volume 4, Philosophies of Religion, Art, and Creativity*, edited by Kevin Stoehr, 1–8. Bowling Green, OH: Philosophy Documentation Center, 1999.*

———. "Post-Kantian Reflections on the Importance of Hermeneutics." In *Disciplining Hermeneutics: Interpretations in Christian Perspectives*, edited by Roger Lundin, 57–66. Grand Rapids, MI: Eerdman's, 1997.

———. "Positive Postmodernism as Radical Hermeneutics." In *The Very Idea of Radical Hermeneutics*, edited by Roy Martinez, 48–63. Atlantic Highlands, NJ: Humanities Press, 1997. (Reprinted in *OCOT*).*

———. "Postmodern Theology." In *Routledge Encyclopedia of Philosophy*, edited by Edward Craig, 583–586. New York: Routledge, 1998.*

———. "Postmodernism and Ethics: The Case of Caputo." In *A Passion for the Impossible: John D. Caputo in Focus*, edited by Mark Dooley, 328–344. Albany: SUNY Press, 2003.

———. "Postmodernism and Religious Reflection." *International Journal for Philosophy of Religion* 38, nos. 1–3 (December 1995): 127–143.

———. "Prayer as the Posture of the Decentered Self." In *The Phenomenology of Prayer*, edited by Bruce Ellis Benson and Norman Wirzba, 13–31. New York: Fordham University Press, 2005.*

———. "The Prereflective Cogito as Contaminated Opacity." *Southern Journal of Philosophy* 45 (2007): 152–177.

———. "Prolegomena to Any Future Philosophy of Religion Which Will Be Able to Come Forth as Prophecy." *International Journal for Philosophy of Religion* 4 (1973): 129–150. (Reprinted in *KCRS*).

———. "Questions from the Prophets." In *The Living and the Active Word of God: Studies in Honor of Samuel J. Schultz*, edited by Morris A. Inch and Ronald F. Youngblood, 59–73. Winona Lake, IN: Eisenbrauns, 1983.*

———. "Reading God the Author." *Religious Studies* 37 (2001): 272–291.*

———. "Recollection and Recognition in Findlay's Thought." In *Studies in the Philosophy of J. N. Findlay*, edited by R. S. Cohen, R. M. Martin, and Merold Westphal, 235–249. Albany: SUNY Press, 1985.*

———. "Recognizing Greed, Nourishing Generosity." *Discernment* 3, no. 2 (Spring 1995): 4–7.*

———. "Religious Experience as Self-Transcendence and Self-Deception." *Faith and Philosophy* 9, no. 2 (April 1992): 168–192.*

———. "Reply to Jack Caputo." *Faith and Philosophy* 22, no. 3 (July 2005): 297–300.

———. "The Return of the Arrogance of Power." *Mississippi Review* 22, no. 3 (Fall 2004): 209–212.*

———. "Ricoeur's Hermeneutical Phenomenology of Religion." In *Reading Ricoeur*, edited by David M. Kaplan, 109–127. Albany: SUNY Press, 2008.

———. "The Search for a Postmodern Ethics." *Research in Phenomenology* 32 (2002): 249–257.*

———. "The Second Great Revolution in Phenomenology." *Journal of Speculative Philosophy* 26, no. 2 (2012): 333–347.

———. "Shame as a Political Virtue." In *Religion in the Liberal Polity*, edited by Terence Cuneo, 231–249. Notre Dame, IN: University of Notre Dame Press, 2009.*

———. "Søren Kierkegaard." In *The Columbia History of Western Philosophy*, edited by Richard H. Popkin, 546–549. New York: Columbia University Press, 1999.*

———. "Søren Kierkegaard, *Concluding Unscientific Postscript* to *Philosophical Fragments*: Making Things Difficult for the System and for Christendom." In *The Classics of Western Philosophy: A Reader's Guide*, edited by Jorge Garcia, Gregory Reichbert, and Bernard Schumacher, 388–394. Oxford: Oxford University Press, 2002.*

———. "Situation and Suspicion in the Thought of Merleau-Ponty: The Question of Phenomenology and Politics." In *Ontology and Alterity in Merleau-Ponty*, edited by Galen Johnson and Michael Smith, 158–179. Evanston, IL: Northwestern University Press, 1990.*

———. "Speech from Beyond the Reach of Language: A Response to Zhang Ianglong." In *Chinese Philosophy in an Era of Globalization*, edited by Robin Wang, 215–229. Albany: SUNY Press, 2004.*

———. "Socrates between Jeremiah and Descartes: The Dialectic of Self-Consciousness and Self-Knowledge." *Philosophy and Theology* 2, no. 3 (Spring 1988): 199–219.*

———. *Suspicion and Faith*. Grand Rapids, MI: Eerdman's, 1998.

———. "Suspicion and Religious Belief." In *Lectures on European and American Philosophy of Religion*, edited by Zhao Dunhua and Melville Stewart, 194–205. Peking: n.p., 2001.*

———. "Taking Plantinga Seriously: Advice to Christian Philosophers." *Faith and Philosophy* 16, no. 2 (April 1999): 173–181.*

———. "Taking St. Paul Seriously: Sin as an Epistemological Category." In *Christian Philosophy*, edited by Thomas P. Flint, 200–226. Notre Dame, IN: University of Notre Dame Press, 1990.*

———. "Taking Suspicion Seriously: The Religious Uses of Modern Atheism." *Faith and Philosophy* 6, no. 1 (January 1987): 277–287. (Reprinted in *SF*).*

———. "Talking to Balaam's Ass: A Concluding Conversation." In *Gazing through a Prism Darkly: Reflections on Merold Westphal's Hermeneutical Epistemology*, edited by B. Keith Putt, 181–205. New York: Fordham University Press, 2009.

———. "Temporality and Finitism in Hartshorne's Theism." *Review of Metaphysics* 29 (March 1966): 550–564.*

———. "A User Friendly Copernican Revolution." In *In the Socratic Tradition*, edited by Tziporah Kasachkoff, 187–191. Lanham, MD: Rowman and Littlefield, 1998.*

———. "Theism and the Problems of Ethics." In *The Philosophy of Gordon Clark*, edited by Ronald H. Nash, 176–201. Philadelphia: Presbyterian & Reformed Publishers, 1968.*

———. "Theological Anti-Realism." In *Realism and Religion: Philosophical and Theological Perspectives*, edited by Andrew Moore and Michael Scott, 131–146. Aldershot, UK: Ashgate, 2007.*

———. "Theology as Talking about a God Who Talks." *Modern Theology* 13, no. 4 (October 1997): 525–536.*

———. "Thinking about God and God-Talk with Levinas." In *The Exorbitant: Emmanuel Levinas between Jews and Christians*, edited by Kevin Hart and Michael A. Singer, 216–229. New York: Fordham University Press, 2010.*

———. "Traditional Theism, the AAR, and the APA." In *God, Philosophy, and Academic Culture*, edited by William J. Wainwright, 21–27. Atlanta: Scholars Press, 1996.*

———. *Transcendence and Self-Transcendence*. Bloomington: Indiana University Press, 2004.

———. "Transcendence, Heteronomy, and the Birth of the Responsible Self." In *Calvin O. Schrag and the Task of Philosophy after Postmodernity*, edited by Martin Matusik and William L. McBride, 201–225. Evanston, IL: Northwestern University Press, 2002. (Reprinted in *LKD*).*

———. "Transfiguration as Saturated Phenomenon." In *Between Description and Interpretation: The Hermeneutic Turn in Phenomenology*, edited by Andrzej Wiercinski, 501–512. Toronto: Hermeneutic Press, 2005.*

———. "The Transparent Shadow: Kierkegaard and Levinas in Dialogue." In *Kierkegaard in Post/Modernity*, edited by Martin Matusik and Merold Westphal, 265–281. Bloomington: Indiana University Press, 1995. (Reprinted in *LKD*).*

———. "The Trauma of Transcendence as Heteronomous Intersubjectivity." In *Intersubjectivité et théologie philosophique*, edited by Marco Olivetti, 87–110. Padua: CEDAM, 2001. (Reprinted in *LKD*).*

———. "Twentieth Century Continental Philosophy: Philosophy of Religion." In *The Edinburgh Companion to Twentieth Century Philosophies*, edited by Constantin Boundas, 603–614. Edinburgh: Edinburgh University Press, 2007.*

———. "Vision and Voice: Phenomenology and Theology in the Work of Jean-Luc Marion." *International Journal of Philosophy of Religion* 60, nos. 1–3 (December 2006): 117–137.

———. "Von Hegel bis Hegel: Reflections on the 'Earliest System Program of German Idealism." In *The Emergence of German Idealism*, edited by Michael Baur and Daniel Dahlstrom, 269–289. Washington, DC: Catholic University of America Press, 1999.*

———. "The Welcome Wound: Emerging from the *il y a* Otherwise." *Continental Philosophy Review* 40 (2007): 211–230.

———. *Whose Community? Which Interpretation? Philosophical Hermeneutics for the Church*. Grand Rapids, MI: Baker Academic, 2009.

———. "Whose Philosophy? Which Religion? Reflections on Reason as Faith." In *Transcendence in Philosophy and Religion*, edited by James Faulconer, 13–34. Bloomington: Indiana University Press, 2003.

———. "William Desmond's Humpty Dumpty Hegelianism." *Clio* 20, no. 2 (1991): 353–370.*

———. "Verzeihung und Anarchie." *Hegel Jahrbuch* (1972): 105–109.*

Edited Volumes

Westphal, Merold, ed. *Method and Speculation in Hegel's Phenomenology*. Atlantic Highlands, NJ: Humanities Press, 1982.*

———. *Postmodern Philosophy and Christian Thought*. Bloomington: Indiana University Press, 1999.*

———. "Religious Significance of Contemporary Continental Philosophy." Special issue, *Faith and Philosophy* 10, no. 4 (October 1993).*

Westphal, Merold, John Caputo, and James Marsh, eds. *Modernity and Its Discontents*. New York: Fordham University Press, 1992.

Westphal, Merold, R. S. Cohen, and R. M. Martin, eds. *Studies in the Philosophy of J. N. Findlay*. Albany: SUNY Press, 1984.*

Westphal, Merold, and C. Stephen Evans, eds. *Christian Perspectives on Religious Knowledge*. Grand Rapids, MI: Eerdman's, 1993.*

Westphal, Merold, Thomas Ludwig, Robin Klay, and David Myers. *Inflation, Poortalk, and the Gospel*. Valley Forge, PA: Judson Press, 1981.

Westphal, Merold, and Linda Martín Alcoff, eds. *Conflicts and Convergences*. Supplement to *Philosophy Today* 42 (1998).*

Westphal, Merold, Linda Martín Alcoff, and Debra Bergoffen, eds. *Remembrance and Responsibility: Special Studies in Phenomenology and Existential Philosophy*. Supplement, *Philosophy Today* 41 (1998).*

Westphal, Merold, and Martin Matusik, eds. *Kierkegaard in Post/Modernity*. Bloomington: Indiana University Press, 1995.*

Contributions to Periodicals

Lipscomb, Ben. "Through a Glass Darkly: An Interview of Merold Westphal by Ben Lipscomb." *Dialogue* 29, no. 1 (September–October, 1996): 6–13.*

Westphal, Merold. "Appropriating the Atheists: An interview of Merold Westphal by Gary J. Percesepe." *Books and Culture*, May–June, 1997: 24–25.*

———. "As If You Really Mean It." *Perspectives*, March 1993: 3.*

————. "Barth's Critique of Religion." *Perspectives*, October 1986: 4–6. (Reprinted in *LKD*).*

————. "Blind Spots: Christianity and Postmodern Philosophy." *Christian Century*, June 14, 2003: 32–35.

————. "Bourgeoisified Buber." *Perspectives*, August–September, 1995: 7–8.*

————. "Chatter: The Protestant Ostinato." *Perspectives*, January, 2001: 3–4.*

————. "Christian Suffering: The Way of the Cross." *Perspectives*, March 1987: 7–10.*

————. "Covenant as Concrete Affirmation." *Perspectives*, September 1988: 4–7.*

————. "Faith at the Beach." *Perspectives*, March 2003: 18–19.*

————. "The Fonda Fallacy." *Perspectives*, February 1991: 3–4.*

————. "The Hermeneutics of Lent." *Perspectives*, February 1986: 8–11. (Reprinted in *SF*).*

————. "Higher Education and Idolatry." *Perspectives*, November 1990: 3.*

————. "How Shall We Escape." *Perspectives*, April 1992: 3–4.*

————. "Identity and Belonging." *Perspectives*, June 1988: 3.*

————. "Interview with Merold Westphal." *Leuven Philosophy Newsletter* 13 (2004–2005): 26–30.*

————. "Lest We Forget." *Perspectives*, February 1996: 10–13.*

————. "A Lifestyle That Reflects Our Faith." *Church Herald*, February 1991: 15–17.*

————. "Living Lives in Grateful Obedience." *Church Herald*, May 2, 1986: 5–7.*

————. "The Manager and the Church." *Perspectives*, June 1989: 3.*

————. "Merold Westphal Replies [to Groothius's 'Postmodern Fallacies']." *Christian Century*, July 26, 2003: 42.*

————. "New Covenant Tithing." *Church Herald*, November 3, 1979: 4–7.*

————. "Not about Me: Prayer as a Work of a Lifetime." *Christian Century*, April 5, 2005: 20–25.*

————. "Of Bumper Stickers and Trolls." *Perspectives*, September 1993: 3.*

————. "Pharaoh's Bankers." *Church Herald*, September 20, 1985: 10–11*.

————. "Prayer as Privilege." *Perspectives*, November 1987: 3.*

————. "Practicing Three Dimensional Prayer." *Church Herald*, December 11, 1981: 10–11.*

————. "The Press Conference Magic Johnson Didn't Hold." *Perspectives*, January 1992: 3–4.*

————. "The Privilege of Touching." *Perspectives*, June–July 2006: 3–4.*

————. "A Reader's Guide to 'Reformed Epistemology." *Perspectives*, November 1992: 10–13.*

————. "Saving *Sola Scriptura* from Rhem and the Rationalists." *Perspectives*, February 1993: 10–11.*

————. "Sing Jubilee." *Other Side*, March 1978: 29–35.*

————. "Singing to Caesar." *Church Herald*, December 12, 1980: 12–13.*

————. "Six Searing Words." *Perspectives*, September 1991: 19–22. (Under the pseudonym Laura Vander Veen).*

————. "Three Dimensional Prayer." *Church Herald*, October 1981: 406.*

————. "'Tis a Task to Be Simple." *Perspectives*, October 1995: 9.*

————. "The Tragedy of RMN." *Perspectives*, August–September 1994: 6.*

———. "Warning: The Great Physician Has Determined That Wealth Is Dangerous to Your Health." *Church Herald,* January 21, 1983: 5–7.*
———. "Will the Real Audrey Hepburn . . ." *Perspectives,* May, 1991: 3.*
———. "Why Gods Die." *Church Herald,* March 9, 1979: 12–13.*

ADDITIONAL WORKS CITED IN THIS VOLUME

Augustine. *Confessions.* Translated by Henry Chadwick. Oxford: Oxford Paperbacks, 2008.
Banwart, Doug. "Jerry Falwell, the Rise of the Moral Majority, and the 1980 Election." *Western Illinois Historical Review* 5 (2013): 133–157.
Barth, Karl. *The Epistle to the Romans.* Translated by Edwyn Hoskyns. Oxford: Oxford University Press, 1966.
Berlin, Isaiah. *Four Essays on Liberty.* Edited by Henry Hardy. Oxford: Oxford University Press, 2002.
Blundell, Boyd. *Paul Ricoeur between Theology and Philosophy.* Bloomington: Indiana University Press, 2010.
Boeve, Lieven. "Richard Kearney's Messianism." In *Between Philosophy and Theology,* edited by Lieven Boeve and Christophe Brabant. Surrey, UK: Ashgate, 2010.
Bromley, David, and Anson Shupe. *New Christian Politics.* Macon, GA: Mercer University Press, 1984.
Burch, Matthew I. "Blurred Vision: Marion on the 'Possibility' of Revelation." *International Journal of Philosophy of Religion* 67 (2010): 157–171.
Caputo, John. "Methodological Postmodernism: On Merold Westphal's 'Overcoming Onto-Theology.'" *Faith and Philosophy* 22, no. 3 (2005): 284–296.
———. *On Religion.* London: Routledge, 2001.
———. *The Prayer and Tears of Jacques Derrida.* Bloomington: Indiana University Press, 1997.
———. "Richard Kearney's Enthusiasm: A Philosophical Exploration of 'The God Who May Be.'" *Modern Theology* 18, no. 1 (2002): 87–94.
———, ed. *Saint Paul among the Philosophers.* Bloomington: Indiana University Press, 2009.
Caputo, John, and Michael J. Scanlon, eds. *God, the Gift, and Postmodernism.* Bloomington: Indiana University Press, 1999.
Caputo, John, James L. Marsh, and Merold Westphal. *Modernity and Its Discontent.* New York: Fordham University, 1992.
Carlson, David Gray. *A Commentary on Hegel's Science of Logic.* New York: Palgrave Macmillan, 2007.
Coakley, Sarah, ed. *Faith, Rationality, and the Passion.* Oxford: Blackwell Publishing, 2012.
Cornell, Drucilla, Michel Rosenfeld, and David Gray Carlson, eds. *Deconstruction and the Possibility of Justice.* New York: Routledge, 1992.
Denzinger, Henry, ed. *The Sources of Catholic Dogma.* Freiburg: Herder & Co., 1954.
Desmond, William. *Hegel's God: A Counterfeit Double?* Surrey, UK: Ashgate, 2003.
Dooley, Mark, ed. *A Passion for the Impossible.* Albany: SUNY Press, 2003.

Ehrman, Bart. *How Jesus Became God*. New York: HarperCollins, 2014.

Evans, C. Stephen. *Kierkegaard on Faith and the Self*. Waco: Baylor University Press, 2006.

Evans, C. Stephen, and George Connell, eds. *Foundations of Kierkegaard's Vision and Community*. Atlantic Highlands, NJ: Humanities Press, 1991.

Faulconer, James, ed. *Transcendence in Philosophy and Religion*. Bloomington: Indiana University Press, 2003.

Ferreira, Jamie M. *Blackwell's Great Minds: Kierkegaard*. Oxford: Blackwell, 2009.

Friedman, R. Z. "Kant and Kierkegaard: The Limits of Reason and the Cunning Faith." *International Journal for Philosophy of Religion* 19, nos. 1–2 (1986): 3–22.

Gadamer, Hans-Georg. *Truth and Method*. Translated by Joel C. Weinsheimer and Donald Marshal. New York: Continuum, 2003.

Gratton, Peter and John Manoussakis, eds. *Traversing the Imaginary: Richard Kearney and the Postmodern Challenge*. Evanston, IL: Northwestern University Press, 2007.

Groothuis, Douglas. "Postmodern Fallacies: A Response to Merold Westphal." *Christian Century*, July 29, 2003: 41–42.

Gschwandter, Christina. *Postmodern Apologetics? Arguments for God in Contemporary Philosophy*. New York: Fordham University Press, 2012.

Guerrière, Daniel, ed. *Phenomenology of the Truth Proper to Religion*. Albany: SUNY Press, 1990.

Hannay, Alastair. *Kierkegaard*. London: Routledge Press, 1999.

Hannay, Alastair, and Gordon Daniel. *The Cambridge Companion to Kierkegaard*. Cambridge: Cambridge University Press, 1998.

Hegel, Georg Wilhelm Friedrich. *Encyclopedia Logic: Part I of the Encyclopedia of Philosophical Sciences with the Zusatze*. Translated by T. F. Geraets, W. A. Suchting, and H. W. Harris. Indianapolis: Hackett Publishing, 1991.

———. *Phenomenology of Spirit*. Edited and translated by Arnold Vincent Miller; John Niemeyer Findlay. Oxford: Oxford University Press, 1977.

———. *Philosophy of Right*. Translated by S. W. Dyde. Kitchener, ON: Batoche Books, 2001.

———. *Science of Logic*. Translated by George Di Giovanni. Cambridge: Cambridge University Press, 2010.

———. *The Philosophy of History*. Translated by J. Sibree. Kitchener, ON: Batoche Books, 2001.

Heidegger, Martin. *Being and Time*. Translated by John Macquarie and Edward Robinson. Oxford: Blackwell, 2001.

———. *Identity and Difference*. Translated by Joan Stambaugh. New York: Harper & Row, 1969.

———. *The Question Concerning Technology and Other Essays*. Translated by William Lovitt. New York: Harper & Row, 1977.

Henriksen, Jan-Olav. "Thematizing Otherness: On Ways of Conceptualizing Transcendence and God in Recent Philosophy of Religion." *Studia Theologica* 64 (2010): 153–176.

Hodgson, Peter C., and Robert H. King. *Christian Theology: An Introduction to Its Traditions and Tasks*. Minneapolis: Fortress Press, 1994.

Horton, Michael S. "Meeting a Stranger: A Covenantal Epistemology." *Weston Theological Journal* 66 (2004): 337–355.

Houlgate, Stephen. *Freedom, Truth, and History*. London: Routledge, 1991.

———. "The Unity of Theoretical and Practical Spirit in Hegel's Concept of Freedom." *Review of Metaphysics* 45, no. 4 (June 1995): 875.

Janicaud, Dominique. "The Theological Turn of French Phenomenology." In *Phenomenology and the "Theological Turn,"* translated by Bernard G. Prusak, 3–106. New York: Fordham University Press, 2000.

Kant, Immanuel. *Critique of Pure Reason*. Translated by Paul Guyer and Allan Wood. Cambridge: Cambridge University Press, 1998.

Kaufmann, Walter, ed. *Existentialism from Dostoevsky to Sartre*. 2nd expanded ed. New York: New American Library, 1975.

———. *Hegel: A Reinterpretation*. South Bend, IN: University of Notre Dame Press, 1965.

Kearney, Richard, and Merold Westphal. "Is There a God after God?" *Boston College Magazine* (2012). http://frontrow.bc.edu/program/westphal.

Kearney, Richard. *Anatheism*. New York: Columbia University Press, 2010.

———. "Enabling God." In *After God: Richard Kearney and the Religious Turn in Continental Philosophy*, edited by John Manoussakis, 39–55. New York: Fordham University Press, 2006.

———. *The God Who May Be*. Bloomington: Indiana University Press, 2001.

———. *On Paul Ricoeur*. Surrey: Ashgate, 2004.

———. *Strangers, Gods, and Monsters*. London: Routledge, 2003.

Kierkegaard, Søren. *Attack upon Christendom*. Translated by Walter Lowrie. Princeton, NJ: Princeton University Press, 1991.

———. *Concluding Unscientific Postscript to the Philosophical Crumbs*. Translated by Alastair Hannay. Cambridge: Cambridge University Press, 2009.

———. *Either/Or Part I*. Translated by Howard Hong and Edna Hong. Princeton, NJ: Princeton University Press, 1987.

———. *Either/Or Part II*. Translated by William Hong and Edna Hong. Princeton, NJ: Princeton University Press, 1987.

———. *Fear and Trembling*. Translated by Howard Hong and Edna Hong. Princeton, NJ: Princeton University Press, 1983.

———. *On Authority and Revelation: The Book on Adler*. Translated by Walter Lowrie. New York: Harper & Row, 1966.

———. *Philosophical Fragments*. Translated by Howard Hong and Edna Hong. Princeton, NJ: Princeton University Press, 1986.

———. *The Sickness unto Death*. Translated by Howard Hong and Edna Hong. Princeton, NJ: Princeton University Press, 1980.

———. *Training in Christianity*. Translated by Walter Lowrie. New York: Harper & Row, 1962.

———. *Works of Love*. Translated by Howard Hong and Edna Hong. Princeton, NJ: Princeton University Press, 1995.

Lacoste, Jean-Yves, ed. *Encyclopedia of Christian Theology*. London: Routledge, 2005.

Levinas, Emmanuel. *Noms propres*. Paris: Fata Morgana, 2014.

———. *Proper Names*. Translated by M. B. Smith. Stanford, CA: Stanford University Press, 1996.

———. *Totality & Infinity*. Translated by Alphonso Lingus. Pittsburgh, PA: Duquesne University Press, 1969.

Mackin, Robert. "Liberation Theology and the Radicalization of Catholic Social Movements." *Politics, Religion & Ideology* 13, no. 3 (2012): 333–351.

Magee, Glenn Alexander. *The Hegel Dictionary*. New York: Continuum Publishing, 2010.

Manolopoulos, Mark, ed. *With Gifted Thinkers: Conversations with Caputo, Hart, Horner, Kearney, Keller, Rigby, Taylor, Wallace, and Westphal*. Bern: Peter Lang, 2009.

Mooney, Edward F. *Knights of Resignation: Reading Kierkegaard's Fear and Trembling*. Albany: SUNY Press, 1991.

Mulder, Jack, Jr. "Re-Radicalizing Kierkegaard: An Alternative to Religiousness C in Light of an Investigation into the Teleological Suspension of the Ethical." *Continental Philosophy Review* 35 (2002): 303–324.

Nietzsche, Friedrich. *Beyond Good and Evil*. Edited by Rolf-Peter Horstmann and Judith Norman, and translated by Judith Norman. Cambridge: Cambridge University Press, 2002.

———. *On the Genealogy of Morals*. Translated by Douglas Smith. Oxford: Oxford University Press, 2008.

———. *On the Genealogy of Morals*. Translated by Samuel Horace. New York: Dover Publications, 2003.

———. *Thus Spoke Zarathustra*. Edited by Adrian Del Caro and Robert Pippin, and translated by Adrian Del Caro. Cambridge: Cambridge University Press, 2006.

Palm, Ralph. *Hegel's Concept of Sublation: A Critical Interpretation*. Leuven: Katholieke Universiteit Leuven, 2009. Dissertation.

———. "Hegel's Contradictions." *Hegel Bulletin* 31, nos. 1–2 (2011): 134–158.

Piper, Henry. "Kierkegaard's Non-Dialectical Dialectic or That Kierkegaard Is Not Hegelian." *International Philosophical Quarterly* 44, no. 4 (2004): 467–512.

Putt, B. Keith, ed. *Gazing through a Prism Darkly: Reflections on Merold Westphal's Hermeneutical Epistemology*. New York: Fordham University Press, 2009.

Ricoeur, Paul. *Figuring the Sacred*. Edited by Mark I. Wallace and translated by David Pellauer. Minneapolis: Fortress Press, 1995.

———. *Freud and Philosophy: an Essay on Interpretation*. Translated by Denis Savage. New Haven, CT: Yale University Press, 1970.

———. *Oneself as Another*. Translated by Kathleen Blamey. Chicago: University of Chicago Press, 1995.

———. *The Symbolism of Evil*. Translated by Emerson Buchanan. New York: Harper & Row, 1967.

Ricoeur, Paul, and Andre LaCocque. *Thinking Biblically*. Translated by David Pellauer. Chicago: University of Chicago Press, 1998.

Schrijvers, Joeri. *Onto-Theological Turnings?* Albany: SUNY Press, 2011.

Simmons, J. Aaron, and Stephen Minister, eds. *Reexamining Deconstruction and Determinate Religion: Toward a Religion with Religion*. Pittsburgh, PA: Duquesne University Press, 2013.

Simmons, J. Aaron, and David Wood, eds. *Kierkegaard and Levinas*. Indianapolis: Indiana University Press, 2008.

Smith, James K. A. *The Fall of Interpretation: Philosophical Foundations for a Creational Hermeneutic*. Downers Grove, IL: Intervarsity Press, 2000.

Stewart, Jon. *Kierkegaard's Relations to Hegel Reconsidered*. Cambridge: Cambridge University Press, 2003.

Taylor, Mark. *Journeys to Selfhood: Hegel & Kierkegaard*. Berkeley: University of California Press, 2000.

Tracey, David. *Plurality and Ambiguity: Hermeneutics, Religion, Hope*. San Francisco: Harper & Row, 1987.

Twiss, Sumner B., and Walter H. Cosner Jr. *Experience of the Sacred: Reading in the Phenomenology of Religion*. Hanover, NH: University Press of New England, 1992.

Webster, John. *Barth's Moral Theology*. New York: T&T Clark, 1998.

INDEX

JUSTIN SANDS is a postdoctoral fellow at North
West University, South Africa. He is cofounder
of the research group Transforming Encounters:
Understanding the Postmodern Self in a South
African and Global Context. He obtained his
doctorate at KU Leuven, Belgium, while studying
the work of Merold Westphal.

CPSIA information can be obtained
at www.ICGtesting.com
Printed in the USA
BVOW03*2344201217
503360BV00001B/2/P

9 780253 031938